Resisting Reagan

Resisting Reagan

LIBERAL STRATEGIES
IN A CONSERVATIVE AGE

Joe J. Ryan-Hume

University Press of Kansas

© 2025 by the University Press of Kansas
All rights reserved

Published by the University Press of Kansas (Lawrence, Kansas 66045), which was organized by the Kansas Board of Regents and is operated and funded by Emporia State University, Fort Hays State University, Kansas State University, Pittsburg State University, the University of Kansas, and Wichita State University.

Library of Congress Cataloging-in-Publication Data

Names: Ryan-Hume, Joe J., author
Title: Resisting Reagan : liberal strategies in a conservative age / Joe J. Ryan-Hume.
Description: Lawrence : University of Kansas, 2025. | Includes bibliographical references and index.
Identifiers: LCCN 2024042776 (print) | LCCN 2024042777 (ebook) | ISBN 9780700638772 cloth | ISBN 9780700638789 paperback | ISBN 9780700638796 ebook
Subjects: LCSH: United States—Politics and government—1981–1989 | Liberalism—United States—History—20th century | Democratic Party (U.S.)—History—20th century | Reagan, Ronald | BISAC: HISTORY / United States / 20th Century | SOCIAL SCIENCE / Women's Studies
Classification: LCC E876 .R93 2025 (print) | LCC E876 (ebook) | DDC 973.927—dc23/eng/20250327
LC record available at https://lccn.loc.gov/2024042776.
LC ebook record available at https://lccn.loc.gov/2024042777.

British Library Cataloguing-in-Publication Data is available.
Authorised Representative Details: Easy Access System Europe
Mustamäe tee 50, 10621 Tallinn, Estonia | gpsr.requests@easproject.com

Contents

Acknowledgments, vii

List of Abbreviations, xi

Introduction, 1

1 Liberalism at a Crossroads: Debating the Future of Liberalism Within the Democratic Party After 1980, 18

2 Protecting Liberalism in Congress: Liberal Legislative Battles in Reagan's First Term, 36

3 Advancing Liberalism on the Ground: Grassroots Organizing in Reagan's First Term, 60

4 Turning Points: The 1984 Elections and the Identity Crisis Within the Democratic Party, 79

5 The Returning Tide of Liberalism: Legislative and Judicial Battles in Reagan's Second Term, 99

6 "Wake Up, Liberals, Your Time Has Come": Reassessing the 1988 Elections, 127

7 Emerging from the Shadow: Liberalism Reconstituted for the Post-Reagan Era, 146

Conclusion: Reckoning with the "Reagan Era," 169

Notes, 177

Bibliography, 241

Index, 257

Acknowledgments

From the moment I scribbled my name down in crayon as the author of my first story at four years old, it has been a dream of mine to become a published author. But without the support of numerous people and organizations, that dream would have remained unrealized. First and foremost, I am indebted to my doctoral supervisors at the University of Glasgow, Marina Moskowitz and Phillips O'Brien, who both inspired and encouraged me to pursue a PhD and provided invaluable support and guidance throughout. Thanks also to Gareth Davies (UCL), who outlined the path to publication, combining rigorous feedback with generous encouragement.

I have been fortunate to have several mentors who supported me on that path. At Glasgow, Dan Scroop provided expert guidance, helping me to scope out the initial parameters of the book and supporting its development since; while a Fulbright scholar at Boston University, Bruce Schulman offered masterful advice and perceptive feedback to improve this project immensely; and finally, while a Government of Ireland fellow at Trinity College Dublin, Dan Geary provided invaluable support as I endeavored to complete it. I am also indebted to many other scholars who offered generous advice and support at various junctures, particularly Patrick Andelic, Jonathan Bell, Stephen Bowman, Elad Carmel, Nicole Cassie, Anthony Eames, Ross Fulton, Robert Mason, Mark McLay, Simon Newman, Priscilla Roberts, and Arun Sood.

The natural home for this book was the University Press of Kansas, and I am incredibly grateful that they enthusiastically supported it from the outset. Expertly guided by such a skilled editor, David Congdon, I am thankful to all the staff at the press. I am also indebted to the reviewers, whose generous, insightful, and constructive comments improved the book significantly.

Like the academic community that made this book possible, numerous organizations supported it in a range of crucial ways. First, this project would have remained a mere annotation on an undergraduate essay had the Arts and Humanities Research Council (AHRC) not provided the financial support to turn it into a work of scholarship. Similarly, I have been fortunate enough to complete several research trips to the United States that, without funding from a range of associations, would have been impossible. Thanks to the British Association for American Studies; the European Association for American Studies; the American Politics Group; and Historians of the Twentieth Century United States. I also presented at conferences associated with these organizations, and I am grateful to the audience members who engaged with my research in various ways.

Equally, several libraries and institutes have supported this project, including grants from the Roosevelt Institute for American Studies in the Netherlands, the John F. Kennedy Institute in Germany, and four presidential libraries in the United States with funding from their respective foundations—John F. Kennedy Library Foundation, Lyndon B. Johnson Foundation, Gerald R. Ford Presidential Foundation, and the Scowcroft Institute at the Bush School of Government and Public Service. The Schlesinger Library at Harvard University deserves a special mention for furnishing the funds to consult their rich archives twice. Without the help of librarians and archivists at each of these institutions and more, this work would have been impossible. I am indebted to them all.

Longer-term fellowship opportunities have provided the space and time to develop this project in immeasurable ways. Thanks to the Fulbright Commission, the Irish Research Council, the Eccles Centre at the British Library, and Hong Kong University. In that regard, I was privileged to find an intellectual home in the John W. Kluge Center at the Library of Congress, first as an AHRC fellow and then as a Kluge fellow. The multidisciplinary nature of the center, coupled with the treasure trove of primary sources at the library, allowed me to cast a far wider net in my research than I thought possible and tackle some of its bulkier questions in innovative ways. Thanks to Travis, Michael, and all the Kluge staff for facilitating such a stimulating and congenial environment.

Across the street, I also held a transformative fellowship at the US Congress while writing this book, which enabled me to test my theoretical understandings of the institution and discuss my research with key practitioners. It was a privilege to work as a legislative fellow for Congressman Juan Vargas, an incredibly generous and thoughtful man, as well as build lasting friendships with several impressive colleagues, particularly Scott, Mariah, Eddie, and Tim. The greatest gift of this congressional fellowship though was the opportunity to meet my future wife.

My deepest debts are to my family. While too numerous to thank each and every individual, I would like to single out a few for a special mention. First and foremost, to my parents, whose contribution to my education has been diverse and immeasurable. Thank you to my mother, Kirsty, who is nothing short of an inspiration and who I genuinely could not have achieved much without; to Campbell, for constantly challenging me to question my assumptions and broaden my outlook; to Sian, for her unwavering support and love from day one; and to my father, Danny, who sparked my passion for history through endless hours of the History channel growing up and whose insight I have relied on ever since. Words cannot express how lucky I am to have them as parents. To my aunt, Kerry, this book is very much a testament to your encouragement and unstinting support. And finally, to my brother, Kavin, who I am proud to also call my best friend, and to my three oldest friends, Robert, Liam, and Jose, who I also consider as brothers. They all have a unique ability to coax me out of the "writing cave" (and usually to the pub!) and to remind me of life's importance beyond the book. Slàinte.

Finally, to my wife, Lian. She has inspired me, encouraged me, and believed in me more than words can capture. Her love has been my guiding light, illuminating the path to help me realize a dream. I truly could not have finished this without her. For that, and much more, this book is for Lian.

Dublin, 2024

List of Abbreviations

ADA	Americans for Democratic Action
AFDC	Aid to Families with Dependent Children
AFL-CIO	American Federation of Labor and Congress of Industrial Organizations
CPE	Committee on Party Effectiveness
CRA	Civil Rights Act
CRRA	Civil Rights Restoration Act
DLC	Democratic Leadership Council
DNC	Democratic National Committee
ERA	Equal Rights Amendment
HDC	House Democratic Caucus
HLA	Human Life Amendment
LCCR	Leadership Conference on Civil Rights
NAACP	National Association for the Advancement of Colored People
NARAL	National Abortion Rights Action League
NHDC	National House Democratic Caucus
NOW	National Organization for Women
NWPC	National Women's Political Caucus
NWRO	National Welfare Rights Organization
PAC	Political action committee
PFAW	People for the American Way
USCCR	US Commission on Civil Rights
VRA	Voting Rights Act

Introduction

Liberalism is at a crossroads. It will either evolve to meet the issues of the 1980s or it will be reduced to an interesting topic for PhD-writing historians.... We must move on to the pressing problems of the 1980s, and we must have answers that seem relevant. Fewer young people are joining the liberal cause in 1980 than in the 1960s.... This is a different generation, and if we do not speak to this generation in its terms, liberalism will decline. And if we do not meet these needs, liberalism should decline.[1]

    Senator Paul Tsongas (D-MA), keynote address at the Americans for Democratic Action 33rd Annual Conference, 14 June 1980

At the dawn of a new decade, American liberalism was about to enter a transitional period. Tracing its lineage as a modern governing philosophy back to President Franklin Roosevelt's use of government to create a limited welfare state and regulate the marketplace through the New Deal in the 1930s, liberalism had evolved significantly over the decades. By 1980, liberalism, broadly defined, reflected a belief in the affirmative power of government to ameliorate social and economic problems, a drive to improve civil liberties and expand equality, and an effort to advocate on behalf of marginalized and disenfranchised groups, particularly after the civil rights movement and the rights revolution it spawned. As both a political approach and a philosophical viewpoint, it should be stated at the outset that "liberalism" is a particularly elusive term.[2] Indeed, historians have grappled with its meaning for decades given its protean and amorphous nature. Nonetheless, while it may not be systematic or logically coherent on every count, some key traits can be identified for the purposes of definition. Generally, liberals favor the use of government action to achieve a greater degree of social and political equality in society through various legislative and programmatic remedies. While this is manifested in a variety of ways in practice, generally modern liberalism can be viewed as a political approach to expand opportunity, create an inclusive and fair society, and address social and economic inequalities through government action; these views stand in contrast to conservatism and its emphasis on individualism, limited government and administrative decentralization, and market-based solutions to assure economic and political freedom.[3]

Speaking that June morning in 1980, Senator Paul Tsongas did not contest these liberal principles; instead, he used his speech to suggest that an updated approach was needed, as many of liberalism's adherents had become "stuck in the past." Given the volatile nature of the American political situation at the time, with poor economic conditions at home and foreign policy crises abroad, Tsongas warned that liberalism needed to meet the moment or it would lose its base of support in the upcoming presidential election of 1980. He had been asked to deliver a speech celebrating liberalism's past achievements by Americans for Democratic Action (ADA)—an organization that had long stood for unreconstructed liberalism.[4] In 1980, the ADA was an enthusiastic backer of Senator Edward Kennedy's insurgent liberal campaign for the presidency, criticizing President Jimmy Carter for his apparent conservative approach to governing.[5] Indeed, on the same morning that Tsongas delivered his address, Kennedy appeared before the convention delegates, many of whom were hoisting up "Kennedy All The Way" signs, to deliver a speech that celebrated the liberal ideal. To the ADA's president, Patsy Mink, the idea had been to present liberalism's stalwart past and its dynamic future, with Massachusetts's two senators bracketing the creed like bookends.[6] Kennedy obliged, using his speech to recount the progress that liberalism had brought to civil rights, women's equality, environmentalism, and labor union laws over several decades, and addressing how the movement would carry principles of egalitarianism and government activism into the new decade. The crowd roared in support.

However, in taking the stage after Kennedy had stirred up the audience, the "other senator from Massachusetts," a thirty-nine-year-old freshman with little clout or seniority, stepped up to the microphone to deliver what some found to be a blunt message: Kennedy-style liberalism was bankrupt. According to Tsongas, older liberals—many of whom were sitting in the crowd—were trapped by rigid dogma in an increasingly outdated approach. Liberals were becoming "blind to reality," noted Tsongas, by not recognizing that the contemporary political situation had changed considerably:

> If we are to mobilize a new generation to move forward with liberal leadership, we must understand that the average young American is just

that—part of a new generation. A generation that never experienced the abuses and injustices that molded us. A generation that takes for granted the social equities that we had to fight for. In short . . . liberalism must extricate itself from the 1960s [and] move on to the pressing problems of the 1980s.

Americans, Tsongas claimed, were becoming increasingly frustrated with the political system and were looking for fresh leadership after years of drift under a Democratic administration. He ended by asking liberals to work for a "new liberalism . . . [one] rooted in the sound values of the past but relevant to the all-too-real problems of the present; I think it means an evolution but so be it."[7] At the core of his message was the contention that liberalism had to be recalibrated to take account of the new economic, social, and political realities that had engulfed the country since the 1960s. At the time, Tsongas's ominous assessment of liberalism's future stunned the wider political community. The symbolism of choosing the ADA, an organization that for more than three decades had proclaimed itself as the living link to the New Deal era and the intellectual home of Cold War liberalism, as the venue to proclaim that liberalism was passé divided opinion along generational lines.[8] Older liberals, such as ADA founder Arthur Schlesinger Jr., accused Tsongas of selling out and betraying Edward Kennedy, while younger liberals, especially those who had entered political office after the tumult of the Watergate scandal in the early 1970s, praised him for exposing liberalism's shibboleths.[9] Editorial responses soon followed, including from *The New Republic,* who scorned his message as "Reaganism with a Human Face," and *Fortune* magazine, who dismissed it as the same old liberal dogma window-dressed as centrism.[10] But to some, the accuracy of his warning was growing increasingly apparent: liberals were losing support and conservatives were on the march. Liberalism, Tsongas argued, had to adapt to the new realities of the moment or it would be placed on the ideological ash heap of history. What happened next is the subject of this book.

By focusing on the nexus of grassroots activism, political ideology, and party politics, *Resisting Reagan* reconstructs and reinterprets the complex reorientation of liberalism and the Democratic Party in the 1980s. In doing so, it illuminates several underexplored or misunderstood aspects of US politics since the 1960s: the impact of the Democratic Party's changing activist and electoral coalition on its political priorities; the means by which liberal grassroots organizations advanced their policy objectives in a supposedly conservative era; and the relationship among partisan politics, coalition building, and the pragmatic brokering of legislation to protect or advance liberalism in an increasingly anti-government environment. Indeed, according to much of the scholarship since, liberalism failed to meet the challenge set forth by Tsongas on that balmy summer's morning. Liberalism, and the principal vehicle of its promulgation, the Democratic Party, is often said to have experienced a sustained period of decline and marginalization after the 1960s; Ronald Reagan's election in 1980 is typically used to evidence liberalism's institutional and ideological collapse.[11] In this view, an increasingly dominant conservative movement overwhelmed the traditional liberal New Deal order in the political realm and forced liberals to retreat. The Democratic Party was only able to regain power, it was argued, by accommodating to the new conservative order and freeing itself from bondage to a liberalism that had become out of touch with mainstream America.

Historian Jeffrey Bloodworth describes the 1980s as the "wilderness years" for liberals, a period characterized by "ideological incoherence and political ineptitude" as liberalism became "moribund."[12] Likewise, historian John Ehrman portrays the decade as a "miserable time for Democrats.... Liberalism became inward-looking, pessimistic, and increasingly out-of-touch with the daily realities of American life."[13] Seemingly incapable of combating Republican dominance and lacking the political means or the agenda to challenge the new conservative order, the Democratic Party and liberals descended into a "gloomy silence" by the 1980s, according to standard accounts.[14] However, these authors are too quick to dismiss the role of liberals in this period and downplay the dissent that rippled throughout the era. Indeed, the declension narrative fails to capture both the creativity and effectiveness of liberals at the time, who learned how to operate in Reagan's shadow by working in broad coalitions, developing sophisticated campaigns, and identifying rare bipartisan opportunities to push back the tide of conservatism. Rather than wandering aimlessly through the political wilderness, struggling to comprehend the full effect of conservatism's ascendancy, liberals were seeking ways to combat the contemporary political environment; and the 1980s ultimately deserves reassessment.

Therefore, by reinterpreting the impact of liberalism during the so-called Reagan Revolution years, *Resisting Reagan* offers a counternarrative, arguing that despite the decade's conservative reputation, there was another 1980s, one in which liberalism had an influence beyond what orthodoxy suggests. Often this involved playing defense, engaging in a tactical struggle to protect hard-won gains through legislative or judicial campaigns. Yet liberals also recorded achievements that exceeded mere holding actions. Identifying these successes, as well as liberalism's obvious constraints, will shed light on a relatively misunderstood decade and add a crucial layer to our understanding of the recent past. This, however, does not mean to suggest that the 1980s was an inherently liberal period that has been misdiagnosed. Clearly, a burgeoning conservative movement reached new heights with one of its chief prophets in the White House, and liberals were therefore forced to operate in a political environment increasingly influenced by Reagan. But in creating a teleological view that overemphasizes the binary relationship between conservatism's rise and liberalism's decline, we are left with an incomplete picture. As historian Julian Zelizer notes, for example, "Many of the books on conservatism treated the Right as if it faced almost no opposition. . . . Liberals were virtually written out of the story."[15] Therefore, by arguing that we should recognize the 1980s more as a period of polarized political contest, than of conservative dominance, this book writes liberals back into the story, showing that liberalism remained viable and dynamic in several crucial ways.

A key issue with how we understand the 1980s has been the centrality of Reagan to the conservative ascent/liberal decline paradigm and his foregrounding in historical interpretations of the decade. Because of this, to a large degree our impression of liberalism in the 1980s is shaped through the prism of Reagan and informed by an understanding of the decade's politics as dominated by the conservative movement he led. Certainly, as an iconic figure, Reagan casts a large shadow; he is held as the triumphant personification of conservatism among its followers, while scholarship on his presidency has flourished as part of the rush to investigate conservatism.[16] Yet this interpretative examination of the period through a biographical lens has caused Reagan to become a synecdoche not only for his presidential term (1981–1989) but also for the decade as a whole, with historians such as Gil Troy and Sean Wilentz referring to it as the Reagan Era or the Age of Reagan.[17] Doing this diminishes the agency of those who organized to resist Reagan, a point Julian Zelizer notes: "Liberalism is the elephant in the room as readers try to understand why Reagan made the shifts that he did."[18] Many factors have been discussed regarding his presidency, but the pressure from liberalism is rarely part of the mix.[19] Instead, within this "rightward bound" historiographical framework, Reagan's landslide victory in 1980 is often used to evidence a supposed political realignment from liberalism to conservatism.[20]

This interpretation largely stems from a cyclical understanding of

American politics, based on the early works of V. O. Key and Walter Dean Burnham, whose theories held that "critical elections" create enduring political realignments, and that of Arthur Schlesinger Jr., who, expanding on the work of his father, reasoned that the political pendulum alternates between thirty-year periods of conservatism and reform.[21] Roosevelt's election in 1932 is regularly heralded as a critical election in this model, but there is sufficient evidence to rebuke the claim that Reagan's election should also be considered as one. As political scientist Everett C. Ladd concluded at the time, it was instead the longer-term process of "dealignment" that gave the 1980 election its distinctive cast, whereby the electorate favored neither Democrats nor Republicans: "Voters moved away from parties altogether . . . as more and more of the electorate became up for grabs."[22] Rather than probing the deeper spatial and temporal currents that flow throughout American politics, scholars have too often used presidential elections to structure narratives of realignment within a conservative/liberal analytical framework, thereby obscuring longer-term transformations and continuities that are equally constitutive of American political life.[23]

Indeed, given the increasing polarization of the political arena and the institutional inertia inherent in the American system, divided government emerged as a persistent feature of national politics after the 1960s, oscillating between parties and largely serving as a framework for policy making and partisan intransigence.[24] For the 1980s, divided government dominated the political environment as Reagan faced a Congress partially—and then fully—controlled by the opposition throughout his presidency.[25] And with the Democratic Party losing much of its conservative wing as the decade progressed—with members either switching party or updating their approach to suit changing demographics—Congress became more liberal as a result, forming a key bastion of resistance and shaping the parameters of partisan conflict across the era. Therefore, by spotlighting the centrality of Congress to liberalism's story at the time, *Resisting Reagan* shows how the declension narrative is challenged when we switch our historical gaze from presidential to congressional politics in the 1980s. Crucially, Congress is a particularly understudied arena in postwar historiography, with historians typically using the presidency as a more suitable vehicle to understand developments in political history.[26] But by demonstrating how congressional actors and liberal groups worked collaboratively to place significant checks on Reagan and his eponymous revolution through congressional action and to incrementally advance their own policies through sophisticated legislative maneuvering, this book shows how the parameters of the Reagan Revolution were negotiated in a nation where liberalism remained a significant force. In doing so, it brings a range of vital but often overlooked actors from Congress and grassroots organizations into the study of political history.

There has been, importantly, a limited revision of liberalism's postwar story recently. Bradford Martin, for example, has challenged the idea of the 1980s as the Age of Reagan by recounting a history of activism on the left buried by the weight of the conservative ascendancy narrative. Martin looks outside electoral politics to illuminate the influential, though often overlooked, movements that flourished in Reagan's America, such as the Nuclear Freeze movement.[27] Timothy Stanley examines the 1980 election through Kennedy's insurgent primary campaign against President Carter to challenge the assumption that its failure necessarily marked the demise of liberalism. Stanley, who argues that Kennedy's defeat was a product of historical accident as foreign policy crises bolstered Carter's support at a crucial juncture in the contest, details the significant degree of support Kennedy was able to attract and shows that the late 1970s was not a period of uncontested rightward drift.[28] Lily Geismer, in *Don't Blame Us* (2014), also challenges the ascent/decline narrative by using the suburbs around Boston in the 1970s and 1980s to examine the increasing importance of white-collar suburbanites to the Democratic Party's electoral fortunes.[29] More recently, Patrick Andelic, in *Donkey Work* (2019), demonstrates how congressional Democrats responded to the conservative challenge from 1974 to 1994 and details the extent to which Congress, as an institution, had a remarkable facility for undermining iconoclasm and stalling policy experimentation.[30]

Resisting Reagan complements and builds on these important works, but crucially, is distinguished by its focus on "identity politics" and its detailed exploration of the broad coalitions that developed around key identity-based issues during the Reagan Era, demonstrating how liberals worked both within and outside formal structures of power to effect change in the political arena. Indeed, existing scholarship largely neglects the story of how the National Organization for Women (NOW) and the Leadership Conference on Civil Rights (LCCR), two of the largest identity-based umbrella organizations in the United States, effectively spearheaded a liberal counterrevolution and drove change from the shadows of the Reagan Era.[31] Yet these grassroots groups, which led innovative coalition-based campaigns throughout the 1980s, fundamentally restructured the politics of the decade, reshaping the contours of liberalism and transforming the policy agenda of the Democratic Party. By refracting and crystallizing the perceived interests of the civil sphere, liberal grassroots organizations served as vehicles of social change across the Reagan Era, exercising civil power by pressuring political institutions and channeling public concerns into the political space. Thus, with a distinct bottom-up approach that emphasizes the grassroots organizing of advocacy groups and their collaboration with politicians within Congress, this book offers crucial context to the story of liberalism by exploring the intersections and impacts of identity, ideology, and political institutions on empowerment and exclusion at the height of conservatism.

Indeed, with Reagan's election signaling a new political age, the prospect of a conservative backlash to liberalism would paradoxically energize liberal coalition groups—both those claiming to represent demographic constituencies, such as NOW, and those engaged in issue-oriented campaigns, such as the National Abortion Rights Action League (NARAL)—into greater political participation. For these groups, the decade's more conservative climate necessitated the ongoing process of building ad hoc factional coalitions to protect or advance their interests. Using diverse methods that covered the full spectrum of activism, from direct action protest to exerting pressure through electoral politics, broad liberal coalitions jelled around key issues during the decade, with the LCCR often at the center as the principal coordinating organization. And central to the development and evolution of liberalism during the 1980s was the extent to which the liberal coalition would alter as the decade wore on, predicated on changes in political demography and geography—shifts that would have powerful reverberations on liberal voting patterns and issue campaigns.

As the decade opened, for example, it became clear that the New Deal Coalition—a coalition forged in the 1930s of labor unions, religious groups, southern white voters, blue-collar workers, and Black voters, among others, to long sustain an electoral majority for the Democratic Party—was continuing to decline, particularly as southern white voters and blue-collar workers had largely supported Reagan's election. However, liberals were still able to succeed in campaigns and elections during the decade by assembling a more consistently left-leaning coalition centered on women, racial minorities, and young professionals.[32] This coalition-building process also had a geographic dimension as liberals sought to attract voters—particularly the swelling Baby Boom generation (the demographic subgroup that would come of age politically in the 1980s)—from growing suburban areas around the country (between 1968 and 1988, the suburban vote, as a percentage of the electorate, grew from 35 to 48 percent).[33] Often thought of as a fulcrum for conservative politics in the postwar decades, suburbia was fertile soil for the growth of liberalism as well.[34] By the end of the 1980s, a reconfigured Democratic coalition increasingly shaped by these liberal constituencies would form the basis of a post–New Deal coalition moving into the 1990s and beyond.

This is not to conflate liberalism entirely with the Democratic Party. As a broad political party, the Democratic Party held a heterogeneous assortment of ideological elements and issue-oriented organizations under its umbrella; the fact that southern conservatives and racial minorities were both key strands of earlier coalitions demonstrates the philosophical diversity of the party's disparate parts. Yet, for a variety of reasons explored through subsequent chapters, by the 1980s both the Republican and Democratic parties had become more effective sorting mechanisms for liberalism and conservatism. Principally, the emergence of social and cultural issues concerning race and gender in the 1960s and 1970s and the rise of assorted movements clamoring for political recognition had forced the parties to assume more polarized stances.[35] Indeed, after the rights-consciousness of various groups was awakened by the drive for civil rights after World War II, the emergence of identity politics—which stresses strong collective identities as the basis of political action—increasingly determined the shape and structure of voting coalitions in ensuing decades.[36]

Similar to liberalism, identity politics is a particularly elusive and contested phrase, often deployed in an American context as a collective rubric for the liberation movements of women, racial minorities, and other marginalized groups who invoked concepts of identity to challenge existing power structures after World War II.[37] Identity politics thus moves beyond a class-reductive analysis of power to capture the notion that one's experience as a member of a social group determines the moral legitimacy of their politics; that one's sense of self in the political arena was shaped by concepts of, and ideas/issues linked to, gender, race, religiosity, or sexuality, for example, rather than purely class-based economic categories.[38] While class certainly remained an important factor, political identity was increasingly informed by subjective choices rather than objective categories, such as occupation.[39] And the emergence of issues linked to those choices, such as abortion rights, dominated political conflict into the 1970s and beyond. The prominence of the abortion issue after the 1960s, for example, was tied directly to the emergence of second-wave feminism and the concept that the "personal is political."[40] As a result, political identities formed around abortion attitudes at the time, with a sense of social connection defined by pro-choice or pro-life stances. This, according to journalist L. A. Kauffman, resulted in "an unprecedented politics of previously non-political terrains; sexuality, interpersonal relations, lifestyle, culture. . . . Identity politics sees these realms, which directly engage the self, subjective experience, and daily life, as crucial sites of political contestation."[41] As will be shown, identity formation through consciousness-raising and the type of issue-based choices directly tied to that process motivated strong identifications with liberalism and conservatism after the 1960s, with a resulting impact on party affiliation as the political environment became more polarized. Indeed, these developments ensured that both parties became more ideologically homogenized as the decade progressed. As the *National Journal* noted in 1985, for example, the politics of the 1980s was "producing very conservative Republicans and very liberal Democrats."[42] Thus, although this work does not shy away from acknowledging the impact that a small number of liberal Republicans played in defending or advancing liberalism in the 1980s, such as Senator Charles Mathias (R-MD) with civil rights, it relates the development of liberalism at party level principally through the lens of the Democratic Party.

Yet, this is not *exclusively* an analysis of liberalism within the Democratic Party either. Rather, this book examines how liberals, both inside and outside of it, leveraged power and influenced the party's direction in an effort to forward their cause. Tensions naturally existed between party leaders, who sought a more cautious approach, and grassroots activists, who pushed the party to assume a more assertive posture against Reagan and the conservative forces he had brought to power. But liberal networks did develop between politicians and political activists at crucial junctures during the 1980s, and a key part of this book's significance lies in its illumination of the relationships forged to sustain liberalism throughout this period. To relate this story, *Resisting Reagan* examines the development of liberalism in the 1980s through three distinct, though interrelated, strands.

First, it explores what is classed as the "intellectual" strand. Reagan's election initiated an intellectual engagement with the very idea of what it meant to be a liberal in the 1980s. Paul Tsongas, for example, was among a cohort of younger, reform-minded liberals who had emerged in the 1970s to grapple with the social and cultural developments of the time and update liberalism accordingly. This was a complicated process; but through an analysis of how these younger liberals sought to evolve liberalism to account for the realities of the 1980s, we can see the intellectual groundwork being laid for subsequent liberal victories at the state, congressional, and, eventually, presidential level. In essence, changing tone and emphasis, instead of substance, allowed these liberals to survive the 1980s, and by exploring this facet of the decade's politics, we gain crucial insights into later developments in both liberalism and the Democratic Party.

Second, it examines liberalism at an "institutional" level. This strand analyzes the organizational developments of both the Democratic Party and liberal grassroots groups in response to the rise of Reagan and the conservative movement. Negotiating liberalism in opposition was a process tied directly to developments in the Democratic Party as liberals sought a political vehicle to resist the conservative challenge and protect established gains. As will be shown, the rights groups that had emerged out of the social and cultural contests of earlier decades, such as the LCCR and NOW, were establishing sophisticated political operations in the 1980s, working in broad coalitions with key liberal officeholders to push back conservative efforts to undo past liberal gains. Grassroots groups and Democratic officials certainly clashed during the era, but the relationships they developed would carry liberalism forward into the 1990s and beyond.

Third, this book details the processes of "mobilization" in the decade. The electoral base of liberalism was shifting in the 1980s as a result of changes in the demography and geography of the electorate. Thus, by focusing on the intersections of grassroots activism and party politics in relation to this, we see how liberals worked to develop an approach capable of building and holding together a diverse coalition of emerging liberal-leaning constituencies—women, racial minorities, professionals—energized by the polarized political environment of the decade. This was not always successful, but the intellectual and institutional reforms were often implemented with mobilization strategies in mind.

What unites these elements is the emergence of identity politics as a transformational dynamic of the political arena. While some of the more traditional New Deal liberals who typically drew their strength from labor unions, such as former Vice President Walter Mondale, struggled to adapt to this new political climate, younger, reform-minded ones like Tsongas and Colorado Senator Gary Hart wrestled with how to incorporate identity-based issues into their liberalism while also trying to emphasize universal issues, such as economic growth, to attract a wider swath of the electorate. This would develop into a generational battle for the soul of the Democratic Party and would dominate intraparty affairs through much of the 1980s. At an organizational level, the Democratic Party reformed its operations to account for the rise in identity-based politics, with quotas inaugurated to increase the representation of previously marginalized groups in the structures of party power. Moreover, grassroots liberal organizations, many of which defined their existence through identity politics, used their shared experiences to build coalitions and push the Democratic Party to legislate for intersectional identities. Finally, social and cultural identity, instead of economic class, increasingly determined the shape of liberalism's developing post–New Deal electoral base as the decade wore on. In examining how these strands interact and intersect, the historical moments explored throughout this book all tackle, in some form or other, the emergence of identity politics within the context of liberalism. Consequently, Tsongas's previously mentioned warning would prove prescient—liberalism was at a crossroads as it entered the 1980s. In seeking to better understand the path that it took, this study examines the ways in which liberals adapted to combat the conservative mood and fashion a more palatable political approach to suit the contemporary moment.

The evolving nature of liberalism during the 1980s means that this study follows a chronological path, with each chapter examining an important development that occurred along the way. While not every chapter examines all three strands of inquiry, the case study format allows for a more in-depth analysis of certain aspects of the argument to explore how they interacted as the decade progressed. Chapter 1, for example, surveys the intellectual response to the 1980 election. Reagan's election created a powerful incentive to rethink the direction of liberalism, and continued Democratic control of the House of Representatives placed that body at the center of the process. Louisiana Congressman Gillis Long and his liberal colleagues in the House Democratic Caucus started to openly debate the future of liberalism in the party and transformed the forum into an instrument of liberal reform. This chapter explores the evolution of liberalism through the prism of these legislators in the aftermath of defeat and details their efforts behind the scenes to reframe their creed and alter their approach. Subsequent policy statements emanating from Long's "Liberal Laboratory" would reflect a retooled Democratic Party, one that affirmed the essence of liberalism but recognized the need for new approaches to achieve traditional goals. Ultimately, chapter 1 details the often-overlooked story of reform that occurred in Reagan's first term, offering insight into how liberals sought to engage intellectually with the parameters of the Reagan Revolution.

But it was not only a period of intellectual debate. While Reagan's election caused younger liberals to seek ways to update liberalism, it also convinced a number of its leaders to stand on principle and protest the incoming conservative wave. As chapter 2 details, liberals in Congress began successfully challenging the Reagan administration as early as 1981. By examining the grassroots and party-led campaigns to protect the Voting Rights Act and the Social Security Act, two legislative symbols of liberalism, this chapter documents the persistent strength of liberalism and challenges interpretations of the early Reagan years as the apogee of conservatism. With the VRA, for example, the eighteen-month campaign to protect the Great Society's brightest jewel from conservative dissection demonstrates how a strong liberal defense had a significant impact on the 1982 midterm elections. Indeed, these campaigns eventually coalesced to form the fairness issue, which was placed at center stage during the midterms. By quickly regrouping after 1980, liberals were able to claw back their losses in Congress, much to the dismay of many on the right who saw their hopes of revolution disintegrating before them. And by choosing to defend certain issues over others, liberals also recognized that the change in tenor after 1980 necessitated a calculated approach—liberals put up less of a defense when Reagan pushed through a comprehensive economic program in his first year that reduced taxes, cut department budgets, and increased defense spending precipitously. Chapter 2 shows that liberals had to make strategic choices to defend their gains in a more conservative climate.

Although the 1980s is often considered an era of retrenchment and backlash, chapter 3 explores how liberal groups representing women and racial minorities grappled with its more conservative climate by focusing their operations, altering their strategies, and collaborating with key legislators.[43] For example, as the Republican Party shifted in a more conservative direction in the 1980s, gender started to correlate with partisan preference/election outcomes in enough contests to give credence to the belief that women were becoming a decidedly liberal voting bloc. This became known as the "gender gap," a term coined in the early 1980s to refer to the electoral phenomenon of women voting for the Republican Party in significantly lower proportions than men for the first time in history. By the middle of Reagan's first term, an administration report had warned that women were "now emerging considerably more liberal and Democratic than men."[44] Contemporaneously, with the equality-seeking movements of the 1970s institutionalizing their operations by the 1980s, liberal women's groups started to exploit this new electoral mandate and moved to ensconce themselves within the internal politics of the Democratic Party. NOW, the largest liberal women's group, proved to be particularly successful in this respect, pushing Democrats to realize the electoral potential of the gender gap and select a woman as their nominee for vice president in 1984.⁴⁵ Chapter 3 also details the extent to which women and racial minorities were disproportionately affected by the curtailment of social welfare programs under Reaganomics and sought further security under the Democratic banner. In doing so, the chapter highlights the growing organizational prowess of grassroots groups and demonstrates how liberals on the ground resisted the conservative challenge and developed a political approach more suited to the Reagan Era.

Chapter 4 uses the 1984 election to explore the turning point for liberalism in the 1980s. Despite Reagan's landslide reelection that year, the Democratic primaries featured a fascinating generational battle that pitted an old-guard liberal, Walter Mondale, against an emergent, reform-minded one, Gary Hart, in a direct contest over how liberalism should respond to Reaganism. Few substantive issues divided them; instead, it became a question of style and appeal. Mondale defended the traditional advocacy role of government and sought to build a coalition reflecting constituencies from the New Deal past, while Hart offered a different coalition-building approach—drawing in independents and "realist" liberals with his "new generation" and "new ideas" rhetoric. Concepts of identity politics were at the center of this battle; and in a close outcome, Hart finished with twenty-five states in his column and 36 percent of the vote to Mondale's twenty-two states and 38 percent. Moreover, once Reagan easily swept aside Mondale, the party increasingly turned to Hart's approach, evidenced initially in the struggle to elect a new Democratic National Committee chairman and the response to the creation of the Democratic Leadership Council, an organization established to move the party away from identity politics and toward a more conservative approach to governance.

Chapter 5 traces these shifts through 1986 and 1987, looking specifically at the 1986 midterm elections and the liberal response to Reagan's nomination of conservative judge Robert Bork to the Supreme Court in 1987. Reagan had tried to make the midterms a national referendum in an effort to recast 1986 as a replay of 1980. However, as the chapter shows, liberals developed mobilization strategies to energize women and racial minorities to turn out in increased numbers to stifle this, providing the voting margins in enough contests to give the Democrats the keys to Congress. Most of the Democrats who ran that year conducted pragmatic liberal campaigns, reaching out in a similar fashion as Hart to the emerging post–New Deal coalition. Furthermore, by chronicling the unfolding of the anti-Bork campaign in 1987, this chapter examines the early and vociferous opposition that the nomination faced from a united liberal movement, both at the grass roots and within the Democratic Party. Bork was a doyen of the right at the time, and his opposition to a raft of liberal issues, including reproductive freedom and civil rights laws, induced liberal groups to launch themselves into the political fray to prevent his confirmation. The forceful and well-organized response from liberal groups and the Democratic Party stunned the Reagan administration; and by using the Bork moment as a detailed case study, this chapter demonstrates how diverse methods of grassroots activism were now utilized alongside polling data, targeted media, and an effective insider game to project power in opposition. This chapter also examines how the "Block Bork" coalition translated their success into other aspects of the liberal agenda by organizing the passage of two crucial civil rights bills in 1988—the Civil Rights Restoration Act and the Fair Housing Act.[46]

Uniting several strands, chapter 6 examines the 1988 elections and the state of liberalism at the close of the Reagan presidency. First, it explores the candidacy of Jesse Jackson, whose trailblazing run for the presidency showcased the increasing power of the so-called Rainbow Coalition of diverse demographic groups. Second, it uses the Democratic primaries that year to examine the evolving nature of liberalism at an intellectual level; Jackson was among a field of liberals jockeying to be the post–New Deal candidate. But it was Michael Dukakis—the Massachusetts governor elected alongside the Watergate Babies in 1974—who emerged triumphant from the contest. Dukakis's pragmatic approach to governance, coupled with his strong commitment to social liberalism, demonstrated the extent to which so-called neoliberalism had taken hold in the party. While 1988 is often remembered for "liberal" being turned into an epithet, this chapter takes a fresh look at both the primaries and Dukakis's candidacy to challenge this view, showing instead that the defeat had more to do with Dukakis's poor campaign and his reluctance to counter Republican attacks. Rather, 1988 is better understood as a missed opportunity, with results outside the presidency continuing to show liberalism's resilience. Indeed, by shifting the historical gaze from the presidency to Congress, it is clear that the emerging liberal coalition continued to fuel Democratic gains; evidence demonstrated that, if cultivated properly, it could propel a Democrat to the White House (Dukakis squandered a staggering twenty-eight-point gender gap months before the election, but it remained the foundation of congressional victories). By exploring the myriad strands of the 1988 elections, this chapter also details the extent to which many liberal grassroots groups had now fully transitioned into partisan operations under a Democratic Party banner.

Finally, chapter 7 explores how, as the curtain fell on Reagan's presidency, clear signs of a nascent, liberal-leaning coalition of women, racial minorities, and young professionals, initially hinted at during the 1986 midterms and energized by the Bork campaign, were now evident as the emerging post–New Deal base of the Democratic Party. With the seeds of recovery planted, the chapter traces these elements into the Bush presidency by detailing how liberals continued to push for expansion of opportunity, especially through the legislative and judicial branches as abortion, civil rights, and other contested identity issues shaped the domestic environment and drove the emerging culture war. It demonstrates how the Democratic Party navigated this environment by continuing to work closely with liberal grassroots groups, courting the developing strands of this new liberal coalition and building on its congressional majorities. Indeed, it details how strategies directly tied to these elements would prove central to the rise of Bill Clinton, whose candidacy is often triumphed for offering a Third Way back to power that moved away from liberalism, but whose route to victory was far more multifaceted. As will be shown, Clinton's rise can be directly traced to the three strands discussed throughout—the intellectual reframing of liberalism in Reagan's shadow, the organizational power of liberal grassroots groups and the Democratic Party, and the emerging coalition of women, racial minorities, and young professionals who formed the demographic foundation of a reconstituted liberalism for the post-Reagan era.

Collectively, these chapters reveal the assorted ways in which liberals challenged the decade's conservative forces, in some cases quite successfully. Crucially, the developments detailed throughout ultimately belie the decade's reputation as an epoch of liberal retreat, instead illustrating the importance of shifting strategies to combat the contemporary political climate. Evidently, liberalism was not an ascendant force during the 1980s, but it was certainly not in terminal decline either. Instead, by using both party members and grassroots organizations as the lens, this book provides insights into the liberal coalitions and networks that formed and developed while in opposition to protect liberalism and help liberals attain success at the state and congressional level, as well as facilitate subsequent triumphs at the presidential level. It demonstrates how negotiating liberalism in the Reagan Era was a process of significant intellectual refinement, organizational collaboration, and demographic mobilization. Indeed, by exploring the tenacity of liberalism through these three interrelated strands, *Resisting Reagan* demonstrates how liberals were able to counter Reagan and the Republicans, maintain the central tenets of major liberal programs and policies, and recalibrate their offer to the electorate to attract emerging constituencies into a liberal-leaning coalition in an era of purported conservative dominance. In doing so, this book provides a fresh perspective on the decade that counterbalances the prevailing notion of liberal decline and offers important historical context for contemporary debates over issues of identity, ideology, and institutions.

1. Liberalism at a Crossroads
Debating the Future of Liberalism Within the Democratic Party After 1980

On Wednesday, 5 November 1980, the nation woke to a new political dawn. Not only was an incumbent president cleared out of office for just the third time in a century, but the Democratic Party lost control of the Senate for the first time in almost three decades. A number of leading liberals in Congress lost their seats in a series of unexpected upsets that some commentators suggested reflected a rejection of liberalism. Indeed, columnist George Will was hardly alone among his contemporaries in greeting Reagan's election as symbolizing a new conservative epoch, noting that "Barry Goldwater won the election of 1964, it just took sixteen years to count the votes."[1] That evening, the *MacNeil-Lehrer Report,* a public television news show, invited three political commentators on to dissect and analyze the outcome. The *New York Times*'s Anthony Lewis assessed the Democratic Party's position gloomily—the party, "without an idea," had been "swept away"' and was now "lost" at sea claimed Lewis. Across the table, Patrick Buchanan, President Richard Nixon's former speechwriter and an ardent conservative, used his appearance to bask in what he described as "a repudiation of the liberal philosophy." The third member of the panel, the *New Republic*'s Morton Kondracke, disagreed with both views. Instead, Kondracke called this "an opportunity." It was, he argued, "a repudiation of Carter'" but "not a rout." Democrats did well at the state and local level, and Kondracke concluded that what was needed now was for the party to adopt "some sort of—what might be called *neo*-liberalism." The cohosts, intrigued, asked Kondracke to expand: "[Neoliberalism] combines traditional Democratic compassion for the downtrodden and outcast elements of society with different vehicles other than categorical aid programs, or quota systems, or new federal bureaucracies."[2]

Kondracke called on liberals to embrace Reagan's election as an opportunity to inject new thinking into their approach. Here, Kondracke was not speaking into a void, but rather was preaching to the choir for many. Indeed, rather than pining for the halcyon days of yesterday, a cadre of youthful, reform-minded liberals sought to use the moment to update and recalibrate liberalism and move the party beyond its past. For decades, liberals had used the success of the New Deal, a set of policies designed to combat the economic and financial turmoil of the 1930s, to rationalize and justify the growth of government to find comprehensive solutions to societal problems.[3] This was at the heart of Lyndon Johnson's Great Society in the 1960s, heralded as the apotheosis of liberal reform. Johnson proposed fiscal policies to maintain full employment and created welfare programs to transfer resources to the poor on the basis of assessed poverty.[4] As amendments to Roosevelt's earlier Social Security program, one of Johnson's most significant legislative achievements was the creation of Medicare and Medicaid, while the Civil Rights Act and Voting Rights Act importantly opened up opportunities to millions of marginalized minorities.[5]

Although these sweeping liberal reforms carried on into the 1970s, due to decisive events—the Vietnam War, economic structural changes, shifts in cultural norms and social values, and a conservative backlash to the liberal legislative agenda—the liberal consensus that Godfrey Hodgson described had fractured.[6] The civil rights revolution had moved race to the center of American politics, and with it, racially inflected issues such as welfare and crime. With Johnson's embrace of civil rights in 1964, followed by the presidential candidacy of southern segregationist George Wallace four years later, a huge swath of white voters moved to the Republican Party. The Republicans, first under Richard Nixon in 1968, and then under Reagan, were able to corral these voters with assurances of low taxes, promises to be tough on law and order, and the use of racially hued rhetoric that tacitly appealed to their fears about civil rights.[7] Among voters, the Democratic Party was increasingly seen as the institutional embodiment of the worst excesses of the 1960s, a view largely solidified by George McGovern's disastrous campaign in 1972.[8] That same year witnessed democratizing reforms to the party's presidential nomination process that opened it up in a more participatory sense by mandating quotas for proportional race, gender, and age delegate representation—developments tied directly to the emergence of identity politics. It was from this context that the "reform liberals" entered the political arena.

In the midst of the Watergate affair, a wave of seventy-five freshman Democrats, termed the Watergate Babies, were elected in the 1974 congressional elections. Most drew their strength from the emerging suburbs across the country by placing social and economic issues at the core of their pitches, and several of them won seats long held by Republican incumbents, including Paul Tsongas, who became the first Democrat from Massachusetts's 5th District in almost ninety years.[9] According to journalist William Schneider, they represented "a new kind of liberal: unorthodox, reform-minded, and iconoclastic."[10] Signaling a generational and cultural shift in liberalism at the time, these Watergate Babies had forged their political identities during the tumultuous 1960s, and this experience would shape their approach to politics. Following the quagmire in Vietnam and the associated failures of the Great Society, these newer liberals sought to recalibrate liberalism for a period of economic strain in the 1970s and update its approach to account for the rise of assorted civil rights movements. More dovish on foreign policy as well, they distanced themselves from the interventionist approach that had characterized liberal internationalism, advocating restraint on the use of military force abroad and major structural reforms to defense budgets instead.[11]

This embryonic search for a new approach would obtain the label "neoliberalism" by the 1980s. Yet, it is important to note that these neoliberals emerged not so much in opposition to the dominant liberalism of the time but as a variant of it—seeking to update rather than replace the creed. Indeed, this generation, and simpatico members elected in subsequent cycles, were engaged in a battle of style rather than substance. The reason, for example, that the ADA invited Tsongas to speak in 1980 was that his voting record marked him as one of the most liberal, if not *the* most liberal member of the Senate.[12] This was true for the rest of the reformist cadre as well. A common neoliberal expression was that "the solutions of the thirties will not solve the problems of the eighties," and for all their skepticism, these newer liberals remained deeply committed to the ameliorative capacities of government and strongly supportive of egalitarianism and social justice.[13] Instead, given the change in tenor after the 1960s, they sensed that there were limits on what liberals could accomplish and claimed that they were engaging in a methodological, rather than ideological, critique of liberalism. To be sure, there was an important political message in the very act of updating their approach; the search for a "new liberalism" reflected the perceived need to move away from the traditional. But the goal was to essentially alter the packaging of their partisan product. Neoliberals suggested that liberalism had to leave the mechanism of the New Deal behind in search of appropriate responses to modern problems. According to Charles Peters, described as the "godfather of neoliberalism" for his advocacy of it through *The Washington Monthly*: "[While] a neoconservative is someone who took a long hard look at where liberalism went wrong and became a conservative, a neoliberal is someone who took that same hard look and decided to correct it, but still retain his liberal values."[14]

Essentially, neoliberalism advocated for a leaner but more activist government and sought to update liberalism to account for the rise in identity-based politics.[15] Senator Gary Hart, who became a leading intellectual light of neoliberalism in the 1980s, summarized the approach pithily: "What is changing are not principles, goals, aspirations, or ideals, but methods."[16] According to these reformers, liberals had been living off the New Deal tradition of priming the pump, which ran counter to the realities of the 1970s, when economic growth had noticeably slowed. Keynesian economic theory—which, among other notions, held that national prosperity required government management of the economy to keep unemployment low, inflation in check, and growth high—had been the guiding liberal principle of postwar economics. However, the "stagflation crisis" of the mid-1970s—a complex mixture of both growing inflation and rising unemployment—brought to the surface tensions inherent in the Keynesian model.[17] The deindustrialization and financialization of the economy, the shift of manufacturing overseas, and the decline of labor unions exacerbated the situation, and as Carter struggled to respond, conservatives laid the blame directly at the liberal state's doorstep, arguing for the use of a supply-side model as a corrective.[18] Reform-minded liberals recognized that New Dealism conflicted with these new realities and started drafting economic proposals that were empirical and pragmatic, rather than doctrinaire, to refine Keynesianism for an age of limits. To them, liberalism was falling out of favor with the electorate because older liberals had become preoccupied with slicing up the economic pie instead of increasing its size. As the *New York Times* noted after the 1980 election, "If a shrinking/non-growing economic 'pie' has turned the public sour on liberalism, then a party that wants to remain liberal should, logically, develop plausible approaches to achieving economic growth."[19] As the decade advanced, an increasing number of liberals embraced this idea that economic growth was a prerequisite for social justice—a reversal of the Great Society tenet that the continuation of growth was secure.

Thus, Reagan's surprise victory created a powerful and immediate incentive to rethink the direction of liberalism, and the noises emanating from these younger liberals only grew louder. As Richard Gephardt (D-MO), who would emerge during the 1980s as a leading neoliberal, noted at the time, such a defeat "tends to focus the mind."[20] Having unexpectedly lost the White House, Democrats now needed to generate new ideas and policy responses to form the basis of an alternative message and agenda for the next election. And given that Carter had appeared to embrace a more conservative approach to governance, liberals argued that the party should rediscover its liberal traditions. Instead of descending into "gloomy silence," as historian John Ehrman suggested, reform liberals, or neoliberals as they were increasingly labeled, were at the forefront of this process to rethink approaches to liberalism and explore new ways of framing it for a changing electorate.[21] By actively responding to the new electoral realities of the time, liberals were proposing policy solutions that were not mere retreads of old orthodoxy, but rather adaptations to new conditions that deserve reassessment. Therefore, this chapter details the important story of reform that took place within the Democratic Party in the early 1980s, looking principally at the intellectual responses that followed the election to show how liberals attempted to reckon with Reagan.

RECKONING WITH REAGAN

With Reagan marking activist government as the cause of society's problems during his inauguration address, some observers wondered whether a political realignment had indeed taken place.[22] But alongside Kondracke's assessment of the situation, other more circumspect commentators probed the deeper complexities of the election, with some noting that the electorate appeared to be neither conservative nor liberal, but instead ready to embrace leadership from almost any angle.[23] Exit polls revealed that only 11 percent of voters crossed the box for Reagan because "he is a real conservative," and many political observers at the time reflected that the defining feature of the election had been rejection instead.[24] Indeed, buried by the landslide narrative is evidence that large percentages of liberal voters rejected Carter.

After a surprising victory over Republican President Gerald Ford in the post-Watergate election of 1976, Carter struggled to win the loyalty and approval of voters and alienated strands of his own party with his tepid support for key liberal legislative goals, such as full employment and national health insurance.[25] Despite running on a decidedly liberal platform, once elected Carter governed very much as a moderate, prioritizing inflation over unemployment and evoking themes of limits and sacrifice.[26] This governing style motivated Senator Edward Kennedy to launch his insurgent primary bid in 1980, noting that Carter's infamous "malaise speech" cemented his decision to challenge a sitting president.[27] Although Kennedy's campaign ended in failure, a correlation quickly grew between Kennedy's primary supporters and the voters who would leave the party in 1980 to become the so-called Reagan Democrats, with particularly large percentages of registered Democrats and independents self-defining as liberal switching to the Republicans.[28] Despite Kennedy's eventual endorsement of Carter, for example, 27 percent of his primary supporters voted for Reagan in November.[29]

Many of the liberal organizations that had campaigned for Kennedy in the primaries also chose instead to support the independent bid of liberal Republican John B. Anderson, who the *New Republic* endorsed as the only candidate able to provide an activist liberal vision for the 1980s.[30] The ADA, who had supported Kennedy and eventually endorsed Carter as the "lesser of two evils," split over whether to back Anderson, with key leaders such as Joseph Rauh arguing that "a conservative moving towards the liberal side is better than Carter moving in circles."[31] Clearly, to many liberals, Carter's economic retrenchment and talk of sacrifice seemed less appealing than Reagan's optimistic rhetoric and promises of more jobs or Anderson's mixture of efficiency and social liberalism.

Carter, the preeminent symbol of the crisis of confidence he had diagnosed, became its foremost victim on election day as members of his own party fled. This paradox is best summarized by a Kennedy supporter asked at the New York primary how he would vote in November: "I'm a liberal... Carter's a disaster. I think what the country really needs is a father figure, so I'm voting for Reagan."[32] Far from the dramatic shift to the right envisioned by ideologues at the time, the electorate largely viewed Carter as the architect of the mess America found itself in as economic stagnation at home and difficulties overseas translated into votes that repudiated his particular brand of leadership. As the *New York Times* noted: "A large share of the 43.2 million Americans who voted for Ronald Reagan appear to have been motivated more by dissatisfaction with President Carter than by any serious ideological commitment to the Republican's views."[33]

Consequently, liberal pollsters were inclined to agree with this interpretation. Democratic pollster Peter Hart, for example, claimed Reagan registered a nonideological victory: "Voters perceived that the status quo was failing and the non-incumbents were the beneficiaries of this dissatisfaction."[34] Certainly, despite the convoluted electoral map, Reagan captured just 50.7 percent of the popular vote, 2.7 percent more than Ford had in 1976, while Carter received 41 percent, and Anderson, dragging numerous liberal voters away from Carter, tallied 6.6 percent.[35] Congressional results also revealed a country that was more deeply divided than the conservative dominance narrative suggests. Although the Democrats lost the Senate, with the Republicans winning twenty of the thirty-four seats at stake, the party actually received 51.8 percent of the nationwide popular vote in all Senate elections against 46.9 percent.[36] The House results were also instructive. Republicans only made gains in either open seats or among Democrats elected prior to 1974, showing that the Watergate Babies escaped much of the upheaval unscathed.[37] In fact, the changing of the guard in Congress allowed the reformist class to oust some of the liberal dinosaurs from important congressional committees.[38] With older liberals, such as Frank Church, chairman of the Senate Committee on Foreign Relations, losing their seats, the election accelerated the rise of neoliberals by producing an opening for them to test new approaches to liberalism from positions of power in the Democratic Party.[39] Some political commentators, such as Arthur Schlesinger Jr., remained skeptical though, viewing the reformist cadre as mere opportunists. Schlesinger, who put himself forward as the last stalwart defender of the great liberal tradition, blasted neoliberalism as an "empty doctrine," whose adherents were "fellow travelers of the Reagan Revolution." Arguing that neoliberals had more or less accepted the political parameters designed by Reagan, Schlesinger mused: "They have joined the clamor against big government, found great merit in the unregulated marketplace, opposed structural change in the economy and gone along with swollen military budgets.... Far from rejecting the Reagan frameworks, they would at most rejigger priorities here and there."[40]

Whether it was praise for entrepreneurs and business leaders, skepticism of government agencies and bureaucracies, or wariness of entitlement programs and services, neoliberalism was, according to political writer Richard Reeves, simply the "survival instincts of young Democrats surrendering to Reaganism."[41] However, to Tsongas and his colleagues, these critics had thoroughly misread their mission. Speaking before the National Press Club in 1982, Tsongas argued: "We [neoliberals] embrace the traditional Democratic views. We're not turning our back on them. If you go through the social agenda, I'm as liberal as they come.... But what we're talking about [is] a different approach. And if you look at the various speeches people are giving, as time goes on they sound more and more like what those of us have been arguing for."[42]

This was a process of repackaging liberalism to suit an electorate that was shifting geographically and becoming increasingly independent in its voting patterns. Following the election, Charles Peters argued that neoliberalism was more equipped to challenge Reagan as it developed new ways to meet traditional ends—justice, fair play, and liberal ideals.[43] Peters later expanded this in the 1983 publication *A Neoliberal's Manifesto*, which outlined how this new liberalism would operate in the decade.⁴⁴ Some of the older liberals who might be classed as "unreconstructed" for their ties to the traditional New Deal formula also accepted the call to fine-tune their approach.⁴⁵ Days after Reagan's election, for example, Kennedy forces started to claim that he represented the new liberalism.⁴⁶ And at an appearance before the ADA in 1981, Kennedy urged his liberal colleagues to "apply our values to new realities."⁴⁷ The ADA's president, Patsy Mink, agreed, describing liberalism's greatest challenge as "remolding our ideals" for the Reagan Era, while former Vice President Walter Mondale, the party's presumptive nominee for 1984, released an article later that year that called on liberals "to re-examine old priorities and shibboleths."⁴⁸ Clearly, with many liberals adapting to new political realities, neoliberalism started to attract a growing audience in the Democratic Party.

Nonetheless, while Reagan's election was not a complete landslide or a profound realignment, it remained a damaging defeat for liberals and the Democratic Party. Indeed, there was a sense among some that the spring of liberal ideas, which had long given the party sustenance, seemed to be drying up. The Republicans, it appeared, were now the party of ideas—a point New York's liberal senator, Daniel Patrick Moynihan, noted, ominously, to colleagues.⁴⁹ Carter's struggle to square the circle of stagflation at home and foreign policy crises abroad contributed to the impression that the party lacked solutions. Thus, with the Democrats seemingly overwhelmed in the arena of ideas, they now had to generate new policies, a coherent agenda, and an effective message to be viewed as a credible alternative to the Republicans. To do so, though, liberals needed a place to debate this intellectual refinement process and propose solutions through established, formal channels in order to effect real change. Here, continued control of the House would prove vital.

LONG'S LIBERAL LABORATORY

The efforts to update liberalism intellectually were given a focus in Congress by Gillis Long. A widely respected southern politician who belonged to a prominent Louisiana political dynasty, Long entered the House in 1963 but lost his reelection bid to his cousin, Speedy Long, over the issue of civil rights in 1964; Speedy Long called him the "man who voted against the South" for his support of procedures to ease passage of that year's Civil Rights Act.⁵⁰ After an interim that included a stint in Lyndon Johnson's government, Long returned to the House in 1972 with significant support from the newly enfranchised African American residents of his district. Although he hailed from the South, Long was not a Boll Weevil—a term, often of derision, applied to conservative Democrats from the South seen as "pests" to the party's legislative agenda. Instead, evidenced by both his early support for civil rights and his subsequent voting record in Congress, he was a liberal-leaning Democrat. His ADA ratings waxed and waned over the years, though they got progressively more liberal during Reagan's first term. Yet, Long also understood the need to reach out to the Boll Weevils, particularly after Reagan's election, to keep them from joining the Republicans. It was this combination—his gradual liberal-leaning record and his conciliatory approach—that led to his election as the new House Democratic Caucus (HDC) chair in December 1980. Long's support came particularly from those hoping to update liberalism, such as California's Norman Mineta, who declared that Long will "help us meet the challenge of pursing a course of fiscal restraint without abandoning our party's fundamental concern for social needs."[51] Seeking to develop a clear response to Reagan's election, Long set out a plan to revive the HDC as an active forum for intraparty debate, and crucially, hand over a significant portion of control on policymaking processes to the younger liberals seeking to develop new approaches to liberalism.[52]

One of the oldest political institutions in Congress—the oldest in the House with exception of the Speakership—the HDC, composed of all Democratic Representatives in the House, traditionally assumed the role of nominating and electing the House Democratic Leadership, approving committee assignments, and enforcing party discipline. By 1980 however, and after years of neglect, the HDC lacked focus and direction.[53] One particular episode on 20 August 1980 showcased this—the caucus had convened for a meeting at 9:04 a.m. but adjourned just one minute later after its chairman, Tom Foley of Washington, explained that it was organized as a formality with no business on the agenda, despite an election three months away.[54] The subsequent meeting in December would mark the beginning of the HDC's new direction. Long began by scheduling regular monthly meetings with substantive agendas and closing caucus gatherings to the media and the public in an effort to spur honest debate among members. One of his first endeavors was to organize an issues conference in January 1981 to address the process of recovery. Taking place at the Capital Hilton in Washington, DC, the conference was especially well attended by the junior liberal members of the caucus. According to historian Karl Gerard Brandt, these liberals convinced Long to establish a new HDC initiative, the Committee on Party Effectiveness (CPE), to provide a focal point for the intellectual reform effort. But the CPE was not simply an informal group; it had the sanction of the entire caucus and the imprimatur of Speaker Thomas P. "Tip" O'Neill.[55] And although it sought to represent "all philosophies and regions," it was principally the younger liberals who made up its membership—of the thirty-seven members, only five had been elected before 1970.[56] The CPE would give free rein to these younger liberals to explore ways to make liberalism more palatable to the wider electorate.

The CPE formed seven thematic task forces (economic, housing, small business, crime, environment, women's issues, and national security) and agreed to meet at least once a week throughout Reagan's first term to discuss new directions. As an example of the type of output the CPE was advancing, liberal representative Geraldine Ferraro (D-NY) used the Task Force on Women—which she headed—to draft a position paper focused on Reagan's economic policies and the impact on women.[57] The ideas from Ferraro's report, and those from the other task force position papers, would form the basis of *Rebuilding the Road to Opportunity*, a CPE publication released in September 1982. Dubbed "the yellow brick road" by its detractors, the booklet—printed with a fluorescent yellow cover—sought to alter the way in which the party packaged its liberal message to the electorate.[58] The report downplayed certain controversial issues, such as abortion and gay rights, and stressed the importance of economic growth and greater opportunity through targeted federal spending initiatives. According to the HDC's executive director, Al From, the yellow booklet was designed to return liberalism to its pre-1968 roots by stressing the "political approach used by JFK—that all Americans, in every group, benefit when the economy grows—the rising tide lifts all boats."[59] Put another way, this might be described as an attempt to return to pre-identity liberalism. However, From's reading of the booklet's intent was only partially correct.

Certainly, instead of focusing on how to appease liberal voting groups on a one-by-one basis, neoliberals were proposing that government should take an active role in directing the nation's industrial growth and investing in new technology first as a means of improving everyone's lot—this is how they attracted the sobriquet "Atari Democrats" after the popular electronics business.[60] Yet, this was not an attempt to downplay the importance of the so-called liberal special interest groups—the label often pinned to the constituencies that emerged during the democratizing reforms of the 1960s and 1970s. Moderate Senator John Glenn (D-OH) acknowledged this in 1983, telling HDC members that "women, minorities, labor are special interests and the historic interests of the Democratic Party. . . . They have been our strength in the past and will be in the future."⁶¹ Rather, the booklet represented an attempt to repackage the way in which the party appealed to these groups by suggesting that little progress on social problems could be expected unless the economy was healthy. According to journalist Fay Joyce, these reform-minded Democrats were simply "liberals with one hand on their wallets."⁶² In a letter to the *New York Times*, Senator Moynihan described this reform effort as a process or a formula for advancing liberalism in an age of fiscal restraint: "I, who have never been anything but a liberal, have been trying to discipline our ideology a little bit."⁶³ Thus, instead of trying to build a coalition by appealing to enough social interests to construct a majority, the reform-minded liberals sought a different approach, one focused on economic interests first.

The economic policy section by neoliberal duo Tim Wirth (D-CO) and Richard Gephardt, "Investing in Our Economy," is a clear example of this. Here, Wirth and Gephardt attempt to move liberalism away from the so-called old ad hockery of redistribution. Asked by reporters to explain what this meant, Wirth conceded that while buyoff was "too strong a word," the politics of redistribution was the way in which the Democratic Party reached out and kept under its broad tent "this group and that group" to hold its coalition together. "We've tried to make a dramatic shift away from that," concluded Wirth.⁶⁴ Recognizing the change in tenor after 1980, this was an effort to reach out and understand the politics of the new professional and middle-class voters less inclined to support redistributionist policies. Wirth himself noted in 1981 that, in his district, suburban college-educated technology workers had replaced traditional blue-collar voters as the base of his coalition.⁶⁵ To pivot the party's focus toward these voting groups, the economic section concentrated on policies that would foster economic growth: policies that, in line with neoliberal thinking, would "grow the economic pie."⁶⁶

Senator Tsongas viewed this shift as key to liberalism's survival, arguing that "the great political tugs and pulls of the past 35 years have concerned the distribution of the golden eggs. . . . In the 1980s and 1990s, we must focus on the health of the goose."⁶⁷ This was not to disavow redistributionist policies—neoliberals still sought to tackle income inequality through progressive taxation, for example—but rather to argue that economic growth should be viewed as a prerequisite for social progress.⁶⁸ By coupling this focus on growth with an emphasis on fairness too, members throughout the party chose to embrace its message.⁶⁹ According to political scientist Jon Hale, there was very little about the report that party members opposed, even those with a supposed orientation toward redistribution.⁷⁰ As the *New York Times* noted, while "growth and fairness may be traditional Democratic goals . . . [together] these proposals could put new life in the old liberal agenda."⁷¹ The focus on growth and fairness as twin pillars of progress would form the foundation of subsequent Democratic presidential platforms.

This economic focus was just one of a range of sections that outlined how to repackage liberalism to chart a path back to power, especially by way of attracting suburban voters. In attempting to summarize the booklet's importance, Long claimed it signaled a commitment to the fundamental principles of liberalism through new strategies for the 1980s.⁷² And the party's receptiveness to it, according to the *Washington Post*, demonstrated just how swiftly political thinking had changed in the years since the Watergate Babies hit the scene: "Ideas looked upon by most Democratic congressional leaders three years ago as diversions from such core issues as national health insurance and welfare have now become the cornerstones of Democratic thinking."⁷³ While, as subsequent chapters detail, liberals were certainly not abandoning this "old gospel," the *Washington Post* recognized the extent to which the Reagan Era had necessitated a change in approach. Although the booklet did represent a break from the past—if not in rhetoric, then in policy focus—it did not seek to undermine the values at the heart of liberalism. Instead, by coupling identity-based policies regarding women, racial minorities, and the environment with those designed to foster economic growth, the booklet blended the concerns of liberals and moderates alike in an attempt to create a new national message that could attract support throughout the party. According to the liberal former Senator George McGovern, who was one of the highest-profile senators to lose his seat in the 1980 elections, the booklet represented "the best guide that the Democratic Party has as to the direction we should pursue in the balance of the 1980s."⁷⁴

Translating these policy statements into a legislative program was immediate. Speaker O'Neill worked with these younger liberals to produce a budget resolution for 1983 that reflected proposals found in the booklet, particularly those on growth and fairness. The booklet would also form the basis of the DNC's televised response to Reagan's State of the Union address that year.⁷⁵ Further, the neoliberal approach outlined in the booklet was on show at the party's 1982 midterm conference in Philadelphia too, with debates focused on policies to spur growth, investment, and entrepreneurship. Senator Kennedy co-opted neoliberal language during his conference address, declaring his support for "a new industrial policy," "a new, simpler tax system," and "investment in basic industry, high technology, and microchips."[76] According to political analyst Michael Barone, because liberals "hardly mentioned the kind of proposals to expand government, which seemed to come automatically out of their mouths a few years ago ... the Philadelphia conference may someday be seen as a turning point."[77] Evidently, neoliberalism attracted a growing audience in the party as members began to recognize limitations on a liberal agenda forced to operate both in opposition and in the economically distressed climate of the early 1980s.

Following this, Long expanded the scope of the CPE by launching the National House Democratic Caucus (NHDC), a group cochaired by a number of prominent liberals, including Speaker O'Neill, and formed independent of Congress to harness the "outside energy and imagination" of the party's "external elements."[78] According to the group's press release, the NHDC would stimulate a "two-way exchange" between party members and supporters to establish a "broad consensus around a workable philosophy of government."[79] It quickly became apparent though that the external elements were not liberal grassroots activists but elected Democrats beyond Congress, including governors, state representatives, and former White House officials. Still, the NHDC proceeded to finance another report, *Renewing America's Promise*, published in 1984 and later submitted to the 1984 Democratic Platform Committee.[80] Written by the same team that designed the yellow booklet, *Renewing America's Promise*, now with a blue cover, was similar in style and content. Again, Long asserted in the preface that the document demonstrated "a clean break with the recent rhetoric, but not the traditional values." Long added, "It is the product of what I believe is an emerging new force within our Democratic Party—made up of members of Congress, young in mind-set if not in age, who will become the next generation of leaders in our country and in our party."[81]

Renewing America's Promise was also more aggressive in tone, focusing on Reagan by cataloguing the social and economic damage supposedly wrought by his policies.[82] Yet, by not including grassroots liberal organizations in this process of policy construction, there was an evident tension between forging a collective message and accommodating the interests of liberal groups within a pluralistic framework. The policy booklets attempted to avoid this tension by focusing on universal issues, such as economic growth and fairness, but when some members of the HDC sought to implement institutional reforms to the party's apparatus in an effort to dilute the power of liberal grassroots groups, liberal activists responded accordingly.

Indeed, at the same time as the intellectual debate over liberalism's future was taking place within Congress, some of the more moderate members in the HDC sought to alter the party's presidential nomination process by bringing elected officials back into the fold, an effort they believed was necessary after the 1980 convention debacle. That year, Kennedy and Carter delegates had, quite literally in some cases, battled it out on the convention floor, and Kennedy forces staged a coup by proposing over twenty-three amendments to the party's platform.[83] In 1981, Ferraro, one of the CPE's rising stars, was appointed to the newly formed Hunt Commission, named after its chair, North Carolina's Governor James Hunt. Here, Ferraro would play a prominent role as a broker between liberal groups and party moderates when plans hit an impasse. Although the commission considered several reforms, one of the most significant and far-reaching was the creation of so-called superdelegates—a term used to describe the elected officials who were automatically assigned to the convention as uncommitted delegates in order to counterbalance the passions of committed delegates. While this returned some semblance of power to party leaders and allowed members to involve themselves more fully in the logistics of party affairs, many perceived it as an attempt to limit the influence of grassroots activists and move away from identity politics altogether.

THE SUPERDELEGATE COUNTERREVOLUTION

As identity-based issues altered the political landscape in the 1960s and early 1970s, Democratic Party reforms were implemented before the 1972 presidential campaign got under way in an effort to open its operations up in a more participatory sense as a response.[84] By accelerating the trend toward grassroots politics driven by Eugene McCarthy's presidential run in 1968, these reforms significantly reduced the role of party officials and insiders in the presidential nomination process, increased the role of caucuses and primaries, and mandated quotas for proportional race, gender, and age representation.[85] At the 1972 convention, for example, 38 percent of the delegates were women (compared to 13 percent in 1968), 15 percent were Black (compared to 5 percent), and 23 percent were younger than thirty (compared to 2.6 percent).[86] This inevitably shifted political power away from a loose alliance of state and local party structures to a universe of activists, often rights-oriented liberal reformers, who were now granted direct access to party machinery.[87]

Later commissions in 1973 and 1978 attempted to scale back these democratizing reforms in an effort to prevent the party from veering too far to the left, but by 1980 the number of elected representatives at the party convention was historically low—the number of Democratic senators had declined to 14 percent, down from 68 percent in 1960, while the number of House members dropped from 39 percent in 1968 to 15 percent by 1980.[88] As columnist Adam Clymer noted the following year, "The issue of who is in charge never plagued the party so much as it has in recent presidential campaigns."[89] Thus, as the Democratic Party was adjusting to incorporate identity politics into its structures of power, some elected officials, stung by their own lack of input in 1980 and fearing a repeat in 1984, banded together to ask that 20 to 30 percent of the delegate total be reserved for party members as uncommitted voting delegates to the 1984 convention.[90] DNC Chairman Charles Manatt supported this, declaring before the HDC in 1981: "Each House Member, Senator, [and] major city mayor must be automatic uncommitted delegates at our national conventions, midterms conferences, and fully involved in the party's work.... It is a two-way street."[91]

Long, who was one of the first to appear before the Hunt Commission in 1981, reasoned that politicians should play a larger role since intrinsic to their status as elected officials was the fact that they represented far broader constituencies than activists or interest groups.[92] But opposition to the proposals came from these liberal organizations and activists, particularly civil rights and feminist groups such as the NAACP and NOW, who believed the reforms diminished their power, according to Ferraro.[93] Opposition also came from liberal supporters of Senator Kennedy, who at the time was expected to make another bid for the presidency. Kennedy supporters feared, with good reason, that a large number of senators and congressional representatives could halt his exploratory run by throwing early support behind Mondale, who incidentally favored the 30 percent figure. Liberal groups, on the other hand, argued that this "un-pledged add on" would create a new category of delegate that, crucially, was not subject to the party's fair participation rules. They described this new status as a "superdelegate."[94] Recognizing that these delegates would be overwhelmingly white and male, Susan Estrich, who later served as Michael Dukakis's campaign manager in 1988, pointed out that there was also the problem of equal power. The superdelegates, because of their flexibility in the choice of a nominee, would have far greater power than any of the delegates committed to a candidate.[95] This impasse was eventually resolved when Ferraro brokered a compromise.

The Ferraro proposal reduced the total number of unpledged delegates to 566, or 14 percent of the convention, which Ferraro argued was a practical solution given the valid concerns of liberal groups.[96] Indeed, as Mark Siegel, Ferraro's colleague on the compromise plan, told the *Washington Post*, Ferraro was effective because she represented the "bridge between the new and old politics, between the feminists and the organization Democrats."[97] Through working closely with liberal groups such as NOW, as well as with officeholders, Ferraro was able to maintain the systems put in place to incorporate identity politics while also balancing the concerns of elected officials.[98] To Ferraro and other liberals in the CPE, the superdelegate battle was as much a contest over image as it was over power. For example, Ferraro credited the drive to bring elected officials back into the fold with the success of the party's midterm conference in 1982. Typically used as a space for passionate, and sometimes rancorous, debate, the midterm conference was a more practical affair in 1982, with Ferraro arguing that it gave liberals the opportunity, once again, to create "realistic political issues" to run on and presented a unified image of the party.[99] Still, as much as Ferraro tried to placate both sides, liberal activists were unhappy with the new arrangements, arguing that the pendulum had swung back in the direction of the "smoke-filled room" method of decision-making (as the decade progressed, liberals would succeed in scaling back these reforms).[100]

This contest over power early in the decade provides an insight into the type of institutional disagreements—and agreements—that would characterize the decade. As liberal groups sought more political clout, and as identity-based issues framed the political landscape, some elected officials moved to incorporate these developments while others attempted to push back against them. As the superdelegate contest demonstrated, tensions between moderate elements in the Democratic Party and liberal grassroots groups often placed party liberals, such as Ferraro, in the middle, balancing the concerns of both. While the superdelegate top-down reform, which in many ways was a conservative reaction to the increasing power of liberal activists, was still implemented, the 14 percent figure was significantly less than what was originally proposed. Still, by guaranteeing a delegation of elected officials working as superdelegates at the 1984 convention, members of the HDC had reformed the process and stood a far better chance of ensuring that the party produced a message grounded in themes advanced by the CPE and NHDC (in fact, all of the announced candidates for the Democratic presidential nomination would appear before the HDC in July 1983 for the first time since the days of Andrew Jackson).[101]

"WE ARE LIBERALS"

As demonstrated, Reagan's election signaled a process of intellectual introspection for liberals, and the emerging neoliberal faction exploited this opening as a chance to test new approaches for the 1980s. While still retaining their belief in the capacity of government to ameliorate the country's social ills, the Watergate Babies matured at the same time that the political realities of Reagan's election necessitated an intellectual engagement with the ideological parameters of liberalism. Recognizing the need to update liberalism's approach for a new decade, these neoliberals found sufficient space to question the party's traditional dogma, and pragmatism effectively became their watchword. Rather than distancing themselves from identity politics and its increasing effect on shaping the party's support base, they sought to incorporate identity issues alongside economic ones by advocating policy planks based on equality of opportunity and placing growth at the center of their approach. By 1982, Paul Tsongas was describing this new liberalism as a synthesis, "an amalgam of the best ideas of both parties, adhering to traditional liberal values."[102] And this drive to rethink approaches to liberalism for the Reagan Era was taking hold throughout the party, evidenced by the number of liberals who subscribed to the process, including such established figures as Senator Kennedy and Speaker O'Neill. Neoliberals were also increasingly moving into positions of power in the party during these early Reagan years, with thirty of the thirty-seven remaining Watergate Babies in the House serving as subcommittee chairs by 1984, while numerous others entered the Senate, including Tsongas.[103]

Still, the reform effort was not without its critics. As shown, many older liberals viewed their younger colleagues as opportunists who practiced a watered-down version of Reaganism, while the liberal grassroots groups representing varied constituencies were concerned that their voice was being diluted by the institutional reform process. In October 1983, Charles Peters organized a conference on neoliberalism in order to address some of these concerns. At the conference, attended by over 350 politicians, journalists, and government officials, including members of the HDC and CPE, Peters used his opening remarks to lay down a marker: "First of all—and most important of all—we are liberals."[104] Yet he also acknowledged that the movement to reform liberalism intellectually needed to do more to reach out to groups whose concerns, in some instances, did not easily mesh with neoliberal viewpoints on certain issues.[105] With the growing importance of racial minorities, women's groups, and other constituency groups to the party's coalition-building efforts, Peters suggested that "the challenge we now face—perhaps the most important one—is how to broaden the movement to include these voices?"[106] Certainly, liberal grassroots organizations worked to ensure that the reform mission was not used as a cover to push the party rightward. By organizing and putting pressure on the Democratic Party to continue espousing a liberal agenda that catered, at least in some way or another, to their interests, the message from grassroots liberal groups was clear from the start of the decade. As journalist David Osborne noted, collectively these groups warned politicians that "if you distance yourself from liberalism, you are going to pay the price politically."[107] This binary development—both neoliberals emerging as a force in the Democratic Party and liberal interest groups engaging more in the political process—would characterize the course of liberalism at both an intellectual and institutional level. Nonetheless, while this battle for ideas was taking place behind the scenes, there was a battle to be waged on the front lines against Reagan and his conservative colleagues, who had begun cutting or threatening to abolish several liberal programs and policies after they entered office. As the next chapter will demonstrate, once again Capitol Hill was at the center of proceedings.

2. Protecting Liberalism in Congress
Liberal Legislative Battles in Reagan's First Term

Unlike previous presidents of the postwar era, Reagan rose to power arguing that government was the root of the nation's social and economic woes. In his inaugural address he famously declared that "government is not the solution to our problem, government is the problem."[1] Once in office, and after a failed assassination attempt hospitalized him months into his presidency, Reagan's popularity sat at over 60 percent by May 1981, and he used the moment to push through his conservative economic program.[2] Reagan engineered the passage of a major tax reduction plan, the Economic Recovery Tax Act, and a far-reaching budget package, the Omnibus Budget and Reconciliation Act, with such speed and efficiency that many subscribed to the idea that his election had ushered in a new revolutionary era. The so-called Reagan Revolution, it seemed, had arrived. However, when Reagan pushed to enact more of his agenda, liberals drew a line in the sand. Indeed, when the new administration set its sights on undermining two of liberalism's most sweeping policies—namely, the Voting Rights Act (VRA) of 1965, pushed through by Lyndon Johnson's Great Society, and the Social Security Act of 1935, one of the core legislative initiatives of Franklin Roosevelt's New Deal—liberals both within and outside of Congress organized to stall the advance of the revolution.

Two liberals with the highest public profiles at the time, Speaker Thomas O'Neill and Senator Edward Kennedy, fronted these defensive actions and constructed a legislative firewall in Congress. First, Kennedy, a member of America's most storied political dynasty, took up the voting rights issue. Voting rights had been the subject of Kennedy's first major address in the Senate in 1965, and like his fallen brothers, issues related to civil rights defined him as a party leader.[3] In 1974, Kennedy faced the issue head-on in his hometown when the controversy over school busing—a federal initiative aimed at redressing prior racial segregation in schools by transporting students to neighboring districts—reached a violent apogee in Boston, forcing the senator to seek refuge in a nearby building.[4] Nevertheless, having sacrificed some of his own popularity for the cause, Kennedy's advocacy for civil rights only strengthened afterward according to his biographer, Peter Canellos.[5] So when the VRA came up for renewal in 1981, perhaps the most famous civil rights measure passed in the wake of his brother John's death, Kennedy led the charge to both renew and strengthen it.[6] The immediacy of the campaign also provided an opportunity for Kennedy to revive himself politically, given that he had damaged his political standing with a quixotic bid for the Democratic nomination in 1980.[7]

Generally, scholars view the 1980s as an era of backlash against the civil rights movement.[8] However, the ability of Kennedy and a constellation of liberal groups to work together to successfully lobby for the renewal and expansion of the VRA complicates the traditional impression of retreat and challenges the idea of the early Reagan years as the apogee of conservatism. From day one, liberals organized, mobilized, and coordinated efforts in anticipation of a difficult legislative battle, and the campaign to push a strengthened VRA bill through a more conservative Congress provides insights into the types of institutional relationships developed between legislators and grassroots organizations that would characterize coalition-building strategies across the decade. Certainly, as Ralph Neas, the executive director of the Leadership Conference on Civil Rights (LCCR), noted, the untold story of the early Reagan years remains "how the broadest and most comprehensive national lobbying effort since the 1960s fashioned such a remarkable victory."[9] These relationships between liberals within and outside of the Democratic Party at such an early juncture in the decade are of particular importance as this triumph had a significant impact on subsequent liberal contests, a notion Neas later acknowledged: "If we had lost that battle, I'm not sure we'd have won anything in the Reagan-Bush era."[10] This chapter examines the eighteen-month campaign that led to that triumph and demonstrates how the formation of coalition-building strategies effectively sustained liberalism through the 1980s.

Contemporaneously, across the halls of Congress, O'Neill set out to mount a similar challenge to Reagan's conservative agenda, this time by effectively using Social Security to reestablish Democratic momentum in the House. O'Neill, an "unabashed liberal" who ascended to the position of Speaker in 1977, emerged as a leading spokesman for liberalism in the early Reagan years. Indeed, with the presidency and the Senate lost in 1980, his position took on an importance far beyond the walls of the Capitol.[11] Initially though, O'Neill had to overcome two immediate obstacles. First, like his liberal colleagues in the Senate, O'Neill returned to the House with his party in a diminished state having witnessed Republicans successfully target the seats of several prominent Democrats. With fewer allies to support him, O'Neill had to choose carefully which issues to throw his weight behind. Second, after several conservative Democrats crossed the aisle to support Reagan's budget cuts, O'Neill was criticized for failing to stop the defection—and thus, the cuts. Yet he told his colleagues that this was part of a wider calculation, believing that if he gave Reagan and his supply-side vision just enough room to operate, it would unravel the revolution. As he told a *Time* reporter: "Wait till Middle America realizes what's happened with these budget cuts.... Am I going to get some Republican scalps down the road? You bet I am."[12] At the center of this debate was Social Security, one of the most sacrosanct liberal programs, around which O'Neill would rally his party and the liberal base. In this way, Social Security started to emerge, for the first time since its founding, as a leading fault line in partisan politics.[13] O'Neill would refer to it as the "third rail" of American politics—like the high-voltage electrical conductors that lie exposed along railway lines, so charged as to be untouchable.[14] Thus, as with the VRA campaign, this chapter uses the Social Security contest to examine the links established between liberals in Congress and at the grass roots to explore the strategies behind coalition-building efforts.

Finally, both rearguard campaigns would coalesce to form the fairness issue, used successfully by liberals during the 1982 midterm elections under the slogan: "It isn't Fair ... It's Republican."[15] Indeed, as the nation entered one of the deepest recessions since the 1930s, in large part thanks to the Federal Reserve's anti-inflation policies, and with unemployment reaching 10.8 percent at its nadir in 1982, Democrats began targeting Reagan and the "unfair" policies of his revolution in an effort to galvanize liberal communities to turn out on election day.[16] Although presidents' parties often lose seats in midterm elections, the Democrats won a notable twenty-six seats in the House, a damaging loss for a president seeking to establish an electoral realignment.[17] The *New York Times* went further, claiming it was one of the most severe defeats suffered by any elected postwar president in a first midterm (the average loss was ten seats).[18] For liberals, the VRA and Social Security pincer movements had worked; the revolution, it seemed, was stalling.

PROTECTING THE GREAT SOCIETY

Using the New Deal as a model, the ambitious legislative and reformist agenda of Johnson's Great Society in the 1960s showcased the height of liberal policymaking, expanding the scope of the federal government considerably and producing a liberal legacy that endures to this day. One of its most significant and defining achievements was the push to translate much of the civil rights agenda into law. Yet, as a son of the South, Johnson understood better than most how this would polarize the electorate. Upon signing the Civil Rights Act of 1964, Johnson is said to have told an aide that with the single stroke of a pen he had just delivered the South to the Republican Party for the foreseeable future.[19] This immediately became a self-fulfilling prophecy when Barry Goldwater carried five states in the Deep South, despite Johnson's overall landslide victory, and captured 55 percent of the white southern vote, making him the first Republican ever to win a majority of white southerners.[20]

However, while the 1964 act did address a number of injustices, the historic marches from Selma in 1965 brought attention to a further component of the movement's agenda—the drive to win access to the franchise. The Fifteenth Amendment, adopted in 1870, had guaranteed the right to vote regardless of "race, color, or previous condition of servitude." But the collapse of Reconstruction in the South and the subsequent implementation of segregation laws, typically referred to as Jim Crow laws, enabled southern states to employ techniques—including literacy tests and poll taxes—to keep racial minorities from voting. It took the enactment of the VRA in 1965, with its considerably stronger protections, to deliver the franchise.[21] In what became one of the crowning achievements of the Great Society—Johnson hailed its enactment as a "triumph for freedom as huge as any ever won on any battlefield"—the VRA was designed to give legal remedies to marginalized citizens, particularly African Americans, who for generations had been precluded from voting by discriminatory state practices.[22] The measures that aimed directly at curbing these practices rankled southern politicians the most.

Under the VRA's section 5, a number of special provisions were established, including the preclearance requirement, which prohibited certain jurisdictions from implementing any voting changes without preapproval from the Justice Department or the DC District Court. Using the "coverage formula," designed to identify jurisdictions that had engaged in egregious voting discrimination practices, these special provisions fell predominantly on the South.[23] Despite intense pressure, particularly from southern conservatives who viewed this as an unwarranted intervention into state sovereignty, Johnson shepherded the bill into law, relying, crucially, on bipartisan support to assure passage.[24] In doing so, he brought about a sudden and significant increase in Black voter registration—in Mississippi, for example, Black registration increased to 54 percent from

7 percent within three years—and cemented a political alliance between African Americans and the Democratic Party.[25] Indeed, the passing of this act precipitated a realignment of the parties, particularly in the South, as a conservative, largely Republican, countermovement emerged in response to the VRA. Among them, Reagan, a Goldwater supporter, opposed the act, describing it as "humiliating to the South."[26]

Fast-forward nearly fifteen years, and Reagan, now a presidential candidate himself, opened his 1980 general election campaign with a speech pledging to defend states' rights at the Neshoba County Fair in Philadelphia, Mississippi—a site where three civil rights workers had been murdered by white supremacists in 1964.[27] Reagan's advisors strategically chose this sore spot on the racial map as it offered an "ideal location" to appeal to "George Wallace-inclined voters."[28] Wallace, who, like Goldwater, appealed to populist and segregationist attitudes, had illuminated the South's resistance to civil rights through his own presidential bids. With a Goldwater protégé appealing to the Wallace-inclined voter, the civil rights community quickly condemned Reagan.[29] Yet, unlike Goldwater, whose opposition to civil rights proved ruinous in 1964, Reagan recognized that subtle opposition provided an electoral advantage in 1980, which spoke to the ways in which racial politics had altered in the intervening years as identity politics polarized the political environment.

Hostility to Great Society liberalism manifested itself in a number of ways, but a central component of the backlash was the issue of race. Johnson and the civil rights revolution had moved race to the center of American politics, and with it, racially inflected issues such as welfare. Liberalism, which had largely been defined by Roosevelt's New Deal as primarily a "race-neutral" economic philosophy of government intervention on pocketbook issues, was becoming more closely associated with issues linked to identity. Conservatism, on the other hand, presented the civil rights movement as symptomatic of liberalism's perilous trend toward egalitarianism, and it sought to reverse its associated "assault" on state affairs and defend against government "overreach." Thus, racial issues started to fuse with political ideologies, providing some of the strongest divisions between liberals and conservatives.[30] Beginning with Goldwater, Republicans started adjusting to this new reality by developing the so-called Southern Strategy, whereby the party would tacitly appeal to the South's fear of civil rights to corral traditionally Democratic white voters. Richard Nixon expanded this strategy beyond the borders of the old Confederacy by appealing to voters across the country that felt victimized by policies such as busing—as the Boston protests demonstrated.

By successfully weaving populist, racial, and law-and-order conservatism into the political construct of the "silent majority," Nixon crystallized a conservative political identity among millions of voters across America.³¹

With a proven template, Reagan rose to prominence, in part, by capitalizing on, and extending, these racially polarizing strategies. Unlike Nixon, who endorsed civil rights while carefully calibrating his appeal to white resentment, Reagan was a Goldwater conservative whose ideological opposition to civil rights was well documented—he had opposed the 1964 and 1965 bills, the push for fair housing legislation, and the drive to create a holiday honoring Martin Luther King Jr., an issue of particular resonance since it represented a symbolic acceptance of the Second Reconstruction.³² To be sure, while running for governor in 1966, Reagan explained that he had opposed the 1964 Civil Rights Act because "it was not as well written as it could have been," while also insisting that he supported the spirit of the law.³³ Still, according to historian Douglas Rossinow, "Reagan rode the white backlash farther than anyone else ever did in American history."³⁴ Lee Atwater, an influential Republican operative, candidly acknowledged as much in 1981, describing race as a key component of Reagan's twin drive to undermine liberalism and expand his coalition. Terming it the "New Southern Strategy," Atwater argued that the Reagan team designed an approach to appeal to "the racist side of the Wallace voter" without antagonizing those who might be offended by such ugly Wallace-style racism:

> You start out in 1954 by saying, "N——, n——, n——." By 1968 you can't say "n——" that hurts you. Backfires. So you say stuff like "forced busing," "states' rights," totally economic things . . . and a by-product of them is [that] blacks get hurt worse than whites. And subconsciously maybe that is part of it . . . because obviously sitting around saying, "We want to cut this," is much more abstract than busing and a hell of a lot more abstract than "N——, n——."³⁵

By the time Reagan entered the White House, a highly polarized atmosphere around civil rights was evident. On election day, an analysis of eleven southern states found that Reagan drew just 3 percent of the 4.3 million Black votes cast.³⁶ Overall, Reagan received 10 percent of the nationwide non-white vote in 1980, which, when contrasted with Nixon's 32 percent in 1960, demonstrates the polarization of the two parties on race.³⁷ It was in this context that the VRA came up for renewal.

The Voting Rights Campaign

The VRA was extended in both 1970 and 1975, with provisions added each time to strengthen it. In 1975, for example, the act was expanded to cover Hispanic, Asian American, and Native American citizens, and bilingual election requirements were added to protect language minority groups.[38] However, the environment had changed considerably by 1981, particularly as the 1980 election saw the addition of twelve new Republican senators, many of whom were ardent conservatives. With Strom Thurmond, the octogenarian senator from South Carolina, whose segregationist views were well documented, assuming the chairmanship of the Judiciary Committee, the VRA was in a precarious position.[39] Indeed, in late 1980 both Reagan and Thurmond had announced that they would seek either to repeal or to substantially modify the VRA to correct what they deemed as unwarranted federal intrusion into local affairs.[40] Liberals knew they had to organize before the 97th Congress convened in anticipation of a difficult renewal battle.

Early in 1981, long before the August 1982 deadline, civil rights leaders, women's organizations, and numerous liberal groups began to cluster under the auspices of the LCCR to strategize and coordinate tactics.[41] The LCCR, the largest and most diverse coalition in Washington, DC, had been the coordinating mechanism for civil rights activities since the 1950s.[42] By 1981, the umbrella organization had grown to include 165 national groups, representing more than 65 million individuals. A powerful political force that wielded significant influence on Capitol Hill, the LCCR was unmatched, according to lobbyist Michael Pertschuk, in its ability to mobilize grassroots activism, structure the media, and formulate and implement legislative strategy.[43] Given the new political environment, the LCCR hired its first executive director in 1981, Ralph Neas, a thirty-six-year-old, white, Catholic, liberal Republican. Operating under Neas's leadership, the LCCR began to work closely with key liberals in the House and the Senate, especially Representative Don Edwards (D-CA) and Senator Kennedy, to draft legislation, sketch strategy, and coordinate approach. In particular, they sought to learn from past mistakes, especially the strategy disagreements that had plagued the push for Fair Housing in 1980.[44] To this end, every LCCR member group designated the VRA as a number one priority and agreed on "a total commitment to maintaining the unity of the coalition."[45]

On April 7, 1981, the coalition drafted and introduced a voting rights bill to Congress.[46] Although identical bills were introduced in the House and Senate, the coalition designated the Democratically controlled House the first line of attack, seeking to win early passage before turning its attention to the more difficult chamber across the hall. However, as they pushed to renew the act, deliberations were complicated by pressures to respond to a Supreme Court case, *Mobile v. Bolden* (1980), which had diluted some of the VRA's provisions and protections by creating the so-called intent standard. *Mobile* held that regardless of whether an electoral procedure resulted in perceived discrimination, an original intent to discriminate must be proven to establish a legal violation. For example, simply showing that no African American had won elective office in a city where they made up a majority of the population was not enough to establish discrimination. Instead, those challenging had to prove that the electoral system was set up with the original intent to discriminate against them. The *Washington Post* described this as a "major defeat for minorities fighting electoral schemes that exclude them from office."[47] Thus, the coalition aimed to use the renewal process to establish a "results" test as a corrective, which would prohibit any voting law that had a discriminatory effect irrespective of whether the law was enacted or operated with discriminatory intent. They did so by introducing an amendment to section 2 that outlined this results standard.

However, as the amended bill came before the House, Henry Hyde (R-IL), the ranking Republican on the Subcommittee on Civil and Constitutional Rights, proposed a substantial alteration to section 5 instead of section 2. As noted, section 5 had long drawn the ire of conservatives, particularly in the South, who viewed preclearance as a stigma for the sins of past generations. To correct this, Hyde sought to localize the preclearance process, giving district courts the power to determine the need for federal intervention. Yet efforts to deny voting to racial minorities had continued despite the VRA and had become more sophisticated over time through gerrymandering procedures or the holding of at-large elections in communities to dilute the minority vote.[48] Following the 1980 census, the process of redistricting and reapportioning opened up the potential for more discrimination, and the coalition set out to demonstrate this in the congressional hearings. As the *New York Times* pointed out, "Although great progress has been made in the South, [the coalition] will show that some of the gains are fragile and could be jeopardized if safeguards of the VRA were removed."[49]

Edwards, the subcommittee chairman, worked closely with the LCCR to line up a series of witnesses in support of section 5, including Reverend Jesse Jackson, who argued: "There are forces in this land who want to turn back the clock, to weaken or destroy this legislation as a first step toward the re-disenfranchisement of black and Hispanic people."[50] By raising the specter of renewed disenfranchisement, the coalition's strategy was to isolate critics of the bill as racists or radical right extremists and lobby members through grassroots pressure campaigns.[51] Certainly, when Edwards held hearings in Alabama and Texas, the coalition organized several witnesses to appear before the committee to detail how systematic, disguised discrimination persisted in their preclearance areas. After hearing this testimony, Hyde withdrew his opposition and urged the president to support the coalition measure: "If you move quickly, you may be able to broaden your constituency by eliminating a fear which plagues the black community most: that the time will soon return when they [are] literally unable to vote."[52]

With the tide turning, the coalition pushed to strengthen the act further by permanently extending preclearance, creating tougher "bail out" procedures that stipulated a "clean record" on voting rights for over ten years, and reaffirming the results standard in section 2.[53] In the end, the House adopted the coalition-sponsored bill by an overwhelming margin of 389–24, a clear demonstration of the liberal coalition's power according to Neas: "[We] led a coalition, unsurpassed in its breadth and depth . . . that lobbied and educated the House, the press, and the public. Ad hoc coalitions to save the VRA were established in all 435 congressional districts. Hundreds of thousands of letters, calls, postcards, and petitions were delivered."[54]

Neas suggested that the outcome in the House was "perhaps the most important civil rights victory in 20 years."[55] Hoping to ride the crest of this victory on the other side of Capitol Hill, Senator Kennedy sought to introduce the House-passed measure immediately, while the coalition encouraged its members to flood the offices of the thirty-nine targeted senators who opposed it.[56] Senator Moynihan acknowledged that this strategy was designed to pressure members before the opposition could organize.[57] However, the coalition was given an unexpected boost days before the hearings began. Although Reagan had announced his position on VRA in November 1981—calling for a limited renewal, a simpler bail out procedure, and a reaffirmation of the intent standard—he had remained fairly hands-off as it made its way through the House.[58] But in January 1982, before it reached the Senate, his administration shrouded itself in controversy by acting in favor of a conservative, evangelical school in South Carolina, Bob Jones University.

A decade earlier, the Internal Revenue Service had concluded that it could no longer maintain tax exemptions for any educational facility engaging in racial discrimination. As a segregated school, Bob Jones had fallen under that ruling and lost its exemption. Following years of legal wrangling, the Supreme Court agreed to review the decision in October 1981; and Reagan, lobbied by Thurmond, a Bob Jones trustee, agreed to reinstate the university's tax-exempt status. Liberal officials responded by denouncing the decision as "part of a pattern of capitulation to segregationists," while the *New York Times* claimed that Reagan had moved "from a lack of interest in fighting racial discrimination to active promotion of it."[59] Under a deluge of criticism, Reagan reversed his decision.[60] The coalition would argue months later that the entire episode helped neutralize administration lobbying against the VRA.[61]

Nevertheless, when Senate proceedings did get under way, attention was focused principally upon the meaning of the coalition's results amendment. Senator Orrin Hatch (R-UT), the chairman of the subcommittee scrutinizing the bill, disagreed strongly with what he believed were efforts to circumvent the intent provision by creating a new, untested standard. In essence, Hatch argued that the results test would alter the electoral landscape by instituting race-based gerrymandering. Hatch's first witness, Attorney General William French Smith, put the Reagan administration firmly on his side, arguing that the results standard would institute quotas.[62] Smith's testimony drew immediate and sharp criticism from liberals, particularly Kennedy, who delivered a lengthy critique of the administration's overall record on civil rights, determining that there was "a crisis of confidence" in its commitment to racial minorities. Smith objected that Kennedy was politicizing the hearings and responded that the president "does not have a discriminatory bone in his body."[63] When the room broke out in laughter, Hatch threatened to clear it.

With Hatch and the administration on one side, the coalition set out to persuade Congress that the results standard was desirable because the alternative was too difficult to prove. According to LCCR chairman, Benjamin Hooks, the administration's proposal would make it "difficult, if not impossible" to ever win a case; the argument, Hooks said, "is code for allowing discrimination to continue."[64] Pointing to the obvious difficulty of determining the collective intent of a group of individuals, such as a legislature, the coalition claimed that the results standard would obviate the unrealistic need to find a smoking gun.[65] Nevertheless, focusing the argument on quotas spoke to a larger conservative critique of the bill—not only did section 2 expand federal power, but it also gave identity issues, principally racial considerations, prominence and relied on outcome instead of process. To Kennedy, this was a pure smoke screen, particularly as the House-passed bill contained a disclaimer that tackled the quota question.⁶⁶ Nonetheless, following what the LCCR described as "an intensive lobbying campaign against the House-passed bill by Hatch and the administration," the subcommittee voted 3–2 along party lines to limit extension and incorporate the intent standard.⁶⁷ Despite effective coalition building in the House, the Republican-controlled Senate was a more challenging arena. A shift in strategy was necessary.

Here, Kennedy and the coalition sought out Republican Senator Robert Dole (R-KS), one of the few remaining undecided members on the committee. Although Dole, a moderate Republican, had shown little interest in the issue beforehand, his presidential aspirations were no secret, and according to one observer, he "decided to put more than a pinch of incense on the altar of the civil rights lobby."⁶⁸ Dole worked closely with Kennedy and the coalition to reconcile the two competing visions, settling on new language for section 2 that proposed to retain the results standard and append a new subsection to describe its parameters in greater detail. However, according to Joseph Rauh, a key figure in the liberal coalition, there "was no compromise at all. We got everything we wanted."⁶⁹ Still, with Dole's seal of approval, several wavering Republicans signed on to assure a veto-proof majority; the Senate eventually accepted it by 85–8.⁷⁰ Senator Jesse Helms (R-NC) threatened to filibuster the bill "until the cows come home," but his filibuster lasted only six days. He was mollified by promises to look at some of his legislative priorities, including abortion restrictions.⁷¹ Surveying the political landscape, the *Christian Science Monitor* pointed to the coalition's clout, even on a "conservative Capitol Hill": "[It] rang clear last week as the Senate, with only eight dissenters, passed the strongest VRA extension since that law was first enacted. The 18 month-long move has successfully mowed down every obstacle in its pathway."⁷²

On 29 June 1982, Reagan signed the bill into law "looking and sounding" like he had been its greatest supporter, according to Neas, who claimed it was "extraordinary chutzpah to take credit for something they fought until the very, very end of the process."⁷³ However belatedly it had appeared to the coalition, Reagan did eventually support the act, and he used the signing ceremony to criticize the "overblown rhetoric" that had exaggerated differences in the legislative battle.⁷⁴ To the coalition though, Reagan's actions spoke louder than his words. According to Hooks, civil rights groups still had no confidence in Reagan or in the prospect that his administration would enforce the new law.⁷⁵ Despite these concerns, the

VRA's enactment was still a resounding victory for liberals. While Reagan had favored a simple ten-year extension, with both the intent standard and easier bail out provisions, Congress extended it for twenty-five years, overturned *Mobile*, and strengthened the bail out measures. In an attempt to explain this success, Neas wrote to a supporter that the result "would be viewed as a major accomplishment in any Congress. But, considering the composition of the 97th Congress and the civil rights policies of the Reagan administration, history will surely judge the enactment as a legislative miracle."[76]

Indeed, in April 1981, the liberal coalition worried aloud about whether it could even slip an extension bill through the House, never mind the Senate, without crippling amendments being attached. With fears of entering a second post-Reconstruction period, the theme of the LCCR's annual dinner that year reflected the mood: "Civil Rights in Crisis."[77] One year later though, according to Hooks, the VRA campaign offered positive signs for liberalism moving forward: "It demonstrates that an informed, active, and committed national coalition can overcome formidable odds and beat back the forces which would have us retreat from the basic principles of fairness."[78] The campaign encompassed not only the historic Black–labor–religious coalitions of the 1960s, but also the identity-based groups that had emerged with force since the VRA: Women, Hispanics, Native Americans. Moreover, from the strategic use of advertisements, press circuits, and direct-mail initiatives to mobilizing supporters at the grass roots, the coalition developed a new set of skills to create a more "highly specialized, complex, lobbying organization than had previously existed."[79] As Neas acknowledged, "In an age of sophisticated mass-mailing techniques and of increased political activity on the state and local level, such tactics will become even more important."[80] As liberals moved on to fight several other battles against Reagan, Neas's prophecy rang true.

Crucially, Neas, who used his political acumen to keep the diverse coalition together and shepherd the bill through Congress, developed close relationships with several liberal legislators, which would prove critical moving forward. Indeed, Neas penned a letter to Kennedy to thank him for his mentorship and support: "Your leadership, commitment, and tenacity were crucial elements in the measure's outstanding success."[81] This was a relationship that continued to blossom; years later, Kennedy would describe Neas as "the 101st Senator for civil rights."[82] In the end, Neas called on the coalition's constituent parts to learn from the VRA campaign: "In the coming months and years, it will be our responsibility to apply the knowledge and experience gained from our recent successes to other civil rights issues. We must continue to galvanize our allies, and set in motion the talent, the resources, and the commitment at our disposal."[83]

On the other hand, Reagan's policies would continue to cause concern among racial minorities, stoking fears that he was against their progress. Indeed, a *Washington Post* poll early in 1982 found that only 8 percent of Black voters approved of Reagan's performance (87 percent disapproved).[84] Inevitably exacerbating these concerns, after the VRA campaign his administration moved quickly to limit the power of the US Commission on Civil Rights (USCCR), an independent advocacy agency created by the Civil Rights Act of 1957 to monitor and investigate civil rights abuses. The USCCR had been critical of Reagan's approach to voting rights, among other policies, and Reagan decided to replace its chairman with Clarence Pendleton Jr., a Black Democrat-turned-Republican who opposed busing and affirmative action as "bankrupt' policies."[85] Painted by his detractors as a lackey for the Reagan administration's "benighted civil rights policies," Pendleton started shifting the direction and focus of the commission to reflect Reagan's policy views.[86] Reagan then proceeded to fill the USCCR with conservatives by firing all of its liberal members, an act the National Organization for Women (NOW) called a "highly unwarranted political shakeup."[87] While these actions were found to be illegal—according to the judge, "You can't fire a watchdog for biting"—this politicization of the commission had a lasting impact; Reagan was eventually able to reconstitute the USCCR in 1983, and according to Neas, "pack it" with conservatives.[88]

Furthermore, despite the overwhelming passage of the VRA, the voting rights issue was revisited in 1986 when the administration signaled a shift in its enforcement policy. In a letter to the attorney general, liberal senators expressed concern over both the inadequate enforcement of the act and the administration's systematic misinterpretation of it to use an intent standard instead.[89] Edwards, who had worked hard to place results at the heart of the 1982 extension, termed the move "an outrageous retreat."[90] Still, efforts to curb or subvert enforcement procedures were also ephemeral in nature, given the fact that a future Democratic administration could simply apply the opposite approach.[91] Moreover, the liberal coalition had succeeded in its immediate objective, which was not only to renew and strengthen the act, but also to do so in a manner that allowed communities to incorporate more racial minorities in the voting process. This was apparent in the 1982 midterms, when liberals used the VRA campaign to mobilize minority support across the country. Contemporaneously though, liberals were forced to launch another far-reaching campaign to protect a key part of their history, the success of which was also evident by the midterms.

DEFENDING THE NEW DEAL

If the VRA was the crowning achievement of the Great Society, then its equivalent for the New Deal was Social Security, designed to insure against the "hazards and vicissitudes of life" for the growing number of destitute citizens during the Great Depression, particularly senior citizens and those unemployed.[92] Amendments would continue to expand its provisions to the point that over thirty-six million people were covered under the Social Security umbrella by 1980.[93] Described by economist Milton Friedman as America's "sacred cow," the nature of the system and the political power of its millions of beneficiaries meant that politicians walked a political tightrope whenever they spoke of "reforming" it, particularly due to its universal coverage.[94] Still, the Reagan administration set its sights on Social Security early, with David Stockman, Reagan's first budget director, describing plans for immediate draconian cuts to the program as "a frontal assault on the very inner fortress of the American welfare state."[95] Reagan fit his critique of Social Security into a wider argument against liberalism, suggesting that liberals had corrupted Roosevelt's original program by turning it into a welfare scheme that kept its beneficiaries dependent on government.[96] Worse still, those dependent on it were now bankrupting it. According to former Social Security Commissioner Robert Ball, in a confidential memo in 1982, this was a calculated ploy to undermine the program: "The Republicans only hope to magnify temporary and quite manageable problems with talk of 'bankruptcy' and 'failure' to justify sweeping cuts."[97]

As recently as 1977, Carter had enacted the largest peacetime tax increase in US history to solve the program's financing problems. This measure failed because poor economic conditions, combined with indexing provisions, pushed the program to an unstable position.[98] In other words, the late 1970s phenomenon of stagflation damaged the Social Security financing system as benefit growth failed to match wage increases and inflation diminished people's purchasing power.[99] While it was clear that something had to be done, Ball warned liberals that Reagan was using this opening to implement an ideologically motivated plan.[100] Indeed, according to Stockman, Reagan's blueprint for economic change required "abruptly severing the umbilical cords of dependency that ran from Washington to every nook and cranny of the nation."[101] In this context, Social Security represented an obvious target; to Stockman, "no single issue was as critical to the success of the Reagan Revolution as Social Security reform."[102] Thus, with claims that Reagan was exaggerating the financial problems and distorting the facts, liberals pointed to his longstanding opposition to Social Security as evidence that his administration wanted to abolish this symbol of liberalism.

To be sure, Reagan was quoted as early as January 1965 saying that Social Security should be made voluntary.[103] Leading up to the 1980 election, he continued to maintain that the system needed restructuring but pledged to "support and defend the integrity" of it.[104] Once in office, Reagan proposed a number of Social Security cuts in his first budget to help compensate for the tax cut and military expenditures. He seemed to have the political capital to push for these cuts, but the severity of them appeared to catch everyone by surprise. Robert Myers, one of Reagan's commissioners on Social Security, said that Roosevelt "had to be spinning in his grave at what they were trying to do."[105] Liberals geared up to stop Reagan.

The Social Security Campaign
In the middle of July 1981, Reagan and Speaker O'Neill exchanged letters on the issue of Social Security. Reagan shared his dismay at the "opportunistic political maneuvering" of the Democrats on Social Security, stating that his highest priority was restoring its integrity. O'Neill wrote back that it was "ill-advised and unacceptable to create and exploit fears about the fate of the social security system so as to make deep cuts in benefit levels."[106] He finished with a warning: "A Democratic administration created the social security system and as Democratic members of Congress we are committed to protecting the system and preserving the security and dignity of those who depend on it."[107]

Months earlier, Reagan had announced his plans to reform Social Security as a two-pronged measure. The first round of cuts, as part of a wider budget resolution that reduced $41.4 billion from eighty-three federal programs, included the abolition of the minimum benefit. In May, the administration proposed additional reductions, the most controversial of which was the immediate 40 percent cut in benefits for those electing early retirement at sixty-two.[108] Disability protection was also to be cut by one-third, overall benefit levels were to be permanently reduced without a phase-in period, and cost-of-living adjustments were to be delayed for months.[109] All told, a low-income worker retiring at age sixty-two in 1982 would see their monthly benefits cut from $248 to $164. As Stockman later admitted, "We just hadn't thought through the impact of making it effective immediately."[110] The White House tasked Health and Human Services Secretary Richard Schweiker with taking the lead, which, according to historians Martha Derthick and Steven Teles, stemmed from the administration wanting to put a certain degree of distance between Reagan and the controversial decision he had just made.[111]

Following the announcement, O'Neill vowed to fight, declaring at a news conference that "for the first time since 1935 people would suffer because they trusted in the Social Security system." A reporter asked if Reagan had made a political mistake, and O'Neill shot back: "I'm not talking about politics. I'm talking about decency. It is a rotten thing to do. It is a despicable thing."[112] Moynihan, picking up the Social Security baton in the Senate, claimed that the proposals amounted to "a breach of contract, startling in magnitude as well as content."[113] Indeed, a vote led by Moynihan in the Senate showed just how badly Reagan had miscalculated. By 96 to 0, the Senate agreed on 20 May not to "precipitously and unfairly reduce early retirees' benefits."[114] The *Washington Post*'s headline, which Stockman declared "planted a permanent political axiom in the Reagan White House," read: "Senate Unanimously Rebuffs President on Social Security."[115] Democrats deliberately began trying to turn Reagan's mistake into a partisan advantage, despite the fact that the Senate was under Republican control when it repudiated the proposals. And liberals in Congress were not the only ones to react. As one of Reagan's advisors on Social Security, John Svahn, later wrote, "Politicians saw the package as a way to get at Reagan [but] interest groups saw it as a fundraiser."[116]

Serving as the coordinating mechanism, Save Our Security (SOS), a liberal coalition group founded by former Johnson Cabinet member Wilbur Cohen in 1979, played a key role. Comprising over two hundred groups, including the American Association of Retired Persons (AARP), AFL-CIO, and numerous other social, labor, and religious organizations, SOS launched a synchronized media campaign to stop Reagan's proposals.[117] In unison, the AARP alerted its leaders to contact lawmakers; the National Council of Senior Citizens denounced Reagan's proposal as "the biggest frontal attack on Social Security ever launched"; and labor began lobbying Congress directly.[118] Numerous other liberal groups got involved as well, including NOW in a direct mail campaign.[119] As Delaware's Republican senator, William Roth Jr., wrote, "We get mail from them constantly, it is their livelihood that's at stake."[120] Certainly, when the increasingly influential Gray Lobby comes to town, politicians sit up and take notice.

Elderly people were a powerful group by the early 1980s, not only because they had the highest political participation rates, but also because they were more concentrated in the so-called Sunbelt states of the South and Southwest. Due to increased migration from the northern Rustbelt as the economy transitioned to a postindustrial landscape, the Sunbelt was becoming a coveted region in electoral politics.[121] Furthermore, Gallup found that Reagan received his largest share of the vote in 1980 from both those closest to his own age bracket and those in the Sunbelt.[122] With serious electoral capital at stake, polls started to show just how vulnerable Reagan was on Social Security. One Harris poll indicated that more than half of the public believed he was being unfair to the elderly, while nearly two-thirds thought he did not care about the hardships faced by older Americans.[123] Under O'Neill's guidance, the House sponsored a resolution to maintain the minimum benefit, with the vote timed to take place while over ten thousand people marched on Capitol Hill against Reagan's cuts.[124] O'Neill began instructing Democrats not to put together their own proposals, nor to work on any in a bipartisan manner, in order to let the issue play out in a way that benefited the party. This was bolstered by Democratic consultants, including Vic Fingerhut, who argued that keeping Social Security in "Democratic vs. Republican terms [means] we win."[125]

In order to calm the political waters, Reagan proposed the creation of a task force, writing in his diary: "I'm withdrawing S.S. from consideration & challenging Tip & the Dems. to join in a bipartisan effort to solve the fiscal dilemma of S.S. without all the politics they've been playing."[126] As Stockman admitted later, the White House was simply cutting its losses, "quickly, completely, efficiently—and ironically, because the Social Security reform plan was the one aspect of the Reagan Revolution . . . that the president understood instinctively and was more than willing to fight for."[127] O'Neill congratulated Reagan on his "new flexibility," while House Aging Committee Chairman Claude Pepper termed the retreat a "major victory."[128] Still, Ball argued that Reagan was only using the commission to get Social Security out of the 1982 elections: "He'll be back after it."[129] The Democrats also calculated that Reagan's mishap could reap continued benefits going forward. Thus, they refused to acknowledge any bipartisan solutions, including the seriousness of the commission, and instead were holding the issue in abeyance for the midterms. As Fingerhut outlined in a strategy memo: "Older Americans and working Americans weren't asleep when the administration tried to slap through anti-Social Security cutbacks; they were alert and we stopped the administration. We must stay alert and keep applying pressure to this issue."[130]

With this in mind, O'Neill's senior aide, Kirk O'Donnell, developed an electoral strategy that placed Social Security at its core.[131] A Democratic National Committee (DNC) poll released months later would confirm the potency of the issue; not only did "Protecting Social Security" rank number 2 in the "most important issue facing the nation" category, but the Democrats held a twenty-five-point advantage on it.[132] To pollster Patrick Caddell, the 1982 battle had arrived on the "changed landscape of public opinion."[133] The conservative offensive, seemingly relentless and irrepressible in early 1981, had stalled. According to Caddell, the Democrats now had an arsenal of electoral weapons to exploit: "For a year the Democratic Party has been an army in retreat. Its test now is whether, given the current opportunity, [it] can skillfully and adroitly shift to the offensive and grasp the potential victory that lies before them."[134]

Early in 1981, according to the *New York Times*, there was a real sense of "anger and frustration" among liberals that Reagan would "shred" the very foundation of liberalism, especially when the VRA and Social Security looked to be in jeopardy.[135] Now, as the nation entered one of the deepest recessions of the twentieth century in 1982, liberal officials widened their net of criticism, framing these issues together with contemporary economic troubles to create the concept of "fairness."[136] And although the VRA and Social Security campaigns had amply demonstrated the continued appeal of liberal programs, they now had to translate these struggles into an electoral victory.

"IT'S NOT FAIR, IT'S REPUBLICAN"

On 9 July 1981, the Democrats won Mississippi's 4th District in an upset special election that caught the nation by surprise.[137] Wayne Dowdy, a thirty-seven-year-old Democrat initially given little chance against a well-financed opponent, was sent to the House by a conservative district that the Republicans had held since 1972. Some commentators pointed to it as a harbinger of the honeymoon's end for Reagan, but it was also a sign of things to come.[138] Two issues were at the center of this upset: the VRA and Social Security. Dowdy's support for the VRA extension, and his opponents' objections to it, became a major focus of attention, with radio ads used skillfully to increase turnout and expand his share of the Black vote: "King died for your right to vote and Ronald Reagan and Liles Williams

[Dowdy's opponent] want to take it away."[139] As journalist David Broder argued, a portion of the white vote was also attracted to Dowdy because of claims that Reagan might jeopardize their Social Security benefits; Dowdy received over 95 percent of the Black vote and roughly 30 percent of the white vote.[140] O'Donnell, using the Dowdy result, pointed to the salience of the VRA issue and its ability to attract the minority vote in his strategy memo.[141]

From this point on, it was clear that the Democrats had found a broad campaign theme going into the 1982 midterms, one that incorporated the successes of both battles and expanded the scope to attract wider support. This was confirmed when the electorate started to turn on the Republicans in the polls.[142] To revive perceived Republican liabilities, Democrats began to use evidence that Reagan's tax cuts had benefited the rich far more than the poor; a Congressional Budget Office report, for example, showed that 85 percent of revenue lost in tax cuts was to households with incomes over $20,000.[143] Furthermore, with the rise of the "deficit issue," which plagued politics for the rest of the decade, Democrats could also attack the Republicans on their handling of the purse strings, particularly when the deficit rose above $100 billion for the first time in history. When the *New York Times* asked Americans to indicate their preferred approach to deficit reduction in 1982, 59 percent favored reducing the scale of the previous year's tax cut and 49 percent endorsed cuts in defense spending; only 29 percent wanted a reduction in antipoverty spending.[144] As historian Gareth Davies shows, even supply-side guru Arthur Laffer was reputedly critical of the anti-poverty impact of the administration's policies.[145] By July 1982, administration officials warned Reagan that the "savage" use of the fairness issue was "badly eroding" his political base.[146]

Moreover, the *Washington Post* pointed out that the perception of Reagan as "anti-Black" from the VRA campaign could bring large numbers of Black voters to the polls "to turn [the] election."[147] By 1980, Black voter registration had reached 60 percent and minority candidates were slowly winning public office. With the VRA campaign providing a prescient warning about where Reagan and the Republicans stood on civil rights, minority communities united to send a message. According to the NAACP's Althea T. L. Simmons: "When you push people's backs to the wall, they fight back.... There was too much Jesse Helms, too much New Right. People who have not spoken out decided to speak out."[148] With nearly fifty congressional districts where the Black population exceeded 30 percent, no Republican midterm strategy could afford to neglect the increasing power of the minority vote.[149] The VRA campaign played heavily on Republicans' minds as the election approached, with one Reagan advisor describing it as an "absolutely unnecessary" self-inflicted political injury: "The most unconscionable mistake we've made as a party was not to be out front on the VRA."[150] As Republican pollster Robert Teeter noted, with only 7 percent of Black voters approving of the president, "Reagan's problem with blacks is going to make it harder for other Republicans this fall."[151]

In addition, the Social Security issue continued to damage the Republican Party's electoral prospects. After the Reagan administration proposed $40 billion in unspecified Social Security savings in May 1982, Moynihan led another effort to block the cuts, and the electorate increasingly placed Social Security as one of the issues that would decide their midterm vote.[152] With limited maneuverability on Social Security, the Republicans changed strategy. Whereas 1980 saw advertisements depicting a large, bloated O'Neill-like character as an allegory to the big-spending federal government, the Republicans sought a simple, positive message for the midterms: "Reagan and his party have made a beginning and should be given a chance to finish the job."[153] The Democrats, on the other hand, went on the offensive, producing a series of thirty-second commercials, including one with an elephant on a destructive path through a china shop smashing plates labeled Social Security. Each captured the essence of their midterm message: "It isn't fair . . . it's Republican."[154] This use of Social Security was starting to pay political dividends for liberals. In the Maine Senate race, for example, liberal George Mitchell came from thirty-five points behind to push ahead in the polls as election day approached. According to Caddell, "All he did was campaign on Social Security for a full year."[155] Moreover, liberal strategists got hold of a Republican fundraising letter that urged recipients to consider voluntary Social Security as a remedy for the system's financial troubles. DNC Chairman Charles Manatt called the letter "the clearest signal yet that Reagan and the Republicans are hell bent on a drastic revision of the Social Security system."[156] Two days later, Kennedy charged that Reagan was planning a "November surprise" to cut Social Security benefits after the election, adding a last-minute spark to the issue.[157]

In the end, by combining Social Security, the VRA, and the economy under a "fairness" umbrella, the Democrats would reap electoral benefits come election day, gaining twenty-six seats to establish a House majority of 267.[158] Not only were these House losses one of the most damaging for a postwar president in their first midterm election at the time, but as House Majority Leader Jim Wright noted, these new members were in fact "real

Democrats—not your boll weevil types" who had supported Reagan in 1981.[159] With most of the newly elected Democrats either moderates or liberals, Ann Lewis, the DNC's political director, claimed that it "proved the liberal coalition is alive and kicking."[160] And many of the blue-collar and elderly voters who had jumped ship in the face of Carter's malaise returned to the Democratic fold. As O'Donnell noted, "Two years ago there was a distinct possibility that there would be a party realignment this election. Instead, traditional prejudices of the public towards the Republicans were reinforced: that they bring about hard times and give preference to the privileged."[161] Clearly, by forming coalitions early to protect the VRA and Social Security and by using these issues to mobilize liberal constituencies on election day, liberals showcased their continued strength and appeal.

Indeed, exit polls demonstrated the success of this campaign strategy. As the *New York Times* reported, unemployment and Social Security were mentioned as decisive issues by 37 and 25 percent of the voters, respectively.[162] Polling demonstrated that Social Security played a role in twenty-four of twenty-seven losses. New York Republican Barber Conable complained afterward that it was his toughest campaign to date: "All my opponent kept saying was 'He wants to cut your Social Security' and all I could say back was 'I do not.' O'Neill's strategy had worked."[163] Because of this resurgence, commentators began calling the septuagenarian Speaker the King of the Hill.[164] Republican governors, with their ranks thinned from twenty-three to sixteen by the results, also criticized Reagan, suggesting that the administration's policies had "scared people to death."[165] Not only did the Democrats make inroads in statehouses and governor's mansions around the country, but they very nearly captured Congress too.[166] Coming "within a whisper" of wrestling back the Senate, as Senator Wendall Ford (D-KY) acknowledged, a shift of just forty-three thousand votes in five states—Nevada, Rhode Island, Vermont, Missouri, and Wyoming—would have given them control of the chamber lost two years earlier.[167] Additionally, several of the liberal senators who looked vulnerable in 1980 easily rolled to reelection, pointing up the unlikely prospects of a conservative realignment. Indeed, Moynihan secured a second term with a seismic thirty-point vote margin, capturing over a million more votes than his Republican challenger in New York.[168] Summarizing the results, Broder wrote: "The election that ended Reagan's domination of Capitol Hill was marked by an increase in voter turnout—reversing a 20-year trend—and by a show of precinct power by Democrats and their labor and liberal allies that had not been seen for years."[169]

Ten million more people—mainly racial minorities and women—went to the polls in 1982 than in the 1978 midterms.[170] Given that Reagan's "unfair" budgetary policies fell disproportionately on women and racial minorities, the combined effect of the cuts and the recession hit these groups particularly hard at the exact moment of the election. As Hooks explained in a letter to Reagan, by the end of 1982 "the jobless rate among blacks was 18.9 percent or nearly twice that of the general population."[171] Moreover, the successful efforts of the coalition to strengthen the VRA had focused renewed attention on the franchise as a key instrument in forwarding minority interests. Using the vote strategically to influence the midterms was the logical extension of that campaign. Moderate Republicans, who had enjoyed minority backing in the past, found that support withering on election day as widespread anti-Reagan sentiment resulted in increased Democratic voting among racial minorities.[172]

Thus, with the election spotlighting both the growing strength and power of minority voters, coalition organizations, rearmed with a powerful suffrage weapon, stepped up efforts to enroll more voters. By 1983, Hooks pointed out that the NAACP had signed up one million new voters and was embarking on a "mammoth campaign" to register two million more by 1984.[173] From Voter Awareness Programs to registration marches across the country, the NAACP sought to tackle voter apathy, register new voters, and "remove the political neanderthals whose minds are wedded to the past."[174] By targeting registration drives and educational activities in congressional districts where the minority population was numerically significant, the NAACP also recognized that the key to change did not lie only in increasing participation but in the effective and strategic use of the franchise.[175] Consequently, from 1980 to 1984 voter registration of racial minorities in the South climbed by 14 percent, with the largest increases occurring in states where VRA measures were implemented: Alabama (37 percent), North Carolina (28 percent), and Mississippi (20 percent).[176]

Furthermore, mobilization strategies were developed as a result of the VRA campaign, and throughout the country minority participation rose in response to active campaigning by minority candidates for political office. The number of Black elected officials nationwide grew by 8.6 percent between 1982 and 1983, for example, the steepest rise in nearly a decade.[177] Increased minority turnout put Black mayors into office in Chicago, Philadelphia, and Charlotte, and helped elect a Hispanic mayor in Denver.[178] And after witnessing the success of the VRA campaign and the midterms, Jesse Jackson set out to turn Black America into a formidable political force by using provisions in the act to register more voters. His presidential runs in 1984 and 1988 would ultimately symbolize the surge in minority political participation in Reagan's America.

Likewise, Social Security would form a key part of the issue stratum that liberals used to build coalitions and mobilize constituencies moving forward. To liberals, more than just Social Security had been at stake. As Moynihan pointed out, the charge that the program was bankrupt was a surrogate for the charge that liberalism and the New Deal had failed.[179] Thus, immediately after the midterms, liberals exploited their new electoral position in negotiations with the Social Security commission. The eventual agreement brokered in January 1983 surprised even Moynihan, especially given the fact the resulting report contained a recommendation that read as a repudiation of Reagan's ideological agenda.[180] At the same time, James Roosevelt, Franklin Roosevelt's eldest son, launched the National Committee to Preserve Social Security and Medicare, believing that Reagan and the Republican Party would not rest until Social Security had been dismantled "piece-by-piece."[181] By 1987, the National Committee had over five million members and described itself as the nation's "fastest-growing, most aggressive grassroots lobbying and educational association."[182] As it grew, it made its presence felt in elections, endorsing candidates and launching a political action committee (PAC)—it contributed to 236 candidates (224 Democrats; 12 Republicans) in 1984 and 309 (285 Democrats; 24 Republicans) in 1986.[183] The PAC's executive director, Keith Tarr-Whalen, called the 1986 campaign "the single largest volunteer effort in senior history."[184] In the end, the overt politicization of Social Security in Reagan's first term turned the issue into a political stick that liberals would beat over Republican heads for decades.[185] Reagan's successor, George H. W. Bush, avoided advocating retrenchment at all costs and promised in 1989 that "we don't touch Social Security—that's off-limits."[186] Social Security, the symbol of liberalism, remains a partisan wedge issue to this day.

Consequently, discussions surrounding the Reagan years often present a distorted picture of his early success. Certainly, Reagan achieved impressive congressional victories at the beginning of his presidency, but from as early as May 1981, liberals were able to frustrate numerous administration attempts to reform government. With highly organized opposition campaigns, spearheaded by liberals both within and outside of Congress, the processes of coalition building were sharpened early in Reagan's reign, and with considerable success. By strategically focusing on broad issues such as the VRA and Social Security, liberals exploited the fact that Reagan's initial popularity did not easily translate into full-throated support for his legislative agenda in order to force significant concessions from him. In the end, the contests over Social Security and the VRA, the emergence of the fairness issue, and the midterm results would have a significant impact on later developments in both liberalism and Reaganism. Some journalists even declared the Reagan Revolution officially over by the end of 1982.[187] While this was a hasty verdict, liberals had, to a degree, reined in Reagan's power. The conceptual foundation of liberalism, and the major programs that embodied it, particularly Social Security and the VRA, would remain a part of Reagan's America.

3. Advancing Liberalism on the Ground
Grassroots Organizing in Reagan's First Term

With the women's movement subject to the same conservative forces that pervaded American political life in the 1980s, many political observers argued that feminism stagnated during the Reagan years. The 1982 failure of the Equal Rights Amendment (ERA), a principal political objective of the women's movement, served to reinforce this dreary assessment. Although a majority of Americans favored the ERA, it was defeated by a highly effective mobilization of grassroots conservatism. Throughout the decade, accounts surfaced in newspapers, periodicals, and academic works with titles such as "The Failure of Feminism," "Post-Feminism," and "Who Stole Feminism?"; and the 1980s is often remembered as a decade of retrenchment for women more generally.[1] Susan Faludi encapsulated this conventional viewpoint in her 1991 bestseller, *Backlash: The Undeclared War Against American Women*.[2] Detailing the defeat of the ERA, the ascent of the antiabortion movement, and the rise of on-the-job sexual harassment and discrimination, *Backlash* painted a bleak picture of feminism in Reagan's America.

Faludi and other popular commentators, however, neglected important developments in feminist politics that had enduring implications for liberalism in particular and electoral politics generally. By examining the activities of the National Organization for Women (NOW) at the time, for example, the largest women's political organization in the United States, we can see how the conservative backlash conversely energized liberal women to greater political participation during the 1980s, both at the ballot box and through effective coalition building and electoral campaigns.[3] Indeed, from 1979 to 1982, which could reasonably be considered the height of Reaganism, NOW significantly professionalized its approach to politics and made the absence of women in the political arena a primary focus. NOW also established eighty-one new political action committees (PACs) across forty states to facilitate and fund the emergence of more female voices in politics; increased its membership threefold to over 220,000 and its annual budget fourfold to over $13 million through effective mobilization strategies; and worked collaboratively with a diverse range of organizations, groups, and politicians to stem the tide of conservatism.[4]

Focusing specifically on Reagan's first term, this chapter shows how NOW helped reshape the political landscape by altering its strategy to grapple with the more conservative political environment of the 1980s, just as the LCCR had with regard to civil rights. Certainly, the decade's more conservative climate necessitated the ongoing process of building ad hoc factional coalitions to protect or advance liberal interests, and NOW positioned itself at the center as one of the principal coordinating organizations. For example, while the ERA struggle had a long history, the 1982 deadline for state ratification offered NOW a focal point to concentrate mobilization efforts at the beginning of the Reagan Era. And although the ratification battle ultimately failed, the organizing work of NOW provided a conduit for the hands-on engagement of numerous activist women in political campaigning, particularly at the state and local level.[5] Indeed, the ERA campaign, and the processes of grassroots organizing tied directly to it, reshaped the contours of women's political participation in the United States and demonstrated the strength and breadth of public support for liberalism and affiliated "women's issues" (those issues deemed, however stereotypically, to have particular importance for women, such as the ERA, abortion, and welfare).

Importantly, the emergence of a new electoral dichotomy at the start of the decade would prove to be a catalyst for the organizing focus of NOW, bolstering their cause and spurring other liberal groups into coordinated action. As an administration report ominously highlighted, women were becoming "considerably more liberal and Democratic than men" in the Reagan Era.[6] By November 1982, Reagan's presidential aide, Lee Atwater, warned that "one of the most severe challenges facing the administration"—one that "could lock the GOP into permanent minority status"—was this "gender gap."[7] NOW's president, Eleanor Smeal, had been the first to identify and examine the gender gap in any great depth, showing that significantly fewer women than men supported Reagan as their 1980 presidential choice.[8] Capitalizing on this, NOW then designed several campaigns throughout Reagan's first term to expand and exploit the emerging chasm, using it as leverage to influence several of the Democratic Party's policy proposals and electoral campaigns. Moreover, the methods and strategies utilized by NOW and its allies through these campaigns would help lay the groundwork for significant future gains. We can see evidence for this by 1992, the so-called Year of the Woman, during which an unprecedented wave of women entered political office.[9] Therefore, by focusing on grassroots organizing and the relationships established between Democratic politicians and NOW in particular, this chapter demonstrates the significance of coalition building and presents a more nuanced picture of the early Reagan years—one that places liberal women at the center rather than on the periphery of Reagan's America.

THE BIRTH OF THE GENDER GAP

The 1980 presidential election results revealed that 9.6 percent fewer women than men voted for Reagan. Men supported the new president by a 56–36 margin over Jimmy Carter, while women gave Carter a narrow 47–45 edge.[10] Not only that, but 1980 was the first year that women voted in equal proportion to men, and demographic trends suggested that women would soon eclipse them (sure enough, in every presidential election since 1980, and in every congressional race since 1986, the proportion of female voters has exceeded that of males).[11] Together, these developments represented important breakthroughs in the political influence of women—albeit as male voting patterns were also becoming more partisan, and thus more influential as well. Surveying the political landscape after the election, Pat Reuss, chief lobbyist for the Women's Equity Action League, noted: "People have not yet appreciated the election result. The same percentage of women and men voted. Yet [there] was an 8-to-10 percent margin in choice. That is a mandate for us to continue our work. Women have separate concerns and they still want to see them pursued."[12]

The 1980 Republican platform represented a marked shift in the party's approach to several so-called women's issues, and liberals were quick to point to this as the reason for the gap's emergence.[13] As the first major party to champion constitutional equality for women, the Republicans put the ERA in their platform as early as 1940. But in 1980, that commitment disappeared.[14] In response, NOW organized over twelve thousand people to march on the Republican convention in Detroit and directed activists to follow Reagan around the campaign trail with ERA placards.[15] While not decisive, the Republican Party's reversal on the ERA issue still had an impact on election day. According to one exit poll, only 32 percent of the women favoring the ERA voted for Reagan. Carter, who had provided lukewarm support to the ERA, still attracted a clear majority of these voters.[16]

At the same time as dropping the ERA from the Republican platform, Reagan backed the Human Life Amendment (HLA). The HLA was a proposed constitutional amendment that aimed to go further than simply overturning *Roe v. Wade*—the landmark 1973 Supreme Court case that enshrined abortion into federal law—by banning abortion and birth control measures outright.[17] Supported by a number of conservative politicians, particularly Senator Orrin Hatch, Reagan's backing increased its legitimacy. In response, NOW launched a nationwide "STOP HLA" campaign, with the slogan "HLA IS A KILLER."[18] By 1982, and in order to halt what they described as a "right-wing attack" on abortion, NOW registered thousands of women to support pro-choice candidates in local elections.[19] As historian Jon Shields observed, Reagan's election in 1980 marked the point when the parties took increasingly polarized stands on the issue of abortion, pushing many pro-lifers into Republican Party politics.[20] Indeed, Richard Viguerie, a pioneer of the New Right, argued that "the abortion issue is the door through which many people came into conservative politics."[21] Certainly, pro-choice supporters walked through the opposite door toward the Democrats, particularly after Reagan's platform pledge on the issue.

While gender differences in presidential voting were not entirely new, it was the magnitude evident from the election results and its persistence across Reagan's incumbency that was unprecedented.[22] By the middle of Reagan's first term, for example, two separate Gallup polls, completed one year apart, demonstrated the staying power of the gap. In July 1982, the survey found that 51 percent of men approved of Reagan's job performance, while only 39 percent of women did. By July 1983, Gallup showed that while 51 percent of men still approved of Reagan's presidency, only 34 percent of women did—a seventeen-point gap.[23] Throughout Reagan's first term an average of 9 percent fewer women than men approved of his performance.[24] *Public Opinion* showed that women gave these lower ratings almost uniformly across age and class groupings.[25] Journalist Adam Clymer pointed out that Reagan's "women problem" seemed to be spreading throughout the Republican Party.[26] However, it was not enough to identify that women were becoming more liberal and more Democratic following the 1980 elections. Rather NOW and its allies, such as the National Abortion Rights Action League (NARAL), quickly recognized that they could use the gendered difference in voting patterns as leverage to better their own political position and, they believed, that of women more generally.[27] Indeed, the gap may have simply remained an interesting statistical anomaly had these liberal organizations not effectively given it political meaning by seizing and promoting it so swiftly.

Taking the initiative in precisely this way, NOW drafted a booklet in early 1981 on the gap and its significance for wide distribution, titled *Women Can Make the Difference*. Designed as part of a conscious effort to push the gender gap into the political lexicon of journalists and politicians, the booklet included a chronological chart of "Reagan's problem with women," pointing to various major polls that documented the issue under the heading "Gender Gap."[28] As the *Washington Post*'s Judy Mann reported, by providing persuasive documentation that a "women's vote" had finally emerged, the booklet was drafted to show Democrats that the opportunity was theirs, as long as they gave genuine support to women's issues.[29] Months later, NOW revised the booklet to account for the gap's significance in the November off-year elections.[30] Additionally, as a way to sustain interest, NOW began releasing a monthly "Gender Gap Update" to several thousand reporters.[31]

The gap also cut across partisan lines, with many liberal Republicans critical of Reagan's policies on equal rights, abortion, and other issues considered especially pertinent to women. The National Women's Political Caucus (NWPC) held a conference in 1983 where its Republican chair, Kathy Wilson, strongly urged Reagan to forego a second term.[32] As Wilson noted, Reagan's approach to women's issues led to a new "coalescing among women's and minority groups" and prompted various nonpartisan groups, including the NWPC, to get behind the liberal effort to defeat him.[33] A central aspect of this effort was to focus attention on Reagan's campaign of welfare retrenchment.

THE "FEMINIZATION OF POVERTY"

As changing norms regarding sexuality, marriage, and workplace roles transformed US society, particularly after the 1960s, the economic fortunes of many women became increasingly intertwined with the welfare state through one or more of its major federal programs—Social Security, Medicare, food stamps, housing benefits, and/or Aid to Families with Dependent Children (AFDC).[34] Yet Reagan had swept to power arguing that government was actually the root of the nation's social and economic problems. With this conviction, Reagan sought to discredit liberalism in general and the liberal commitment to welfare provision in particular. In this way, he skillfully exploited growing hostility across the country toward big government in the late 1970s. This is perhaps best captured by the so-called welfare queen—a racially charged trope used by those on the right, including Reagan, to vilify women receiving federal assistance for supposedly living off the largesse of the taxpayer.[35] Indeed, by helping to foster the notion that welfare fraud was a nationwide epidemic, the "welfare queen" provided a convenient villain that enabled conservatives to sell voters on their public spending cuts and on reducing the role of government.[36]

Significantly, in what economists Ann Mari May and Kurt Stephenson termed the "inequalities of sacrifice," women constituted a majority of Reagan's targeted programs: 61.6 percent of Social Security, 64.8 percent of Medicare, 56.7 percent of food stamps, 70 percent of housing, and most significantly, 81.1 percent of AFDC users.[37] The welfare program that suffered the largest decline in spending from 1980 to 1988, at 11.2 percent of its allocated budget, was also the one that had the highest percentage of women as clients or recipients, AFDC. A joint federal–state cash assistance program enacted as part of a New Deal legislative wave in 1935, AFDC provided financial support for needy children in the case of death, incapacity, or absence of a providing parent. As social norms regarding marriage and job roles changed rapidly, with rising divorce rates and more women in the labor market, the number of female-headed AFDC families increased considerably.[38] Between 1961 and 1979, for example, the number of AFDC families headed by women more than quadrupled, from 635,000 to 3 million.[39]

Rising unemployment during Reagan's first term, which peaked at 10.8 percent in 1982, also had a disproportionate effect on women, particularly as women comprised an estimated two-thirds of all minimum wage earners in the country.[40] A *Congressional Press* report determined that the recession was most severely felt by the growing numbers of single, divorced, and widowed women supporting themselves and their children through welfare and low-paid work.[41] According to Ann Lewis, women were "the miners' canaries of economic conditions: the first to feel the damaging effects of any ill winds."[42] The US Commission on Civil Rights reported in May 1983 that households headed by women had witnessed their median income dip to $10,950, while those headed by males rose to $25,065.[43] The National Advisory Council on Economic Opportunity declared, ominously, that this "feminization of poverty" would be complete by the year 2000, arguing that, by then, the poverty population would be composed entirely of women and their children.[44]

In an effort to expand the gender gap, NOW honed in on this data and argued that Reagan's policies had not only failed to tackle the problem, but were actively accelerating it.[45] Historically, there had been a class and racial divide between NOW and organizations such as the National Welfare Rights Organization (NWRO).[46] NOW's initial campaigns to "liberate" women from the monotony of households was largely a middle-class endeavor and presented a false dichotomy to groups like the NWRO, who fought instead for a guaranteed adequate income, regardless of whether women worked in factories or were at home raising children.[47] Moreover, while NOW's Bill of Rights demanded "that poor women be given the same access to opportunities as men, without prejudice based on their status as mothers," Black women, and Black men for that matter, clearly had far less access to opportunity, regardless of parental status.

Yet, by the 1980s, with the reality of Reagan's welfare cuts on full display and the NWRO no longer in existence, NOW assumed the mantle of welfare state defender, laying blame for the poverty situation squarely at Reagan's doorstep and launching a targeted "feminization of poverty" campaign to encourage anti-Republican sentiment.[48] Indeed, in a 1982 interview, NOW's president blasted Reaganomics as a "direct and frontal assault on women and their economic security."[49] A White House report that year showed that this strategy was working: "The fear of losing government benefits appears to be causing women to oppose the administration."[50] An impression that Reagan was moving to weaken, cut back, or abolish federal programs and laws designed to protect women spread; Congresswoman Patricia Schroeder (D-CO) spoke for many when she argued that Reagan had "all but declared war on women."[51] By 1983, a 21 percent gap appeared in a *CBS News/New York Times* poll when respondents were asked about Reagan's handling of the economy.[52] At the same time, NOW was reporting that more than four million women and children had sunk below the poverty line since 1980 because of Reagan's cuts.[53]

In this period, an increasing proportion of women became reliant on the welfare state for subsistence, protection, and expansion of opportunity at the very same time as the Republican Party was driving a process to curtail it. NOW used campaigns and strategies to spotlight the feminization of poverty, attack Reagan and the Republicans on the issue of fairness, and encourage Democratic voting as a result. Moreover, the defeat of a central piece of feminist legislation only months before the 1982 midterm elections would lead NOW to couple this approach with what could be termed the feminization of politics strategy.

THE FEMINIZATION OF POLITICS

At the outset of the 1980s, the ERA fight commanded the bulk of feminist energies. After women secured the right to vote through the Nineteenth Amendment in 1920, suffragist leader Alice Paul introduced the

ERA to Congress in 1923, affirming the Constitution's equal application to all persons regardless of their sex. Perpetually consigned to congressional committee, the ERA was introduced in every Congress from 1923 to 1971 without success. Released from committee shackles in 1971, and swiftly approved by Congress, the ERA passed thirty of the required thirty-eight state legislatures in under one year. However, the pursuit lost considerable steam following the emergence of a powerful and organized opposition movement, led in part by social conservative activist Phyllis Schlafly, who raised the specter of unisex bathrooms and women fighting on the frontlines.[54]

Schlafly, who launched the "pro-family" interest group Eagle Forum in 1972, was one of the ERA's principal opponents and derived her authority from an ability to mobilize women at the grassroots level to support conservative causes.[55] Significantly, in order to defeat the ERA, Schlafly and anti-ERA forces were able to link it explicitly to the highly divisive abortion issue.[56] After the remaining states failed to ratify it, Schlafly claimed that she had sealed its defeat by "deliberately hanging around its neck the albatross of abortion."[57] Polls, however, still showed that a majority of the electorate favored the ERA; in 1981, Gallup found that 63 percent supported it, whereas 32 percent opposed it.[58] And NOW tried to link the ERA campaign with the gender gap's emergence in an effort to mobilize more women into politics. Indeed, while many commentators were predicting that the ERA defeat would be the death knell for feminism, others were persuaded by NOW's claims that it would politicize more women to join the process. A sampling of national headlines suggests this: "ERA Defeat Prompts New Interest in Elections" (*New York Times*) and "With ERA Off Its Back, White House Senses Trouble at Its Heels, Polls Show Women Voting More and Liking Reagan Less" (*Washington Post*). NOW aimed to reframe the ERA defeat as a catalyst for action, particularly with the 1982 midterms approaching.

In 1982, NOW, a bipartisan organization, began endorsing Democratic men supportive of the ERA over Republican women opposed to it, despite its tradition of not providing endorsements to specific candidates. The most prominent examples were the endorsements of Barney Frank over Margaret Heckler in a Massachusetts House race and Frank Lautenberg over Millicent Fenwick in the New Jersey Senate race. NOW released a report designed to contradict claims that it had become the "National Organization for Democratic Women," but its policy to endorse Democratic men over Republican women was illustrative of the contemporary political environment.[59] As the two parties became increasingly polarized on certain issues, the gender gap showed that women, by and large, found a more welcoming home under the Democratic banner. In fact, between the ERA's demise and the welfare state's retrenchment, the 1982 elections represented something of a referendum on the Reagan administration for many women, and the results highlight that the gender gap proved pivotal.

A *New York Times* election analysis found a gender differential in seventy-three of eighty-five state-wide races, deciding the winners in several closely contested governors' races, including Democrats Mario Cuomo in New York, Mark White in Texas, and Richard Blanchard in Michigan, three of the largest states in the country.[60] Blanchard's race is particularly illuminating. His opponent, Republican Richard Headlee, was not only anti-ERA, but during his campaign he had allegedly mocked women for supporting "women's issues."[61] In contrast, Blanchard chose the so-called Mother of the ERA, former Congresswoman Martha Griffiths, as his running mate and treated women's issues, such as childcare and welfare programs, seriously on the campaign trail.[62] On election day, the gender gap reached 8.5 percent while Blanchard won the overall vote by 6.8 percent.[63] Providing the winning margins in several races also enabled NOW to challenge claims that the gap was only due to Reagan's warmongering image. Certainly, while most Republicans categorically denied that the ERA had anything to do with the gender gap, Reagan himself apportioned blame to it in an interview just before the midterms. Asked about his "women problem," Reagan responded by saying: "I have a hunch that part of it has been inspired by the ERA movement."[64] What every top-level official denied, Reagan confirmed. Liberals now seemingly had enough evidence to claim that a gender gap provided victory based on women's issues. Consequently, NOW released an updated booklet: *Women DO Make the Difference*.

NOW also pointed to the significance of its Countdown Campaign, launched just before the midterms, as further evidence that the gender gap was now a major factor in political calculations.[65] By monitoring and publishing gender differences in polls, NOW used their Countdown Campaign to raise the value of women's issues and convince the Democratic Party to take notice. According to one midterm analysis, the Democrats listened, seeking to capitalize on the gap by urging members to "tailor campaign materials to women, to shake hands in hospital parking lots ... and to make sure that women staffers are visible on hustings."[66] Accordingly, as NOW reported to its activists at the beginning of 1983, the ERA campaign increased "our political effectiveness" and allowed women to emerge as a political force "to be reckoned with."[67]

Having launched its first-ever multimillion-dollar advertising campaign, organized campus events, and expanded its door-to-door canvasing project, NOW could point to the success of its ERA rallies in over 180 cities as evidence of its organizational prowess.[68] Statistics corroborate that the campaign had impressive results on the ground—for example, NOW's membership surged from 40,000 in 1977 to over 220,000 by 1982; at the same time, its annual budget climbed from $500,000 to over $13 million.[69] Not only did NOW increase its membership and finances considerably throughout this period, it is clear that it became far more professionalized in the process. In surveying the political landscape after the ERA defeat, for example, NOW's Toni Carabillo determined that women had "learned so many skills we never knew before": "We know political organizing down to the prescient level; we know how to raise money—we're experts on direct mail and fundraising phone banks; [and] we have the largest liberal mailing list of any organization in the country. . . . The reality is the long struggle has only made us larger, stronger, and more skilled."[70]

NOW's ability to turn what was still a crushing defeat into a political launch pad for women evidenced their newfound prowess. Understandably, frustration about their inability to convince male-dominated state legislatures to pass the ERA led NOW to question its position in politics. In a report on the ERA's demise, NOW declared that "we must elect many more feminist women to sit in the legislative halls of this nation."[71] To do so, NOW launched a number of PACs to raise money for these campaigns, establishing forty-six new PACs in twenty-seven states to boast a total of more than eighty across the nation by the 1982 elections.[72]

Results were immediate, as record-breaking numbers of women filed for legislative seats in 1982. As the *Los Angeles Times* observed, "NOW, battered in the ERA fight, appears to have taken a good deep breath and regrouped."[73] The promise to "Remember in November" after the ERA defeat became "We'll remember every November" as NOW used the energy from the Countdown Campaign to drive its strategy, increase its clout, and mobilize turnout.[74] Having honed their political skills in the losing campaign for ERA, NOW and its allies had particular success in several states where the ERA had been contested until the ratification deadline, including Florida, where women doubled their number in the state senate from four to nine.[75]

Portending significant electoral trouble ahead for the Republicans, an internal party report demonstrated that in 1980 and 1982, for the first time ever, women cast more votes than men in all but one of the twenty-five largest states. Crucially, the report found that the number of women voters in the southern states had grown from 49.8 percent in 1978 to 55.9 percent in 1982, and strategists argued that national trends demonstrated that women now held the key to success in future elections.[76] With the emergence of the gender gap, the defeat of the ERA, and the impact of the feminization of poverty campaign, NOW clamored for a new kind of politics: one that, importantly to them, featured more women in positions of power. They also began to seriously discuss an audacious concept—placing a woman on a major nationwide ticket. According to Smeal, while the 1970s was the decade in which women increased their participation in the workforce, the 1980s would be the decade when they did so in politics.[77]

THE FERRARO FACTOR

In October 1983, NOW organized a symposium in Washington, DC, on "Women in Politics" and invited the full field of Democratic presidential contenders. One question proved more significant than any other: "Would the candidates pledge to name a woman running-mate?" NOW justified this interest in a woman nominee with reminders of the gender gap and the potential excitement level that such a candidacy might elicit. NOW's new president, Judy Goldsmith, made it clear that the promise to name a woman running mate would be considered alongside a host of issues to justify the organization's first endorsement of a presidential candidate in its seventeen-year history. When the candidates met NOW, they all claimed that they would give serious consideration to the proposal. Former Vice President Walter Mondale, for example, described himself as a feminist, while Senator Gary Hart declared that he would be proud to serve on a ticket with a woman "at either end."[78]

Not a year had passed when on 17 July 1984 New York Congresswoman Geraldine Ferraro became the first woman nominated as vice president by a major political party. Ferraro, addressing the crowd at the Democratic convention that year, spoke to the historic nature of her candidacy: "By choosing a woman to run for our nation's second-highest office, you send a powerful signal to all Americans. . . . If we can do this, we can do anything."[79] For many, this signaled a significant advance for women in politics; however, for a dedicated few in the crowd, this was also the culmination of a year of campaigning.

The origins of Ferraro's vice presidential nomination lay in both the ERA defeat and the electoral significance of the gender gap. As Goldsmith declared to the Democratic convention in 1984, the move to get a woman on the ticket was grounded in the political realities of the time: "recognizing both the historic movement of women onto center stage of the political arena and the strong and growing public support for a woman vice-president."[80] Described by Goldsmith as "possibly the most significant political phenomenon of this century," the gender gap enabled NOW and its allies to use the emerging voting clout of women as leverage to convince the Democrats to take notice.[81] For example, the NWPC organized its own conference in 1983 and invited the Democratic field. Previously, those invited would simply send position papers, or even their wives, to the conference; but, apparently impressed by the gender gap, five male contenders agreed to appear. One NWPC member called this a "quantum leap" in women's influence.[82]

With growing influence came increasing calls for a seat at the top of the table. Citing the gender gap as evidence, NOW argued that adding a woman to the Democratic ticket would strengthen it by widening its political reach. Since there had never been a female nominee, this was an untested claim, but by linking it to increasing participation and voter turnout, the idea of a woman vice president began to take hold.[83] Reinforcing this impression that women could determine the outcome, Census Bureau data estimated that eight million more women than men were projected to vote in 1984.[84]

Despite the fact that women served in positions of power across the world at the time, Mondale pledged only to seriously consider a female running mate. But this assurance still proved enough for NOW, who endorsed him in December 1983.[85] In justifying this endorsement over the rest of the field, especially Jesse Jackson, who had the strongest program on women's rights and social justice issues and was the only candidate to actually promise to choose a female running mate, NOW pointed to the perceived electability of Mondale.[86] Still, critics argued that the choice not to endorse Jackson was part of an underlying racism inherent in both the organization and the Democratic Party; this reality was also evidenced in the primary campaign, where gender gaps quickly evaporated and were replaced by racial gaps, with white women and white men largely voting together against Jackson. In the New York primary, for example, 89 percent of Black women and 83 percent of Black men supported Jackson, while white women and white men each gave Jackson only 6 percent of the vote.

Both the endorsement and the use of electability as a criterion for support demonstrated the distance NOW had traveled in a relatively short space of time.[87] In common with several women's rights groups, NOW was formed as a bipartisan organization in the mid-1960s, yet the polarized nature of the Reagan years had pushed it in a more partisan direction, driving the organization to establish clear institutional links with the Democratic Party. While some quarters of its membership had pushed for the organization to use its first-ever presidential endorsement to make a radical statement, Smeal reasoned that an overarching determination to defeat Reagan was at the core of the endorsement decision and that, by choosing Mondale, activists could solidify behind a front-runner early and work within a wider coalition to "turn out the gender gap."[88] It would also, seemingly, increase the organization's bargaining power and enhance their ability to have him select a woman as a running mate. The outcome of the primary contest demonstrated the wisdom of this strategy: Mondale secured the nomination and Ferraro became the vice presidential nominee. The test, however, was for NOW to deliver the women's vote as promised.

To do so, NOW organized an extensive registration drive and set out to raise over $3 million through its PACs.[89] Working together with the Women's Vote Project, the LCCR, and other liberal organizations, NOW formed a coalition that specifically targeted women and racial minorities.[90] Arguing that "registration is the key to mobilizing the power of the gender gap," NOW combined this drive with a new campaign, the "Women's Truth Squad on Reagan."[91] As an internal memo to its state and local chapters advised, Truth Squad brochures were to be used to "identify potential anti-Reagan voters . . . register them, ask them to join NOW, and re-contact them in [the] fall get-out-the-vote drive."[92] A key facet of this drive was to continue linking Reagan to the welfare state "crisis." As documented, social spending cutbacks provided strong anti-Reagan incentives for millions of women trapped by the increasing feminization of poverty. Identifying this, a strategy document released by NOW argued that only through exercising collective power at the polls could the budget cuts that had "so heavily and negatively affected women" be stopped.[93] Finally, NOW and its allies focused their energy on the states Reagan won by less than 10 percent in 1980, purporting that registering more women in just a few of them would make the difference in 1984.[94]

Yet registration drives and targeted campaigns could not undo decades of prejudice. Although Ferraro's candidacy was trailblazing in many ways, stereotypes regarding her "weaknesses" on national security and foreign policy dogged the campaign. As Ferraro later noted, "It was so endlessly annoying being presumed as weak and indecisive simply because I was a woman."[95] To be sure, she likely faced these criticisms not just because she was a woman, but also because she was a liberal woman, particularly as conservatives were increasingly attacking liberals as weak on foreign policy after the Vietnam imbroglio. Indeed, that year Jeane Kirkpatrick, Reagan's UN ambassador and a prominent neoconservative, famously lambasted Democrats as the "Blame America First" party in a rousing speech to the Republican convention.[96] Still, what was supposed to be a bold move to exploit the gender gap had instead dissolved into controversy. Come election day, the massive vote that proponents of a female vice president expected failed to come to fruition. Despite Ferraro's groundbreaking candidacy, the aphorism that people mainly vote the top of the ticket endured. As one voter in Cleveland said, "Ferraro is one hell of a lady. I just wish Reagan was with her."[97] A postelection study also found that 33 percent of male Democrats who rated Ferraro higher than Mondale on a likability scale defected from their partisanship to vote for Reagan.[98] Mondale was not a particularly popular candidate from the outset, and Ferraro's dynamic placement on the ticket may have actually strengthened negative perceptions of him.[99] Mondale trailed Reagan in most major polls conducted in 1984, and Theodore White's joke that only Florence Nightingale or Joan of Arc could have saved his campaign effectively captured the mood.[100]

Additionally, after the midterm losses in 1982, the gender gap took on a new measure of importance for Reagan and the Republican Party.[101] Shortly after the midterms, Reagan made two high-profile appointments of women to cabinet positions—Elizabeth Dole as Secretary of Transportation and Margaret Heckler to head the Department of Health and Human Services.[102] According to the *Washington Post*, these appointments were driven by political calculations: "The president is seeking to neutralize this 'gender gap' by including women in the upper reaches of his administration, according to White House aides."[103] The administration also launched the Working Group on Women, and Dole was put in charge of publicizing Reagan's new efforts to improve the status of women. As Dole later explained, "This was the first time we'd had a lot of assistants to the president working on women's issues."[104]

In attempting to bridge the gap, Republicans also began to profile women voters, allowing strategists to reject the concept of women as a uniform category and concentrate on finding those subgroups that would be most receptive to the Republican message. While NOW was largely treating women as a monolithic voting bloc to increase its own influence, Republican strategists began to divide women into eight subgroups, named alphabetically from Alice to Helen, the latter being the most anti-Reagan—unmarried, unemployed women under twenty-five.[105] Writing off the anti-Reagan groups, television ads, direct mail initiatives, and campaign appearances were targeted at the demographic subgroups considered most responsive to Reagan's message. As James Lake, Reagan's campaign press secretary, claimed at the time, "It is foolish for us to try to attract the 'Gloria Steinems of America,'" but certain Reagan initiatives—reversing his opposition to taxes that benefit women, appointing cabinet-level posts, and putting the first woman on the Supreme Court—were designed to appeal to Alice and her friends.[106]

Consequently, by not addressing the issues that underpinned the gender gap for fear of inadvertently alienating male voters, the Mondale campaign left an opening that Republicans were able to exploit. According to journalist Ellen Goodman, the Mondale camp mistakenly believed that Ferraro's presence on the ticket alone would sufficiently motivate women to vote Democratic: "They played to the women's vote only at the end.... It was as if the Mondale people expected Ferraro to win women's votes based on mysticism."[107] Additionally, while NOW had been able to convince the party to place Ferraro on the ticket, they were essentially unable to influence the campaign's agenda in any dynamic way afterward due to Mondale's strategy.[108] Indeed, although NOW had traditionally operated by pressuring their agenda from the outside, they were clearly maneuvering from inside the system now. Even Judy Goldsmith, who now traveled with the campaign, admitted that she had assumed "an insider's role."[109] Inevitably, while NOW was establishing important institutional links with the Democratic Party, there were clear limits to how far they could push the party to forward their interests.

Nevertheless, NOW could point to the fact that the gender gap persisted despite the existence of factors that should have eliminated it. Although an overall majority of the electorate voted for Reagan, the National Election Study recorded a gap of 8 percent, with 63 percent of men and 55 percent of women voting for Reagan. According to the *New York Times*, this gender gap cut across several demographic indicators, including race (white vote, 4 percent; Black vote, 6 percent), age bracket (eighteen-to-twenty-nine-year-olds, 6 percent; thirty-to-forty-four-year-olds, 8 percent), and marital status (married, 5 percent; unmarried, 13 percent).[110] Still, the Democratic Party had to face the fact that a majority voted for Reagan, albeit with reservations from more women. In the end, Mondale ran a relatively uninspiring campaign focused on notions of collective sacrifice, while Reagan's optimistic rhetoric focused on peace, prosperity, and patriotism. Voters responded accordingly. Even Mondale reflected afterward that Reagan "was selling Morning in America and I was selling a root canal."[111]

Across Pennsylvania Avenue though, the gender gap would play a more decisive role. In the Senate, it stretched from 5 percent, allowing Iowa Democrat Tom Harkin to beat a Republican incumbent, to 18 percent for Massachusetts Democrat John Kerry.[112] Helping to keep Reagan's coattails short, the women's vote proved key in a number of other important local and state-wide races too, including Senate seats in Illinois and Michigan, and the Vermont gubernatorial contest, where NOW had assigned its largest contribution.[113] NOW immediately released a memo with the headline: "Gender Gap Saves Congress and Major Seats for Democrats."[114] With this gender differential in voting now seemingly established, the Democrats had to learn how to cultivate it better at the presidential level.

Despite the result, the Ferraro candidacy remained representative of the increased power liberal women's groups like NOW wielded in the early Reagan years. As Smeal declared, "Perhaps the most important outcome of the Ferraro nomination is that when women leaders sit down to strategize, we will take ourselves more seriously. We know how to play the game."[115] Indeed, NOW's campaigns helped register 1.8 million more women for 1984.[116] Certainly, in its use of political influence, access to politicians and the media, and control of information, particularly polling data, NOW demonstrated its development into a major political force. Crucially, Reagan's 1980 victory prompted a change in political approach for NOW, who were transitioning from a confrontational, bipartisan organization pressuring politics from the outside to a coalition-based, partisan body working within the formal structures of power.[117] By interviewing candidates and making endorsements, NOW employed the tactics that were traditionally associated with interest/lobbying groups such as labor.[118] Democratic candidates reacted to the prospect of a NOW endorsement in the same way they did to one from the AFL-CIO. But many supporters believed that NOW had made a strategic miscalculation in assuming such an insider role, which became a key focal point of the organization's 1985 leadership contest.

Launching a campaign that surprised many observers, previous president, Smeal, criticized her protégé, Goldsmith, for turning NOW into a wing of the Democratic Party and promised to return the organization to its more radical past if elected. While not a battle for the soul of NOW, the contest would still signal the movement's direction. Though NOW's national board and state chapters supported Goldsmith by a 2 to 1 margin,

Smeal roused delegates at NOW's convention and won by 839 to 703 ballots. Smeal did "take NOW to the streets" by organizing mass marches and pressuring both parties through campaigns afterward, but the significance of the gender gap and Reagan's "anti-women" stance ensured that the organization remained closely affiliated with the Democratic Party.[119] Indeed, despite frustration with the organization's influence in 1984, NOW did not have an alternative political vehicle available to it, and the Reagan Era had clearly illuminated the necessity of pragmatic coalition building. While NOW would continue to function as a grassroots movement pressuring politics from the outside, Reagan's first term clearly demonstrated that it had also become, for the first time, an institutionalized interest group pursing politics from within.

"MORE LIBERAL AND MORE DEMOCRATIC"

Following the 1984 election result, liberals wondered aloud how Reagan had been able to sweep the electoral map despite a majority of voters disagreeing with his conservative views. As Gloria Steinem mused: "A large majority of men and a slender majority of women went to the polls and voted for a President whose major positions—from disarmament talks to deficit spending, from illegal abortion to reduced environmental controls—a majority of Americans don't share."[120]

A Gallup poll taken two weeks after the election confirmed Steinem's argument, showing that public opinion was still heavily in favor of a nuclear freeze, increased spending on social programs, and ERA passage.[121] As the Democratic Party tried to find reasons to explain their defeat, some members pointed blame at Ferraro, even though vice presidential candidates rarely make an impact. As journalist Flora Davis highlighted, a member of Mondale's inner circle insisted that "the party got a gun put to its head by women to choose a woman for Vice-President. They overpromised what they could not deliver." One of the party's top consultants, Patrick Caddell, added fuel to the fire by warning that "we can't afford to have a party so feminized that it has no appeal to males."[122] However this was a search for scapegoats rather than a discovery of causation.

As the next chapter explores, Mondale lost due to a variety of factors. In particular, after a difficult primary battle, Mondale emerged to challenge Reagan's optimistic rhetoric as a wounded candidate discussing notions of sacrifice. Ferraro suggested that voters rewarded Reagan for telling them only the good news, while punishing Mondale for bringing them the bad.[123] Moreover, the party, at the presidential level at least, evidently ignored several of the issues that had created the gender gap; and Republican strategists, not Democratic ones, proved astute at disaggregating its complexities for a national campaign. Accordingly, the problem was not with Ferraro, but rather with the party's confused message and strategy. Liberalism was in a state of transition by the mid-1980s, and Mondale struggled to construct a message that appealed to both the newer liberal constituencies—women among them—that emerged out of identity politics battles of earlier decades, and the voters that had provided the party's New Deal base in the past. Nevertheless, these internal disputes over the defeat should not detract from the fact that the campaign to nominate a woman vice president was still an effective means of organizing power and projecting presence in the political arena; and together with the ERA battle before it, these struggles laid the groundwork for later developments.

Evidently, the debut of the gender gap enabled an alphabet soup of liberal groups, from NOW to NARAL, to develop more politically sophisticated operations in Reagan's shadow, particularly with regard to establishing ties with the Democratic Party. By working directly with the party, for example, NOW developed effective coalition-building strategies and mobilized voters throughout Reagan's first term to make the absence of women in politics a more potent issue. As a result, they increased their financial and political reach, steadily entrenching their operations and working closely with key legislators to advance movement goals. By the end of Reagan's first term, and in large part because of the strategies implemented by NOW, women had increased their political visibility and legitimacy considerably, and with lasting impact. Indeed, as a consequence of the groundwork laid by NOW, the number of women in the House of Representatives more than doubled between the elections of 1980 and 1992, expanding from twenty-one to forty-eight, and the tally of female US senators went from two to seven.[124]

Crucially, greater political participation rates among women fueled these developments and were the direct result of NOW's voter registration drives in the years prior; between 1980 and 1984, women accounted for 60 percent of newly registered voters and "Democratic women accounted for most of that increase."[125] As an internal report by NOW noted, women were now "more likely than men to support candidates with an activist view of government against candidates who think government is too big"—a clear philosophical preference that favored the Democrats.[126]

By the close of Reagan's presidency, polls demonstrated that women were now "more inclined to vote for Democrats, even male Democratic incumbents, over female Republican challengers."[127] In the end, the fact that women became more liberal and more Democratic is an important and often overlooked aspect of Reagan's America.

4. Turning Points
The 1984 Elections and the Identity Crisis Within the Democratic Party

It was "Morning Again in America" in 1984. After the most severe recession since the Great Depression, the economy had gradually improved in the years that followed 1982. Unemployment and inflation dropped to 7.5 percent and 3.5 percent, respectively, by 1984, while the rate of real disposable income rose by 2.5 percent in 1983 and 5.8 percent in 1984—the largest election year increase since 1936.[1] Reagan's personal popularity rose in conjunction with these trends, from 35 percent at the beginning of 1983 to 57 percent as the election year opened.[2] The president proceeded to conduct a successful campaign based around the themes of peace, patriotism, and prosperity, and his famous "Morning in America" television advertisement seemed to capture the mood of the nation at the time.[3] By connecting viewers to a mythical present, the ad provided a poignant view of American life through gauzy images of small-town America awakening to a new dawn.

However, while it was morning again in America for Reagan and his supporters, for many liberals at the time it may have seemed more like twilight. Not only had Geraldine Ferraro's historic candidacy failed to affect the election outcome in any serious way, but Walter Mondale's crushing defeat to a president perceived, from his first term at least, as trying to undermine every program and policy that underpinned liberalism was a particularly difficult loss for liberals. Indeed, liberals were concerned that Reagan, without a reelection campaign to worry about, would move to implement some of the more controversial aspects of his conservative agenda, including limiting abortion rights.[4] Still, hidden from view by this landslide defeat were a number of important developments for liberalism that deserve closer examination—developments that may not have seemed significant at the time, but that would effectively determine the shape of liberalism in Reagan's second term.

Indeed, the Democratic primaries that year showcased the ways in which liberalism had adapted and responded intellectually to Reaganism and illuminated a central problem facing the Democratic Party at the time: what message could be deployed to attract the increasing number of independent voters without alienating traditional liberal constituencies? Mondale and his main challenger, Colorado Senator Gary Hart, offered two different ways to sell liberalism to the electorate and build a winning coalition. Mondale, a protégé of Senator Hubert Humphrey and a strong supporter of New Deal/Great Society programs as a senator himself in the 1960s and 1970s, seemed to embody most of the liberal principles of the previous half century. He had campaigned for civil rights, pushed the government to strengthen aid to the poor, and called for restraint in the exercise of American might abroad.[5] Yet his past involvement as an establishment warrior in these liberal battles and his attempts to unite the fading strands of the party's New Deal coalition were used against him. Whether unfairly or not, he was characterized by his opponents as an unreconstructed, old-style liberal: his close relationship with labor; his attempts to gain the endorsements of various liberal organizations; and his proposed solutions to some of the country's most trenchant issues—he infamously offered voters higher taxes in response to the growing national deficit—damaged his campaign and contributed to his image as an old "tax and spend" liberal.[6]

Hart, on the other hand, represented the emerging neoliberal strand of the party and offered a liberalism full of "new solutions" and "new ideas" to distinguish himself from Mondale. As with the rest of the neoliberal cohort, Hart was engaging in a battle of style rather than substance. Hart remained true to the central tenet of liberalism—that, used wisely, government was an invaluable tool for the amelioration of social and economic ills—and his record marked him as one of the most liberal elected officials in the nation at the time. Yet, in light of Reagan's election and the successful implementation of aspects of his agenda, Hart argued that the time had come for "a new generation to take over."[7] The inexorable facts of demography foretold that the children of the baby boom, well seasoned from a political education during the Vietnam era, would soon decisively affect the electoral process.[8] Less wedded to political parties and institutions than their elders, these voters—typically young, urban professionals (or Yuppies as they came to be known)—would have a marked impact on the presidential race as Hart tried to give them an identity and a political focus.[9] As one pollster noted to Speaker O'Neill: "It is clear that the message of the Hart campaign, not the Mondale campaign, is much more dangerous to Reagan, probably more helpful to other Democratic candidates, and more likely to be successful."[10] Moreover, the *Wall Street Journal* declared that Hart's efforts to engage with liberalism's approach would be the "lasting phenomenon" of his campaign.[11]

On November 6, as liberals watched Reagan flood the electoral map in a sea of red, this prophecy proved accurate. Senator Paul Tsongas, whose staff tried to convince him to release a simple statement saying "I told you so" after Mondale's defeat, would use Hart's campaign to argue that the party could only win at the presidential level with a neoliberal platform.[12] And by 1985, early speculation on the potential contenders for the 1988 election focused almost entirely on members of the neoliberal cohort, with Hart as the clear front-runner.[13] Thus, in 1984 a battle for the liberal soul of the party took place that would shape the development of liberalism into Reagan's second term and beyond.

MONDALE

The 1982 midterm results were, in some ways, a victory for liberals. With twenty-six "Reagan Republicans" ousted from Congress, as well as favorable results at state and local levels, the Reagan Revolution seemed to run aground much earlier than anticipated. While some quarters of the Democratic Party had predicted liberalism's demise in 1980—Ohio's Democratic chairman, Paul Tipps, said at the time that "any public official who is a liberal Democrat has two choices: find another job or change his philosophy"—the 1982 results altered the debate.[14] Instead, talk was of revival as political commentators, such as Fred Barnes, pointed to the resurrection of liberalism: "Liberal ideas, despite the obituaries, are not dead. They were only in hibernation."[15] These results also seemed to encourage several Democrats to revert to the party's traditional New Deal moorings, even though some, including Mondale, had started to embrace the neoliberal effort to update liberalism at the time.

After the 1980 elections, for example, Mondale had announced that he was undertaking a reeducation program in order to position himself among the new thinkers of the party. Yet as political commentators John Judis and Ruy Teixeira noted, just as Mondale was moving to embrace the neoliberal approach, he was emboldened by the midterm victories to eschew new proposals and adopt a standard liberal attack against the "unfairness" of Reagan's program of government.[16] Internal party polls at the time demonstrated that the issues Americans worried most about favored this traditional stance. According to pollster Peter Hart, the number one issue was "jobs/unemployment and Democrats are seen better at handling it than Republicans by 53-to-20 percent."[17] As the nation emerged from a damaging recession, these results were understandable, but as Mondale would discover, the concept of fairness took on a new meaning when the economy started to recover. A DNC poll after the 1984 elections, for example, found that some voters, particularly middle-class suburban voters, viewed "fairness" as a "code word for giveaway."[18]

The midterms had also convinced Mondale to move quickly to gain the endorsements of key constituency groups, political leaders, and elected officials. As demonstrated, liberal organizations were increasingly injecting themselves into the political fray in the early 1980s. Labor unions, for example, had endorsed a raft of liberal candidates in 1982, and in an effort to raise their profile further, the AFL-CIO announced a break with its tradition of not endorsing a candidate before the primaries by throwing its weight behind Mondale, a strong ally of labor.[19] Like many interest groups during the Reagan years, the AFL-CIO was not only adapting its approach but was redefining itself as a partisan political force. Given that this endorsement carried some, though not decisive, weight with union members, a critical component of the New Deal base, Mondale was already ahead before the primaries formally began. More endorsements came—from women's groups, teachers' unions, environmentalists, and politicians—but polls also demonstrated that voters were wary of Mondale's brand of politics.[20] By practicing his coalition-building process in the full glare of the electorate, Mondale's search for endorsements accentuated the connection between seeking votes and promising benefits. Some commentators thus claimed that Mondale was becoming beholden to special interest groups—a perception fed by his opponents as the election calendar advanced.[21]

Still, as the anointed front-runner, Mondale plotted his route to the nomination early, hoping to use name recognition and endorsements to ensure a quick victory.[22] But his first electoral test—the Iowa caucuses—exposed his shortcomings. Although Mondale won the Iowa caucuses with almost 50 percent of the popular vote, there were problems hidden in the figures. Particularly weak among younger voters, winning only 19 percent among those under the age of thirty, he was seen as lacking in new ideas and as overly influenced by special interests.[23] Equally significant, the "surprising showing" of Hart, who scored 16.5 percent, was the beginning of what would become an insurgent campaign that pushed Mondale all the way to the convention. By coming second, however distantly, Hart became the unofficial candidate of the "not-Mondale" contingent—voters who were younger, more educated and affluent, and disenchanted with the orthodoxies of the party.[24] Enlivening the race were six other candidates, including Ohio's moderate Senator John Glenn, who, as a former astronaut and the first American to orbit the earth, had high name recognition but scored a contrastingly weak 3.5 percent in Iowa, and Reverend Jesse Jackson, whose historic bid gave a voice to racial minorities and spotlighted the Democrats' dependence on their votes.[25]

As the *New York Times* noted before the New Hampshire primary a week later, Mondale was still the front-runner: "He holds the most commanding lead ever recorded in a presidential nominating campaign by a non-incumbent."[26] Nevertheless, Hart's claim that he would beat Mondale became a self-fulfilling prophecy as he swept the Granite State to inflict a "Hart attack" on the Mondale campaign.[27] This came as a surprise to nearly everyone, with Mondale later admitting that the result "stunned us."[28] But it should not have. Months earlier, Mondale had hired pollster Peter Hart to test his prospects in New Hampshire by using biographical and political profiles similar to his own and those of Hart, Glenn, and a number of others looking at the race. The results revealed by an overwhelming margin that respondents chose the "Hart" candidate: young, liberal, western, and full of new ideas.[29] Hart captured 38 percent to Mondale's 28, Glenn managed only 12 percent, and the other candidates divided the remainder. Spelling trouble for Mondale, Hart swept every category of voter, except those sixty years or older.[30] Polls also showed that Hart gained more support from women than men, suggesting that he was better positioned to exploit the gender gap.[31]

Speaker O'Neill concluded that it was the biggest surprise since Eugene McCarthy took on Lyndon Johnson in 1968, while journalist David Broder determined that Hart had found Mondale's weakness: "In the voting booth, Mondale's claim that 'I am ready' proved far less appealing than Hart's claim that 'I am new.'"[32] The field eventually winnowed down to three, or, in effect, two since Jackson's unguarded remarks, particularly those referring to Jews as "Hymies," derailed his candidacy and all but destroyed his political viability, no matter how much he apologized.[33] Still, Jackson's campaign would spotlight the importance of building a Rainbow Coalition—a multiracial liberal coalition united across intersectional issues—and laid the foundation for a far more successful run in 1988.

Consequently, by Super Tuesday—nicknamed to capture the large number of states from geographically and socially diverse regions that hold primaries and caucuses on the same Tuesday, typically in March—the political calculus of the nomination had changed significantly. Mondale was losing support, and Hart, a relatively unknown candidate, was quickly becoming the cynosure of the nation.

HART

Hart, who managed George McGovern's presidential bid in 1972, entered political office as a leading member of the Watergate Babies in 1974.[34] McGovern's nascent campaign, for all its glory and pathos, had given Hart a crucial insight into both the nominating process and presidential politics, allowing him to develop the grassroots organizational skills that earned him the reputation as a political genius.[35] After emerging from the McGovern crucible, Hart conducted his own autopsy of the campaign and reflected that "the fount of specific proposals and programs was running dry.... American liberalism was near bankruptcy." The Democratic Party, he concluded, needed new thinking and new leadership or its intellectual creativity would dry up: "The soil is worn out. Liberals better pull their socks up and get back in the game.... New ideas must be found to solve old problems."[36] When Hart ran for the Senate in 1974, his major stump speech was titled "The End of the New Deal"—a title more interesting for what it suggested politically than for its historical accuracy.[37] Clearly, the political framework created by the New Deal had not disappeared by the mid-1970s, nor was Hart calling for liberals to wholesale abandon it (he strongly supported Social Security, Medicare, and other key aspects of the New Deal tradition). Instead, this was a form of rhetorical positioning that mirrored the language employed by the reformist liberals arriving in Washington after 1974. By warning liberals to avoid clinging to New Deal shibboleths, Hart would quickly become a leading intellectual light of the neoliberal brigade.

Consequently, by 1984, Hart was engaging his liberal competitor in a battle of style rather than substance. Indeed, Mondale and Hart had near identical voting records in the Senate, and by 1982, the American Civil Liberties Union gave Hart the highest liberal score of any senator: 96 percent.[38] That year, Hart also used a speech in Iowa to lay claim to Edward Kennedy's liberal supporters from 1980, telling onlookers that in the "shameful" stampede to pass Reagan's programs in 1981, only two National Democrats voted against every aspect of Reaganomics: "Kennedy was one and I was the other."[39] According to political commentator John Farrell, "Amid the tide of the Reagan Revolution, Hart cast his votes as a liberal, refusing to bow to pressure."[40] Thus, as the primaries would make evident, few substantive issues divided Hart and Mondale; instead, it was a question of approach. Hart himself acknowledged this:

> In the great sweep and flow, basically Mondale and I have the same beliefs, the same principles. The question is how we act those out. The fault line of the party is now between those who have been in office for 20 or 25 years and those who have come into office in the last 10 years and who are less tied to the arrangements dating to Roosevelt and Johnson. This is not a contest over values, but a contest over methods and process and control.[41]

This generational aspect of liberalism became key to Hart's appeal. From his earliest campaigning days, Hart had used the same slogan to capture this notion of change: "They had their turn. Now it's our turn."[42] When announcing his presidential candidacy in 1983, Hart used the occasion to showcase this fusion of ideological and generational elements: "Our problems worsen while some retreat to an unfair past and others debate old remedies and contend over shop-worn policies. In this decade—in the term of the next President—we must build a bridge to a new era and master its possibilities."[43] Although only nine years separated Hart and Mondale in age, they gazed at one another across a generational divide. As historian Steven Gillon argues: "Mondale and Hart would look at the audience and see two different realities.... Mondale would see people by age, occupational status and deduce political leanings. Hart would see alienation, and a need for generational change."[44] Mondale's political consciousness had been forged by the New Deal, and he drew his strength from labor unions. By contrast, Hart's was reflective of the skepticism and pragmatism that grew out of Vietnam and Watergate. As Hart himself attests, "My political roots are in the John Kennedy wing of the Democratic Party—pragmatic liberalism as opposed to the ideological liberalism of Adlai Stevenson."[45] In practice though, Hart reached out to the exact same voting constituencies as Mondale and sought the same endorsements from liberal interest groups. An early strategy memo among Hart's staff members captured this: "Priority constituencies should be: Dem Party, teachers, blacks, Chicanos/Hispanics, labor, activist seniors, environmentalists, feminists; Geographic priority: Strengthening base in the West, ten largest states [which control 53.1 percent of delegates], early foray into the South to test market Hart's appeal there.... Must begin strengthening base among core constituencies (a politer way to say 'special interests.')"[46]

The memo, clearly conscious of identity politics, noted that one of the key objectives was to present Hart as the leader of the post–New Deal liberals.⁴⁷ Candidly, Hart's staffers acknowledged that they did not know what this really meant. Indeed, as noted, the process of updating liberalism intellectually was an ongoing one, and efforts to develop a post–New Deal liberalism represented an attempt to synthesize the economic and welfare state driven model of the New Deal with the social and cultural issues that were increasingly impacting the political environment. And given that Hart and Mondale agreed on most issues, how this post–New Deal concept translated into political practice was difficult to discern. Nevertheless, Hart still sought possible points of conflict to capture the concept and differentiate himself from Mondale over issues as well as style. Consequently, Hart decided to use the role of organized labor—a foundational component of the New Deal—as an attack measure, despite earlier seeking their endorsement. Mondale had racked up a record of consistent support for labor and its causes, but this, alongside the AFL-CIO endorsement, was used by Hart to create an impression that Mondale was their lackey.⁴⁸ In a live debate before the Iowa caucuses, for example, Hart asked Mondale to name just one issue on which he and organized labor disagreed. Mondale, refusing to play Hart's game, sidestepped the question, but his inability to name an issue only served to support this impression of him.⁴⁹ Hart, who had relied on strong labor support in the past, was calculating that both Mondale's previous ties and labor's decreasing influence in a transitioning economy could be used to his advantage, particularly in his efforts to frame his liberalism through a past/future prism.⁵⁰ By attacking Mondale as a creature of the past and as a symbol of the old Democratic Party, Hart struck a powerful chord with primary voters.⁵¹

In a further effort to position himself as a post–New Deal liberal, Hart attempted to wrap his liberal ideas in language meant to appeal to emerging constituencies of the postindustrial landscape. Neoliberals increasingly drew their strength from the suburbs, where the knowledge worker had replaced the autoworker and where the baby boom generation had significant electoral power. Baby boomers, comprising two of every five voters by 1984, were more likely to identify as independents, which made them readily susceptible to new strategies and arguments.⁵² Hart targeted his campaign toward them, believing he gave them a voice: "They don't want a messiah. They don't want me to personalize an entire generation's yearnings—just to be the vehicle for its expression."⁵³ In fact, Hart was already claiming this victory before the primaries had even begun: "I've already won one race, and no one has written about it. . . . That is the race to become the spokesman for my generation in the mid-1980s."⁵⁴ In the same way that John F. Kennedy gave harder edges to the coalition first mobilized by Adlai Stevenson, Hart was hoping to galvanize the generation awakened by Camelot.

By calibrating his approach to appeal to these voters, Hart argued that his message was a two-pronged push "beyond the twin pasts being offered by Reaganism and by the worn-out, but redecorated policy ghosts of the other Democratic candidates."[55] At the center of this pitch was his "new ideas." Hart championed more economic growth and less regulation, a more efficient military—breaking the Left–Right dichotomy of "more is better" or "less is better" by simply saying "better is better"—and a government that invested in schools, industry, and skilled workers instead of worrying about redistributing income.[56] Like his colleagues in the House Democratic Caucus (HDC), Hart's goal was to change the image of liberalism, not liberalism itself. Indeed, as he argued before the HDC in 1983, the focus should be on economic growth first: "If we go into the next national referendum as the party with only the slogan of redistributing more fairly a stagnant economic pie, we will lose, and I think we will deserve to lose."[57] Thus, by emphasizing alternative approaches to both economic and social equity issues, Hart was hoping to offer an intellectual bridge from the idealistic 1960s to the pragmatic 1980s.[58] This was welcomed by the HDC, with Texas Representative Martin Frost noting at the time: "The broad appeal of Hart's call for 'new ideas' [may] have caught much of the nation's political establishment off guard. But for many members of the HDC, the allure of Hart's message both validated and reinforced our own, parallel efforts to bring about the intellectual renovation of the party."[59]

Primary results would demonstrate the "allure" in Hart's approach. While Mondale was a favorite among the traditional New Deal groups—labor unions, low-income workers, the unemployed—Hart did better with independents and young professionals, particularly those in the suburbs, and among voters who disliked labor unions.[60] Notably, their support with women and racial minorities was broadly similar, due largely to the fact that they each embraced emerging identity-based issues.[61] As the primaries progressed, Hart argued that Mondale's strength among the more traditional groups should not be overrated as those voters, many of them strongly anti-Republican, would vote Democratic whether the nominee was Mondale or Hart. Mondale, on the other hand, claimed Hart was all style and no substance. Days before Super Tuesday, Mondale leveled a memorable—and quite damaging—criticism against Hart during a debate in Atlanta by borrowing a line from a famous Wendy's fast-food advertisement. As Hart was discussing new ideas to stimulate entrepreneurship and foster economic growth, Mondale interrupted him to say: "When I hear your new ideas, I'm reminded of that ad: 'Where's the beef?'"[62] Seemingly crystallizing the anxiety some voters felt about Hart's "new ideas" rhetoric, this became a criticism he struggled to shake, even though he had laid out substantive details in his book *A New Democracy*.[63] Seeking to respond, Hart posed for a photograph with this book between two burger buns the following day and claimed on an evening news show that "the reason a lot of people cannot digest that beef is because it is not grown on special interest cattle."[64] Tortured metaphors aside, Hart was still seeking support from the same groups as Mondale, and this "special interest" criticism was essentially a form of rhetorical cover. Nevertheless, the attack proved damaging as Hart began to lose the momentum he had gathered from early primary victories.[65]

From Super Tuesday to the beginning of June, the contest remained tumultuous. During this time, Hart hoped to exploit the party's delegate rule changes to his advantage and convince the superdelegates, who were designated on an uncommitted basis but had pledged support to Mondale early on, that the "moral imperative of beating Reagan required them to switch."[66] Strengthening Hart's case, pollster Bill Hamilton used evidence to show that Hart led Reagan 47–44 percent, while Mondale lost to the president 37–55.[67] Republicans also started to admit that they feared the prospect of facing Hart more; the Republican National Committee ran several campaign advertisements against Hart in an effort to reach out to the demographic groups supporting his candidacy.[68]

In the end, Hart argued that his total string of victories—"amounting to 25 primaries and caucuses, a sweep of all primaries West of the Mississippi, a sweep of New England, a win in Florida, Ohio and Indiana, and just about an even number of votes with those cast for Mondale"—gave him a stronger geographic and demographic spread.[69] Speaker O'Neill, praising Hart for "attracting a new group into politics," urged the senator not to play the role of spoiler.[70] But Hart vowed to continue the fight all the way to convention, declaring to a crowd in California: "Welcome to overtime."[71] While Hart's efforts fell short, he still used his prime-time speaking slot at the convention to take a final shot at Mondale: "Our party and our nation needs new leadership, new direction and new hope. . . . You will continue to hear from us. . . . This is one Hart you will not leave in San Francisco."[77] Beyond rhetorical flourish, Hart was also setting his marker down for 1988, recognizing that the wide support his approach had attracted put him in a strong position to assume the party's leadership mantle if Mondale lost the election.

With such a divided outcome, the primaries had effectively illustrated the crossroads that liberalism now found itself at. Mondale, representing the traditional Democratic coalition with labor at the core, did little to dispel suspicions that his candidacy was bound to the past. He struggled to retain the allegiance of the New Deal voting blocs without shaking off the image of the New Deal itself, and with it, the implication that his vision was a half-century old. He won fewer primaries, and the five he carried by a large margin were all situated in the industrial Northeast—New Jersey, New York, Pennsylvania, Maryland, and West Virginia. His most loyal supporters were union members, those over sixty, and those who did not possess a high school diploma—the voters least likely to be a part of the new postindustrial economy.[73] Hart, on the other hand, provided a vehicle for the embryonic neoliberalism of the early 1980s, and his bid demonstrated the political traction of such an approach. While Mondale was talking about union busting and protest movements of the past, Hart was attempting to provide a bridge to the future by discussing technology, the information revolution, and the increasing impact of globalization. Evidenced by his primary victories, Hart's message was highly attractive to westerners, middle-class suburbanites, and young professionals who disagreed with Reagan but sought a "realist" liberal alternative.[74] As the *New York Times* pointed out, voters saw in Hart "many qualities they see in themselves: independence from old ideas and political structures; pragmatic, non-ideological approach to problems and a rejection of the cynicism that developed in the Vietnam and Watergate eras."[75]

Moreover, Hart's message had a more immediate impact on proceedings as well because Mondale incorporated aspects of it into his convention speech, particularly the argument that the nation's fiscal problems could not be solved solely from taxing the rich, but required a plan to grow the economic pie first.[76] Mondale also gave Hart's chief spokesman on the platform committee, Tim Wirth, a prominent voice in the drafting process, ensuring that economic growth, prosperity, and opportunity were emphasized as the party's central goals.[77] But Mondale surrogates on the committee still included the obligatory references to all the interest groups that had supported his candidacy; and Mondale's own search for a running mate—an exercise Jesse Jackson derided as a "P.R. parade of personalities"—did little to dispel the image of him as a captive of special interests.[78] Essentially, Mondale's efforts to blend old and new ideas into a homogenized document produced a bulging platform of nearly forty thousand words.[79] Moreover, with the convention marking the pivot toward the general election, the mood throughout the party was largely fatalistic. While roaming around the convention floor, political journalist

William Greider reported that he could not find a single person who felt Mondale could win in November.[80] As historian Douglas Rossinow has demonstrated, during the course of 1984, 101 major polls matched Reagan and Mondale: "Mondale won only one, by a margin of two points, conducted immediately after the Democratic convention."[81] Mondale was not a particularly strong candidate, and Hart had illuminated weaknesses in his approach that Reagan would exploit shrewdly.

Consequently, Reagan swept every state except Mondale's home state of Minnesota (which he lost by a margin of only 3,761 votes no less) and Washington, DC. Racial minorities and the poor largely voted for Mondale, while everyone else, in percentages that rose directly with income, voted for Reagan.[82] He amassed the largest Electoral College total in history (525 votes), and his popular vote margin (18 percent), while lower than Nixon's in 1972 (23 percent) or Johnson's in 1964 (22 percent), represented a significant rout.[83] With exit polls indicating that roughly one-third of Hart's primary voters supported Reagan, calls for a new approach only grew louder.[84] In the aftermath, Hart spoke to the historical significance of his campaign:

> It is not accidental that I was one of the two serious final candidates. . . . Something is going on out there. There is a strong desire for new leadership—that is more than just a slogan; it represents a new way of thinking. The shift is coming about in the electoral process, in the governorships, in the Congress, certainly in State legislatures. About all we haven't done is occupy the White House—and that's the last and most difficult.[85]

Hart called on liberals to "learn from our losses if we are not to repeat them . . . to broaden our base in recognition of the nation's changing demographics . . . young voters as well as older ones, independents as well as traditional Democrats."[86] In the end, the election represented a watershed moment for liberalism—a time for one generation to fade and another to take its place. Mondale had been beaten, Kennedy had committed himself to Congress, and O'Neill had announced his retirement. A newer breed of liberals, Hart among them, would now have their turn. As Mondale noted, 1984 was a "transitional time for the liberalism I believed in."[87] Mondale, who according to his issues director, William Galston, had felt trapped between two liberal worlds—Humphrey's liberalism of the past and Hart's liberalism of the future—would be the last Democratic presidential candidate whose political lineage could be traced back to the New Deal.[88]

"PURPOSE AND SOUL"

The day after the election, liberal Congressman Tony Coelho wrote a letter to supporters and detractors in an effort to set the tone of analysis:

> Reagan won a popularity contest yesterday, but that's all he won.... Sure enough, [Republicans] will soon form a circle and start shooting inward. Teflon is non-transferable, so before you start writing obits about the Democratic Party, you might take a look at the other side. Our party is strong. We need to continue making progress in terms of financial and technical health of the party, and we will. And we will aggressively look forward to 1986, when I believe we can make major gains. We recognize that we have some problems, but we can solve them as we always do, and today we look forward to the future, not to the past.[89]

Despite defeat, the party could find some consolation in the 1984 elections. They retained a commanding, if diminished, majority in the House (253–182); and they not only gained seats in the Senate (47–53) but also believed, according to political analyst Alan Baron, that they could retake the chamber in 1986.[90] State-level results were also positive: the Democrats won control of over two-thirds of governorships and state legislatures—facts somewhat masked by Reagan's electoral landslide. Moreover, political scientists Thomas Ferguson and Joel Rogers found that on issues of social welfare, civil rights, and government intervention, "mass opinion has actually moved slightly leftward since Reagan assumed office."[91] Exit polls confirmed that on virtually all the important issues identified with the Reagan Revolution, public opinion ran against the president. Additionally, of those voting for Reagan only 6 percent (compared to an already low 11 percent in 1980) directly identified his conservatism as the influencing factor, showing that a slim minority of voters took a doctrinaire approach to the election.[92]

Thus, liberals argued that Reagan had won a personal victory. As O'Neill mused, Reagan was one of the most popular figures in history, "I don't believe if we had Paul Newman this year, we could have beat this fellow, to be perfectly truthful."[93] Others subscribed to this idea as well, including Reagan's chief of staff, James Baker, who said after the election: "It was a victory for him personally, but I'm not sitting here claiming it's a big mandate."[94] Liberals in the House, bolstered by the 1982 midterm results, could also point to the success of their campaign strategy to shorten the length of Reagan's coattails. As Coelho, one of the principal architects of the strategy, noted:

> Just as "fairness" was the prominent 1982 theme, our decision to develop the "insurance policy" theme seems to have worked. Our polls in 1983 and 1984 showed clearly that while voters like Reagan personally, they were nervous about his unfair policies at home and trigger-happy policies abroad. Voters wanted a "check" or a "balance" against Reagan. They would sleep better at night knowing that a Democratic House would moderate his agenda.[95]

Crucially, a near record of 190 districts split their vote between Reagan for president and a Democrat for Congress in 1984.[96] In a sense, just as conventional wisdom tells us that voters chose change rather than conservatism in 1980, it was neither conservatism nor change, but continuity that characterized the 1984 election. Neither party could claim majority status; instead, the split-level partisan alignment of government that had defined the era's politics continued.

Nevertheless, while this helps explain why the Democratic losses outside the presidency were not as pronounced, the election still convinced Democrats that a broader effort was needed to redefine both the party and how it reached out to voters. As Kennedy observed, the party had a perception problem at the national level: "There is a difference between being a party that cares about labor and being a labor party . . . a party that cares about women and being a women's party. And we can and we must be a party that cares about minorities without becoming a minority party. We are citizens first—and constituencies second."[97] Mondale's endorsements had only served to amplify the party's supposed groups-based approach to politics, and Reagan was able to exploit this opening by criticizing him as the candidate of special interests. According to Stuart Eizenstat, Carter's former domestic policy advisor, if Mondale's loss tells us anything, it is that "we must speak directly to the voters whose votes we seek and not filter our message solely through groups claiming to represent them."[98] Indeed, despite Mondale's ties to labor, almost 50 percent of union households voted for a supposedly anti-union president.[99]

Therefore, the 1984 elections made clear that liberals could not hope to win back the presidency if they nominated a candidate whose appeal was limited demographically to traditional party constituencies and restricted geographically to the northeastern corridor.[100] Instead, Hart's efforts to use liberalism to attract new constituencies, while still retaining the allegiance of the party's traditional voting groups, seemed to provide a clearer path back to power. Indeed, while Mondale argued in his concession speech that "every defeat carries the seeds of victory," it was actually in Hart's defeat that the seeds were sown.[101] As the ADA's Ann Lewis acknowledged, Hart "set the tone, if not the language, of the party.... I don't know who the nominee will be in 1988, but I know Gary Hart will have written his script."[102] Not only did Hart himself emerge as the front-runner for 1988, but his reformist brand of liberalism, with its "new generation" orientation, became the template that the rest of the field would employ.[103] The eventual nominee, Massachusetts Governor Michael Dukakis, who subsumed Hart's campaign apparatus after Hart exited the race, placed particular emphasis on knowledge workers and Yuppies. Likewise, Hart's regional strategy was at the forefront of election postmortems. As Coelho noted, for example, "We need to focus on the South and West.... The Democratic Party must be willing to come of age—and fast."[104] This debate about how the party should respond was placed front and center in the search for a new party chairman after Charles Manatt's abrupt resignation in the aftermath of defeat.

Representing another iteration of factional division within the party, with the contest divided along regional, racial, and gender lines, the battle for the DNC chair initially attracted a seven-person field. With 367 votes of the national committee at stake, the pack effectively was winnowed to two in the weeks leading up to the election: Nancy Pelosi, a former California Democratic chair who had won the endorsement of the outgoing party chair, and Paul Kirk, a lawyer and former Kennedy chief of staff from the Northeast. Kirk had a strong liberal background, having served under the close tutelage of Kennedy; first as Kennedy's political director, then as chairman of his 1980 presidential campaign, Kirk helped the senator craft his image as a "liberal warrior" on civil rights, equality, and a host of other issues.[105] Pelosi, who had gained her political education from another revered liberal, California's Phillip Burton, was also a vocal supporter of liberal issues and challenged Kirk on his party-building skills, not his liberal credentials.[106]

That two liberals emerged as the front-runners in the contest convinced southern party leaders to pursue an alternative course. To them, both Kirk and Pelosi had inescapable handicaps that sent the wrong signal to their region: Kirk carried the liberal baggage associated with Kennedy into a contest that was fast becoming a referendum on liberalism itself, while Pelosi was a female at a time when the loss of white males, particularly in the South, was preoccupying the party.[107] Although both candidates were moderating their liberal rhetoric and emphasizing the same thing—the importance of nuts-and-bolts party building and the need to look south and west to expand the base—southerners remained skeptical. Fearing a repeat of 1984 with a woman or a Kennedyite at the helm, these southern leaders—Governors Charles Robb (Virginia) and Bruce Babbitt (Arizona) among them—convinced former North Carolina Governor Terry Sanford to enter the race at the eleventh hour.[108] Sanford's candidacy was the product of a pervasive feeling among southern officials—and neoconservatives under the auspices of the Coalition for a Democratic Majority—that only a move to the right could stall realignment.[109]

As the contest entered its final week, Pelosi endorsed Sanford, explaining that "many didn't think the right message would go out if a woman was elected chairman," as did a number of the other candidates.[110] But Kirk, who received a boost when the national leadership of organized labor called on all DNC union members to back him, started to emerge as the front-runner.[111] Kirk had forged ties with labor unions and liberal groups as the manager of Kennedy's campaign in 1980, and he used these connections to his advantage.[112] Liberals, both Mondale and Hart supporters, united behind his candidacy, and he toppled Sanford by over fifty votes (203 to 150) in balloting that, according to journalist David Lightman, was "marked by color and controversy unusual for a generally little noticed election."[113] Chastened southerners left town complaining that Kirk's election had done nothing to reach out and appeal to disgruntled voters. As Texas Democratic chairman Bob Slagle said afterward, "I doubt seriously that people in Texas will think electing a Kennedy chief-of-staff is a moderate signal."[114]

In many ways, Kirk's election was the straw that broke the camel's back for a number of these officials. Months earlier, a group of southern and western Democratic senators, governors, and House members held a series of meetings to discuss reforming the party and moving it away from liberalism. As a direct outgrowth of Gillis Long's efforts to influence the party, Long's unexpected death in January 1985 and the failure to elect a southern chair the following month convinced this group that the national party was not the best venue to pursue reform.[115] Instead, by operating outside the institutional restraints of the DNC and the hierarchical systems of Congress, which were seen to stymie iconoclasm, these members could pursue a more muscular approach to reform.[116] Moreover, Long was a liberal-leaning Democrat and had worked to ensure that the party maintained its commitment to liberal constituencies during the HDC reform process. His death, along with the perception that the 1984 elections demonstrated that voters had lost their thirst for liberalism, led these members to form the Democratic Leadership Council (DLC) in February 1985 to pressure the party to moderate its impulses and move its philosophical focus in a more rightward direction. To be sure, this type of soul-searching after an electoral defeat was not new—the ADA, for example, had pointed to the folly of moving rightward in the aftermath of the McGovern defeat in 1972 when similar ventures were being discussed—but the DLC did represent a bold new iteration in this intellectual space.[117] The DLC's membership, which contained forty founding members, included a number of those prominent in the unsuccessful fight to elect Sanford.[118]

The principal purpose of the DLC, according to Senator Sam Nunn, a DLC signatory, was to "lay a foundation, intellectually and politically, on which a moderate Democrat can run for president in 1988."[119] Indeed, to former DNC chairman John White, the DLC was formed to act as a counterbalancing force to the liberal ADA.[120] This effort to shift the party intellectually was, in many ways, an attempt to move it away from the identity politics battles that were increasingly polarizing the electorate. In DLC policy booklets and press releases, for example, they placed emphasis on the economic deficiencies of liberalism by targeting big government largesse and advocating that the private sector should drive economic planning. But there was almost no mention of either race- or gender-based issues, which, more than the economy, were increasingly defining the differences between liberals and conservatives in the 1980s.[121] Instead, the DLC categorized women, racial minorities, and the other emerging identity groups as special interest caucuses and described policies targeted at these groups as special interest legislation.[122] In response, liberals labeled the DLC "crypto-Republicans" and criticized their operation as a "white-male caucus" (Jesse Jackson branded it "Democrats for the Leisure Class").[123] Hart, who turned down numerous requests to join the DLC, also questioned the group's motives: "You've got this DLC group that wants to move the party to the center. [But] what does the center mean? Apparently for some of them it means financing contra aid in Central America and voting for Reagan economic policies. Well, if that's what they define the center as being, we shouldn't have a Democratic Party. . . . It's Reagan in Franklin Roosevelt's clothing."[124]

Certainly, the tendency of DLC members to argue at a level of abstract generalization that the party was the captive of special interests permitted them to leap over some facts that otherwise would have punctured their case. As documented, women and racial minorities were quickly becoming indispensable to Democratic gains at congressional and state levels, and while reforms had been brought in to counterbalance the situation, the grassroots structure of the party was still heavily weighted toward the activist cadres on the left. Indeed, past elections had demonstrated that it was these campaigners who rang the doorbells, organized the precincts, and raised the money.[125] As the *Washington Post* mused, "If the DLC's main argument is that government has an important, but limited role, who is going to wear a campaign button that proclaims 'Important but limited?'"[126] Others criticized the impulse to shift rightward after 1984 too, including the ADA's outgoing director, Leon Shull, who wrote that while the proclivity of liberal activists to make "extreme demands" on Democratic candidates had to be reined in to some extent, driving them out of the process or making them inactive would lead to certain political decline. According to Shull, the party's "purpose and soul" stems from the ability of liberals to dictate its agenda and stop it from becoming a pale imitation of the Republicans: "Some positions are more important than electoral success. . . . We mustn't be terrified of the prospect of losing if we have a reason to lose. . . . There are certain immutable principles."[127] For liberals, the DLC was clearly swapping the party's principles for quick electoral success.

The creation of the DLC also frustrated Kirk, who feared that further fragmentation of an already weakened party would send the wrong signal and affect his own plans to refurbish its image. While Kirk was a liberal, wholly against the DLC's attempts to push the party rightward, he was also the party's chairman, with the key responsibility of ensuring unity. In an attempt to dissuade disillusioned members that he was an old-style liberal wedded to the past, Kirk sounded similar themes to Hart and surprised many with his deference to the southern Democrats who had opposed him—doing nothing to discourage them from organizing a regional presidential primary, and endorsing the notion that the party needed a southern candidate on its 1988 ticket.[128] Like Hart, Kirk understood the importance of tilting the party's electoral strategies toward the South and West, politically muscular regions that cast 272 of the 538 Electoral College votes. Kirk also announced the formation of the Democratic Policy Commission (DPC) in 1985, which, driven predominantly by neoliberals, was tasked with finding solutions to the party's bulkiest problem—how to maintain its decade-long commitment to fairness and equity without always talking about big government.[129] Kirk had supported the earlier efforts of Long and others to repackage liberalism and saw the DPC as an extension of that process.[130] Similarly, in his drive to improve the party's image, Kirk scrapped the Democratic midterm convention—which had often been a site of disharmony rather than a show of party cohesion—and abolished the DNC's caucus system, which had balkanized the party into several demographic and thematic groups.[131]

However, Kirk pushed back when some of his detractors tried to implement resolutions and rule changes designed to lessen the influence of liberal activists. For example, Illinois's Cook County chairman, Edward Vrdolyak, called on the DNC to scrap its racial and gender quotas in the party's delegate selection process. Although quotas had served as a powerful metaphor to capture the discontent of some white voters, who saw the party serving racial minorities at their expense, Kirk opposed the measure and it was voted down.[132] In a series of further actions, Kirk moved to reaffirm the party's commitment to liberal constituencies. In one of his first major addresses, he stated that while the Democrats "will concentrate on policies that unite us as a majority, we will never abandon our commitment to minorities."[133] He increased the presence of racial minorities in the DNC, including appointing the first Black female treasurer, and convinced the Congressional Black Caucus to endorse his vision of reform.[134]

Moreover, while Kirk welcomed the increasingly important role of liberal interest groups in the party, he also cautioned that the early endorsements in 1984 had been a strategic mistake. Although these groups were displaying shrewdness in their organizational and political action skills, Kirk argued that by endorsing Mondale before voters had the chance to cast their ballots—and in some cases, without polling their own members first—the AFL-CIO, NOW, and others had only fed the impression that Mondale was an establishment lackey trading votes for benefits. Hart had an equally strong record of liberal support and attracted much of the rank-and-file membership of these organizations, for example. Thus, Kirk urged constituency groups to hold off endorsing a candidate before the 1988 primaries: "Let the candidate use the primary process to develop and to demonstrate their own broad appeal and their own strong political base before giving one your full and united backing."[135] Some initially viewed this as evidence that the party was attempting to undo the institutional links it had developed with these groups, but most eventually accepted the wisdom of Kirk's point.[136]

In the end, Kirk's maneuvers, like those of Hart or the HDC, represented another iteration in the decades-long attempt of liberal officials to bridge the chasm between the party's traditional values and its newer political imperatives, including how to appeal to the baby boom generation, which would constitute one of the largest voting blocs in American history by 1988.[137] Still, some believed that Kirk was ceding too much ground to the DLC in his efforts to keep the party together. At the beginning of 1986, for example, more than a thousand liberals, mostly women's groups, civil rights activists, and labor leaders, rallied in Washington to denounce what they saw as the party's swerve to the right after 1984. Speaking that day, Jesse Jackson charged that the party was producing "schizophrenic leaders who want to look like John Kennedy with hair flowing to the left and act like Ronald Reagan with behavior flowing to the right."[138] Additionally, a Jackson ally, former Atlanta Mayor Maynard Jackson, appeared before the DLC in 1986 to remind the group that the liberal constituencies at the heart of the party's coalition should not be undervalued: "We cannot be praised for playing a key role in the success of the Democratic Party and then be asked to sit over in the corner and be quiet."[139] Texas commissioner, Jim Hightower, weighed in, warning that an out-of-power party makes a strategic mistake when it tries to "recapture the national agenda with an offering of me-too-isms."[140]

Still, liberals now not only had to face Reagan and the Republican Party in the aftermath of a damaging defeat, but also a resurgent conservative challenge from within as the DLC attempted to push the party away from identity-based politics. This complicated the process of liberal recovery; but liberals, both within and outside the Democratic Party, continued to build ad hoc coalitions to protect or advance their interests after 1984. Indeed, as the next chapter highlights, developments in 1986 and 1987 would remind members across the spectrum of the strength of liberalism, especially from the grass roots.

5. The Returning Tide of Liberalism
Legislative and Judicial Battles in Reagan's Second Term

With Walter Mondale's crushing defeat in 1984 and the corresponding efforts of some to shift the Democratic Party's political focus rightward, the prospect for liberal recovery at the start of Reagan's second term seemed bleak. Indeed, in contrast to the earlier success reauthorizing the VRA, liberals struggled to convince Congress to pass the Civil Rights Restoration Act (CRRA) in 1985, legislation that contained identity politics issues at its core (the bill was designed to broaden the scope of earlier civil rights laws and tackle discrimination based on gender, race, age, and/or disability). Fast-forward to 1987, however, and the political outlook for liberals was quite different. After an intense period of organizing, liberals mobilized turnout, particularly among women and racial minorities, to secure significant gains at the 1986 midterm elections and give the Senate—and thus full control of Congress—back to the Democratic Party. As many political commentators argued at the time, these electoral victories undermined the notion that the party had to move right to be competitive.[1] And by winning back control of Congress, the liberal community now had enough support to pass the CRRA.

Moreover, an opening on the Supreme Court in 1987 triggered a titanic struggle that pitted liberals in a direct philosophical contest with conservatives over the ideological composition of the court following Reagan's nomination of Judge Robert H. Bork, one of the staunchest conservative judges in the country. In what many viewed as an effort to tilt the court's ideological balance in his favor, Reagan's nominee galvanized the emergence of a coordinated grassroots liberal movement to block the appointment. This forceful and well-organized response offers evidence that a liberal recovery of sorts was under way by the mid-to-late 1980s. According to one of the most prominent liberals at the time, for example, the civil rights stalwart Joseph L. Rauh, "The tide of liberalism that ebbed in the Reagan years seems ready to come in again."[2] Therefore, by using the Bork moment as a case study and spotlighting the importance of coalition building behind the scenes, this chapter showcases the relatively unexplored history of how liberals were able to mount such a successful campaign during Reagan's second term.³

To begin, it examines the processes that built to Bork, taking as its first focus the push to enact the CRRA and the effort to win back the Senate for the Democrats, where voter registration drives and the political strategies concerning the gender gap would prove crucial. Following an in-depth examination of the Bork moment, it concludes by detailing how the liberal coalition that battled Bork moved swiftly to translate their success into other aspects of the liberal agenda. Indeed, as a consequence of their organizing work, liberals helped ensure that Reagan's legislative success rate in the latter part of his tenure was the lowest for a president since *Congressional Quarterly* began tracking the data in 1953.⁴

Importantly, while the placement of the Bork episode aligns with the chronological development of this book's argument, it also serves a larger purpose, demonstrating in one moment the confluence of earlier strands of enquiry. To be sure, the chapter focuses predominantly on the institutional developments of liberalism by Reagan's second term—detailing how the professionalization of liberal groups and the relationships established with the Democratic Party allowed a coordinated liberal coalition to emerge quickly, while arguing that the efforts to modernize political strategy enabled them to conduct a sophisticated campaign through working together. However, it also demonstrates that the process of repackaging and marketing liberalism was, as well, impacting liberal grassroots groups, who were becoming increasingly conscious of the language and strategies used to attract support in a changing electorate.

BUILDING TO BORK

The origins of the CRRA can be traced to a little-known conservative educational outpost in Pennsylvania, Grove City College. In 1976, this conservative Christian college refused to sign a federal compliance form mandating antidiscrimination measures, pointing to its historic tradition of rejecting state and federal assistance to preserve its institutional autonomy and protect its conservative principles. The college did enroll students who received government-sponsored grants though, which triggered the application of Title IX of the 1972 Education Amendments in particular—designed to tackle gender discrimination in education—and the requirement to sign the compliance form in general. Believing that an overbearing government was threatening its institutional freedom, the college argued that accepting this Assurance of Compliance meant more than a pledge of nondiscrimination; it would have allowed the government jurisdiction over all its operations.[5] Following various lower court judgments, the Supreme Court ruled in the college's favor in February 1984, arguing that the receipt and use of federal grants "does not trigger institution-wide coverage under Title IX."[6] Instead, it found that the college was only liable to such regulations at the specific entry point of federal funds—which, in Grove City's case, was the financial aid/admissions department.

As with the Bob Jones case in 1982, the Reagan administration sided with the conservative school, arguing before the Supreme Court for this program-specific application and terming the result a "major victory."[7] Though the ruling only affected Grove City's admissions department, it had implications far beyond the college grounds since the "program-specific" interpretation logically threatened a host of similar civil rights statutes. Title IX had been modeled after Title VI of the 1964 Civil Rights Act, which prohibited discrimination on the basis of race, color, and national origin in programs/activities receiving federal assistance. Section 504 of the 1973 Rehabilitation Act, prohibiting discrimination on the basis of disability, and the Age Discrimination Act of 1975 also adopted the same model. Emboldened by the decision, the Reagan administration immediately started dropping discrimination complaints across the country.[8] Given the wide-ranging ramifications, a large liberal coalition of over 225 organizations quickly developed, including all the major women's, civil rights, labor, senior, disabled, and religious advocacy groups. Again, the Leadership Conference on Civil Rights (LCCR) was the organizing mechanism on the ground, and Senator Kennedy was the principal advocate on Capitol Hill.

In the first instance, the coalition sought immediate corrective legislation. By working closely with Kennedy, the LCCR's drafting committee honed the language of a new bill, clarifying that federal financial assistance benefiting one program or activity of an entity (such as a school) would trigger institution-wide coverage. Symbolically referred to as the "Civil Rights Act of 1984," the coalition set out to return all four affected statutes to their original purpose, using words from President Kennedy to signal their mission: "Simple justice requires that public funds, to which all taxpayers of all races contribute, not be spent in any fashion which encourages, entrenches, subsidizes, or results in racial discrimination."[9] The Democratically controlled House passed this legislative remedy by a wide margin, 375–32, in June; and with over sixty cosponsors in the

Republican Senate, the bill seemed destined for passage. Yet, according to the coalition, the Reagan administration and the conservative movement were vigorously opposing the measure by conducting a "stalling strategy coupled with a campaign of scare tactics."[10] The conservative opposition hoped to bottle the bill in Senator Orrin Hatch's committee (Labor and Human Resources), believing the measure was a liberal smoke screen for a vast expansion of federal power. Hatch, who labeled it the "Civil Privileges Act of 1984," claimed that the bill was one of the most dangerous pieces of legislation in years, "opening the door to federal intrusion" in all facets of life.[11]

At the same time, women's groups criticized Reagan for his perceived hypocrisy on equal rights. When opposing the ERA earlier in the decade, Reagan had argued that he preferred a statute-by-statute revision of laws to eliminate discrimination and enshrine equality. Given that the proposed bill did just that, NOW questioned the sincerity of Reagan's argument: "It is peculiar that Reagan has not come out strongly in favor of the proposed legislation—legislation that makes clarifying changes in existing statutes."[12] Republican Senator Robert Dole did propose a compromise bill that more explicitly focused on Title IX, but according to the LCCR, this was an effort to divide and conquer the liberal coalition.[13] While a key priority for liberal women's groups had been reestablishing the power of Title IX, particularly given its seminal role in the development of the women's movement, the LCCR proposed that the coalition sign a pact of solidarity as the compromise was too specific. NOW, which had been criticized in the past for focusing too narrowly on the interests of middle-class white women, supported this all-or-nothing stance. As NOW's Pat Reuss wrote, "In the current atmosphere of backtracking on civil rights, every group needed one another, you can't have civil rights for some and not for all. We stuck together."[14] Although this show of solidarity reflected the improved coalition-building skills of liberals at the time, the bill was still defeated in the Senate, an action for which Senator Kennedy chastised his fellow members: "Shame on this body. . . . We are . . . [tucking] discrimination under the mattress until next year."[15]

Efforts to pass the bill fared no better in 1985, despite the liberal coalition characterizing their new legislative push as the "Civil Rights Restoration Act"—a title to show that they simply planned to restore the law to its preexisting state.[16] The US Conference of Catholic Bishops had challenged the bill on the grounds that it expanded the scope of abortion rights, despite claims from the coalition that they had written "abortion neutral" language into it.[17] Abortion was a controversial issue—one that had the ability to split the coalition given the religious organizations within it—so the LCCR refused to take a position, instead vowing to oppose "any efforts to turn the act into a vehicle for anyone's agenda."[18] But the issue would effectively arrest the debate for the rest of the session.

With limited maneuverability, the coalition's focus shifted to winning back the Congress for the Democrats, and thus, ensuring more liberal voices on key committees. NOW, for example, claimed they were going to tie the CRRA directly to the 1986 midterms in an organizing effort that would "make the extension campaign for the ERA look small."[19] To press home the importance of this effort, the coalition released two reports months before the election to show the severe impact that *Grove City* was having on civil rights across the country.[20] Both reports presented evidence that the Reagan administration was using the decision to undercut the machinery and procedures put in place to tackle gender, race, disability, and age discrimination practices—at least sixty-three discrimination cases were "closed, limited, or suspended" by the administration in 1985 while an unknown number continued to go unenforced.[21] These reports were designed to galvanize the communities affected by the ruling and push them to elect Democrats to change the trajectory of the bill.

The 1986 Midterms
As the sun set on election day in November, retiring House Speaker O'Neill triumphantly declared to the press that the midterm results had produced one clear message: "If there was a Reagan Revolution, it's over."[22] While liberals had tried to claim this at earlier points in the decade, Reagan had framed the midterms as a pivotal ideological contest to protect the revolution, presenting the election to the public as a decision "whether to hand the government back to the liberals or to move forward with the conservative agenda into the 1990s."[23] Moreover, Reagan believed he was in a strong position going into the midterms. He entered 1986 with historically high levels of support (66 percent in a *Washington Post*–ABC News preelection poll), and the economy was finishing its third year of unbroken growth.[24]

Nevertheless, the Republicans suffered heavy congressional losses on election day. Although seat losses in the House were, at five, not particularly damaging, the Democrats' gains left them with a large majority there (258–177). More significantly, a net loss of eight seats in the Senate returned the majority to the Democrats (by a margin of 55–45). With the Democrats now in full control of the legislative branch for the first time during his presidency, the Reagan Revolution seemed to be stalling. The Republican class of 1980 witnessed seven of its twelve freshman senators lose their reelection bids, a development the *New York Times* noted was an indication that the power of Reagan and his revolutionary guard "had crested and fallen back."[25] While midterms are often difficult for a sitting president, few had predicted the sweep of the Senate, with the election proving particularly significant because it shored up Democratic strength in the South and West—two areas the party was increasingly pivoting toward—and showed that self-described liberals could win in a number of close contests despite the Republicans' substantial advantage in money and technology.[26]

The Democrats elected to the Senate that year ran the ideological gamut. On the liberal side, former House Representatives Barbara Mikulski (D-MD) and Tim Wirth (D-CO) had cumulative vote ratings of 89 and 86 percent from the ADA, while Richard Shelby (D-AL) and John Breaux (D-LA) scored 15 and 17 percent for the conservative side.[27] Still, instead of moving rightward, a majority of the Democrats elected that year had focused broadly on liberal issues, albeit to varying degrees. With Democrats focused on advocating redistributionist economic policies, expanding civil rights legislation, and protecting access to abortion, rather than offering "Republican-light" platforms, the outcome led the *Boston Globe* to describe the election as a "defeat for Me-Tooism."[28] Moreover, the constituencies that helped elect these legislators were part of the newly emerging liberal coalition: women, racial minorities, and young professionals. Together, they sent Reagan a powerful wake-up call on election day that it was not "Morning in America" for them.

In the Colorado Senate race, for example, which featured two contenders whose ideological differences were as "clear and sharp as Venetian glass" according to journalist Scott Armstrong, these constituencies tipped the liberal candidate over the edge.[29] The contest between Tim Wirth and Republican Ken Kramer was thought to be a precursor to the 1988 presidential campaign, in which a Reaganite Republican and a neoliberal Democrat were likely to emerge as the parties' standard-bearers.[30] Colorado, a conservative-to-moderate state where the Republicans held an iron grip on the legislature, had voted only once for a Democratic presidential candidate since 1952. Nonetheless, like Gary Hart, Wirth carefully calibrated the way he espoused his liberalism to the electorate, focusing on broad-based issues such as jobs and the environment while targeting the inequities at the heart of Reaganism. This "progressive pragmatist" approach enabled him to attract enough support to win by a margin of one percentage point: 49–48 percent.[31] In addition to racial minorities and young professionals, Wirth relied heavily on women to provide his slim margin of victory (despite only winning by one percentage point overall, Wirth finished with a 5 percent gender gap advantage over his rival).[32]

Significantly, a gender gap emerged in every statewide contest that year, appearing in all forty-two senatorial and gubernatorial races.[33] Indeed, in 1986, the *New York Times* confirmed that women were now reliably more liberal and more Democratic than the opposite sex. One poll, for example, found that while men were evenly split in their support for both parties, women were now solidly Democratic.[34] According to NOW, more than any other single factor the surplus of women's votes accounted for the Democrats recapturing the Senate in 1986; the Democrats that were elected each received less than 50 percent of men's votes, but won because they secured 50 percent or more of the women's vote.[35] By using Census Bureau data to suggest that six million more women than men voted in 1986, NOW pointed to the growing strength of the women's vote and the importance of mobilizing turnout to ensure maximum impact of the gender gap.[36]

Furthermore, 1986 had also witnessed "a particularly dramatic increase," according to NOW, in the number of women who ran for statewide office themselves (sixty women ran in 1986, three times the number of 1984).[37] Notably, these women candidates gained their support from the other demographic strands of the emerging liberal coalition—younger people, professionals, and minority constituencies.[38] It was this support that provided the winning margin for Barbara Mikulski, who was the first Democratic woman to win election to the Senate without having previously been appointed to fill an unexpired congressional term. With Mikulski's election representing yet another crack in the figurative glass ceiling, Eleanor Smeal described 1986 as a historically significant year for women in politics.[39] Crucially, it was liberal women's groups who helped fuel these gains, working behind the scenes to support and fund these victories.

Indeed, following Geraldine Ferraro's defeat in 1984, NOW reevaluated its political strategy and decided to shift focus away from the top of the Democratic ticket by expanding its earlier push to elect more women at all levels of government. Tied in with its efforts to pass the CRRA, NOW launched a new campaign, the Feminization of Power, which aimed to "flood the ticket . . . from top to bottom" and challenge the conventional notion that only a slow, incremental approach resulted in success.[40] This was still an ideologically driven operation though—the goal was not simply to elect more women, but to elect more liberal ones. Smeal acknowledged as much when, in 1987, she launched a concomitant political organization, the Feminist Majority Foundation, designed to recruit and support as many liberal women as possible.[41] Others joined the cause too, including Ferraro herself, who in 1985 formed a political fundraising committee that concentrated on getting liberal women elected to Congress in 1986. That year, Ferraro's committee focused its efforts on ten women candidates for Congress, eight of whom were elected.[42] Furthermore, by 1986 an entirely new liberal organization had arrived on the scene, inspired by the earlier efforts to push women into politics and formed as the result of one defeat in particular.

In the 1982 Missouri Senate race, Harriet Woods had initially struggled to raise money to support her candidacy. Though donations from traditional sources such as labor eventually arrived, Woods had been forced to limit her campaigning and pull her political advertisements from the air before election day. Despite this lack of funds, coupled with the challenge of unseating an incumbent in a Republican-leaning state, Woods almost won, receiving 49.1 percent of the vote (26,200 votes fewer than Republican Senator John Danforth).[43] Out of Woods's narrow loss emerged the impetus behind EMILY's List, a political action network launched in 1985 by Ellen Malcolm, the former press secretary of the National Women's Political Caucus.[44] Malcolm, and a host of other liberal activists, believed that early contributions targeted in a strategic way could have swayed the election, and thus, the name, EMILY, an acronym for "early money is like yeast," was born.[45] Reflecting the contemporary political environment, EMILY's List was created as a partisan operation, and the first campaign it supported was Mikulski in 1986, contributing a quarter of a million dollars to her Senate campaign ($1 out of every $5 raised).[46] Thus, by funding candidates, organizing voter registration drives, and fueling the gender gap, the efforts of EMILY's List, NOW, and a host of other liberal women's groups clearly had an impact on the 1986 midterms.

Finally, demographic shifts in the South were also an important aspect of the 1986 midterms, demonstrating to a host of southern Boll Weevil Democrats that they could not possibly hope to win elections without attracting significant support from the more liberal-leaning constituencies in their regions. In particular, with southern whites continuing to defect to the Republicans, Black voters were becoming increasingly central to the Democratic Party's electoral fortunes in the once-solid South, often providing the margin of victory in close races. Former Governor Terry Sanford, who had previous ties to the DLC and was now running for the Senate seat in North Carolina, tackled this by enlisting Jesse Jackson to ease tensions with minority communities during the campaign.[47] As part of a wider effort to harness the power of the Black vote, liberal groups also started stressing to voters that control of Congress would determine the shape of policy and politics for the rest of the decade. As the *New York Times* pointed out, liberals, particularly those in civil rights organizations, argued that the election would "determine whether the CRRA, bills to create jobs and other measures favored by blacks are passed.... And because the Senate can confirm nominees for the Federal judiciary, civil rights advocates look to the Senate to be a bulwark against attempts to appoint right-wing conservatives."[48] Given the fact that the two principal Senate committees that dealt with these issues were chaired by staunch conservatives—Senator Hatch (Labor and Human Resources) and Senator Strom Thurmond (Judiciary)—liberals argued that regaining the chamber would give them the power to set and control the flow of legislation and structure the judicial confirmation process. Only months earlier, Reagan had been able to get the Supreme Court's most conservative justice, William Rehnquist, confirmed as chief justice, despite vocal opposition from liberals both on and off the committee.[49] Thus, liberals aimed to convince voters that the stakes were high in 1986.

In the end, according to the Joint Center for Political Studies, minority voters provided the edge in six Senate races (Alabama, Georgia, Louisiana, North Carolina, Nevada, and California—where the candidates each received less than 50 percent of the white vote) and helped boost the margins in the two other contests (Maryland and Florida).[50] But the question became whether these newly elected Democrats would be responsive to minority voter interests. Immediate signs suggested that the new officials would—Senator Breaux, for example, quickly pledged to remember that "he could never have won without the black vote" (he had attracted nearly 90 percent of the Black vote, as compared to 40 percent of the white vote).[51] Clearly, despite the DLC's attempts to push the party rightward, some of its most loyal adherents had to juggle efforts to advance the organization's cause while respecting the changing electoral dynamics of their regions. Some, like Shelby, would eventually switch party as a result, while others, like Sanford, would compile a more liberal voting record as the decade progressed.

In the immediate term though, the midterms provided a significant boost to the liberal coalition seeking passage of the CRRA. Not only did the arrival of more Democratic senators provide new allies, but by winning back the Senate, liberals secured control over the all-important Labor and Human Resources Committee, with the bill's most ardent supporter, Senator Kennedy, taking over the chairmanship. As NOW noted, the change in control of the Senate "from Reaganite Republicans to liberal Democrats has enhanced significantly the prospects for passage of the CRRA."[52] Given this new political environment, the coalition pursued a fast-track strategy, believing that the CRRA had received adequate scrutiny over the years.[53] And by June 1987, passage seemed inevitable: it had been reported out of committee by a 12–4 vote (with all weakening amendments defeated by a 2–1 margin) and had the support of over seventy senators.[54] According to the LCCR's Ralph Neas, this showed the importance of shifting the power balance in the Senate: "Now you see what happens when you have a civil rights champion in charge."[55] However, just as they were preparing for victory, the coalition's calculus changed abruptly when Reagan announced the Bork candidacy that same month. This relegated and delayed consideration of the CRRA as the coalition agreed to throw everything behind the effort to defeat Bork.[56]

BORK'S CONTESTED NOMINATION

On 26 June 1987, Supreme Court Justice Lewis Powell unexpectedly announced his retirement. Having already successfully nominated two justices to the apex of the judicial system—Sandra Day O'Connor in 1981 and Antonin Scalia in 1986, the latter at the same time he named Rehnquist his chief justice—Reagan was determined to use the vacant seat to ensure that his conservative philosophy would outlast his administration. Indeed, federal judgeships had been campaign issues for the Republican Party throughout the 1980s, with Reagan pledging to appoint only those supportive of "traditional" family values and opposed to judicial activism.[57] As Reagan's Attorney General Edwin Meese claimed, the administration aimed "to institutionalize the Reagan Revolution so it can't be set aside no matter what happens in future presidential elections."[58]

Moreover, the timing of Powell's retirement also gifted Reagan a much-needed opening to reinvigorate his administration, which was caught in the maelstrom of scandal at the time. Breaking just months earlier, the Iran-Contra scandal was a complicated affair that eventually revealed the details of a covert and potentially impeachable operation conducted at the White House. As the nation would discover, not only had his administration violated an arms embargo with Iran under the pretext of securing the release of American hostages, but the president had also circumvented a congressional amendment and used the proceeds from such sales to fund anti-communist rebels in Nicaragua covertly.[59]

However, Powell had voted with liberal justices on a variety of issues in the past, and decisively, in his last two terms on the court he had cast the crucial vote in rejecting positions of the Reagan administration in cases involving affirmative action and abortion.[60] Thus, with liberal principles regarding civil rights and equality at stake, the fight over who would fill Powell's seat was deemed all the more critical because many commentators described him as the moderate swing vote on the court. After Powell's announcement, Senator Kennedy immediately warned that Congress was going to "ensure that Reagan does the right thing instead of the *far right* thing in filling the vacancy," while Senator Joseph Biden (D-DE), the new chairman of the Judiciary Committee, pledged to "resist any efforts by this administration to . . . impose an ideological agenda upon our jurisprudence."[61] Biden was also a presidential aspirant at the time, and opposing Reagan's nominee would become the cause célèbre of the party's base.[62] Nonetheless, Reagan did not heed these warnings and announced Judge Robert Bork.

An accomplished federal appeals court judge in Washington, DC, and a leading conservative legal theorist, Bork was in many ways the doyen of the right at the time. More than any other candidate Reagan could have nominated, Bork was a symbol of Reagan's conservative campaign, an intellectual crusader for the revolution. By 1987, Bork had established himself as a chief spokesman for the conservative legal movement—his extensive writings on both antitrust law and constitutional originalism had become preeminent in their respective fields—and he had amassed a substantial body of work from various political, judicial, and academic roles over the years. Thus, there was a palpable fear that Bork would swing the balance of the court and overturn important liberal victories if confirmed; the liberal Advocacy Institute even labeled him "a right-wing loony."[63] Kennedy understood the political implications of Reagan's choice, using a Senate speech moments after the announcement to paint a bleak picture of a nation with Bork at its judicial helm:

> Robert Bork's America is a land in which women would be forced into back-alley abortions, blacks would sit at segregated lunch counters, rogue police could break down citizens' doors in midnight raids, schoolchildren could not be taught about evolution, writers and artists would be censored at the whim of government, and the doors of the federal courts would be shut on the fingers of millions of citizens for whom the judiciary is often the only protector of the individual rights that are the heart of our democracy.[64]

This hyperbolic statement was merely one of the opening shots in a battle that consumed the summer and autumn of 1987 as liberal groups, working closely with Kennedy, quickly set out to prevent confirmation. Once again, the LCCR and NOW would play leading roles in uniting and organizing a broad-based liberal coalition to defeat Bork, using the groundwork laid by the CRRA campaign and expanding the scope considerably.

The Groundwork
When Bork was nominated, it was largely assumed that he would sail through the process; not only were his professional credentials and intellectual qualifications as impressive as any candidate's, but as history revealed, rejection of Supreme Court nominees was rare.[65] Moreover, Bork was a sitting court of appeals judge, whose elevation to that bench had required confirmation by the Senate in 1982. As members of the liberal community noted, blocking Bork's nomination would be a long shot.[66] Still, instead of mounting a quixotic bid, Bork's opponents set out to show that the battle was winnable if the focus could be turned to his judicial philosophy, as Kennedy had sought to do with his harangue on the Senate floor. Bork's supporters criticized this emphasis on philosophy, saying the Senate's duty was only to examine a nominee's credentials and character, but polls revealed that the public generally sided with those wanting to scrutinize his judicial beliefs.[67] For liberals, pushing the Senate to reject the nomination represented a "last-chance saloon" to prevent Reagan from fundamentally changing the philosophical makeup of the judiciary.[68]

With the departure of Powell, liberals could count on only four justices on the high court to back their agenda judicially.[69] Concerned that Reagan would swing the balance of the court, liberals pointed to the president's record of appointing judges of only a conservative hue. As legal scholar Ronald Dworkin argued at the time, "for the last seven years" the Reagan administration had conducted "an open and inflexible campaign of ideological appointments on all levels of the federal courts, hoping to make them a seat of right-wing power long after the administration ends."[70] When announcing his nomination, Reagan also made no effort to disguise the political character of it, noting that Bork "shares my view" and "is widely recognized as the most prominent and intellectually powerful advocate of judicial restraint."[71] For Bork's opponents, that was precisely the problem. With the Supreme Court deemed the most important judicial forum, given its power to set precedents, those challenging the nomination did not question Bork's credentials but rather what they saw as his extreme views.

Indeed, Bork had a longstanding paper trail of speeches and articles studded with provocative, inflammatory postures and phrases.[72] In a 1963 article, for example, he had called civil rights demonstrators "a mob" that coerced "other private individuals in the exercise of their freedom."[73] He also repeatedly claimed that the court's long string of decisions implementing the "one man, one vote" principle to tackle malapportionment and enshrine equal legislative representation was seriously mistaken.[74] Given such past racial insensitivity, the civil rights community quickly threw down the gauntlet, declaring: "We will fight Bork all the way until hell freezes over and then we'll skate across the ice."[75] Beyond a penchant for hellish hyperbole, Bork's opponents would exploit his earlier writing shrewdly by designing a southern strategy to capitalize on the anxieties among many southerners about inciting the racism that had plagued—and still plagued—the region.

Furthermore, outside the realm of Black civil rights legislation, Bork's stance on women's rights and privacy issues also roused his opponents. Bork regarded the 1965 Supreme Court decision in *Griswold v. Connecticut*, which established a broad right of privacy not stated in the Constitution, as simply "one more slogan" employed by judges "writing their own tastes into law." Equally significant, he was an ardent foe of *Roe v. Wade*, the 1973 case that had guaranteed women the right to have an abortion, calling the decision "a serious and wholly unjustifiable usurpation of state legislative authority."[76] The courts, he felt, should not thwart the will of the popularly elected lawmakers, and judges ought not to substitute their values for the "original intent" of the Constitution's framers. To many, this approach threatened decades of rulings that broke down the barriers of discrimination.

To be sure, liberals recognized that these issues were already under threat from the executive and legislative branches—the inability to pass the CRRA was a case in point. And when a case involving privacy and sexual freedom reached the Supreme Court in 1986, a closely divided bench ruled 5–4 in favor of the constitutionality of a Georgia sodomy law that criminalized certain sexual acts in private and was clearly targeted toward homosexuals.[77] With fears that the "last bastion of liberalism" was now also under threat from a right-wing backlash, liberals could sense the way the wind was blowing and reasoned that Bork, more than any other candidate, could complete Reagan's transformation of the Supreme Court.[78]

Aside from ideology, Bork's opponents also raised the specter of Watergate and the role that Bork, as President Nixon's solicitor general, played in the so-called Saturday Night Massacre as further justification of his unsuitability.[79] Following the resignations of Attorney General Elliot Richardson and his deputy, William Ruckelshaus, who had both refused to execute Nixon's order to fire the Watergate special prosecutor, Archibald Cox, Bork, as acting attorney general, complied and fired Cox. Cox had asked the White House to hand over tapes of Nixon's Oval Office conversations, a request that would eventually unravel a presidency; and this episode, on 20 October 1973, became the infamous Saturday Night Massacre. Thus, in a report sent to activists, the liberal group People for the American Way (PFAW) wrote that Bork:

> chose to follow a President who sought to obstruct justice rather than follow the rule of law, and he rationalized his actions on the basis of a technicality. Particularly in these times of turmoil created by the actions of this Administration in the Iran-Contra scandal, Bork's actions raise serious questions about the extent to which he, as a justice on the nation's highest court, would require the federal government to adhere to constitutional and other legal limitations.[80]

To liberal groups, Reagan, it seemed, was trying to reach from the muck of Iran-Contra (or Irangate as it was also known) into the muck of Watergate to appoint a principal person of the affair to the highest court in the land. As a result, liberals launched a Block Bork campaign and framed the nomination as the most consequential political battle of the decade. Democratic Representative Richard Gephardt captured the immediacy of the moment: "Just as we were ready to put Reagan behind us, his power of judicial appointment has, like a hand from the grave, reached far into the next century to threaten all the progress of the last 50 years."[81]

Certainly, there was a pro-Bork campaign too, with conservative pressure groups raising money to support it and the right-wing *New York Post* challenging liberals to "make our day" by opposing it, but their counterattack was impeded by the White House from the start.[82] Over the objections of many who welcomed forceful conservative support, the administration attempted to recast Bork's record to make him appear moderate. In a July speech, Reagan even equated his nominee with Powell, despite Bork's past attacks on Powell's opinions.[83] The LCCR was quick to undercut this strategy, pointing out that "to make Bork over in the image of a Lewis Powell, a Robert Jackson, or a Felix Frankfurter . . . rather than seeing him in the tradition of a Sutherland, Reynolds, or Rehnquist, is to give the lie to Bork's public extra-judicial professions of his beliefs."[84] As the liberal coalition made clear, the "real Robert Bork" would be placed front and center.

At the same time as the pro-Bork campaign clashed over how best to present their nominee, the Block Bork campaign resisted all efforts to add, or substitute, goals other than to block confirmation. For example, consumer activist Ralph Nader wanted to use the campaign as a launching pad for a national progressive movement, but members argued that any suggestion along these lines would reduce the coalition's effectiveness by allowing pro-Bork forces to claim that only special interests and extreme left-wingers opposed Bork.[85] In fact, although the coalition did attract support from across the liberal spectrum, they were also highly effective at lining up support from groups not viewed as traditionally liberal in order to avoid this appearance.[86] The campaign was able to register the opposition of numerous law associations, law school deans, and constitutional law professors, for example.[87]

With broad support, this ad hoc coalition developed a three-pronged approach to defeat Bork: first, raise the stakes of the nomination by focusing on Powell's swing vote status; second, argue that Bork's judicial philosophy was too extreme; and finally, and perhaps most importantly, strategically use his controversial views on civil rights, women's issues, and privacy against him to mobilize public opinion and generate enough pressure to ensure that senators simply had to oppose him.[88] To do so, the coalition would employ an array of new techniques to take the campaign directly to the people.

The Campaign
Having played the leading role in several legislative battles in the Reagan years, the LCCR quickly became the center of gravity for the anti-Bork forces. Neas, who had proven his reputation as an effective advocate for liberal causes, assumed the leadership role. Neas immediately released a statement on behalf of the coalition, describing Bork as an ultraconservative and the nomination as a historic moment when senators will cast the "most important and far-reaching vote" of their careers.[89] Not only was Neas setting the tone, but he was also signaling to senators that this judicial battle would be like no other. He also enlisted the help of Senator Kennedy once again, whose support proved crucial. Kennedy sent thousands of letters and made hundreds of telephone calls to political leaders across the country, especially to Black political leaders, warning them that "everything we have worked for in the past quarter century may

be jeopardized if Bork is confirmed." According to Anthony Podesta, the founding president of PFAW, if Kennedy had worked as hard during the 1980 Democratic primaries as he did to defeat Bork, "he might well have been nominated."[90]

With the foundations established, Neas developed a grassroots strategy packet that outlined the general approach of the coalition. Here, Neas highlighted the need for a broad-based effort and a "generic theme" to attract diverse groups and appeal to the wider public, while consciously not diminishing the importance of individual group identities.[91] Indeed, controlling the narrative was critical from the outset, and Neas utilized an Advocacy Institute report to detail the "principal areas of symbolic conflict."[92] The report noted that alongside framing Bork as "an extreme ideological activist serving as Reagan and Meese's political agent," opponents must cast themselves as the "true conservatives: conservers of personal rights—the privacy of the bedroom, restrainers of excessive government intrusion."[93] Liberals, clearly recognizing Reagan's ability to set an agenda through symbolism and mood, were attempting to play the president at his own game.

This is illustrated further by the coalition's decision to temper some of its rhetoric and downplay some of the more contentious liberal issues. For example, as the CRRA campaign had demonstrated, drawing attention to the abortion question would not only spur a conservative backlash but might also divide the coalition, given its diverse membership. Therefore, at a grassroots meeting in August, Neas urged members from a wide variety of civil rights, feminist, labor, environmental, religious, and public interest groups to de-emphasize controversial issues, such as abortion, and to "push but not pressure" senators into a decision.[94] Instead of abandoning reproductive rights or attempting to silence the pro-choice groups within the coalition, Block Bork strategists sought to embrace and subsume abortion rights within the more generalized principle of privacy. In doing so, the coalition were effectively providing cover to politicians, shielding them from the controversy attached to some issues while allowing them the space to reject Bork on more innocuous grounds.

Controlling the narrative in this way reflected a keen awareness of marketing in the Reagan Era: a critical component of the coalition's media advocacy strategy was the identification of themes or symbols, such as privacy, that had broad universal appeal.[95] This approach touched a powerful chord, as evidenced by the large number of senators who gave prominence to the privacy issue in their speeches opposing Bork.[96] Classic left-wing tactics—marches, demonstrations, sit-ins—were also discouraged as the

Block Bork movement sought to develop a unifying campaign. Arthur Klopp, PFAW president, expanded this point afterward: "We did this without the traditional liberal saber-rattling and protest marches because that was not the impression we wanted. . . . Once the progressives started using mass media and moving away from the old-fashioned politics of confrontation, the right-wing began to lose its grip."[97] In presenting a united front, the coalition demonstrated its political skill by deciding to focus on a few major areas—the media and grassroots organizing—and to hammer Bork's record on broad issues, such as civil rights and privacy.

With a clear and coherent strategy in place, the next step was to get Bork's controversial record out in the public eye. Since there existed no published compilation of Bork's views, the coalition began researching and organizing his record into a single document. This mammoth excavation enabled the movement to base their opposition on Bork's own writings and opinions so that when the White House or supporters tried to claim that Bork was a moderate, the coalition had amassed the materials into a Book of Bork to say: "No, he's not! And here's why."[98] By taking Bork's words and decisions, and paring away the subtleties, complications, and shadings, liberals successfully constructed an extreme image of Bork devoid of context. And by compiling Bork's record into a single document, the coalition was able to flood media and political offices with convincing evidence detailing Bork's "extreme" opinions. According to the *New York Times*, with the press largely persuaded by the thrust of the opponents' vast fabric of documentation and analysis, "It was the 'Book of Bork' that defeated Bork."[99] Efforts to compile and disseminate the Book of Bork not only brought to light critical elements of Bork's record, but crucially, it provided intellectual legitimacy and weight to the liberal campaign against him.

As well as releasing the Book of Bork, the coalition employed an array of newer techniques to ensure its strategy was successful, using focus groups and public opinion polls to ascertain the issues that could best be exploited and hiring media consultants to promote favorable coverage.[100] To this end, the coalition conducted a blitzkrieg in the media, collecting over $2 million and producing a series of advertisements to communicate their agenda.[101] One ad in particular, which became known as the "Gregory Peck ad" since the revered actor provided the narration, proved highly effective. By warning of dreadful consequences under a Bork-influenced Supreme Court, the ad's subliminal skill was in its ability to invoke the image of Peck as the noble defender of civil rights, Atticus Finch, in the film *To Kill a Mockingbird*. With a voice that, arguably, Americans subconsciously trusted, Peck warned viewers of Bork's opinions on privacy and civil rights, before ending with a rallying cry: "Please urge your senators to vote against the nomination."[102]

The imagery of the Gregory Peck ad was just as powerful as its statement. By opening with a positive message that captured the awe of the Supreme Court, and with the image of a typical nuclear family standing at its footsteps, the ad was able to underscore Peck's key points. Visually, by having these two symbols interact—the archetypal American family and one of the shrines of American democracy, the Supreme Court—the ad juxtaposed a looming Bork in the background as a threat to them both. With this media blitz, the movement aimed not so much to influence senators by direct appeals or representations, but rather to mobilize public opinion and generate mass pressure, which, it was hoped, senators would find impossible to withstand. In a press release immediately before the Judiciary Committee hearings began, for example, the liberal coalition, as if to remind senators of its broad support, claimed that the opposition comprised organizations with more than twenty million members.[103]

Through an effective public relations campaign that moved beyond the realm of classic left-wing tactics, liberals transformed what might otherwise have been a rubber-stamp appointment into a national issue, showcasing their organizational and political prowess and defining the parameters of the debate from the outset. By recognizing the importance of rhetoric, staged events, and Madison Avenue–style advertising techniques, the coalition communicated its message directly to the people and controlled the narrative presented in the media. By the time the nomination entered the committee stage, a developed structure was in place and the coalition's efforts would dictate proceedings.

The Outcome
Bork's nomination would only gain approval in the Senate if the Republicans remained united and if sufficient Democratic defectors could be found. At the beginning of his presidency, Reagan was able to convince southern Democrats to support his conservative agenda, but by 1987 the situation was different. With Iran-Contra damaging Reagan's appeal and with losses in Congress handing the Senate majority—and therefore control over the confirmation machinery—back to the Democrats, Reagan was in a precarious position going into the most important stage of the nomination battle. The administration had lagged and stumbled through the summer in developing its thematic thrust, struggling to square the circle of presenting Bork as a moderate while galvanizing the conservative

base to support him. Nevertheless, they were hopeful that when Bork appeared on television for the hearings, his intellect and bearing would impress viewers and influence the outcome. The Block Bork coalition were conscious of this, fearing that Bork's testimony would elicit the same flurry of support that National Security Council staff member Oliver North received after his appearance in full military regalia at the Iran-Contra hearings. In a letter to activists, the coalition urged campaigners to intensify opposition activities in the days leading up to the hearings: "Remember the wave of so-called 'public support' generated for Ollie North after he first testified? We hope that a massive outpouring of calls and telegrams to senators on the first few days of the Bork hearings will generate a similar public presence and visibility for those of us opposed to Bork."[104]

But these fears proved unfounded as opinion polls revealed that Bork's negative ratings increased after his appearances. Bork came across as "pedantic and passionless," in the words of historian John Ehrman, seeming to confirm his opponents' caricature of him as someone who could "bloodlessly roll back the rights of Americans."[105] When Wyoming's Republican Senator Alan Simpson, an ardent Bork supporter on the committee, asked Bork why he wanted to serve on the Supreme Court, he replied by saying: "It would be an intellectual feast." Kennedy retorted that it might be a "feast for Bork, but millions of our fellow citizens would be starving for their rights in his America."[106] Bork's critics also professed doubts about some of the opinions he expressed because they were at such variance with his past positions. Senator Patrick Leahy (D-VT) even asked if Bork had undergone a suspicious "confirmation conversion"—like the proverbial deathbed conversion, subject to justifiable skepticism.[107] The Block Bork's so-called War Room in the basement of the Russell Senate Office Building was quick to react. Position papers were brought out overnight to illuminate how the "new Bork" contradicted "the old one," and to feed questions and information to senators during the hearings.[108] By exposing and highlighting the flaws in Bork's testimony for committee members and framing the import of it for the media, the Block Bork campaign was undermining Bork's credibility from the outset.

During the hearings, Bork also stumbled when questioned about his previous cases regarding women, particularly his 1984 ruling that a company's position on forced sterilization in order for women to remain employed was lawful.[109] Polls by the coalition demonstrated that this ruling was political dynamite, and when questioned in the hearings, Bork closed his testimony by saying: "I suppose the five women who chose to stay on the job with higher pay and chose sterilization—I suppose that they were glad to have the choice."[110] Spurred on by the coalition, the lawyer for Betty Riggs, one of the plaintiffs, had her send a telegram to the committee saying: "I cannot believe that Judge Bork thinks we were glad to have the choice of getting sterilized or getting fired.... Only a Judge who knows nothing about women who need to work could say that.... I had no choice."[111] As the coalition argued, this was yet another example of Bork's "incomprehensible insensitivity to the plight of women."[112]

Indeed, the coalition's use of polls to shape strategy and influence the vote was significant. For example, pollster John Marttila surveyed the entire country and discovered that in addition to high proportions of minority voters against Bork, the last thing southern whites wanted to do was to refight the civil rights battles of the 1960s—which they believed a Bork confirmation would trigger.[113] With the shifting realities of electoral politics providing a prescient warning to many senators, especially those who owed their margin of victory to minority voters in the 1986 midterms, the Block Bork movement placed heavy pressure on them to oppose the nomination, sending a clear signal that significant political costs were associated with a vote for Bork.[114] Speaking on behalf of the coalition, Reverend Joseph Lowery of the Southern Christian Leadership Conference reminded wavering Democrats that: "The people who support Bork will forget how you vote, but we will never forget."[115] A widely circulated poll by the *Atlanta Journal-Constitution* confirmed the South's opposition to Bork.[116]

Likewise, polls also showed that women disapproved of Bork's nomination more than men, demonstrating the emergence of a clear gender gap ranging from 8 to 9 percent.[117] The Block Bork coalition used these figures to advance their cause by designing reports specifically targeted at women. Before the hearings, for example, they released a report, *Setting the Record Straight: Judge Bork and the Future of Women's Rights,* warning that Bork threatened "women's role in the workplace, their access to educational opportunities, their health and reproductive rights, their status as citizens with full rights to equal treatment by our government, and even their rights as parents."[118] During the hearings, the liberal coalition worked to keep attention focused on Bork's "dismal record" concerning these issues to widen the chasm of opposition further. Kennedy, for example, created a series of statements seemingly crafted for the evening news, including: "In Robert Bork's America, there is no room at the inn for blacks, and no place in the Constitution for women."[119] Similar statements and reports were utilized to intensify opposition pressure and help seal Bork's defeat.

Finally, following Bork's lukewarm appearance, the coalition took another calculated, yet unprecedented step—they decided not to testify at the hearings. Not only did this signify a break from the past, but it also represented a departure from the coalition's strategy up to that point, since testifying could provide a national platform to potentially further the anti-Bork cause, recruit new members, and reinforce fund-raising appeals. However, a consensus emerged that testifying could actually prove counterproductive, as it would provide an opening for pro-Bork forces to manipulate the groups' appearances and redirect the Senate's animus away from Bork and toward the coalition as a "lynch mob."[120] *The Washington Post* labeled the decision "the supreme sacrifice," arguing that Neas engineered the "most effective disappearing act in the history of Washington lobbying" by keeping the entire coalition off the witness stand.[121] Senator Simpson, who hoped to have coalition members at the hearings "screaming about abortion," called it an "awesome move."[122]

Yet the Block Bork campaign would still play an important role. By working closely with Chairman Biden, who decided the structure of the witness list, the coalition helped secure witnesses who would bolster their cause and add fuel to the firestorm brewing in the country. Ironically, the most eagerly sought-after witness was William T. Coleman, a prominent Black Republican attorney and a strong supporter of Reagan. Coleman was first approached by administration officials to testify in Bork's favor, but Biden and the coalition knew he had reservations about the nominee and convinced him to appear.[123] In a *New York Times* op-ed, Coleman outlined his reasoning for speaking out: "When it has counted, Bork has often stood against the aspirations of blacks to achieve their constitutional rights.... Too much is at stake for the Constitution, for blacks, for women—indeed, for the entire country—to go forward with a nomination raising such extraordinary doubts."[124] Alongside the testimony of other prominent figures, such open and frank discussions on Bork's views regarding race and gender helped convince wavering senators to outright oppose the nomination.[125]

For example, after the testimonies of Coleman and others, the one undecided Republican on the committee, Senator Arlen Specter (R-PA), announced his reluctant decision to oppose Bork because of doubts about the nominee's views on equal protection.[126] Alabama's Democratic Senator Howell Heflin, who was one of the Reagan administration's most reliable supporters on the committee, noted that the intensity of pressure stirred up by the liberal coalition influenced his last-minute decision to oppose the nomination, despite Reagan having personally invited him to the White House to lobby for his vote. By early October, Heflin said his office had received more than fifty thousand cards and letters to vote against Bork (by comparison, he received only two thousand during the Iran-Contra investigation).[127] According to his Alabama colleague, Senator Shelby, the most significant source of opposition had come from two groups: Blacks and women.[128] As part of their southern strategy, the liberal coalition used the electoral arithmetic of the region to argue that these Democratic senators had far more to lose in the Bork fight. Ultimately, the southern bloc voted against confirmation, which Congresswoman Barbara Jordan argued was a clear reflection of the "growing political strength of the region's black voters, empowered by the very civil rights laws and Supreme Court decisions which Bork had opposed."[129]

Following two weeks of witness testimony, the judiciary committee voted nine to five against Bork's appointment on 6 October, and the full Senate rejected him 58–42 on 23 October—the largest number of votes ever cast against a nominee at that point.[130] From Kennedy's initial work with liberal leaders to organize a coalition to Biden's efforts with them behind the scenes to structure the hearings, liberal activist groups outside of Congress had effectively joined hands with liberal officials within to paint a picture of Bork as a threat to civil rights and civil liberties and to help convince moderate senators to vote against confirmation. A clear case of grassroots democracy in action, the Block Bork campaign strategically and successfully navigated the court of public opinion to politicize the nomination and ensure that Bork remained a footnote in Supreme Court history.

The Aftermath
In the final stages of the nomination fight, Reagan had tried to rally his supporters by presenting Bork in the context of a philosophical battle with liberalism: "Many of them [liberals] viewed the courts as a place to put judges who would further their agenda. . . . It is because those groups are gravely concerned that Judge Bork's appointment will mean a Supreme Court that practices judicial restraint as our forefathers intended that the nomination has produced a distorted, unseemly political campaign."[131]

After the defeat, Bork and conservative activists blamed the White House for allowing liberals to effectively hijack the process. To them, Bork lost because of the "slick, shrill propaganda of liberal special interest groups."[132] The shock defeat, coupled with the reactions of those on the right, persuaded Reagan to nominate Bork's conservative colleague, Judge Douglas Ginsburg—Reagan had vowed to put forward a nominee that would upset liberals just as much as Bork had.[133] Yet the Bork II battle, in Washington parlance, had a lifespan of just nine days following revelations about Ginsburg's private life; and the nominee eventually confirmed in Bork's stead, Judge Anthony Kennedy, proved more liberal on precisely the issues—sexuality, civil rights—that Bork's critics emphasized in their attacks. While ideologically conservative, Kennedy's expansive view of constitutional rights was sufficient to placate most of the liberal groups who fought against Bork—only NOW seriously opposed him, arguing that his views on employment discrimination and school desegregation, among other issues, were flawed.[134]

In fact, Reaganites apparently suspected Kennedy's moderate leanings as well, identifying some "disturbing aspects" in his record on questions of sexual freedom and civil rights.[135] Reagan, when introducing Kennedy as his nominee, also emphasized that he "seems to be popular with many senators of varying political persuasions."[136] Thus, with Kennedy's conservatism proving sufficiently amorphous to calm the waters after Bork, he sailed through the confirmation process with a vote of 97–0. As *CQ Press* acknowledged years later, Kennedy's appointment and his opinions since "vindicate both the fears of Reagan's advisers about him and the liberal forces that opened the path to his nomination all those years ago."[137] Indeed, Kennedy cast the determining vote and wrote the majority opinion in *Obergefell v. Hodges* in 2015, in which the court held in a 5–4 decision that the fundamental right to marry was guaranteed to same-sex couples by the Fourteenth Amendment. Speaking after the *Obergefell* ruling, Nan Aron, the founder of Alliance for Justice, an organization that had opposed Bork, told *CQ Press* that "one of the benefits—significant benefits— of defeating Robert Bork was the confirmation of Anthony Kennedy. . . . There's no question that the Bork defeat paved the way for the Supreme Court decision in the same-sex marriage case."[138]

Therefore, in many ways the Bork contest symbolized more than simply a vote for or against Robert Bork; it represented something of a referendum on the Reagan Revolution as a whole. Bork's constitutional theories, if carried to their logical conclusion, threatened to break down the legal barriers blocking the implementation of conservative approaches to a host of issues, including abortion and affirmative action. And by confirming Bork, Reagan would have decidedly tilted the court rightward and ensured that his agenda far outlasted his administration. In the Reagan Era, liberals viewed the Supreme Court as a last bastion for the defense of hard-won civil rights and social justice battles of the previous decades, and they scored a major symbolic victory in defeating Bork. Certainly, more than any other moment in the 1980s, the outcome of the Bork controversy signaled the continued strength of liberalism. Sandwiched in between Reagan's electoral landslide in 1984 and the election of his vice president in 1988, the ability of liberals to coordinate and defend their legacy challenges the impression of the decade as one of liberal drift.

More specifically, the Bork battle amply displayed how liberals had honed their coalition-building and advocacy skills in the shadows of Reagan's presidency. By operating under one umbrella, each liberal organization became part of a greater whole, enabling leaders and groups to subordinate personal and institutional interests in order to focus on the common goal and speak authoritatively with a unified voice. In doing so, the campaign framed the conflict in a way that resonated with the broader public and provided the necessary cover for wavering senators to stake out opposition positions without appearing to capitulate to the "ultra-liberal crusaders" and special interests that the right had characterized as leading the anti-Bork cause. Therefore, by establishing links with the Democratic Party, integrating national leadership figures and outside networks, and utilizing the full range of political skills and techniques, liberals developed a model of how to run a sophisticated liberal campaign in the Reagan Era.

The use of polls to shape strategy, the importance of refining the message as the battle evolved, and the consciousness of symbols, labels, and language demonstrated that the coalition had not only mastered the techniques of the right but had successfully combined them with a coordinated grassroots effort to outmaneuver Reagan and the conservative movement. When surveying the battlefield afterward, the LCCR's vice chairman, William Taylor, understood the significance of the moment for the liberal community: "No battle has brought more diverse groups together. That's part of the legacy, because once people have worked together and found that they can work together, it provides a basis for doing so again."[139] While dissent was present, as Taylor acknowledges, the Bork campaign brought groups together to forge new, and in some instances, highly unlikely alliances.

Arguably, the liberal reaction to the Bork nomination can be seen as a defining moment in the process of liberal recovery in the 1980s. In an immediate sense, it reminded a potentially rightward-bound Democratic Party that their liberal constituencies still held significant political leverage. According to the *Washington Post*'s Mary McGrory, for example, liberal voting groups, previously derided as "special interest groups," were now being discussed in Democratic circles as "constituencies" once again. "Blocking Bork," McGrory wrote, demonstrated that "liberal issues still sell."[140] It also had a more lasting impact, a notion corroborated by members of the Block Bork coalition afterward. According to former Secretary of Labor Robert Reich: "Without the nomination of Bork, there would have been no resurgence of leadership on the American left.... Bork was a spark that touched off the wild fire; Reagan was the arsonist."[141] Equally, Neas argued that keeping Bork off the court "ranks among the most important achievements of the progressive coalition over the past seven decades."[142] Individual liberal groups also gained a surge in both membership and fundraising capabilities as a result; the National Abortion Rights Action League (NARAL) attracted eleven thousand new members and raised $1.3 million during the battle, for example.[143]

Thus, the Bork victory, as well as the alliances formed during the battle, reenergized the liberal movement after years of slow progress. Afterward, liberal activist Ann Lewis talked of her surprise at the renewed sense of confidence and empowerment that the Bork campaign gave to political veterans, while Reverend Lowery argued that Bork's defeat proved "that the civil rights movement is alive and the era of activism is not concluded."[144] Indeed, efforts immediately moved to translate this success into other aspects of the liberal agenda, with NOW and the LCCR at the forefront once again.

LIBERALISM RESURGENT? DEVELOPMENTS AFTER BORK

Instead of dispersing after the Bork battle, the reenergized liberal coalition refocused attention on the CRRA. On 20 January 1988, just weeks before Anthony Kennedy was to be confirmed, key actors from the Block Bork effort—particularly Neas and Senator Kennedy—wrote to senators to lobby for quick passage of the CRRA.[145] By 8 March, both the House (315–98) and the Senate (75–14) had passed the measure by wide margins, and the liberal coalition was now writing to the president to urge him not to veto it: "A presidential veto of a bill to end federal funding of discrimination would leave a terrible and lasting stain on your presidency."[146] Despite this, alongside warnings from Republicans that a veto would damage their election prospects, Reagan became the first president in 122 years to veto a civil rights bill (the nation's first civil rights law had passed in 1866 over a presidential veto).[147] Reagan argued that the bill would unjustifiably extend federal government power over the decisions and affairs of private organizations: "The truth is, this legislation isn't a civil rights bill.... It would force court-ordered social engineers into every corner of American society. I won't cave to the demagoguery of those who cloak a big government power grab in the mantle of civil rights."[148]

In response, liberals lobbied hard for senators and representatives, including those on the Republican side, to override the veto. On 22 March, the Senate voted 73–24 (all Democrats present voted in favor, with a 21–24 split for the Republicans) and the House voted 292–133 (House Democrats split 240–10, while the Republicans voted 52–123) to do so.[149] Kennedy claimed passage sent an unequivocal message that the nation rejected Reagan's "narrow view of civil rights."[150] Certainly, by reaffirming past civil rights statutes, its passage was a repudiation of the Reagan administration's approach. Not only did it restore the traditional practice of denying federal funds to discriminatory institutions, but it broadened protection for women, racial minorities, the elderly, and those with disabilities—all key Democratic constituencies.

Following this success, the liberal coalition pushed Congress to legislate in another area where discrimination was rampant: housing. To liberals, the 1968 housing bill, enacted as Title VIII of the 1968 Civil Rights Act, was not strong enough and new legislation was needed to improve it. In 1980, Congress came close to enacting strengthening measures, but a conservative filibuster sealed its demise.[151] By 1988, the situation with housing, liberals believed, had worsened. The Reagan administration, which the LCCR charged with leading opposition to fair housing throughout the decade, had cut funding to a number of agencies tackling housing discrimination.[152] The overall budget of the oversight agency, the Department of Housing and Urban Development (HUD), was cut from $36 billion in 1980 to $15 billion in 1988, the largest drop of any federal department during the decade.[153] At the same time, cases of housing discrimination were rising, with HUD estimating that over two million cases of unlawful victimization occurred in 1986 alone.[154] In particular, as with the CRRA, those most affected were often racial minorities, women (especially single women with children), and people with disabilities.[155] Thus, the liberal coalition redesigned the original housing bill by enlarging and strengthening HUD's enforcement provisions and expanding coverage to prohibit discrimination specifically against these groups. It also broadened the scope to cover various financial transactions involving residential real estate, a compromise brokered with the National Association of Realtors, who had become believers in the LCCR's power after Bork.[156] Together with the CRRA, passage of the Fair Housing Amendment Act of 1988 represented "the most significant and dramatic improvement in civil rights laws in two decades," according to Neas; and it demonstrated that despite "fierce opposition," the 1980s will be remembered "as an era of reaffirmation of our civil rights laws and remedies."[157]

Thus, as the sun began to set on the Reagan presidency, the LCCR reflected that "while the Reagan administration continued to compile the worst civil rights record of any administration . . . the 100th Congress was one of the most successful and productive Congresses in our nation's history."[158] Indeed, alongside passing historic civil rights bills, the liberal majority in the 100th Congress also limited Reagan's legislative success rate to only 43.5 percent in 1987 and 40.6 percent in 1988—the lowest rates for a president since *Congressional Quarterly* began tracking in 1953.[159] Still, as the LCCR acknowledged, "despite the considerable successes, one cannot gainsay the fact that there was also a tremendous downside to the Reagan years on civil rights matters."[160] Jesse Jackson agreed, telling the NAACP's 1987 conference that Reagan shifted the civil rights climate from "we shall overcome" to "we shall overturn."[161] Scholars too weighed in, with Norman Amaker arguing that Reagan, unlike his immediate predecessors, both Democrat and Republican, operated in defiance of, rather than adherence to, the prophylactic goals of national civil rights law.[162]

In the end, Reagan's actions across the decade clearly spurred the emergence of coordinated liberal countermovements and drove the development of politically sophisticated coalitions, with the LCCR building and refining the concept of coalition politics. In doing so, these liberal groups established direct ties with officeholders and increasingly moved in a partisan direction, forming strong institutional links with the Democratic Party as a result. The Bork defeat and the passage of two significant pieces of civil rights legislation exemplify this point. While each of these developments alone represents a substantial—and not necessarily predictable—victory, taken together they showcase the extent to which liberals, both within and outside the Democratic Party, had strengthened their political position by Reagan's second term. By modernizing their political operations, honing their coalition-building processes, and updating their approach, liberals had clearly developed strategies during Reagan's presidency to mobilize their supporters and compete—successfully at times—with conservatives in the political arena. As historian Nicholas Laham notes, by the end of the Reagan Era "federal antidiscrimination laws and the groups representing the interests of minorities and women proved to be sufficiently powerful and durable to withstand assault from the most conservative administration in modern American history."[163]

Nevertheless, taking back control of the Congress had only given liberals a greater degree of maneuverability in the legislative arena. While doing so had provided a bulwark against the conservative agenda in the final years of Reagan's presidency, attention began to shift toward winning back Democratic control of the executive branch, and thereby securing a platform to actually set the national agenda. As the next chapter details, the 1988 elections witnessed a number of important developments for liberalism, both intellectually and institutionally, including the trailblazing run of a Black preacher who galvanized marginalized communities across the country in the Democratic primaries and the nomination of a northeastern governor who used Gary Hart's "new generation" approach to reach out to suburbia.

6. "Wake Up, Liberals, Your Time Has Come"
Reassessing the 1988 Elections

Ahead of the 1988 elections, liberal stalwart Arthur Schlesinger Jr. wrote an op-ed in the *Washington Post* titled "Wake Up, Liberals, Your Time Has Come."[1] Declaring that "the next liberal hour impends," he used the piece to administer last rites to the Reagan Revolution: "Reaganism is finished, bankrupt, used up, over. At last, it is bedtime for Bonzo. The Reagan Revolution—or, more precisely, the Reagan Counter-Revolution—is evaporating." Whether 1988 would represent an epitaph for the revolution was still uncertain at this point, but the article captured the wider mood of the liberal community at the time. Following the historic defeat of Robert Bork, alongside the legislative successes of the 100th Congress, both the Democratic Party and grassroots organizers were inspired, and in some cases even surprised, by their ability to coordinate such successful campaigns against Reagan and the conservative movement. No longer sailing against the wind, liberals seemingly had the wind at their backs going into the 1988 presidential elections. But rough waters lay ahead.

First though, history would be made. Jesse Jackson ran an impressive campaign for the presidency that year, showcasing the significant progress made by racial minorities in the political arena during the Reagan Era. Jackson registered over two million new voters, won seven million votes in the primaries, and challenged the eventual nominee, Massachusetts Governor Michael Dukakis, all the way to the party convention while championing a clear liberal message.[2] The *New York Times* would declare 1988 the "Year of Jackson"—the year when, for the first time in American history, a Black candidate made a serious bid for the White House and was taken seriously by the electorate.[3] By examining Jackson's primary campaign in depth, this chapter demonstrates how the support that his progressive agenda attracted, especially while some Democrats were attempting to move the party rightward, further complicates the impression of the period as one of liberal drift. Certainly, as the Democratic primaries illustrated, liberalism was still in a state of intellectual transition, and Jackson was among a pack fighting for ownership of the post–New Deal mantle—a candidate with liberal values electable as a "new generation" Democrat and salable in the South and West. However, the support his candidacy attracted, particularly from white southerners, challenges the rightward-bound narrative of groups like the DLC and demonstrates the continued centrality of race to the development of liberalism across the 1980s.

In many ways though, 1988 was a missed opportunity for liberals. With no incumbent running, the election was the first in nearly twenty years to start with a relatively wide-open race, and the issues of the day seemed to favor the Democratic Party. Yet, Dukakis lost a significant postconvention lead after a series of tactical and strategic miscalculations. In particular, Dukakis opted to run a nonideological campaign, which in many ways was a consequence of the efforts to update liberalism intellectually. Dukakis framed his candidacy around competence, rather than his liberal views, in an attempt to move beyond the debate. By doing so however, he left a philosophical vacuum that his opponent, George Bush, effectively filled with an extreme version of liberalism, painting the governor as a dangerous liberal whose views were outside the mainstream. And at the precise moment that his campaign started to implode, Dukakis threw caution to wind and embraced the liberal label—and crucially, started to recover. This may not have saved his candidacy, but results in other political arenas continued to show the persistence of liberalism, particularly in Congress, where women and racial minorities powered Democratic gains across the country. By 1988, signs of a nascent coalition of women, racial minorities, and young professionals, initially hinted at during the 1986 midterms and energized by the Bork campaign, were increasingly evident. And the Democratic Party, working together with liberal grassroots organizations, was establishing electoral strategies to mobilize these groups.

"THE JACKIE ROBINSON OF AMERICAN POLITICS"

Winning is new people running . . . new voters.

Winning is winning Congressional districts across this country that progressives have never won, which gives us the ability to change the face of Congress.

Winning is knowing that I have the ability to compete at this level.

We're not just running for an office. We're running for freedom.[4]

Jesse Jackson, "On Winning"

Jesse Jackson, a Baptist minister who grew up in the racially segregated South, played a key role in Martin Luther King Jr.'s civil rights operation during the 1960s. After King's assassination in 1968, Jackson picked up the leadership baton and created his own organization in 1971, Operation PUSH, to drive the movement for civil rights further. Fast-forward to the 1980s, and the successes of the Voting Rights Act campaign in 1982 and Harold Washington's victory in the Chicago mayoral election of 1983 convinced Jackson that a new national approach was needed. Jackson had helped mobilize and register thousands of voters for Washington; using that election as a model, he argued that racial minorities should seek more than simply the coattails of white liberals to advance their agenda by leveraging minority power inside the party.[5] According to one of his close advisers, Frank Clemente, while Jackson sought merely to advocate the idea of a Black presidential candidate, he flung himself into contention after hearing crowds chant "Run Jesse Run" during his 1983 Southern Crusade—a registration campaign that increased the Black electoral roll by 30 percent between 1982 and 1984.[6]

Although Jackson failed to clinch the nomination in 1984, his focus on voter registration and his efforts to translate King's concept of the poor people's crusade into a national political campaign ensured that his campaign had a lasting impact on minority politics. Drawing upon a baseball metaphor, California Assemblyman Willie Brown concluded that Jackson had become the "Jackie Robinson of American politics," predicting that "a whole lot of little leaguers" will someday join Jackson in rising up to the political big leagues.[7] Even Jackson regarded his 1984 candidacy as largely symbolic: "seizing the opportunity to register new black voters and raise their consciousness."[8] Moreover, he used his convention speech that year to transcend his pigeonholed image as the candidate of Black America and put his stake in the ground as the candidate for liberal America:

> Our flag is red, white, and blue, but our nation is a rainbow—red, yellow, brown, black, and white. America is not like a blanket—one piece of unbroken cloth, the same color, the same texture, the same size. America is more like a quilt: many patches, many pieces, many colors, many sizes, all woven and held together by a common thread. The white, the Hispanic, the black, the Arab, the Jew, the woman, the Native American, the small farmer, the businessperson, the environmentalist, the peace activist, the young, the old, the lesbian, the gay, and the disabled make up the American quilt.[9]

Here, not only was Jackson establishing identity politics as the foundation of his approach, but he was also setting his marker down for 1988. After 1984, Jackson institutionalized his campaign apparatus by transforming it into a permanent political organization, the National Rainbow Coalition.[10] He continued his voter registration drive, bringing in over two million new voters between 1984 and 1988. As he told *Jet* magazine: "I registered more voters as Democrats than anyone alive... which led to the Democrats regaining the Senate in 1986 and [defeating] Bork in 1987."[11] Indeed, according to political analyst Andrew Kopkind at the time, "One after another, Southern Democrats, who wouldn't have dreamed of supporting Northern liberals in a straight ideological struggle 10 or 20 years ago, joined in the vote against Bork.... The difference, this time, was Jesse Jackson."[12] All this groundwork became the basis of a stronger attempt at the nomination in 1988 as Jackson aimed to draw more colors into his rainbow. While in 1984 some Black leaders committed their support to Walter Mondale—given his track record on civil rights—there was more unity behind Jackson in 1988 since none of his rivals had the credentials to compare. But Jackson would still face a familiar foe, one who enjoyed a substantial lead over him and the rest of the Democratic field, early in the polls.

Senator Gary Hart, who launched his 1988 campaign as a New Generation Democrat, was immediately crowned the front-runner. According to Gallup, Hart had a double-digit lead over the rest of the Democratic field and was beating Bush by thirteen points in early previews of the election.[13] Sounding many of the same themes from 1984, Hart defined himself early in a 1985 speech in Boston, telling the crowd that while traditional liberalism had "protected and preserved our national values for more than 50 years," to advance those same values it was now time to "accept change."[14] Again, this was a debate over the method and process of delivering a liberal vision in Reagan's America, rather than an overall critique of the values and principles that underpinned the philosophy. Indeed, Hart maintained a strong liberal voting record. In 1985, for example, the *National Journal* declared him to be the most liberal member of the Senate.[15] Thus, by positioning himself as a post–New Deal liberal, Hart was establishing the same rationale for his candidacy in 1988 as he had in 1984—the process of updating liberalism intellectually in response to Reaganism and the challenges of the 1980s.

By the time that the primary campaign got under way, Hart had also used the intervening period to address some of his earlier shortcomings. He launched a think tank, the Center for New Democracy, to survey the state and local landscape and create an almanac of innovative policies.[16] According to the *New York Times*, "The candidate who suffered from the question 'Where's the beef?' now has enough of the stuff to supply Wendy's for a decade."[17] Hart also moved quickly to embrace key segments of the Democratic Party and hired several liberal campaign veterans, including Mondale's 1984 political director Paul Tully. Clearly, Hart was establishing a serious campaign organization, but more significantly, he was also getting credit, if belatedly, for having been right in 1984 about liberalism's need to embrace new ideas and a new approach.[18] As the *New York Times* wrote:

> [Not only] was Hart way ahead in the polls, [but] every Democrat seems to have listened to him. Other contenders are sounding so many of Hart's 1984 themes that quite a few politicians have described the '88 race as one among different versions of Gary Hart. The new Democratic conventional wisdom seems to have been built from planks in the '84 Hart platform, [which] include... above all, a sense that it is possible for Government to attend to social needs without producing copies of New Deal and Great Society programs.[19]

Evidently, Hart's efforts—and, by extension, that of neoliberals—to update liberalism had taken hold in the party. But while Hart was ahead in the polls and several journalists were describing him as destined for the White House, the emergence of rumors concerning an alleged affair effectively derailed his candidacy.[20] Other Democratic contenders, sensing that voters were still keen for Hart's message, just not for Hart himself, scrambled to assume his mantle. While, for a moment, it looked as though Hart's 1984 campaign cochairman, Colorado Representative Patricia Schroeder, would carry on his crusade, she eventually decided against a run, despite a raft of liberal women's groups throwing their support behind her.[21] Still, it was not lost on observers at the time that Schroeder's serious consideration amply demonstrated the progress women had made in Reagan's shadow; Schroeder herself paid homage to Geraldine Ferraro for altering the nation's attitude toward women in politics.[22] The natural heir to Hart's approach was Michael Dukakis, confirmed by the large movement of Hart staffers to his campaign.[23] With the Baby Boom generation coming of age politically and making up almost half of the electorate by 1988, Dukakis presented himself as the new generation candidate "who has made new ideas work."[24] Hart did reenter the race at the end of 1987, but many interpreted this self-resurrection as the height of folly, if not hubris. He lacked an organizational structure, and his hopes hinged on winning New Hampshire, where Dukakis soundly defeated him.[25]

After Hart's implosion and with the Democratic field lacking a clear front-runner, the media took to referring to this relatively untried group as the "seven dwarfs." Although Jackson was winning most run-off polls at this stage, he was not declared the front-runner, a point *Ebony* magazine attributed to his race: "Front-runner status, if you happen to be Black . . . comes with an asterisk next to your name that means 'not seriously expected to win.'"[26] A *New York Times* article completed the point: "Most political analysts give [Jackson] little chance—partly because he is black, partly because of his un-retrenched liberalism."[27] Hart had shown the importance of carefully calibrating a liberal message at the national level to attract the less-partisan voters in society, and Jackson's own experience in 1984 had demonstrated the limits of a minority candidate running a minority issue-based campaign. Yet, many commentators failed to recognize that Jackson was also learning how to play liberal politics in the Reagan Era, even co-opting some of Hart's themes to do so. Those who did, including journalists at *Newsweek*, picked up that Jackson was moving from "Jesse Jetstream" to "Jesse Mainstream" and remarked that some of Jackson's speeches could "almost have been Hart's."[28] Jackson also appeared before the DLC in 1987 to claim common cause with the organization; and his campaign downplayed its labor alliances, "lest we be accused of Mondale-type interest group politics" according to a Jackson staffer.[29]

Still, Jackson soundly rejected the "me-too" positioning of some Democrats looking to move rightward at the time and placed his liberal vision at the center of his campaign. Of all the competitors, Jackson was the most unabashed advocate of increased government spending for social programs, and his candidacy was, in many ways, the direct response to Reaganism. Indeed, the curtailment of social welfare programs and increasing levels of poverty in minority communities were key factors in Jackson's decision to run.[30] But he combined this emphasis on social justice with an economic populist message that transcended easy pigeonholing. Irrespective of race or social class, Jackson sought to fashion a message that linked struggling rural farmers with displaced industrial workers to forge a multiracial coalition. By fighting on behalf of marginalized groups, as well as the middle class, and by actively seeking out white audiences to emphasize his multiracial appeal, Jackson was articulating a liberalism refashioned for the Reagan Era; his refrain to blue-collar workers that when "the plant lights go out, we all look the same in the dark" struck a powerful chord.[31] By mobilizing a liberal, multiracial coalition, Jackson would transition from a rank outsider to a serious player in Democratic politics within a matter of months.

Initially though, a candidate running a very similar campaign to

Jackson's clinched the nation's first contest of the season. Representative Richard Gephardt won the Iowa caucus by positioning himself as the antiestablishment insurgent running against "them"—the Reagan administration, Wall Street, etc.—and placing liberal issues of social and economic justice at the center of his campaign.[32] This was perhaps surprising, particularly given that Gephardt had voted for aspects of Reaganomics earlier in the decade and was a member of the political establishment in Washington. He had also served as the first chairman of the DLC, although he suggested to journalist Sidney Blumenthal that he never viewed the organization as a vehicle to move the party ideologically but rather as an "ideas center" to design a palatable liberal agenda.[33] Certainly, as the decade progressed, Gephardt changed his stance on a number of issues to reflect a more liberal viewpoint.[34] Additionally, instead of using DLC staffers, Gephardt filled his campaign with liberal veterans, including Hart and Kennedy aides.[35] The clearest sign of Gephardt's gradual drift toward liberalism is evidenced by his ratings from the ADA: from 45 percent in 1981 to 90 percent in 1988.[36] Senator Paul Simon (D-IL), who ran third behind Gephardt and Dukakis in Iowa, latched on to this apparent transformation, airing attack ads that contrasted the earlier, more conservative incarnation of Gephardt with the now "reliably liberal" one.[37] Yet, going from representing a predominantly white suburb in St. Louis to running a national campaign, pragmatism dictated a change in approach. And regardless of whether Gephardt had undergone a liberal conversion or was simply a practitioner of situational politics, it is clear from his philosophical migration that liberalism remained attractive to Democrats in the late eighties.

Moreover, despite work by conservatives and moderates under the auspices of the DLC to dilute the liberal vote in the primaries, the inverse occurred. As part of the DLC's Super Tuesday Education Project, fourteen border and southern states agreed to hold primaries on the same day for 1988. According to the DLC, this would heighten the "relevance and quality of the public policy debate, increase voter interest and turnout," and help foster the selection of a more conservative standard-bearer to lead the party.[38] Yet, this new regional primary did more for the most liberal candidates in the field, Jackson and Dukakis, than it did for the DLC's choice, southern Senator Al Gore (D-TN); Jackson won sixteen first- or second-place finishes of the twenty races that day, while Dukakis managed twelve and Gore eleven. Jackson attracted the largest share of the popular vote (2,547,302) and won majorities or pluralities in the Black vote (91 percent), labor vote (35 percent), women's vote (30 percent), and the younger generation's votes (33 percent of eighteen-to-twenty-nine-year-olds).[39] Just as significantly, over half a million white southerners marked Jackson's name on their ballots twenty-four years after the Civil Rights Act.[40]

Arguably, the DLC's efforts to alter the mechanics of the primary system overlooked the shifting ideological voting dynamics in the region. According to Patricia Ireland, NOW's executive president, with women again voting in larger numbers than men, the Super Tuesday results confirmed the fallacy of the DLC's argument: "They were looking at the South for what it was, not what it is.... The northern liberal band was not supposed to be the beneficiary."[41] Indeed, polls demonstrated that southern Democrats were "virtually indistinct from Democrats elsewhere."[42] Furthermore, Senator Sam Nunn of Georgia, who was considered by his colleagues as the ideal conservative Democratic candidate, polled particularly poorly in the South in 1987 and decided to stay out of the race.[43] Despite the best efforts of the DLC and its allies, the Democratic Party was still a predominantly liberal party, and its source of support continued to come from the more liberal elements of society, even in the "conservative" South.

Consequently, the field winnowed to two following Jackson's surprise victory in Michigan, where all indications had pointed to a close race between Dukakis and Gephardt. Together with his Super Tuesday returns, the win in Michigan legitimized Jackson as a serious candidate and pushed him to the front of the polls again.[44] While Dukakis eventually recorded enough victories to secure the nomination, Jackson ended with more than seven million votes to register one of the strongest second-place showings in history. Significantly, by stepping into the vacuum Hart left, Jackson captured the "new generation," winning the eighteen-to-twenty-nine-year-old vote outright and running even in the thirty-to-forty-four-year-old category. As a Jackson staffer noted to CBS, "Jackson is the future of the Democratic Party; if you don't believe me, go ask your kids!"[45] More broadly, at a time when some strategists were urging Democrats to trim their liberal sails, Jackson reminded them of their identity as the party of economic populism and social liberalism.[46] As the *New York Times* wrote, "Jackson's positions pull on many liberal Democrats tired of suppressing their thirst."[47] Jackson himself acknowledged the significance of his campaign in a letter to his staff afterward: "You have helped me set the agenda" for November, moved American politics in "a progressive direction," and "helped bring the civil rights movement to life as a force in national electoral politics."[48]

With this foundation, Jackson was able to march into the convention center in Atlanta and leverage his power, forcing the party to commit to real policy and institutional changes—winner-takes-all primaries were eliminated in a number of states, the share of superdelegates was cut by over one-third, and of the thirteen platform planks in dispute between the two campaigns, Jackson lost just two and negotiated and won major portions of nine.[49] Finally, Jackson secured a prime-time speaking slot at the party convention and used it to reflect on the heightened power of racial minorities in politics. Indeed, his own political journey mirrored the transformation of the Democratic Party over that same space of time: racial minorities, women, and professionals were now shaping a party that had segregationist southerners as its base when Jackson started out.

Afterward, Jackson used his position to broker further leverage for racial minorities in the Democratic Party. The immediate symbol of this was the election of Ronald Brown, Jackson's campaign manager, to the DNC chairmanship in 1989, the first African American elevated to the position. With Jackson's support, David Dinkins would also become the first African American mayor of the nation's preeminent city, New York, that same year. Furthermore, like Ferraro's candidacy in 1984, Jackson's campaign was a national civics lesson, enlarging the idea of who could and should aspire to be president. As the *New York Times* noted, Jackson's bid "registered a social and cultural shift ... that enables us all to entertain the possibility of a black President."[50] The historic election of the first Black president, Barack Obama, in 2008 reflected the realization of this shift. That year, Obama, who forged his political identity in the 1980s, echoed Jackson's words in his victory speech, itemizing the party's diverse coalition by promising to lead "young and old, rich and poor ... black, white, Hispanic, Asian, Native American, gay, straight, disabled and not disabled."[51] While Obama's election took decades to cultivate, Jackson played a seminal role in planting its seeds, as well as those of many other victories over the years. As *The Nation* reflected in 2010: "Jackson inspired more young people and minorities to vote than anyone—and given that almost all of them registered Democratic, it is very likely that Jesse has helped elect more Democrats than any other political figure. No one has done more to put 'flesh' on the 'spirit' of the Voting Rights Act."[52]

In the end, Jackson's candidacy was an important moment for the development of both liberalism and the modern Democratic Party. First, given the perceived abandonment of civil rights by the Reagan administration and the tough economic conditions facing racial minorities, Jackson provided a conduit to express the accumulated frustration of minority groups after years of slow progress. Second, Jackson's impressive campaign reflected the heightened power of racial minorities as a voting constituency, particularly within the Democratic Party. By conducting voter registration drives, campaign organizing events, and strategy sessions with political veterans, racial minorities developed strong institutional ties and became "intimately familiar," according to historian Steven Lawson, with party rules and structures through Jackson's candidacy. As Lawson notes, they learned valuable lessons about "fundraising, media relations, and the myriad tasks of preparing a candidate to stump through the country in search of support."[53] Jackson had also established himself as a national spokesman for minority issues; as Democratic strategist Ted Van Dyk argued at the time, "Without Jesse's support, no white Democrat can accomplish much on a national scale."[54] Finally, after both the 1986 midterms and the Block Bork campaign, Jackson's candidacy again reinforced the political importance of racial minorities to the party's coalition-building efforts and challenged the notion that its members had to travel rightward to garner electoral support.

"COMPETENCE, NOT IDEOLOGY"

Michael Dukakis, the son of Greek immigrants, grew up in the prosperous suburb of Brookline, Massachusetts, and became a rising star in the state's political arena during the 1960s. Serving as governor of the Bay State in the late 1970s and early 1980s, Dukakis's rise to national prominence aligned with efforts by Democratic insiders to bring more governors into the process of party recovery. As the *New Republic* argued weeks after Mondale's defeat, for example, "If any one group ought to be elevated in influence, it is the party's governors, who have shown a remarkable ability to win elections while national candidates have been losing."[55] In 1986, Dukakis was reelected to a third term with 69 percent of the vote and was designated the most effective governor in America by his peers.[56] Crucially, Dukakis had shown an ability to attract suburban voters, typically independents or young professionals, in his home state.[57] With the center of political power shifting from the metropolitan city to the emerging suburbs of the postindustrial landscape, the suburbanization of the electorate was becoming particularly evident by 1988 (48 percent of the nation's population lived in suburbs by then).[58] In an effort to pivot the party toward the suburbs, DNC chairman Paul Kirk commissioned a report to examine Dukakis's suburban policies in depth after his 1986 reelection.[59] Citing what Dukakis had accomplished in Massachusetts, Kirk used the governor's alternate approach to welfare policy—where work requirements were combined with the continuation of benefits—as an example of a pragmatic approach to a liberal goal that appealed to suburban voters.[60]

In the space of a decade, the Bay State had been transformed under Dukakis's watch from a high-tax, slow growth, mass unemployment area into one of the most robust industrial states in the nation. Dukakis's activist, liberal approach to government was at the center of this economic renaissance, which was labeled the Massachusetts Miracle.[61] Proposing to replicate this on a national scale, Dukakis was a quintessential neoliberal—his campaign slogan was "idealism that works."[62] In Iowa, where he positioned himself as "a very strong Democrat, a liberal Democrat, a progressive Democrat," a reporter asked him how his liberalism differed from that of Hubert Humphrey. "Not at all in values and goals," Dukakis replied, "but we've learned something about implementation over the years."[63] Indeed, by employing the approach championed by Hart, Dukakis mixed liberal idealism with pragmatic reform, supporting civil rights, women's equality, and abortion rights, among other issues, while carefully calibrating his rhetoric to attract emerging constituencies and clinch the nomination.

With an electoral model predicated on a suburban strategy, Dukakis sought to balance the ticket geographically and ideologically by naming moderate-to-conservative Texas Senator Lloyd Bentsen as his vice presidential choice. Fully aware that an electoral majority would be difficult to assemble without breaking the Republican grip on the South, Dukakis put pragmatic politics ahead of his liberal reformer image. A well-respected senator, Bentsen was a strategically sound choice, but given Jackson's impressive run, minority voters had hoped Dukakis would give Jackson serious consideration. Still, in seeking to revive the Boston–Austin axis from 1960, Dukakis's choice was also part of a wider effort to resurrect the ghost of President Kennedy.[64] From the earliest primary, Dukakis had not been shy about invoking the memories of "another man from Massachusetts." Believing the mood in 1988 reflected that of 1960, with a popular president on the way out and the country open to change, Dukakis employed Kennedy's "we can do better" theme to try to capture the memory of Camelot; he also hired Kennedy's former wordsmith, Theodore Sorensen, to wax lyrical about the comparison.[65]

Certainly, Dukakis was not the only liberal to recognize the political potency of reigniting the Kennedy torch. Indeed, the Kennedy cadence and imagery formed a crucial part of the neoliberal drive to modernize liberalism. By 1988, Kennedy's revival was, in many ways, a reflection of the generational change that was occurring within the Democratic Party.

With the majority of presidential hopefuls under fifty that year, identifying with Kennedy became a way for these younger liberals to differentiate themselves from their older colleagues who celebrated Franklin Roosevelt and the New Deal.[66] But where other neoliberals had embraced the liberalism inherent in their approach, Dukakis tried to suggest that labels were "meaningless" as he pivoted toward the general election, using his convention speech to declare that the election would be about "competence, not ideology."[67] Believing that voters had developed a taste for nonideological politics following the perceived excesses of the Reagan years, Dukakis sought to appeal to the head rather than the heart and asked voters to judge his competence as an administrator.

However, Dukakis had compiled a strong liberal record as governor and won the nomination by relying on support from the liberal community. Moreover, his decision to soft-pedal his political views and run a determinedly nonideological campaign left a vacuum that Bush would effectively fill with an extreme version of liberalism devoid of reality. By assembling and deploying a range of symbols and images to control and direct the discourse, it was conservatives, not liberals, who offered definitions of liberalism in 1988, and the Bush campaign utilized this strategy to reduce the seventeen-point lead that Dukakis held coming out of the convention.[68] First, Dukakis's veto of a bill in 1976 that required public school teachers to lead their students in a daily recitation of the Pledge of Allegiance was used to question his patriotism and present an image of liberalism as "anti-American." Second, Bush sought to paint Dukakis's Massachusetts Miracle as a mirage by using the pollution of Boston Harbor to criticize the governor's record.[69] He also focused attention on Dukakis's foreign policy experience, using a photograph of Dukakis in an M1 Abrams tank with a "Snoopy-style" helmet on as a metaphor for liberals pretending to be tough on security.[70] But of all the strategies deployed, the focus on Dukakis's law and order credentials formed the principal measure through which Bush sought to distort liberalism.

The impression that liberals were soft on crime had become a thorn in the Democratic Party's side since the Great Society and the expansion of criminal rights under Earl Warren's Supreme Court in the 1960s. To exploit this, Bush criticized Dukakis for being "a card-carrying member of the American Civil Liberties Union" and questioned his position on capital punishment.[71] This became a flashpoint during the second presidential debate when the moderator, Bernard Shaw, asked the governor if his wife were raped and murdered, would he favor an irrevocable death penalty for the killer? Dukakis produced an unemotional, policy-orientated response that many—including the candidate himself—would argue seriously damaged his campaign.[72] Expecting a law and order question, campaign manager Susan Estrich, and close advisor Arkansas Governor Bill Clinton, had coached Dukakis on how to use his past experience of crime to relate to viewers. Dukakis's brother had been killed in a hit-and-run incident, and his father had been robbed and beaten in his medical office by a drug addict. However, Dukakis's passionless response seemed to confirm the "ice man" stereotype Bush had constructed; poll numbers dropped from 49 percent to 42 percent in one night.[73] Perhaps most damaging though, the Bush campaign was able to project this law and order issue through a racial prism and tap into a racially influenced fear of crime that, as demonstrated, had led many suburban white voters to support the Republicans after the 1960s.

To do so, Republicans focused on one story in particular from Massachusetts in 1986. While serving a life sentence, convicted murderer Willie Horton was allowed a weekend pass under the state's furlough program, but he fled and brutalized a couple in Maryland, raping Angela Miller and torturing her partner, Clifford Barnes, before being caught. As with the pledge issue, Dukakis had vetoed a bill in 1976 that forbade furloughs for first-degree murderers, sensing that the courts would deem it unconstitutional. Bush's campaign manager, Lee Atwater, decided to place this threatening archetype—a black man as the rapist of a white woman—at the center of the law and order attack.[74] At the time, an anonymous member of the Bush campaign was quoted as saying of the Atwater strategy: "It's a wonderful mix of liberalism and a big black rapist."[75] While Atwater maintained publicly that Horton was never a racial symbol, he perhaps alluded to his true feeling in a speech to Republicans during the election: "There is a story about a fellow named Willie Horton who for all I know may end up to be (sic) Dukakis' running mate.... On Monday, I saw in the driveway of [Dukakis's] house Jesse Jackson. So anyway, maybe he'll put this Willie Horton guy on the ticket after all is said and done."[76]

As was noted at the time, Atwater was clearly equating Jackson with Horton because both happened to be Black. He acknowledged as much in an interview only three years later, apologizing to Dukakis for the "naked cruelty" of his campaign to "make Horton his running mate."[77] The Bush campaign would use the Horton story in series of notorious and effective political advertisements.[78] The "revolving door" TV advertisement, for example, portrayed a line of convicts walking in and out of prison through a revolving door while the narrator recited Horton's crimes without explicitly mentioning him by name. Significantly, the ad was designed to emphasize the African American in the lineup, who was the only one to look up at the camera.[79] *CBS/New York Times* polls showed that the "revolving door" ad had the greatest impact on respondents in 1988, with a correlated effect on how they viewed each candidate on crime issues.[80]

There was the more explicit use of Horton as well: the Maryland Republican Party disseminated a political flyer pairing photographs of Horton and Dukakis with the message, "Is this your Pro-Family Team for 1988?" Bush also took to reciting Horton's crimes in detail on the campaign trail and used his primetime convention speech to criticize Dukakis's furlough program—this was despite the fact that the federal government ran the largest furlough program.[81] Dukakis eventually responded, releasing an attack ad titled "Bush's Furlough from the Truth" and pointing out that the federal government had allowed thousands of drug kingpins out on furlough while Bush was in charge of the War on Drugs.[82] The Dukakis team even found their very own Willie Horton, a heroin dealer named Angel Medrano who had raped a pregnant white woman while on a weekend pass. However, as an internal campaign memo mused, the decision to go on the offensive was probably too late.[83]

Throughout the campaign, Bush attacked Dukakis as an old-fashioned liberal trying to masquerade as a man of the center. In September, the *Atlanta Journal-Constitution* warned that Dukakis's decision not to respond "could cost him the election."[84] Indeed, polls confirmed that the negative attacks—and Dukakis's refusal to counter them—were affecting his candidacy badly. In May, for example, Dukakis registered a 71 percent favorability rating, with only 16 percent of voters having a negative opinion of him; by October, 43 percent of voters held an unfavorable opinion while his favorability dropped to 50 percent.[85] His seventeen-point lead had all but evaporated. By avoiding ideology in the hope of promoting "competence," Dukakis allowed Bush to project a caricatured version of liberalism—one that promoted an anti-family agenda that threatened the moral fabric of America and an intrusive government that endangered the individual liberty of its citizens. In doing so, Republicans were able to use the word liberal strategically as an epithet to foster negative associations of Democratic social and economic policies. Indeed, on the campaign trail, Reagan was one of its chief proponents, deploying this attack line effectively to cement these negative associations: "Their views can only be described by the dreaded 'L' word: liberal, liberal, liberal. That once-proud party of hope and affirmation has become the party of obstruction and negativism."[86] Though it mattered little that this characterization did not mesh with Dukakis's record, by his failure to respond accordingly, this damaging discourse began to take hold.[87]

"I'M A LIBERAL"

Dukakis, acceding to advice to reclaim the party's liberal traditions, eventually dropped his resistance and accepted the label just two weeks before election day. At a campaign stop in California, Dukakis told the crowd: "I'm a liberal in the tradition of FDR and Truman and JFK."[88] Though he had hoped to conduct a campaign devoid of ideology, Dukakis told the *New York Times* that he was unwilling to "let the Republican Party pervert that word [liberal] or give it a meaning that it doesn't have."[89] He still suggested that his version of liberalism was different from the past, a point former Speaker O'Neill also sought to make by arguing that liberals of his generation were now "a thing of the past. . . . Today, you're a progressive. . . . Do I consider Dukakis a liberal of my stripes? Absolutely not. He's a progressive."[90] But like Hart in 1984, this was essentially a form of rhetorical positioning, an effort to package liberalism in a way to attract moderates and independent voters as well. Indeed, the issues at the heart of Dukakis's campaign reflected his liberal credentials. He deployed the Social Security issue, for example, attacking Bush as being "four-square behind [Reagan's] efforts to slash Social Security" and positioning himself as the program's guardian.[91] As noted, Social Security had become a third rail issue and Dukakis sought to benefit from the widespread liberal support the program attracted.

Dukakis also sought to link Bush to Reagan's "abysmal record" on civil rights, pointing to Bush's opposition to the VRA extension in 1982 and his support of Reagan's veto of the CRRA in 1988.[92] Dukakis, his campaign material suggested, would restore the role of the federal government as protector by demonstrating an "unyielding commitment to affirmative action, equal opportunity, and social justice."[93] Dukakis also enlisted Jackson to help rescue his campaign in the final weeks. Jackson worked hard for the campaign, defending Dukakis's liberal values and aligning them with his own: "When Dukakis stands for decent health care for all, for day care, for equal rights for women and minorities, he stands for hope."[94] But Dukakis had damaged his relationship with Jackson's supporters over his vice presidential choice. A Gallup poll found that more than 40 percent of African Americans believed Jackson was mistreated and more than half of those indicated that it made them less enthusiastic about Dukakis.[95] Come election day, although racial minorities still supported Dukakis over Bush, turnout was particularly low. Indeed, over one million more minority voters would go to the polls for Clinton in 1992.[96]

Finally, Dukakis resurrected the specter of Robert Bork in a late effort to reach out to his base, warning that Bush would appoint a "court full of

Borks" if elected.⁹⁷ With the campaign stalling, the Dukakis team hoped to reignite the Bork controversy a year after it had blazed through America. Pointing out that Bork was one of the "few visceral issues we have," an internal memo argued that "if we can convince [anti-Bork forces] that their rights and freedoms are on the line in this election, then we will tap a powerful source of support."⁹⁸ Dukakis sent an appeal letter to those involved in the Block Bork coalition, asking them to join in the effort to Block Bush and protect the "integrity of the Court and Constitution."⁹⁹ The campaign also hired the grassroots coordinator for the LCCR, Mimi Mager, to energize interest groups and reach out to dignitaries from the Bork campaign: "Can we reinvigorate the Bork coalition in some form?" an internal memo asked.¹⁰⁰ To many activists though, the last-minute decision to exploit the Bork issue was too little, too late—"a missed opportunity" according to Nan Aron, a Block Bork veteran.¹⁰¹

In the end, by failing to defend his liberal views until late in the game, Dukakis left himself open to a fusillade of attacks; he later acknowledged that he lost because he chose "not to respond to the Bush attack campaign, [which] in retrospect, was a pretty dumb decision."¹⁰² Indeed, it was only when Dukakis boldly stated that he was a liberal that his campaign started to recover—from that point on, crowds swelled; he reversed his steady decline in the polls; and, as the *New York Times* reported, undecided voters began to break in Dukakis's favor.¹⁰³ But the damage had been done. Come election day, not only was turnout low among some of the more traditional liberal constituencies—racial minorities, labor, the poor—but the voting groups that were becoming increasingly important to the Democratic Party's coalition-building efforts—in particular, women and professionals—slightly broke Bush's way.¹⁰⁴ Still, although Dukakis lost the election, it quickly became apparent that Bush failed to win convincingly.

Despite the fact that Bush was the heir to a popular president at a time of relative peace and prosperity, Dukakis won ten states (and Washington, DC) and lost twelve others by a margin of four percentage points or less. The Democratic ticket did best in the Northeast, upper Midwest, and the Pacific states of California, Oregon, and Washington, providing the basic outline of what would become a winning combination in 1992.¹⁰⁵ In California, the prototypical suburban state that would become an anchor for later Democratic victories, Dukakis lost by only three points and fewer than three hundred thousand votes of nearly ten million cast.¹⁰⁶ Moreover, Bush had no coattails whatsoever. The Democrats gained two seats in the House to cement their dominance (260–175), leaving Republicans with only 40 percent of the chamber—the smallest share ever won by a party winning the presidency.[107] They also gained a seat in the Senate, added another governor's mansion to their roster, and kept their commanding majority in state legislatures—facts that augured well for redrawing the boundaries after the 1990 census. With this, the results cemented a paradox of the decade—Democrats had now lost three successive presidential elections, but they had also improved their position in Congress significantly as the decade wore on.

Still, the results seemed to suggest that the election was a real missed opportunity for liberals, a point some Republican strategists noted as well. Kevin Phillips, a former strategist for President Nixon, argued that the gap between Dukakis's "July vista of victory" and his "November margin of defeat" would "represent the most fumbled opportunity since 1948 when Thomas Dewey ignored emerging issues and booted a fifteen-point poll lead."[108] *Time* magazine posed the rhetorical question on everyone's lips: "If Dukakis was such a competent manager, why was his campaign so poorly managed?"[109] It was an election that was winnable—and it was not won. But the Dukakis defeat was also not, as some scholars have suggested, the last hurrah of liberalism.[110]

Indeed, while Dukakis lost, support for liberalism did not necessarily decline. As the ADA's director, Ann Lewis, pointed out, while liberals were "tempered by some of the realities of the last decade"—particularly on the question of raising taxes to fund large social programs—the waning years of the Reagan administration had witnessed a drift leftward on several issues. Citing evidence of a drop in public support for increased defense spending, heightened skepticism about free-market solutions, and a renewed desire for a more activist domestic policy, Lewis highlighted an emerging thirst for liberalism.[111] Beginning in 1976, *CBS/New York Times* surveyed the electorate's receptiveness to the philosophical bigger/smaller government question. In March 1980, when conservatism was on the rise, voters chose smaller government, 54–32 percent. By 1988 however, polls showed that 44 percent supported a larger role for government while 43 percent preferred a less intrusive role. As the *New York Times* wrote: "Bigger government has not been this popular since November 1976, which is also the last time the Democrats won a presidential election."[112]

Equally, consider the Democratic field in 1988. All the candidates, to varying degrees, pushed the traditional liberal argument that an activist government was needed to tackle national social needs. The ADA was said to be "incredibly pleased" with the field, stating that the DLC had "misread the mood" of the nation.[113] If all these candidates could be broadly classified under the liberal rubric, regardless of some policy differences, then it is undeniable that liberalism dominated national Democratic discourse by the end of the 1980s. Even Gore, who the *New York Post* endorsed as the moderate Democrat, had a voting record and ADA rating that was as liberal as Senator Kennedy's.[114] Dukakis's reluctance to embrace the liberal label certainly evidenced limits in the effort to update it intellectually, but given the nature of political contest in the 1980s, the Democratic Party was a predominately liberal party by the close of the Reagan Era, whether politicians openly accepted this as fact or not. Additionally, not only was Jackson's campaign manager—and longtime Kennedy ally—Ron Brown installed as DNC chair, signaling the continuation of liberal management at the highest echelons of the party, but Gephardt, whose liberal conversion was well documented, was elected House Majority Leader in 1989 to serve as spokesperson and present "an image of what the party stood for."[115]

WHAT NOW?

Evidently, as the sun set on Reagan's presidency, a liberal dawn was yet to come. But it was clear that the seeds of a liberal recovery had been planted in its shadows, and the 1988 elections reflected the myriad ways in which it was beginning to sprout. For example, Jackson's trailblazing campaign amply showcased the increasing power of racial minorities in the Democratic Party. Indeed, although minority groups had largely focused on attaining and retaining access to the franchise in previous decades, the 1980s witnessed several of their leaders seek and achieve positions of significant power in politics—Brown being elected DNC chair is a case in point. Moreover, congressional results continued to highlight the robust nature of liberalism across the country and spotlight the importance of constituencies that would shape its future. As the next chapter details, for example, the gender gap continued to shape the political arena in a multitude of ways; and as the party sought a route back to executive power in 1992, women would eventually be taken seriously as an integral component of electoral success.

Still, at an intellectual level, the picture was more complex. Clearly, the neoliberal approach was taking hold throughout the party, evidenced by the contest over the post–New Deal mantle in the primaries. But the eventual nominee distanced himself from the liberal label and conducted a campaign devoid of ideology. And given the polarizing nature of the 1988 campaign, elected officials increasingly recalibrated their approach to certain issues, such as crime, in its aftermath. Some of the younger liberals, who were already looking for ways to fashion a post–New Deal liberalism for emerging regions outside the Northeast, updated their nomenclature accordingly, utilizing terms such as "progressive" or "New Democrat" in the 1990s. Still, it is important to note that the values at the heart of their approach largely remained the same for many—support for civil rights, women's equality, an activist federal government, and public spending on a host of programs. Moreover, although Dukakis had been unable to pull a liberal electoral coalition together to clinch the presidency, evidence continued to suggest that the party's emerging post–New Deal voting base could elect a Democratic president if the message was relayed correctly.

Finally, polls showed that the electorate was becoming more liberal in several crucial ways as the decade wore on. An *ABC/Washington Post* survey in 1989 found that voters were restive about market-based solutions and supportive of a broader role for government, seeking increased federal spending on, among other things, Medicare (72 percent), Medicaid (61 percent), and Social Security (58 percent); they also had little interest in increased military spending (18 percent). Warren Miller, a political analyst, addressed the paradox of the decade's politics: "The shift toward the Republicans occurred in the face of generally increasing support for liberal policies."[116] As the curtain fell on the Reagan presidency, it was clear that liberalism had not been an ascendant force during his tenure, but it was certainly not in a state of terminal decline either. Instead, it had adapted in several fundamental ways, both intellectually and institutionally, and remained electorally robust, rooted in a newer, emerging coalition of voting constituencies who had provided its strength in campaigns throughout the decade and would provide its power in contests of the future.

7. Emerging from the Shadow
Liberalism Reconstituted for the Post-Reagan Era

With George Bush entering the White House, liberals sensed a "third" Reagan term on the horizon. But it was unlike the dawn of the Reagan Era—the political calculus had changed within the span of eight years. Having developed strategies in Reagan's shadow to protect and advance their cause, liberals were now in a much stronger position than they were at the opening of Reagan's presidency. Indeed, by building upon the foundations established during the intervening years, liberals moved into a more offensive posture and pushed for expansion of opportunity in a range of areas during the Bush presidency, especially through the legislative and judicial branches as abortion, civil rights and other contested identity issues shaped the domestic environment and drove the emerging culture war.

Once again, for example, women played a key role in sustaining liberalism, and their migration to the Democratic Party accelerated as the decade came to a close. Across the Reagan Era, liberal women's groups had mobilized women voters and made the absence of women in politics of central importance, increasing their financial and political reach considerably. Thus, when a Supreme Court decision early in Bush's presidency threatened their interests, they were now in a much stronger position to respond, utilizing the relationships developed with the Democratic Party and energizing voters to affect election outcomes across the country in the 1990 midterms and beyond.

Congress too would continue to play a central role in liberalism's story, providing a bulwark against conservative retrenchment, broadening the scope of equality through significant pieces of legislation, and increasing the power of the federal government to ameliorate social and economic ills. At the start of the 1990s, for example, a landmark civil rights law that expanded and strengthened antidiscrimination legislation—the Civil Rights Act (CRA) of 1991—was passed following a coordinated campaign by liberal officeholders and coalition groups, with the LCCR leading the charge once more (this was despite the fact that Bush had vetoed an earlier version of the bill).[1] At its height, civil rights leaders were describing the prolonged battle as a "struggle for the soul of America."[2]

Finally, this chapter explores how strategies directly tied to these elements would prove central to the rise of Bill Clinton, whose candidacy is often heralded for offering a Third Way back to power that moved away from liberalism, but whose path to victory was far more multifaceted. Indeed, central to Clinton's ascension would be elements of the three strands discussed throughout—the intellectual reframing of liberalism in Reagan's shadow, the organizational power of liberal grassroots groups, and the emerging coalition of liberal-leaning constituencies who would fuel Democratic victories, both in 1992 and far beyond.

"IGNORE THE GENDER GAP AT YOUR PERIL"

While many observers focused on Michael Dukakis's ability to throw a seventeen-point lead away during the 1988 presidential elections, a less well-known, though far larger figure was also squandered. At one stage, according to a June 1988 poll, Dukakis enjoyed a seismic twenty-eight-percentage-point gender "gulf" over his opponent; he would eventually lose the women's vote to Bush by 2 percent, 51–49.[3] Evidently, the Democratic Party still had not grasped the potency of the gender gap, even though its power had just been demonstrated by the 1986 midterms, a fact that was not lost on liberal women's groups.

Indeed, combined with their Feminization of Power campaign, launched to convince more women to run for elected office, NOW used demographic indicators from the 1986 midterms to argue that it would be folly for the Democrats to try to "out-Reagan Reagan" in 1988.[4] In other words, despite the efforts of the DLC to push the party rightward, liberals had fueled the Democratic gains that year and would fuel them again in 1988 unless the party became a pale imitation of the Republicans. According to NOW, by moving rightward the party would alienate the very voter base that "soundly defeated the Reagan dream machine in 1986" and handed back the keys to Congress. Speaking before the Democratic Platform Committee, NOW's new president, Molly Yard, suggested that the lesson for 1988 was clear: "Ignore the gender gap at your peril. Ignore the fact that the gender gap is an 'issue' vote at your peril. Abandon, diffuse or obfuscate the issues at your peril."[5] The National Women's Political Caucus, a liberal group working closely with Democratic officials, organized a conference around the gender gap to "underscore the obvious": women held the power to determine the outcome in 1988 as ten million more women than men were projected to vote.[6]

Nonetheless, it was Bush who set out to build a bridge across the gap by implementing a "kinder, gentler" vision for America to repeat what Reagan had achieved in 1984.[7] By seizing the symbols of family and opportunity, and developing the themes of economic empowerment and security, Bush used the Republican convention to showcase his appeal. As pollster Linda DiVall noted, this strategy proved effective as "the numbers that moved the most after the speech were with women."[8] Moreover, while Bush's policies on childcare, education, and parental leave were well received, his famous "revolving door" advertisement was said to have had a particular impact on women voters, according to Dukakis's campaign manager, with polls showing that the gap had been whittled down to a mere percentage point by October 1988.[9] As NOW's Eleanor Smeal mused, by distancing themselves from the liberal label and assuming their base would remain robust, the Democratic Party's hot pursuit of southern Democrats and Reagan Democrats—both terms frequently used as euphemisms for white males—effectively lost Dukakis his "colossal" gender advantage.[10]

Despite a late focus on what the Democrats perceived as "women's issues"—the ERA, childcare, sexual discrimination—and an endorsement by *Ms. Magazine* following his embrace of liberalism, Dukakis was unable to reopen the gap.[11] In repeating the mistakes of 1984, Dukakis wrongfully assumed that he had "pocketed the gender gap" according to the *Washington Post*.[12] But the phenomenon still persisted at the congressional level in 1988, and women's groups could justifiably point to these trends as evidence that, if cultivated properly, the gap could help elect a Democrat in 1992.[13] Having lost huge leads in 1984 and 1988, trial and error naturally caused the Democratic Party to rethink its presidential strategy. The gender gap would eventually become a foundational element on which the party constructed victory in the ensuing decades. But before that could happen, the Supreme Court agreed to consider *Webster v. Reproductive Health Services* in April 1989—a case to determine the constitutionality of state legislation to restrict abortion practices, including the use of state funds or facilities to perform them, and codify the principle that life starts at conception into law. The resulting battle would galvanize a new generation of women into liberal politics, fueling the gender gap for decades thereafter.

In 1973, the Supreme Court's controversial reasoning in *Roe v. Wade* relied on an implicit right to privacy rather than an explicit constitutional mandate. While this enshrined abortion into law, its ambiguous reasoning all but guaranteed conflict between pro-choice and pro-life factions. By 1980, Reagan's election marked the point at which the parties took increasingly polarized stands on the issue of abortion. And as the decade progressed, the issue became one of the most divisive matters in Reagan's America, particularly after the Supreme Court strongly reaffirmed *Roe* in the 1983 case *City of Akron v. Akron Center for Reproductive Health,* by invalidating the provisions of an ordinance enacted by the Akron City Council to regulate the performance of abortions.

Afterward, the anti-abortion movement became more vocal—and in some cases, more violent—as a result. It became common for some pro-life groups to picket, vandalize, and destroy property at abortion clinics.[14] A coalition of pro-choice groups worked to "fight, organize, and mobilize women and the pro-choice majority against this all-out assault."[15] Describing pro-life tactics as a "campaign of emotional manipulation, vicious harassment, and outright terrorism," NOW launched a Campaign to Save Women's Lives in 1985 and led the first March for Women's Lives in 1986, which drew over 150,000 people.[16] Women's groups also challenged Reagan on his "half-hearted response" to anti-abortion terrorism and demanded that he use the presidency as a pulpit to condemn it.[17] However, although Reagan spent little political capital on the issue, the wider pro-life movement enjoyed rhetorical support from him, illustrated in 1980 and 1984 when he pledged to outlaw *Roe*.

Fast-forward to 1989, and after years of lip service, pro-lifers finally had their day in court. But liberal forces responded by mobilizing over six hundred thousand protesters to march on Washington, DC.[18] According to the National Abortion Rights Action League (NARAL), *Webster* awakened the "sleeping giant" of pro-choice activism.[19] Between April and July 1989, for example, NOW's membership increased by forty thousand, with the strongest surge coming from younger women.[20] For NARAL, the numbers were even more stark; membership almost doubled from two hundred thousand to nearly four hundred thousand between 1989 and 1990.[21] Beyond bolstering its army, NARAL also adapted its political strategy by increasingly endorsing Democratic men supportive of abortion rights over pro-choice Republican women in a clear partisan effort to influence the dynamics of Congress, especially with Supreme Court nominations in mind. During the 1990 Illinois Senate race for example, NARAL endorsed pro-choice Democrat Paul Simon over pro-choice Republican Lynn Martin, arguing that "Simon's reelection would put us one important step closer to a Senate majority that places principles above party loyalty."[22] Accordingly, an internal White House memo noted that such an action demonstrates "how central a political issue the next Supreme Court nomination will be, because of its possible effect on *Roe v Wade*, and therefore a useful reminder of the need to be prepared for the fight."[23]

In the end, while the court eventually upheld parts of the Missouri statute in a 5 to 4 vote, thus empowering conservatives to chip away at existing abortion laws in states across the country, the result, paradoxically, became an organizing windfall for liberal groups.[24] Not only did NOW organize rallies across the country, challenging politicians with "your help or your job," but *Webster* galvanized thousands to join the liberal movement and caused the first substantial shift in public opinion on the issue for two decades.[25] From 1972 to 1988, for example, views on abortion hardly budged according to polling data from Gallup.[26] After *Webster*, a significant number of those who had supported abortion only under limited conditions started to liberalize their opinions. Between 1988 and 1992, the percentage agreeing that abortion was a matter of personal choice increased from 36 to 47 percent.[27]

This shift had an immediate electoral impact, evidenced in the Virginia governor race just four months after *Webster*. Democrat Douglas Wilder placed abortion at the center of his campaign, using television advertisements and speeches to attack his pro-life opponent, Marshall Coleman.[28] Wilder was bolstered by NARAL, who produced their own advertisement featuring a Virginia doctor recalling the days of back-alley abortions and pointing ominously to their return under Coleman.[29] According to exit polls by *CBS/New York Times*, abortion was the single most important issue to Virginia voters on election day; pro-choice advocates also helped the Democrats in the New Jersey governor race and New York City mayoral contest.[30] Frank Greer, a Wilder advisor, said there was a "sea change" among young voters after *Webster*, allowing Wilder to overcome a fifteen-point deficit and surge ahead by eight points.[31] With the political winds shifting on the issue, the House of Representatives also approved Medicaid funding for abortions in extreme cases for the first time in the 1980s.

Moreover, according to exit polls taken during the 1990 midterms, it was only because of the gender gap—intensified by *Webster*—that the Democrats were able to retain control of Congress. In contests for the Senate, men voted Republican 53 to 45 percent, whereas women swung in exactly the opposite direction; in the House, men split their votes evenly, while women voted Democrat 54 to 46 percent. Due to demographics, in both cases women's votes decided the outcome.[32] As with the 1986 midterms, these results did little to confirm the argument that the Democrats had to be more like the Republicans to win elections. Finally, as political scientist Martin Wattenberg has highlighted, the *Webster* decision also had an impact on the 1992 presidential election. In 1988, Dukakis's support for abortion rights had a detrimental effect on his campaign, with voters more likely to oppose him due to it, whereas in 1992 Clinton actually attracted support, rather than lost it, because of his pro-choice stance.[33] By throwing the controversial issue back into the political arena, *Webster* reshaped the abortion debate and had a clear impact on subsequent elections.

By the close of the decade, and in large part thanks to liberal groups, the gender gap and the battle over *Webster* reflected the fact that women had significantly increased their legitimacy in politics. By 1992, both houses of Congress featured more than double the number of women legislators that they held in 1980.[34] California, the largest electoral state, saw the emergence of a trio of liberal Democratic women—Dianne Feinstein, Barbara Boxer, and Nancy Pelosi—who have had a significant impact on national politics since; Pelosi, for example, served as the first woman Speaker of the House from 2007 to 2011.[35] Furthermore, where the Democrats and Republicans had been in close parity among women legislators in 1980 (in total, there were eleven Democratic women and twelve Republican women in Congress after the 1980 elections), the increased presence of women in politics was the direct result of developments within the Democratic Party traced throughout this book. By 1992, for example, three-quarters of congresswomen and five out of the seven women senators were Democrats (in total, there were forty Democratic women and fourteen Republican women in Congress after the 1992 elections).[36] Throughout the Reagan Era, women moved increasingly under the Democratic banner, and the party eventually learned how to better exploit this advantage after some testing errors. Certainly not a monolithic voting bloc, women still became more liberal and more Democratic in Reagan's America, emerging as a central component of the party's post–New Deal base.

CIVIL RIGHTS AFTER REAGAN

The 1990 midterms had seemingly cemented a positive year for liberals. Not only did the Democratic Party retain strong control of Congress—in large part thanks to the gender gap—but they picked up a Senate seat and the governorships of two Sun Belt states, facts that augured well for succeeding battles over reapportionment.[37] Moreover, the 1990 amendment of the Clean Air Act (enacted in 1963) significantly strengthened environmental protections, introducing sweeping new regulations in a host of areas, including acid rain and air pollution, and expanding the role of the federal government considerably. To be sure, this moment had been years in the making. Environmental organizations had boomed in size as a result of conservative efforts to dismantle environmental protections throughout the 1980s, and they proved critical in the drive to pass the Clean Air amendment. The Sierra Club grew its membership from 182,000 in 1980 to 550,000 by the 1990s, for example, while the Wilderness Society had grown from 50,000 to 330,000 members across the same period.[38]

Likewise, 1990 also saw the passage of one of the most significant civil rights measures ever enacted—the Americans with Disabilities Act. This new law implemented a wide array of federal protections and mandates, expanding civil rights to individuals with disabilities (an estimated forty-three million Americans) in line with those provided through earlier acts on the basis of race, color, sex, national origin, age, and religion. Beyond extending protections, the act also tackled the broad structural (and artificial) barriers that those with disabilities experienced across society, from transportation access and employment opportunities to urban planning and architectural design. According to Senator Tom Harkin (D-IA), the act represented "the emancipation proclamation for persons with disabilities."[39] The culmination of decades of advocacy, passage of such a comprehensive and expansive piece of social legislation in a conservative era represented a seismic achievement for the liberal community. Indeed, campaigners drew a direct line to earlier conflicts in the Reagan Era to situate their success within the broader context, particularly the Civil Rights Restoration Act (CRRA) where discrimination issues sat at the core.[40] But as had been the case through much of the 1980s, moments of progress in the political realm were typically juxtaposed with those of retrenchment, and 1990 was no different. In the same year that a historic expansion in the parameters of equality was realized, a Republican president also vetoed a civil rights bill for only the second time in more than a century.

The genesis of this moment can be traced back to several Supreme Court decisions restricting the reach and remedies of federal antidiscrimination laws from the preceding year. One example was the *Wards Cove Packing Co. v. Atonio* decision in June 1989, which made it harder for workers to prove indirect job discrimination by shifting the burden of proof away from the employer; instead of employers having to show that there was a legitimate business necessity for challenged practices, workers were required to prove that there was not.[41] Such practices included physical tests and academic requirements, which were ostensibly neutral but often had an adverse impact on women or racial minorities.[42] Another, *Patterson v. McLean Credit Union*, limited the scope of Section 1981, which prohibited racial harassment and bias in the workplace.[43] Collectively, these decisions represented a marked shift in the parameters of equal employment law, limiting the effectiveness of statutes established over the preceding decades and narrowing job discrimination remedies. According to Ralph Neas, the Supreme Court "did more damage to civil rights laws in four weeks in June than had occurred in the previous four decades."[44] To the liberal community, the impact of a "Reaganized" judicial system was now on full display.[45]

Thus, a coalition quickly formed to nullify the decisions by introducing the CRA of 1990. But as with prior campaigns, this one presented an opportunity not only to safeguard protections but to expand them as well. Indeed, as the 1980s had demonstrated, civil rights had been an area where the Democratic Congress found Republican administrations vulnerable; and the liberal community, led by the LCCR once again, sought to mirror the successful approach employed in earlier battles, namely the VRA and CRRA campaigns. Here, the LCCR coordinated early to set the tone, outlining the thrust of their message in a letter to Congress:

> Last year, America's progress toward the goal of equal opportunity for all was threatened by a Supreme Court out of step with our society and our times. As a result of a series of ruling decided by razor-thin majorities, millions of Americans can no longer count on the protections . . . dating back to the 1960s—and the 1860s. In order to repair the damage to our civil rights laws, leaders from both Houses of Congress will introduce the [CRA]. This key legislation will restore and strengthen protections of the civil rights of every American, and send a clear message that Congress—and the American people—do not intend to reverse our national commitment to equal justice for all.[46]

On a cold winter's morning during the first weekend of February, leaders of the liberal coalition assembled on Capitol Hill to officially launch the CRA campaign. Coretta Scott King, the widow of slain civil rights leader Martin Luther King Jr., was the special guest, offering a powerful reminder of her husband's unfinished agenda.[47] PFAW released a report to coincide with the launch, titled "Justice Denied," which detailed the severe consequences of the court's actions and urged swift passage of the bill to "rebuild, brick by brick, the protections all Americans deserve."[48] The Women's Legal Defense Fund added that the CRA was one of the most important pieces of legislation for women since 1964, arguing that the court's rulings "demonstrated a view of working women that is almost as unrealistic as the plot to 'Back to the Future.' But this is not a movie, and nobody's laughing.... The [CRA is] a vehicle that will take us back to the real future."⁴⁹ With the stakes so high, the LCCR designated the CRA "the number one legislative priority of the 185 national organizations" in its orbit, while House majority whip, William H. Gray III (D-PA), declared it "the top priority on the Democratic Party agenda."⁵⁰

The CRA also proved to be the first real test for Bush on civil rights, but within weeks the coalition was criticizing his response as "seriously inadequate," noting that his administration was, in several respects, less supportive than Reagan's.⁵¹ Although the bill was, on its face, about reestablishing prior protections, a furor erupted over affirmative action, with emotions inflamed by the White House labeling the CRA a "quota bill." The LCCR had anticipated this quota angle, detailing in an early letter to Hill staff: "We already know that the Far Right will attempt, as they always do on civil rights measures, to turn this bill into a debate over quotas.... This bill will have nothing to do with quotas or any other affirmative action remedy."⁵² Still, it was a potent attack, demonstrating that the campaign would be an uphill battle from the start.

To counter, the LCCR developed grassroots and lobbying strategies to drive the campaign and diffuse conservative attacks, holding weekly task force meetings with key leaders in DC and distributing materials to state and local affiliates to "activate grassroots networks" across the country.⁵³ As in the past, direct mail initiatives and media strategies proved the most immediate, with lobbying targets updated weekly to focus attention on certain members of Congress.⁵⁴ The media task force also worked closely with committee witnesses to expand the reach of their testimony, strategically placing op-eds in national and local media markets while organizing television and radio interviews to build broad support for the CRA.⁵⁵ William T. Coleman Jr. took to the *Washington Post* to rebut the quota attack, for example, while Jesse Jackson blasted the Bush White House across media outlets for its "continued use of emotionally charged 'code words' such as racial 'quotas' to distort and confuse issues that involved equal opportunity in hiring and promoting women and minorities."⁵⁶ According to *US News & World Report*, however, with conservatives "still smarting" over the CRRA battle from years earlier, they had also begun organizing "unusually early ... determined not to be stampeded ... [by] the liberal onslaught" this time around.⁵⁷ Thus, the stage was set for a titanic battle.

With the campaign being waged at the grassroots level and across the media space, Senator Kennedy was the coalition's field marshal in Congress again, skillfully shepherding the CRA through committee hearings and markups. But he would face a familiar foe as the bill advanced—Senator

Orrin Hatch. Kennedy and Hatch had led their respective sides in the CRRA fight, and with familiar faces came familiar passions. Hatch charged that the CRA would "open the door to quotas and a spoils system," while Kennedy countered "Quotas, schmotas . . . quotas are not the issue; job discrimination is the issue."[58] Procedural maneuvers by Kennedy to limit amendments further frustrated Hatch and his colleagues, who blasted the Democrats for treating the Republicans like "a bunch of bums."[59] In the end, the Senate voted 65 for (all 55 Democrats voted in favor, as did 10 Republicans), while 34 Republicans voted against it.[60]

Despite the rancor, bipartisan support seemed to suggest that the bill was now on a path to victory, but the White House signaled its position clearly in the wake of Senate passage to burst that balloon. According to White House spokesman Marlin Fitzwater, "The President wants a bill that ends discrimination, not one that starts a quota system."[61] This was despite the fact that the bill now contained explicit wording deeming the use of quotas an unlawful employment practice.[62] Indeed, inclusion of this provision, considered superfluous by many, was supposed to act as a fig leaf, but with the White House maintaining its opposition, the coalition concluded that the quota issue was simply a red herring. Across the halls of Congress, the debate also proved acrimonious and deeply partisan, with Democrats accusing Republicans of being against equal opportunity while Republicans labeled the bill a "fraud" and the Democratic approach a "charade."[63] Still, the House passed the bill 272–154 (with 32 Republicans joining 240 Democrats in the affirmative; 142 Republicans and 12 Democrats against).[64]

Despite passage in both chambers, the threat of a presidential veto loomed large as the threshold had not been met to assure an override, so the campaign transitioned to focus grassroots operations on building a sustained majority. Neas wrote to all members: "We cannot rest. . . . The Bush administration is lobbying hard against the bill. . . . Please activate your grassroots networks. . . . We must both communicate how important the [CRA] is and convey a sense of urgency." Enclosed in this rally call were "targets lists and messages," "informational materials," and strategies to "flood the White House with phone calls, letters, mailgrams etc."[65] The rhetoric ramped up as well, with the LCCR declaring that "just as the Bob Jones fiasco defined the Reagan presidency on civil rights, so would a veto of the [CRA] define the Bush presidency."[66]

An impasse seemed broken when the principal opponent of the bill, Senator Hatch, became its advocate at the House–Senate conference stage after securing compromises designed to make it more palatable to the

White House.⁶⁷ Moreover, key personnel associated with the administration started pleading with the president to support the bill, foremost among them Arthur Fletcher, Bush's appointed chairman of the US Commission on Civil Rights. Fletcher was considered by many to be "the father of affirmative action" for his work on the Philadelphia Plan in 1969, which established the foundations of affirmative action. In a letter to Bush, Fletcher compared the president's choice to that of President Lincoln ahead of the Emancipation Proclamation, adding, "Today, as a result of over 125 years of civil rights struggles, accomplishments, and setbacks, our country is disenfranchised once again. You ... can make it whole again by signing the [CRA] ... in the Abraham Lincoln bedroom."⁶⁸ Still, despite the brokered language and emotive pleas, Bush vetoed the bill, maintaining that it would lead to quotas.⁶⁹ To the LCCR, this demonstrated that "George Bush is a Ronald Reagan in sheep's clothing. ... He capitulated to the right wing [and] deprive[d] millions of American the protections of strong and effective civil rights laws."⁷⁰ With the 1990 midterm elections approaching, California congressman Don Edwards concluded, "We'll name that for what it is. Politics and racism. It's to get votes."⁷¹ And despite coordinated efforts to override the veto, the Senate failed to do so by a single vote. The year would end with a dark cloud hanging over the civil rights community.

After the defeat, the coalition regrouped and revived their fight in early 1991 with a new political strategy: a sales pitch to women. The administration's quota angle had proved pivotal, so the coalition decided they would no longer make equal opportunities for racial minorities the central thrust of their campaign. As *CQ Press* noted, "By promoting the bill as a help to working women, advocates hoped to build a broader base of support and defuse charges that the job protections would lead to quotas."⁷² The House Education and Labor Committee proposed several changes to the original bill to reflect this, including adding a Glass Ceiling commission to tackle artificial barriers in the workplace for women and racial minorities; setting up a pay equity study to examine wage disparities; and, perhaps most symbolically, changing the bill's title to "The Civil Rights and Women's Equity in Employment Act of 1991."⁷³

This shift was also reflected in the upper echelons of the coalition itself. In January 1991, the LCCR Women's Caucus was formed, with a twofold purpose: "to provide a formal mechanism for input into LCCR decision-making on women's rights issues; and to help us be more effective in mobilizing our constituents and members in supports of the broader LCCR agenda."⁷⁴ The new iteration of the LCCR's grassroots strategy packet also included significantly more materials focused on women, particularly the intersectional layers of discrimination that working women experience—gender, race, national origin and/or disability.[75] As PFAW acknowledged, rather than getting drawn into the quota debate again, "a real important lesson for all of us [is] to communicate what the legislation does."[76]

Alongside this updated strategy, the LCCR sought to build a bridge to the business community by working directly with the Business Roundtable, a consortium of chief executives from two hundred large companies. However, by May the coalition was complaining that the White House had "succeeded in scuttling the discussions ... [by] exert[ing] tremendous pressure on the leadership of the Roundtable." In a memo to the national press, the LCCR wrote: "The sabotaging of these discussions should make it obvious to everyone that the White House does not want a meaningful civil rights measure enacted into law. Rather, it wants a political issue that will serve the same purpose that Willie Horton served in 1988."[77] Indeed, in a joint statement a few weeks later, prominent civil rights leaders united to condemn Bush's continued use of racial politics and symbols to structure the debate: "The narcotic of racial polarization is once again being peddled in the halls of Congress and the White House. The time has come to just say 'no.'"[78] Beyond the rhetorical subverting of Nancy Reagan's famous "just say no" campaign, these civil rights leaders were warning that the creation and manipulation of racial animosity for political purposes was now dominating political discourse. Crucially, this dynamic would sit at the center of another firestorm brewing in the background.

In June, Judge Thurgood Marshall, the first Black Supreme Court justice, unexpectedly announced his retirement, citing advanced age and ill health. A champion of civil rights and a doyen of liberalism, Marshall's retirement sent a shock wave through the liberal community. Liberal Senator Alan Cranston (D-CA) immediately warned that if Bush "picks another right-wing ideologue like Robert Bork, he can expect another Bork-like fight."[79] Like Reagan, Bush did not heed these warnings and nominated Judge Clarence Thomas, a conservative Black lawyer who he had appointed a year earlier to fill the seat vacated by Bork on the DC federal appeals court.[80] Following the announcement, the House Congressional Black Caucus, which noted its "special responsibility" to "speak out" with no Black representation in the Senate at the time, captured the overall mood of those on the left, condemning Thomas's "dismal civil rights record and his absolute disdain and disrespect of Congress and its laws."[81] Parallels to the Bork fight were clear. Certainly, in learning the lessons of

1987, the Bush White House and Republicans in the Senate approached the Thomas nomination as an all-out political campaign, while for liberal groups opposing Thomas, the campaign to defeat Bork largely served as a model for the Thomas battle. At NOW's 1991 conference, one activist even said of Thomas, "We're going to 'bork' him."[82] But the battle differed in two distinct, and decisive, ways.

First, while Bork's record and testimony confirmed the caricature that liberal groups had been promoting, Thomas essentially established a jurisprudential vacuum during his confirmation process. As the *New York Times* reported, following five days of "full and often contentious questioning, Judge Thomas's views remain elusive.... Several Democrats ... complained that Judge Thomas was being purposely vague and even disavowing his extensive record to win confirmation."[83] Liberal stalwart Joseph Rauh argued that in over half a century as a Supreme Court observer, he had never seen such a case of "weaving and bobbing," describing Thomas's testimony as "inconsistent, incredible, and inoperative."[84] As with the Bork battle, the liberal coalition pounced on this, distributing materials labeled "Clarence Thomas: Then and Now" to congressional offices and media outlets in the hopes of spotlighting his "extremely significant contradictions."[85] Abortion activists were particularly incensed by Thomas's responses, especially his claims "not to have read" a 1986 White House report that he signed onto calling for the overturning of *Roe*. To NARAL, the conclusion was "inescapable": if confirmed he "will take the right to choose away from women in America."[86] Yet by making it more difficult to decipher his jurisprudence, Thomas muddied the confirmation process and offered less political cover for moderate senators to oppose him than Bork had.

Second, by framing his nomination through a racial prism, the White House strategically deployed racial symbols to advance the confirmation and avoid questions about Thomas's lack of experience or judicial philosophy. For example, according to the LCCR, the White House ran "an extraordinary public relations campaign" to avoid this scrutiny by focusing on his relatively humble beginnings in segregated Georgia.[87] In opposing Thomas, the NAACP said that it "repudiated the patronizing assumption that black Americans—and the Senate—should apply some kind of color test to Thomas's life, setting a different, weaker standard for a nominee whose skin is black."[88] Rather than "separate and unequal treatment," the coalition sought to focus the Senate on the "reality of a man whose public service has been devoted to placing obstacles in the path of equal justice."[89] Adding fuel to the fire was the fact that the American Bar Association rated Thomas the least qualified of all judges nominated to the court since 1955, including the three nominees previously rejected—Haynsworth, Carswell, and Bork.[90] Here, the LCCR blasted Bush for his "ironic" use of quotas: "Bush professes to be a staunch opponent of quotas . . . vowing to veto the [CRA] . . . on the unfounded basis that it would lead to hiring quotas. Yet by nominating an unqualified individual to the Supreme Court, Bush is engaging in the very quota practices he claims to abhor."[91]

But it was in the closing stages of the nomination that this racial dynamic proved particularly significant. After allegations emerged of sexual harassment against Thomas by his former colleague, Anita Hill, Thomas angrily accused the committee of conducting a "high-tech lynching for uppity blacks who in any way deign to think for themselves."[92] Sitting in front of an all-white, all-male judiciary panel, Thomas purposely shifted the narrative to the racist stereotyping of Black men, rather than the sexual harassment of a Black woman, and deployed the potent symbol of lynching to flip the focus onto the tactics of the committee members instead.[93] With his vehement denial of Hill's charges, the hearings ended inconclusively and went forward to a full Senate vote. With solid support from Republicans and scattered votes from Democrats, mostly from southern states with large African American populations, Thomas won a bitterly close confirmation 52–48.

Yet, like the *Webster* case, the fallout from the confirmation battle would have far-reaching consequences. As the *Wall Street Journal* wrote, Hill became a "catalyst" for the candidacies of women across the country, whose chances were bolstered by the work of financing operations that had emerged in the Reagan Era. In just one year, for example, EMILY's List increased its membership from thirty-five hundred at the time of the hearings to twenty-two thousand and raised more than $4.5 million for candidates in 1992, up from $1.5 million in 1990. In the Illinois Senate race, Carol Moseley Braun unseated the incumbent Democrat, who voted for Thomas, and raised more money than any other Senate candidate that year.[94] As Representative Patsy Mink (D-HI) noted at the time, women were "tired of taking a backseat. . . . The only way to gain equality is to gain power."[95] To be sure, the foundations for this rise in women's participation had been built in the decades prior, but the Thomas hearings, alongside the *Webster* case, demonstrated acutely why the work of liberal organizations such as NOW seemed so necessary.

In a more immediate sense, the Thomas nomination would also have an impact on the CRA outcome. According to *CQ Press*, in the wake of the Thomas hearings, the White House withdrew its CRA opposition to avert a brewing confrontation that threatened to divide Senate Republicans and intensify tensions over race and gender issues: "While both sides claimed victory, the administration appeared to have made the most concessions as it tried to avoid a veto fight it was not certain to win."[96] The strong showing of Ku Klux Klansman David Duke in the Republican primary for the Louisiana governor's race likely contributed too. Quotas had been a potent issue for Duke, and Bush clearly did not want to be caught reading from the same script. As Texas congressman Craig Washington mused during a House floor debate, for example: "Where did the quotas go? They swam upstream, as red herrings often do. . . . David Duke took the sheet off that [quota] argument."[97]

Consequently, according to William Coleman and Vernon Jordan in a *Washington Post* op-ed, the coalition "won virtually everything that civil rights advocates first sought two years ago."[98] On the burden of proof question, for example, the new law returned the burden to employers, reinstating the requirement from *Griggs v. Duke Power Co.*, the 1971 ruling that hiring and promotion requirements be related to job performance. Among other achievements, the act established the Glass Ceiling Commission, it made the 1964 Civil Rights Act more inclusive, and it allowed for more expansive approaches to damages relating to discriminatory employment practices. According to James Simon, "most of the conservatives' narrow victories in civil rights cases were blunted by the [CRA]."[99] To be sure, by reversing all or part of more court rulings than any other piece of legislation in recent history at the time, the CRA represented a significant accomplishment for the liberal community. But the battle also reflected the wider paradox of progress in the Reagan Era—liberals were often forced to operate on the defensive, protecting past achievements while advancing their agenda only through incremental change. Indeed, liberal stalwart John Lewis, who had been on the frontlines of the civil rights movement since the 1960s, summarized the CRA pithily: "It is not perfect. It is not a panacea. But it is a step in the right direction."[100]

Issues of identity were often at the heart of conflicts in the Reagan years; and, as battles during the Bush presidency confirmed, they were now a bedrock of political discourse in America. But with a presidential election quickly emerging on the horizon, liberals started wondering aloud whether they could actually end the Reagan Era once and for all. Here, the LCCR sought to focus attention on Bush's "terrible" record with race and gender issues, arguing: "History will remember George Bush for playing racial politics with Willie Horton, the Clarence Thomas nomination, and the [CRA] of 1990/1991."[101] Alongside a host of issues, the 1992 elections would be fought on this terrain, but not in the way that Bush might have hoped. As Elizabeth Drew argued afterward, for example, "One of the smartest things the Democrats did was to refight—and win—the battle of 1988: to say enough times that the Bush campaign would be dirty, and to remind people of the Willie Horton issue enough that the Bush campaign was at least somewhat inhibited."[102] Indeed, liberals went on the offensive from the outset, accusing Republicans of trying to mimic the tactics of 1988 through the "Hortonization" of several issues, from homosexuality to abortion.[103] The CRA battle had clearly demonstrated the prism through which Bush sought to frame the 1992 election, but it was the Democrats who would shape its parameters instead.

THE CURIOUS CASE OF CLINTON

Reaching nearly 90 percent following his successful adventures in the Persian Gulf, Bush's popularity ratings—the highest since presidential opinion polling began in the 1940s—narrowed the Democratic field in the run up to the 1992 election.[104] Capturing the mood at the time, prime time's *Saturday Night Live* ran a skit titled "Campaign '92: The Race to Avoid Being the Guy Who Loses to Bush." Those who did decide to venture in were immediately written off as "the Democratic B-team—the end-of-the-bench substitutes who get to play only when the game is presumed to be hopelessly lost."[105] However, the seeds of Republican disintegration were already germinating by this point.

Alongside the damage wrought by the Thomas hearings, a deep recession followed the Gulf War to discredit supply-side economics, which Bush had already discarded by breaking his ironclad 1988 campaign promise, "Read my lips, no new taxes."[106] Patrick Buchanan's primary challenge from the right disclosed profound internal schisms over social policy and produced the damaging view that the Republican Party was divided and disorganized. Indeed, ideological purity tests had increasingly been imposed on Republican leaders by the party's more conservative members, and Bush had struggled throughout his presidency to pass several of them. Newt Gingrich, a conservative leader in the House, storming out of the White House over the 1990 budget compromise deal exemplified this.[107]

A darling of the New Right, Gingrich had become the cynosure of Washington after leading the charge to oust the Democratic Speaker of the House, Jim Wright (TX), one year earlier.[108] To be sure, unlike his predecessor Tip O'Neill, Wright was no "Man of the House." An enigma to most of his Democratic colleagues, Wright had failed to establish the type of kinship necessary to keep the wolves away and was widely regarded among his peers as "cold, tightly wound, [and] short-tempered."[109] But it was his heavy-handed procedural maneuvering that infuriated the opposition most, politicizing even the more moderate Republicans. Congressman Bill Gradison (R-OH), who had been the sole Republican to help the Democrats pass a budget in 1987, reportedly told the press: "It takes a lot to politicize me. Wright's done it. I'm partisan as hell now."[110] Smelling blood, and understanding more than most that the modern age of media politics was as much about perception as substance, Gingrich launched an ethics crusade against Wright, using House rules as a partisan bludgeon to drive a coordinated campaign against "the most corrupt Speaker" in history, even though there was little evidence to substantiate this.[111] With Washington engulfed in a media frenzy, allegations about potentially shady financial dealings in Wright's past metastasized into a full-blown political scandal.

As the ethics morass threatened to envelop him, Wright opted to resign before the process could run its course, hoping his departure would heal the partisan rancor.[112] Instead, the episode inspired a new confidence in Gingrich's style of tactical warfare and laid the foundations for his storming of the House in 1994, when the Republicans secured unified control of Congress for the first time since 1952.[113] Indeed, by tarring the Democrats as corrupt, Wright's defeat was part of a larger campaign by Gingrich to weaken voter faith in government and build popular support for a conservative program of retrenchment, exemplified by his Contract with America agenda. Still, in a more immediate sense, though it did not have a significant electoral impact as the Democrats comfortably retained the House in the 1990 midterms, Gingrich's campaign catapulted him atop the conservative movement as its national leader. This made his clashes with Bush all the more damaging as the firebrand helped fuel "a tidal wave of anger" from the right to undermine the president's credibility.[114]

Pouring more gasoline on the fire, Buchanan's blistering "culture wars" speech at the 1992 convention showcased how little progress conservatives had actually made on their core issues since 1980.[115] As historian Marcus Witcher has demonstrated, for "revolutionaries on the frontlines of the conservative movement," the Reagan Era had clearly not ushered in the types of radical policies that they desired.[116] Following a bitter factional primary fight, Bush ran a lackluster campaign that failed to convert his successes abroad into a convincing argument to reelect him at home.

Furthermore, unbeknownst to the Republicans at the time, the

Democrats had an ace in the hole. Bill Clinton, a charismatic young southerner who earned a reputation as a serious thinker on domestic and economic issues, had already come far in politics.[117] By 1992, he had been governor of Arkansas for twelve years and was widely hailed for improving the state's education, roads, and health care, despite the largely hostile conservative legislature he had to contend with.[118] This political education in a culturally conservative state taught Clinton valuable coalition-building skills; he learned how to attract diverse racial coalitions to secure (and resecure) the governor's mansion through imaginative combinations of issue stances. As he sought to pivot to a national campaign, Clinton found an initial home in the DLC, serving as its chairman from 1990 to 1991. According to Kenneth Baer, the DLC's director, Al From, used the organization's fundraising prowess as a blandishment to attract Clinton to the role.[119] In addition to financial support, Clinton was able to use the DLC as a springboard, with his tours to found DLC chapters in various states becoming the basis for his national support network in the presidential campaign.[120] But to label Clinton a devout DLC disciple is to miss the wider point.

To be sure, Clinton did put forward several DLC-style arguments that emphasized civic responsibility, law and order, and welfare reform, insisting on pragmatism and moderation in government programs.[121] But Clinton's political philosophy drew on several disparate and seemingly contradictory political strands to weave together a liberal and centrist Democratic worldview that had the ability to appeal to a wider range of constituencies. For example, with the economy faltering, Clinton tapped the New Deal legacy to promise new jobs and greater economic security; he invoked traditional populism with his campaign slogan "putting people first"; and he sounded sixties-era liberal commitments to protect the environment and defend women's rights and civil rights.[122] Clinton, who launched his political career by working on George McGovern's quixotic liberal quest for the presidency in 1972, combined DLC ideas with the key tenets of liberalism to form a compelling political philosophy, appropriating aspects of both and combining them alchemically to garner significant public support. Indeed, as David Greenberg demonstrates, "Clinton's policy solutions creatively blended liberal and conservative elements in ways that shored up Democratic vulnerabilities without undermining progressive values."[123]

With an amalgam of nostrums, Clinton's approach reflected an ability "to break through the either-or choices that characterized the debate between liberals and conservatives and find some 'both' solutions, some win-win solutions."[124] Clinton never believed there was an inherent conflict between the traditional objectives of liberals and his own approach, which can be evidenced by the political coalition he formed during the 1992 campaign. For example, along with support from the DLC, Clinton relied equally (or more) on other networks, such as the National Governors Association, civil rights and feminist organizations, and the celebrated Friends of Bill ensconced in political and intellectual power centers nationwide.[125] Since these networks included as many liberals as moderates, Clinton's election represented a vindication of his own distinctive blend of liberalism and DLC-style moderation. According to journalist Richard Rothstein, Clinton shrewdly assembled an electoral coalition in 1992 by positing a program that both liberals and centrists convinced themselves mainly represented their own views.[126]

Crucially then, Clinton's rise to power should be understood within the context of the reformist strand that emerged from the early 1970s.[127] As noted, Clinton cut his political teeth in the McGovern campaign and rose to prominence as the successful governor of a conservative state by stressing new ideas and rejecting outdated models, mirroring the approaches blazed by his neoliberal peers at the time, such as Gary Hart. He campaigned heavily for Dukakis in 1988—Clinton was often described by journalists that year as a southern liberal—and worked closely with key liberals in 1992, including the new liberal DNC chairman, Ronald Brown.[128] After his election, Clinton would select Brown as his secretary of commerce while many prominent neoliberals from the 1980s would also hold powerful positions in his administration, including Robert Reich as secretary of labor. Clinton's path to victory was multifaceted, part of a complex process of restructuring that can be traced back to the younger, reform-minded liberals who emerged as a cohort after the Watergate imbroglio. Indeed, Clinton very nearly became a member of the congressional class of 1974, losing Arkansas's 3rd District by less than four points that year (48.17 percent to 51.83 percent).

Moreover, Clinton would face a trailblazer from that cohort in the 1992 Democratic primaries, Senator Paul Tsongas, and the battle amply displayed the ways in which the Democratic Party had evolved over that period, as well as showcasing Clinton's political instincts and philosophical approach. As was clear from the outset, both drew from a similar ideological fountain, embracing experimental approaches to economics while championing liberalism's commitment to social issues and foreign policy. Their similarities meant Clinton strategically moved to the left of Tsongas, running a populist liberal campaign emphasizing the New Deal and Great

Society. Clinton charged Tsongas with a lack of faith in Social Security, and promised a large middle-class tax cut, massive public investments, and a nationalized health service.[129] He avidly courted labor unions, racial minorities, and senior citizens, while his opponents lambasted him as just another tax-and-spend liberal—hardly an appropriate caricature for someone leaning to the right. Instead, as historian Patrick Andelic has argued, the 1992 primaries effectively "revealed the extent to which the 'neoliberal' ideas that had emerged from the class of '74 had come to dominate the party-wide conversation and define what was considered 'mainstream' Democratic thinking."[130] Indeed, while Clinton eventually bested Tsongas for the nomination, in a real sense Tsongas wrote the script from which Clinton acted. Midway through the Clinton administration, for example, the *New York Times* would argue that Clinton practiced and preached much of what Tsongas outlined in his book *The Road from Here*, which expanded on his 1980 ADA speech.[131] *The Baltimore Sun* even contended that Tsongas blazed the path for Clinton by holding a mirror up to liberalism with that ADA speech.[132]

In the twelve years that elapsed between Tsongas's speech and Clinton's victory, liberals, particularly the younger cohort, had begun laying the intellectual groundwork by rethinking how to update liberalism for a changing electorate. Certainly, of the three strands explored in this book, the process of rethinking liberalism at an intellectual level proved the most challenging for liberals. Although the neoliberal approach gained prominence as the 1980s progressed, the emergence of the DLC, the durability of the Reagan coalition—until 1992 at least—and the struggle to develop a message that encompassed both identity-based and economic-based issues in equal measure highlighted the limits these younger liberals faced in their efforts to engage with liberalism intellectually. Indeed, as liberalism entered the 1990s, Clinton and a host of other Democratic politicians would distance themselves—rhetorically at least—from the liberal label during campaigns, despite clear preferences for liberal goals. Alongside the use of updated monikers, such as New Democrat and "progressive," this inevitably led some political commentators to declare that liberalism had disappeared by the 1990s.[133] Still, while Clinton's approach was too protean to be neatly categorized, as noted, he clearly subscribed to the central tenet of liberalism, seeking to use government as a facilitator to improve equality in society, albeit to a lesser degree than many of his Democratic predecessors.[134]

Moreover, the institutional developments in the 1980s, particularly the movement of liberal grassroots groups further under the Democratic umbrella, had a clear impact on Clinton's election and in shaping what would become the party's new electoral base. By 1992, for example, the twelve-year Republican occupancy of the White House had driven several bipartisan liberal groups in a partisan direction. The Federation of Business and Professional Women, a previously Republican-leaning organization, used its first-ever presidential endorsement to back Clinton after a decade of "anti-woman, anti-choice" Republican administrations (the gender gap would play an important role in Clinton's election, providing him with an 8 percent advantage over Bush).[135] Racial minorities, too, played a foundational role in Clinton's coalition, with increased turnout across the board fueling his victory and the Black vote in particular helping provide margins of success in several key states, which *Black Enterprise* attributed in part to Jesse Jackson's extensive voter registration campaigns.[136] Thus, while attracting back some of the white working-class, blue-collar voters who had fled the party to become Reagan Democrats, Clinton drew most of his electoral support from the emerging constituencies of the post–New Deal base—women, racial minorities, and young professionals—and he pursued a suburban strategy similar to that of Hart and Dukakis.

Once in office, rather than reject identity politics, as the DLC may have hoped, Clinton would famously ensure that his administration "looked like America"—with historic levels of women, Black, Hispanic, and other minority communities represented—and the policies he initially pursued were decidedly liberal, regardless of whether or not he couched them in centrist rhetoric.[137] During his first week, for example, Clinton signed a group of executive orders that lifted restrictions on the federal government regarding the funding, access, and provision of abortion.[138] One DLC member, Congressman Rob Andrews of New Jersey, would later lament that Clinton "ran like Jack Kennedy and governed like Ted Kennedy."[139]

Additionally, the electoral inroads made by Ross Perot as an independent candidate in 1992 would highlight the tenuous nature of Clinton's victory, further underscoring the importance of the liberal-leaning coalition that helped elect him.[140] Perot, a self-made billionaire, attracted millions of alienated voters with his stance as an outsider and his staunch opposition to the North Atlantic Free Trade Agreement (NAFTA); he scored 19 percent of the popular vote, the strongest showing of a third-party candidate since Theodore Roosevelt in 1912.[141] Clinton received just 43 percent of the popular vote, some 3 percent less than Dukakis had garnered in 1988, when the DLC caricatured him as an out-of-touch liberal.[142] Of particular significance, voters in 1992 believed that Clinton was just as liberal as Dukakis according to polling data.[143] Thus, the constituencies that helped elect Clinton in 1992 could rightfully expect that he would govern in their image.

Furthermore, the developments traced at the congressional level through the 1980s were also evident during the 1992 election. Not only did the Democratic Party retain control of both houses of Congress, effectively ensuring that liberals, in part, held the reins of power in the federal government (until 1994 at least). But 1992 was also popularly referred to as the Year of the Woman following the elections of an unprecedented wave of women to political office, in large part thanks to the groundwork laid by liberal women's groups in the 1980s.[144] As the *Los Angeles Times* highlighted, for example, EMILY's List, which had become "the nation's largest funder of federal campaigns," played an instrumental role in 1992 by contributing record levels of support to women candidates through its donor base.[145] As noted, strategies concerning the gender gap became more sophisticated as the 1980s wore on, and liberal women's groups, by 1992, had established themselves as key political operatives in the Democratic Party.

Collectively, these developments facilitated the Democratic Party's control of both the Congress and the executive branch in the early 1990s, and for a brief interregnum at least, liberals came close to establishing a national health service, an objective long described as the "holy grail of modern liberalism."[146] That failure and the midterm elections in 1994, when the Democrats suffered significant losses, highlighted the volatility of the political environment in the 1990s as well.[147] Certainly, 1994 was a transformative election, with Gingrich, once again, the architect of a landmark Democrat defeat. Armed with the Contract with America, a legislative blueprint to shrink government and limit spending, Gingrich nationalized the midterms, framing them as a referendum on Clinton and his "failed" agenda. With both houses of Congress now controlled by Republican lawmakers for the first time in forty years, the results were a damaging indictment of Clinton.[148] But as the foot soldiers of Gingrich's Revolution would quickly find out, while reducing government in the abstract may have worked as a campaign slogan, anti-statism often dissipated when the crosshairs were positioned on specific programs.[149] Indeed, just as the Reagan revolutionaries discovered during the Social Security debacle, the liberal leviathan was firmly ensconced, and Americans expected extensive protections from their government. Hence, when Gingrich presented an ultimatum to the president in 1995—either approve cuts to Medicare, Medicaid, and other programs, or he would shut down the government—the ensuing shutdowns were an embarrassment for Gingrich and a victory for Clinton, who the public applauded for protecting their interests.[150]

Moreover, while Clinton clearly moved rightward after the 1994 rout to accommodate Washington's new balance of power, this was not without retaining his commitment to traditional liberal goals.[151] For example, when former liberal Representative Barney Frank (D-MA) was asked whether Clinton compromised too much of the party's soul during his presidency, he responded with a simple rebuttal: Clinton "stuck with us on affirmative action, on choice, on gay rights, on immigration. What was our soul?"[152] Thus, although we can hardly pretend that liberalism was an ascendant force after the 1980s, subsequent developments continued to demonstrate its importance. With the old New Deal coalition largely supplanted by a new, more consistently liberal-leaning one comprising women, racial minorities, and young professionals, these constituencies would form the Democratic Party's bedrock, growing in prominence as the decades progressed and increasingly shaping its political priorities. The 1992 election was only the beginning.

Conclusion
Reckoning with the "Reagan Era"

How should we view liberalism during a conservative age? Certainly, at a time when the Republicans controlled key instruments of government, liberalism was not an ascendant force, nor did it enjoy the levels of support that it had garnered in earlier decades. However, it was not, as many have suggested, in terminal decline either. Instead, buried underneath the weight of the Reagan Revolution and "conservative ascendancy'" narratives are examples of how liberalism recovered and strengthened in several fundamental ways across this era. Rather than the "wilderness years," the 1980s should be understood as a period when liberalism played a significant and influential role in shaping the decade's politics. Indeed, Reagan may have entered the White House atop a conservative wave, but he found it increasingly difficult to implement a conservative agenda when negotiating the political realities of exercising power, thanks in large part to the opposition work of liberals.

At first glance, Reagan's revolution certainly appeared to have unstoppable momentum; he passed an historic tax cut, began a massive defense build-up, and accelerated the process of deregulation in his first year. However, the federal leviathan actually grew under his watch—federal spending reached record heights, and the number of employees on the federal payroll increased considerably—and liberals were clearly able to push back and unravel significant parts of his agenda as the decade progressed.[1] Indeed, Reagan's rhetorical assault on the role of government effectively energized liberal communities across the United States, many of whom had been long searching for a sense of direction and a common opponent after the malaise of the 1970s.[2] Moreover, despite repeated attempts by those on the right to dismantle government programs or departments, the period was instead characterized by considerable continuity as bureaucratically well-established structures, now largely entrenched in the fabric of society, remained in place.[3] In constructing a narrative of conservative triumph and liberal exhaustion, scholars have too often overlooked these limits and contradictions.[4] Evidently, the parameters of the Reagan Revolution were negotiated in a nation where liberalism remained an important and significant force, with liberals clearly able to place several roadblocks in Reagan's path during his drive to remake politics.

For example, the Social Security and Voting Rights contests at the start of Reagan's presidency represented clear conservative attempts to undo signature liberal achievements; and liberals responded accordingly. Led by Senator Edward Kennedy and Speaker Thomas O'Neill, liberals in Congress, supplemented by the activism of liberal groups on the ground, were able to force significant concessions from Reagan at the apparent height of conservative power; and their ability to protect and even strengthen these core liberal policies challenges the conventional impression of the decade's early politics. As Reagan and the conservative movement learned, the electorate's seeming antipathy toward government was complicated by durable support for many of its programs, a paradox noted as early as 1968 by Lloyd Free and Hadley Cantril that Americans were becoming "ideologically conservative but operationally liberal."[5] Liberals were able to bait the Republicans on Social Security and Voting Rights and frame the 1982 midterms through a "fairness" prism with particular electoral success, a development that paints a more complicated portrait of the early Reagan years than the ascent/descent paradigm. As Julian Zelizer argues, for example, "The survival of domestic policies created in the 1930s and 1960s was not inevitable, nor was it inertia. In the 1980s, conservatives faced formidable liberal opponents who fought to defend the American social welfare state."[6]

Moreover, as Reagan recalibrated his approach to welfare state retrenchment, focusing on liberal programs that enjoyed more tenuous support and offered less-tangible benefits to the majority of Americans—principally, those targeted at women and racial minorities in society—the communities disproportionately affected by these cuts started to seek greater security under the Democratic Party's umbrella as a result. As detailed throughout *Resisting Reagan*, race and gender increasingly correlated with ideology and partisanship in the 1980s, defining the difference between liberals and conservatives, shaping the presidential and congressional coalitions of the Democratic and Republican parties, and providing a new dimension to policy battles throughout the decade. Clearly, Reagan's conservative approach would energize women and minority communities to form grassroots coalitions to protect past gains and strengthen their political clout to effect change in the political arena. The arrival of the gender gap in the 1980 election and the ascent of conservative lawmakers to powerful positions in government was the catalyst that helped galvanize a broad movement of liberal groups to campaign against the type of societal restructuring they feared conservatives would implement. Indeed, as the notion of identity became increasingly central to contemporary political discourse during the 1980s, commonality of experience and intersectionality among consciousness-raising groups led to the formation of sophisticated political coalitions as tools of opposition.

For example, several of the liberal groups that had emerged with force out of the social movements of the 1960s and 1970s, such as NOW and the LCCR, worked together during the decade on issues of common cause. In doing so, these groups professionalized and strengthened their operations and employed a range of new political tactics to forward their agenda, combining symbolic displays of opposition with grassroots political action designed to elect lawmakers who shared their point of view. The increasing numbers of women and racial minorities holding—or at least running for—positions of political power as the decade wore on was, in many ways, the result of these efforts, with voter registration drives and targeted grassroots campaigns impacting all levels of government. Certainly, the 1980s was a difficult period for liberal coalition groups, but as demonstrated, it was often at times of defeat in the policy realm that they learned some of the most valuable strategy lessons.[7] For example, the battle over the ERA demonstrated to liberal women's groups the importance of using the gender gap as leverage to increase their influence and push more women to run for elected office. Additionally, the struggle for the Civil Rights Restoration Act focused attention on winning back Democratic control of Congress in 1986.

Reckoning with Reagan reached new heights during the Robert Bork nomination of 1987, which, more than any other moment in the decade, effectively demonstrated the significant strides that the liberal movement had made in Reagan's shadow. By then, liberals had honed their coalition-building and advocacy skills, mastered the techniques of modern political campaigns, especially through the use of polls to shape strategy, and recognized the importance of symbols, labels, and language to conduct a successful campaign. Additionally, as the Gregory Peck advertisement and the use of carefully crafted sound bites demonstrated, liberals developed powerful media strategy skills during the 1980s, understanding that media professionals were as essential as community organizers to the liberal project. Effectively, the Bork nomination provided a liberal template of attack in the Reagan Era, the success of which became a galvanizing force for liberals moving forward, evidenced by the renewed sense of confidence and vigor with which coalition groups and liberal officeholders fought together on a raft of ensuing issues. While the decision to wage an ideological battle against Bork had profound consequences that continue to reverberate to this day, in the specific context of the Reagan Era, the ability of liberals to reassert themselves forcefully and successfully, surprising conservatives and moderates alike, challenges the notion of decline and shows instead the significant progress that liberals had made in the 1980s, particularly through effective mobilization and coalition-building strategies.[8]

The Bork moment also underscored the growing polarization among the parties on cultural issues and social identities, and the extent to which they had both assumed more ideologically homogenized characters as a result by the closing stages of the decade. Indeed, a theme that permeates each chapter in this book—the emergence and significance of identity politics in the 1980s—proved central to the Bork story and effectively set the stage for what became known as the culture wars in the 1990s, a political era dominated by polarizing controversies regarding issues of race and gender, among others.[9] From Willie Horton to the Civil Rights Act of 1991, in many ways the Bush presidency would cement the prominence of the culture wars in the political arena. With concepts of identity increasingly conditioning attitudes toward politics, debates over issues of morality and cultural views shaped policy conflict and electoral behavior into the 1990s and beyond. Here, the institutional developments surveyed across *Resisting Reagan*, particularly the relationships established between liberal legislators and grassroots organizations, would enable liberals to protect or advance their interests across this deeply polarizing political space as well.

Yet this period not only saw liberals mobilize at an institutional level, but it also witnessed the equally important efforts, particularly by younger liberals, to study some of liberalism's limits. As stated, Reagan's election had created a powerful incentive to rethink the direction of liberalism, and the changing socioeconomic context of the decade necessitated intellectual engagement with the contours of Reaganism in order to fashion an appropriate response. To do so, the younger liberals who had emerged during the Watergate imbroglio sought to construct a broad and comprehensive vision of progressive politics capable of commanding majority electoral support in a changing electorate, both demographically and geographically. These Watergate Babies—or neoliberals—had typically earned their support from the emerging suburban regions of the country by conducting issue-oriented, reform-minded campaigns that consciously sought to distance liberalism from the old-style politics of the New Deal. This change in intellectual tenor was not an attempt to abandon liberal values or beliefs, but to repackage them for the 1980s and adapt their applicability to the realities of the age. This was evidenced early in the House Democratic Caucus, where these younger liberals proposed policy solutions that were not mere retreads of old orthodoxy, but rather adaptations to new political conditions.

By combining liberal stances on civil rights, feminism, and the environment with a commitment to stimulating entrepreneurship and economic growth, these neoliberals sought to update liberalism to account for rights-based issues that had risen to prominence in the 1970s. As identity politics began to impact the political landscape, neoliberals incorporated the language of social justice and equality into this newer vision of liberalism for the 1980s, one updated to deal with the expressed concerns of a postindustrial society. What ensued was a generation-based struggle in the Democratic Party between traditional New Deal liberals and younger neoliberals over how to act out liberalism's core principles; the struggle was nowhere more vividly illustrated than in the contest for the presidential nomination between Walter Mondale and Gary Hart in 1984. Evidently, as the decade progressed, the party's center of gravity started shifting from its traditional urban base toward suburban areas, with women, racial minorities, and professionals increasingly supplanting blue-collar workers and labor union members as its core constituencies. Democratizing reforms in the early 1970s had brought a host of new activists into the political process, and the mobilization strategies implemented to attract the emerging liberal-leaning coalition started clearly benefiting liberal candidates as the coalition grew in both size and influence. The 1984 Democratic primaries, in many ways, signaled this turning point, with party liberals increasingly adopting Hart's approach afterward in an effort to reach out to this newer coalition, while Jesse Jackson's trailblazing campaigns would serve to underscore the importance of its "rainbow" foundations.

Still, the 1984 elections were significant for another development directly related to liberalism's story. Reagan's electoral landslide that year convinced the remaining conservative elements in the party to launch an offensive under the auspices of a new organization, the Democratic Leadership Council (DLC), to prevent the party from supposedly veering off a left-wing cliff over identity politics issues. This contest for ideological control of the Democratic Party would continue well beyond the historical parameters of this book, but what is clear from an initial reading of the DLC's impact is just how limited it proved to be. Not only did liberals succeed in retaining control of the Democratic National Committee (DNC) by placing one of their own in the party's driving seat with Paul Kirk as chairman, but the DLC's institutional reforms for 1988, particularly the regional Super Tuesday contest in the South, did more for the two most liberal contenders in that year's contest, Jesse Jackson and Michael Dukakis.

Moreover, with the party as a whole becoming more ideologically cohesive in its commitment to liberalism as the decade progressed, evidenced by collective ratings from the liberal organization Americans for Democratic Action (ADA), the DLC had a limited pool of elected officials to draw from. By its second year of operation, it was forced to employ a big-tent policy to recruit new members. Numerous elected liberals agreed to tie their flag to the DLC's mast at this point, recognizing the wisdom of discussing ways to make party positions more palatable but rejecting the DLC's efforts to alter it ideologically. In other words, the motivation to use this moderate outlet was, at least partially, more a branding exercise, an effort to balance liberal convictions with pragmatic politics. By 1987, forty-eight of the one hundred DLC House members had ADA ratings of more than 75 percent.[10] Certainly, the DLC provided a political vehicle for those hoping to implement an ideological realignment after 1984, but their ability to do so was limited by liberal opposition, both from within and outside the party, and by the electoral realities of the party's shifting voter pool, which was becoming more liberal as the decade progressed.

Yet, in terms of historical memory, the DLC has often occupied a central role in the story of Democratic recovery by the 1990s. Indeed, a significant part of the "liberalism in decline" interpretation has been what might be described as the "DLC as savior" narrative, with Kenneth Baer's *Reinventing Democrats* foremost among this school of thought.[11] This account details how a collection of moderate-to-conservative Democratic politicians and policy technocrats, under the aegis of the DLC, worked to free the party from its bondage to a liberalism that was out of touch with voters. In this interpretation, only by becoming a centrist rather than a liberal party were the Democrats able to attract support and win elections. As Jeffrey Bloodworth has argued, for example, "Republican dominance" was reversed in the early 1990s only because Democratic moderates came together under the DLC to establish an "organizational foothold" and "slowly alter party orthodoxy."[12] Central to this tale are the ideas found in *The Politics of Evasion*, a booklet released in 1989 by two Democratic policy advisers, William Galston and Elaine Kamarck, which lays out the political case against liberalism. For the DLC, the Dukakis defeat provided sufficient evidence that liberalism had to be read out of the party, despite Dukakis's attempts to distance himself from the label. Galston and Kamarck argued that the party had become dominated by its extreme left wing, whose rigid adherence to a so-called liberal fundamentalism predicated on identity politics was out of touch with mainstream America.[13]

Accordingly, with *Politics of Evasion* as its guiding political manifesto, the DLC found a Moses to lead the Democratic Party out of the electoral desert when it recruited Bill Clinton, who served as DLC chairman from 1990 to 1991. This argument is certainly persuasive. Clinton did run as a New Democrat, and he presented his approach as a centrist amalgam that transcended both liberalism and conservatism by offering a Third Way back to power. However, as noted, Clinton was too protean a character to be contained in a DLC mold. Certainly, using the term "New Democrat" enabled Clinton to distance himself from the line of previously unsuccessful Democratic contenders, but the New Democrat label, like Hart's New Generation Democrat in 1984/1988, was campaign rhetoric concocted by a team of strategists. Although Clinton moderated his views on several issues, such as crime and welfare, and his economic approach included more market-based solutions, he forthrightly endorsed civil rights; supported abortion, the ERA, and certain aspects of the gay rights movement; and promised an ambitious national health care program to provide coverage to all uninsured people.[14] And as demonstrated, his route to victory relied as much on these liberal viewpoints and policies as it did on his use of the DLC as an electoral vehicle.

Once in office, rather than becoming a prisoner of the Reagan Era, with his choices and policies shackled by Reagan's conservatizing of the political space, Clinton managed to remake the image and operations of the Democratic Party in ways that effectively undermined the Reagan Revolution. Indeed, while certainly informed by the Reagan years, Clinton moved clearly away from its attempts to immobilize government; and the essential principle of his agenda—leaner, activist government—was the result of a rethinking of the future of both liberalism and the Democratic Party.[15] Here, by bookending Paul Tsongas's ADA speech in 1980 with Clinton's election in 1992, *Resisting Reagan* traces this complex process of rethinking and showcases the myriad of ways in which liberalism recalibrated, reconstituted, and refined across that period.

Furthermore, the demographic and geographic trends explored throughout *Resisting Reagan* would continue to fuel liberal politics for decades thereafter. Indeed, not only did the more liberal-leaning constituencies help elect Clinton in 1992, but they would also prove crucial to another future Democratic Party leader, who was gaining his political education that year through a voter registration drive in Illinois. Barack Obama coordinated a campaign in 1992 that secured over 150,000 new voters in Chicago alone, mostly from minority communities, to help elect both Clinton and the first female Black senator in history, Carol Moseley Braun.[16] And the so-called coalition of the ascendant that powered Obama's historic presidential victories in 2008 and 2012 was centered on the demographic components of the coalition mobilized in the 1980s—racial minorities, women, and professionals (groups that continued to grow in the electorate, hence the ascendant moniker).[17]

With the 1980s and early 1990s forming the era in which Obama and many of his allies became politically active, it is arguably impossible to understand their historic rise to power without an examination of the political environment that first nurtured them.[18] To be sure, the road from 1992 to 2008 is far more complicated and convoluted than a straight line, but it is clear that the foundations for these later victories were being built in Reagan's shadow. In the end, liberals survived—and in some cases thrived during—the Reagan Era by changing tone instead of substance; building powerful coalitions, both at the grassroots level and directly within formal party structures; and designing strategies to exploit emerging trends in political demography and geography. In resisting Reagan, liberals protected their past and planted the seeds of a future recovery.

Notes

INTRODUCTION

1. Paul Tsongas, *The Road from Here: Liberalism and Realities in the 1980s* (New York: Alfred A. Knopf, 1981), 253–256.

2. As historian Douglas Rossinow has remarked, for example, in American politics "left, liberal, and progressive are terms whose meanings shift and float. Clintonite centrists, anti-imperialist peace agitators, and labor-union activists alike call themselves progressives, and no one can say definitely that any of them are wrong." Douglas Rossinow, *Visions of Progress: The Left-Liberal Tradition in America* (Philadelphia: University of Pennsylvania Press, 2008), 1. Moreover, while liberalism can also be defined by ideologies that seek more radical systemic change, this book uses liberalism to describe the political approach of working within the established democratic system to advance egalitarian goals.

3. Like liberalism, modern conservatism is a broad philosophical and political doctrine with deep historical roots and ideological tensions, mirrored in the diverse constituencies that support the cause—from New Right religious activists to public intellectuals under the auspices of *The National Review*.

4. In 1974, the ADA's national director, Leon Shull, summarized the key tenets of liberalism: "Liberalism is a passionate conviction that equal opportunity, equal justice and freedom for all are the foundation stones of the social structure we all seek to build." Leon Shull, "Ultimate Solutions, Day-to-Day Work," *ADA World*, April–May 1974, 29, nos. 4/5, Peter R. Rosenblatt papers, folder marked "ADA," Lyndon B. Johnson Presidential Library (LBJ Library), Austin, TX, 4.

5. Jeff Jacoby, "Liberalism's Debt to Paul Tsongas," *The Baltimore Sun (BS)*, 29 January 1997.

6. Randall Rothenberg, *The Neoliberals: Creating the New American Politics* (New York: Simon & Schuster, 1984), 42.

7. Tsongas, *Road from Here*, 253–256.

8. David S. Broder, "Politically Passé?" *The Washington Post (WP)*, 25 June 1980. Progressive social reform and anti-communist internationalism formed the twin pillars of the ADA, fleshed out in Arthur Schlesinger Jr.'s seminal book, *The Vital Center*. Arthur M. Schlesinger Jr., *The Vital Center: The Politics of Freedom* (New York: Houghton Mifflin, 1949).

9. Jacoby, "Liberalism's Debt."

10. Robert M. Kaus, "Reaganism with a Human Face," *The New Republic (TNR)*, 25 November 1981; David Osborne, "The Other Senator from Massachusetts," *Mother Jones*, July 1982, 24–58.

11. See, among others, William G. Mayer, *The Divided Democrats: Ideological*

Unity, Party Reform, and Presidential Elections (Boulder, CO: Westview, 1996); Kenneth S. Baer, *Reinventing Democrats: The Politics of Liberalism from Reagan to Clinton* (Lawrence: University Press of Kansas, 2000); and Donald T. Critchlow, *The Conservative Ascendancy: How the GOP Right Made Political History* (Cambridge: Harvard University Press, 2007).

12. Jeffrey Bloodworth, *Losing the Center: The Decline of American Liberalism, 1968–1992* (Lexington: University of Kentucky Press, 2013), 2.

13. John Ehrman and Michael W. Flamm, *Debating the Reagan Presidency* (New York: Rowman & Littlefield, 2009), 55.

14. Ehrman and Flamm, *Debating the Reagan Presidency*, 55; Also see John Ehrman, *The Eighties: America in the Age of Reagan* (New Haven, CT: Yale University Press, 2005); Michael Schaller, *Reckoning with Reagan: America and Its President in the 1980s* (Oxford: Oxford University Press, 1992); and Gil Troy, *Morning in America: How Ronald Reagan Invented the 1980s* (Princeton, NJ: Princeton University Press, 2007).

15. Julian E. Zelizer, "Reflections: Rethinking the History of American Conservatism," *Reviews in American History* 38, no. 2 (2010): 367–392, (380).

16. See Ehrman, *The Eighties*; Schaller, *Reckoning with Reagan*; Gil Troy, *The Reagan Revolution: A Very Short Introduction* (Oxford: Oxford University Press, 2009). Recent scholarship on the era has also importantly explored the limitations of applying a conservative lens to Reagan's legacy. Marcus Witcher, for example, in *Getting Right with Reagan* examines the development of a "mythical Reagan" since the 1980s, arguing that he came to "represent the purest form of conservative principles, and his pragmatic governing style was forgotten." Marcus M. Witcher, *Getting Right with Reagan: The Struggle for True Conservatism, 1980–2016* (Lawrence: University Press of Kansas, 2019), 3.

17. See Troy, *Morning in America*; Sean Wilentz, *The Age of Reagan: A History 1974–2008* (New York: HarperCollins, 2008); and Steven F. Hayward, *The Age of Reagan: The Conservative Counterrevolution, 1980–1989* (New York: Three Rivers, 2009).

18. Zelizer, "Reflections," 387.

19. Bruce J. Schulman and Julian E. Zelizer, *Rightward Bound: Making America Conservative in the 1970s* (Cambridge: Harvard University Press, 2008).

20. James Sundquist argued that Reagan "accelerated the realigning forces that had been making continuous, though relatively minor changes in the composition of parties and the nature of the party struggle." James L. Sundquist, *Dynamics of the Party System: Alignment and Realignment of Political Parties in the United States* (Washington, DC: The Brookings Institution, 1983), 437. Also see Craig Shirley, *Rendezvous with Destiny: Ronald Reagan and the Campaign That Changed America* (Wilmington, DE: Intercollegiate Studies Institute, 2009); Matthew Dallek, *The Right Moment: Ronald Reagan's First Victory and the Decisive Turning Point in American Politics* (New York: Free Press, 2000); and Andrew Busch, *Reagan's Victory: The Presidential Election of 1980 and the Rise of the Right* (Lawrence: University Press of Kansas, 2005).

21. V. O. Key, "A Theory of Critical Elections," *The Journal of Politics* 17, no. 1 (1955); Walter Dean Burnham, *Critical Elections and the Mainsprings of American Politics* (New York: W. W. Norton, 1970); Arthur M. Schlesinger Sr., "The Tides of National Politics," *Paths to the Present* (New York: Macmillan, 1949); and Arthur M. Schlesinger Jr., *The Cycles of American History* (London: Houghton, 1987).

22. Everett C. Ladd, "The Brittle Mandate: Electoral Dealignment and the 1980 Presidential Election," *Political Science Quarterly* 96 (1981): 1–25. Hedrick Smith described dealignment as the movement of voters away from one party without firmly fixing onto another. Hedrick Smith, "Republicans See Opportunity," *The New York Times (NYT)*, 4 February 1985.

23. Brent Cebul, Lily Geismer, and Mason B. Williams, eds., *Shaped by the State: Toward a New Political History of the Twentieth Century* (Chicago: University of Chicago Press, 2019), 6.

24. Here, Byron Shafer argues that American politics after the 1960s was shaped by the "cross-cutting" allegiance of voters to a variety of liberal and conservative issue stances and that the institutions of American government accommodated these divisions through the device of split partisan control. According to Shafer, many traditional Democrats are liberal on social welfare issues but conservative on cultural issues, with the former tending to be to the fore in the context of legislative elections, but the latter in the case of presidential elections. Byron E. Shafer, *The Two Majorities and the Puzzle of Modern American Politics* (Lawrence: University Press of Kansas, 2003).

25. Richard S. Conley, *The Presidency, Congress, and Divided Government: A Postwar Assessment* (College Station: Texas A&M University Press, 2003), 126–141.

26. This is despite the fact that historian Thomas Cochran described this presidential-centered approach, understood as the "presidential synthesis" theory, as a failure in 1948. Thomas C. Cochran, "The 'Presidential Synthesis' in American History," *The American Historical Review* 53, no. 4 (1948). See also Kenneth Kato and Elizabeth Rybicki, "Congressional History: A Literature Review," *OAH Magazine of History* 12, no. 4 (1998): 5–12. There has, however, been some important recent scholarship on congressional history, such as Julian E. Zelizer, ed., *The American Congress: The Building of Democracy* (New York: Houghton Mifflin, 2004).

27. Bradford Martin, *The Other Eighties: A Secret History of America in the Age of Reagan* (New York: Hill and Wang, 2011); Michael Stewart Foley, in *Front Porch Politics*, also demonstrates how grassroots activism across the political spectrum was robust in the 1980s, typically involving citizen participation and political action when local issues posed a threat to people's families, homes, or dreams, often from the vantage point of a front porch, whether actual or figurative. Michael Stewart Foley, *Front Porch Politics: The Forgotten Heyday of American Activism in the 1970s and 1980s* (New York: Hill and Wang, 2013).

28. Timothy Stanley, *Kennedy vs. Carter: The 1980 Battle for the Democratic Party's Soul* (Lawrence: University Press of Kansas, 2010); Stanley and Jonathan Bell also bring together a collection of essays that showcase the myriad of

ways in which liberalism influenced policy and governance during the supposed rightward-bound years of the 1960s and 1970s. Jonathan Bell and Timothy Stanley, eds., *Making Sense of American Liberalism* (Champaign: University of Illinois Press, 2012).

29. Lily Geismer, *Don't Blame Us: Suburban Liberals and the Transformation of the Democratic Party* (Princeton, NJ: Princeton University Press, 2014).

30. Patrick Andelic, *Donkey Work: Congressional Democrats in Conservative America, 1972–1994* (Lawrence: University Press of Kansas, 2019).

31. Like the liberal individuals explored throughout this book, the organizations examined in depth, such as the LCCR and NOW, worked within the established democratic system to disrupt oppressive structures and drive societal change. But they also absorbed—and resisted—the radicalism of the social movements that birthed them in significant ways. NOW, for example, whose name is synonymous with second-wave feminism, was not purely an organization of liberal feminists; rather, it was a broad church that housed members with diverse political views and pursued both radical and moderate change across its history. And as conduits that channeled energy from grassroots activism into formal politics, they offer crucial insight into the era.

32. "Racial minorities," "women," and "professionals" are blanket terms that should be approached with caution. Typically, this book explains the interests of minoritized voters—racial and ethnic groups that are underrepresented and systemically oppressed—through the African American experience, both because they were the largest minority group at the time and they had the strongest institutional foundations. But the issues focused on throughout—voting rights, discrimination—affected all marginalized groups and were championed by organizations that reflected this. Likewise, women were not a monolithic voting bloc; it was working, single, and highly educated women who tended toward liberalism during the decade. Chapter 3 specifically addresses this problem and shows the complicated nature of gender politics in the 1980s. Finally, this book defines "professionals" in line with authors John Judis and Ruy Teixeira: "highly-skilled, white-collar workers, typically with a college education, who produce ideas and services [ranging from] architects and engineers to scientists and lawyers." The rise of the postindustrial professional class coincided with the growth of suburbia; and, as Judis and Teixeira note, their "politics shifted [as a result]. In 1960, professionals supported Nixon over Kennedy 61-to-38 percent.... By 1988, professionals were supporting Democratic candidates an average of 52-to-40 percent." This was more pronounced with women, who also favored Nixon over Kennedy but, as subsequent chapters demonstrate, began voting more Democratic and more liberal. Racial minorities were already quite liberal voting groups by the 1980s, but the fact that they increased both their presence and participation in politics during the decade is important. Finally, it is crucial to note that these umbrella terms are, of course, not mutually exclusive, with voters often simultaneously encompassing all three. John B. Judis and Ruy Teixeira, "Majority Rules: The Coming

Democratic Dominance," *TNR*, 5 August 2002, 18–23. Also see John B. Judis and Ruy Teixeira, *The Emerging Democratic Majority* (New York: Scribner, 2002).

33. Thanks in large part to the Baby Boom generation, the roughly seventy-two million people born between 1946 and 1964, the 1992 election was the first in which the suburban vote reached a majority. Thomas Byrne Edsall, "Race," *The Atlantic*, May 1991.

34. See Lisa McGirr, *Suburban Warriors: The Origins of the New American Right* (Princeton, NJ: Princeton University Press, 2001). For a recent exploration of the suburbs from a liberal context, though limited in historical scope to the 1940s–1970s period, see Jonathan Bell, *California Crucible: The Forging of Modern American Liberalism* (Philadelphia: University of Pennsylvania Press, 2012).

35. Like "liberalism," "gender" and "race" are elusive terms open to interpretation. Both are social constructs of identity and language shaped by culture and social dynamics, such as power and hierarchy. At a basic level, gender, unlike sex, which is based on biological characteristics, describes the organization, both socially and culturally, of relationships between males and females in society. Race, broadly, refers to the grouping of people into subgroups based on certain features or markers, skin color being a well-known, though not determinative, element. While this book does not shy away from acknowledging the complexities of these terms, it tries to situate each in its contemporary cultural context, using Joan Scott's definition of gender to mean "a constitutive element of social relationships based on perceived differences between the sexes" and viewing race as a similar category of historical analysis that helps us to understand how inequalities of power are organized along certain axes. Joan W. Scott, "Gender: A Useful Category of Historical Analysis," *The American Historical Review* 91, no. 5 (1986): 1053–1075, (1067).

36. Courtney Jung, "Why Liberals Should Value 'Identity Politics,'" *Daedalus, Journal of American Academy of Arts & Sciences* 135, no. 4 (2006): 32–39.

37. For early discussions on identity politics, see Karen A. Cerulo, "Identity Construction: New Issues, New Directions," *Annual Review of Sociology* 23 (1997): 385–409; and Stanley Aronowitz, *The Death and Rebirth of American Radicalism* (New York: Routledge, 1996), 83–90.

38. Political scientist Ronald Inglehart described this shift in emphasis as one from materialist to "post-materialist" values. Ronald Inglehart, *Culture Shift in Advanced Industrial Society* (Princeton, NJ: Princeton University Press, 1990).

39. Byron Shafer argues that after the 1960s, a growing segment of the Democratic Party became "less concerned with the old redistributional issues that had underpinned the New Deal Democratic coalition and more concerned with an aggregate of social, cultural, and behavioral issues—less with the 'quantity of life' and more with the 'quality of life.'" Shafer, *Two Majorities*, 12.

40. June Hannam, *Feminism*, 2nd ed. (New York: Routledge, 2014), 5.

41. L. A. Kauffman, "The Anti-Politics of Identity," in *Identity Politics in the Women's Movement*, ed. Barbara Ryan (New York: New York University Press, 2001), 23.

42. William Schneider, "Politics of the '80s Widens the Gap Between the Two Parties in Congress," *National Journal*, 1 June 1985, 1268–1282.

43. The "backlash" theory holds that the rights groups who flooded into the political process during the 1960s and 1970s to fracture the New Deal coalition triggered an electoral backlash in the 1980s. See Norman C. Amaker, *Civil Rights and the Reagan Administration* (Washington, DC: Urban Institute, 1988); Thomas B. Edsall, *Chain Reaction: The Impact of Race, Rights, and Taxes on American Politics* (New York: W. W. Norton, 1991); Susan Faludi, *Backlash: The Undeclared War Against American Women* (London: Vintage, 1992); and Nicholas Laham, *The Reagan Presidency and the Politics of Race* (Westport, CT: Praeger, 1998).

44. Lee Atwater, "'The Gender Gap': A Postelection Assessment," 23 November 1982, in Julian E. Zelizer and Meg Jacobs, *Conservatives in Power: The Reagan Years, 1981–1989: A Brief History with Documents* (Boston: Bedford/St. Martin's, 2011), 114–117.

45. Research drawn from this chapter has been recently published: Joe J. Ryan-Hume, "The National Organization for Women and the Democratic Party in Reagan's America," *The Historical Journal* 64, no. 2 (March 2021): 454–476. Copyright © 2020, Cambridge University Press; Reprinted with permission.

46. Research drawn from this chapter has been recently published: Joe J. Ryan-Hume, "The 1986 Midterms: The End of the Reagan Revolution?" in *Midterms and Mandates: Electoral Reassessments of Presidents and Parties*, ed. Patrick Andelic, Mark McLay, and Robert Mason (Edinburgh: Edinburgh University Press, 2022). Copyright © 2021, Edinburgh University Press. Reproduced with permission of Edinburgh University Press Limited through PLSclear.

CHAPTER 1. LIBERALISM AT A CROSSROADS

1. Quoted in Steven F. Hayward, *The Age of Reagan: The Fall of the Old Liberal Order, 1964–1980* (New York: Random House, 2001), xii.

2. Quoted in Rothenberg, *Neoliberals*, 15–17.

3. See, among others, Sidney M. Milkis and Jerome M. Mileur, *The New Deal and the Triumph of Liberalism* (Boston: University of Massachusetts Press, 2002); and Alonzo L. Hamby, *Liberalism and Its Challengers: From F.D.R. to Bush*, 2nd ed. (Oxford: Oxford University Press, 1992).

4. Lyndon B. Johnson, "Remarks at the University of Michigan," 22 May 1964, The American Presidency Project (APP), https://www.presidency.ucsb.edu/documents/remarks-the-university-michigan.

5. See, among others, John A. Andrew, *Lyndon Johnson and the Great Society* (Chicago: Ivan R. Dee, 1999); and Sidney M. Milkis and Jerome M. Mileur, *The Great Society and the High Tide of Liberalism* (Boston: University of Massachusetts Press, 2005).

6. Godfrey Hodgson, *America in Our Time: From World War II to Nixon—What Happened and Why* (Princeton, NJ: Princeton University Press, 1976), 67–99; Also see Schulman and Zelizer, *Rightward Bound*, 1–13.

7. Douglas Rossinow, *The Reagan Era: A History of the 1980s* (New York: Columbia University Press, 2015), 8–9.

8. See Bruce Miroff, *The Liberals' Moment: The McGovern Insurgency and the Identity Crisis of the Democratic Party* (Lawrence: University Press of Kansas, 2009).

9. Ronald D. Elving, "Rebels of '94 and 'Watergate Babies' Similar in Class Size, Sense of Zeal," *CNN*, 24 January 1998; Also see John A. Lawrence, *The Class of '74: Congress After Watergate and the Roots of Partisanship* (Baltimore, MD: John Hopkins University Press, 2018).

10. William Schneider, "JFK's Children: The Class of '74," *The Atlantic*, March 1989, 35–53.

11. According to one member of the cohort, Senator Gary Hart (D-CO), military reform was needed to ensure that the United States had "a defense that is the most effective and not simply the most expensive." Reflective of his class, Hart would also say that Vietnam taught him "that there simply isn't an American answer to every problem in the world." Gary Hart, "Democratic National Party Conference Address," 25 June 1982, Thomas O'Neill papers (TON papers), Boston College, Chestnut Hill, MA, Kirk O'Donnell Files (KOD files), box 22, folder 3, 2; Michael Kramer, "Where Does Hart Stand?" *New York Magazine*, 9 April 1984, 32.

12. ADA Voting Records: http://www.adaction.org/pages/publications/voting-records.php. The ADA's annual Liberal Quotient rating ranges from 0, meaning complete disagreement with ADA policies and, thus, a strong conservative stance, to 100, representing the opposite.

13. Rothenberg, *Neoliberals*, 27.

14. Quoted in Rothenberg, *Neoliberals*, 68–69.

15. Osborne, "The Other Senator," 27.

16. Quoted in Fay S. Joyce, "Hart Sees Triumph for His Ideas, If Not for Himself," *NYT*, 22 July 1984.

17. Stagflation represented a significant ideological crisis for Keynesianism, as rising unemployment and inflation simultaneously was seemingly impossible under the economic theory underpinning it—the Phillips curve, which presupposed an inverse relationship between the two.

18. See Bruce Schulman, "Slouching Towards the Supply-Side: Jimmy Carter and the New American Political Economy," in *The Carter Presidency: Policy Choices in the Post–New Deal Era*, ed. Gary Fink and Hugh Davis Graham (Lawrence: University Press of Kansas, 1998); and W. Carl Biven, *Jimmy Carter's Economy: Policy in an Age of Limits* (Chapel Hill: University of North Carolina Press, 2002).

19. Tom Wicker, "Democrats in Search of Ideas," *NYT*, 25 January 1981.

20. Richard Gephardt, minutes from Organizational Meeting of House Democratic Caucus (Minutes), 25 March 1981, House Democratic Caucus Records (HDC papers), Library of Congress, Washington, DC, box 14, folder 1, 34.

21. Ehrman and Flamm, *Debating the Reagan Presidency*, 55.

22. Hedrick Smith, "Reformer Who Would Reverse the New Deal's Legacy," *NYT*, 21 January 1981.

23. Adam Clymer, "Displeasure with Carter Turned Many to Reagan," *NYT*, 9 November 1980.

24. Meg Jacobs, "The 1980 Election: Victory Without Success," in *America at the Ballot Box: Elections and Political History*, ed. Gareth Davies and Julian E. Zelizer (Philadelphia: University of Pennsylvania Press, 2015), 200–201.

25. Julian E. Zelizer, *Jimmy Carter* (New York: Henry Holt, 2010), 77–84.

26. The ADA argued that "Carter ignored principles at the very heart of the Democratic Party. . . . His warped budget priorities reflect a thoroughgoing desertion of the 1976 platform." Joseph L. Rauh Jr. and Arthur M. Schlesinger Jr., Letter to ADA National Board, 13 September 1980, Patsy T. Mink papers (Mink papers), Library of Congress, Washington, DC, box 856, folder 5.

27. Kennedy said in his autobiography: "I watched the televised talk with mounting incredulousness and outrage. This message was contrary to—it was in conflict with—all the ideals of the Democratic Party that I cherished. . . . I tried to imagine President Kennedy or Bobby Kennedy ever abandoning their optimism in the face of adversity and giving vent to sentiments remotely this melancholy." Edward M. Kennedy, *True Compass: A Memoir* (New York: Twelve, 2009), 367.

28. Steven V. Roberts, "Blue-Collar Democrats Slipping to Reagan," *NYT*, 20 April 1980.

29. "How Americans Swung to Reagan," *U.S. News & World Report*, 17 November 1980.

30. Kennedy backers who switched to Anderson included the New York Liberal Party: "New York's Top Democrats Backing Anderson," *NYT*, 4 July 1980; and the National Organization for Women: "NOW Parley Dominated by Politics," *NYT*, 4 October 1980; Editorial, "John Anderson for President," *TNR*, 4 October 1980. Arthur Schlesinger Jr., who wrote in his diary that "Carter was a disaster to both the party and the country," also decided to support Anderson in what he described as "the general doldrums." Arthur M. Schlesinger Jr., *Journals, 1952–2000*, ed. Andrew Schlesinger and Stephen Schlesinger (London: Atlantic Books, 2008), 498–503.

31. Rauh Jr. and Schlesinger Jr., "Letter"; ADA National Board Document, "1980 Presidential Election," 21 September 1980, Mink papers, box 856, folder 5.

32. Quoted in "Of Kennedy, Carter, the UN and the Money Gap," *Newsweek*, 24 March 1980, 9.

33. Clymer, "Displeasure with Carter."

34. Peter Hart, "The Regeneration of the Democrats," [n.d.], TON papers, KOD files, box 21-2, folder 4–5.

35. 1980 Election results, *APP*, https://www.presidency.ucsb.edu/statistics/elections/1980.

36. In large part, this was due to significant Democratic majorities in Senate contests in California (1.6 million), Ohio (1.6 million), and Illinois (619,006), and some razor-thin margins in Republican victories (six of their twenty victories were achieved by margins of less than 1 percent). Tom Wicker, "Democrats in Search of Ideas," *NYT*, 25 January 1981.

37. Kirk O'Donnell, memorandum, "Political Agenda for House Democrats," 4 August 1981, TON papers, box 13, folder 16, 1.
38. A report prepared for the ADA presented convincing evidence that length of service was more significant than ideology as dissatisfaction with the status quo led voters to "throw the rascals out." Indeed, Barry Goldwater—the dean of conservatism—came close to losing his seat during a supposed conservative tidal wave. Kamber Report, "The Political Prognosis for the 97th Congress," [n.d.], Mink papers, box 852, folder 3.
39. David Rogers, "A Tale of Two Democratic Parties; One Looks to Labor; The Other to High-Tech Future," *The Boston Globe (BG)*, 28 November 1982.
40. Quoted in Rothenberg, *Neoliberals*, 19.
41. Quoted in Ehrman, *The Eighties*, 76.
42. Paul E. Tsongas, "Speech Before the National Press Club," 5 October 1982, Paul E. Tsongas Congressional Collection (Tsongas papers), University of Massachusetts Center for Lowell History, Lowell, MA, box 1B, folder 23, 8–9.
43. Rothenberg, *Neoliberals*, 20.
44. Charles Peters, "A Neoliberal Manifesto," *The Washington Monthly*, May 1983.
45. Roscoe Drummond, "Is Kennedy's Future Behind Him?" *The Christian Science Monitor (CSM)*, 9 July 1980.
46. According to Bob Shrum, while Kennedy was being "pigeonholed as a kind of knee-jerk liberal . . . nothing could be further from the truth." Quoted in Michael Kramer, "See How They Run—Already," *New York Magazine*, 24 November 1980, 11.
47. Edward Kennedy, ADA Speech, 4 April 1981, Adam Clymer personal papers, John F. Kennedy Presidential Library, Boston, MA, series 4, box 13, folder 1.
48. Patsy Mink, University of Houston Speech, 1 February 1981, Mink papers, box 855, folder 7; Walter Mondale, "The Re-Education of Walter Mondale," *NYT*, 8 November 1981.
49. "Of a sudden, the GOP has become a party of ideas." Letter from Congressman Ted Weiss to Senator Daniel P. Moynihan (quoting Moynihan's remarks), 20 November 1980, Daniel P. Moynihan personal papers (DPM papers), Library of Congress, Washington, DC, part II, box 2, folder 3; The rise of so-called advocacy think tanks as part of the conservative movement's ascendancy, who acted as institutional incubators for these ideas, compounded the problem. According to the Heritage Foundation, they were "the intellectual shock troops of the conservative revolution." Amy Wilentz, "On the Intellectual Ramparts," *Time*, 1 September 1986.
50. Long was the distant cousin of Huey P. Long, a former governor and US senator; of Earl, Huey's brother and also a governor; and of Senator Russell B. Long. Joan Cook, "Rep. Gillis Long, 61, Louisiana Liberal, Dies," *NYT*, 22 January 1985.
51. Minutes, 8 December 1980, HDC papers, box 12, folder 16, 11–12.
52. Karl Gerard Brandt, "The Ideological Origins of the New Democrat Movement," *The Journal of the Louisiana Historical Association* 48, no. 3 (2007): 273–294, (281–283).

53. Brandt, "Ideological Origins of the New Democrat Movement," 281.
54. Brandt, "Ideological Origins of the New Democrat Movement," 281.
55. Brandt, "Ideological Origins of the New Democrat Movement," 284.
56. Jon F. Hale, "The Making of the New Democrats," *Political Science Quarterly* 110, no. 2 (1995): 207–232 (210). Regionally, the CPE reflected both the foundational strength of the Democratic Party, with eighteen representatives from the Northeast and Midwest, and the emerging powerhouse of the Sunbelt, with nineteen representatives from the South and West. CPE report, "Rebuilding the Road to Opportunity: A Democratic Direction for the 1980s," September 1982, HDC papers, box 63, folder 2.
57. Geraldine Ferraro, "Report of the HDC Special Task Force on Women's Economic Issues," 2 August 1982, HDC papers, box 63, folder 1, 1–12.
58. Hale, "New Democrats," 210.
59. Al From, memorandum to Representatives Gephardt and Wirth, 12 September 1982, HDC papers, box 63, folder 1; Baer, *Reinventing Democrats*, 42–43.
60. Thomas B. Edsall, "'Atari Democrats' Join Party Conflicts Revived by Gains," *WP*, 7 November 1982. According to the *New York Times*, "When the Atari Democrats first emerged in the early Reagan years, their commitments to investment won them much criticism from older liberals, who considered their neoliberalism as warmed-over Reaganism." E. J. Dionne, "Greening of Democrats: An 80's Mix of Idealism and Shrewd Politics," *NYT*, 14 June 1989.
61. Minutes, 13 July 1983, HDC papers, box 18, folder 5, 17.
62. Joyce, "Hart Sees Triumph."
63. Letter from Daniel P. Moynihan to Tom Wicker, 27 June 1980, DPM papers, box 2, folder 3.
64. Quoted in Rothenberg, *Neoliberals*, 161–162.
65. Steven V. Roberts, "Democrats: An Aye for Business," *NYT*, 1 March 1981.
66. To Gary Hart, these new ideas were allowing liberals to develop a "comprehensive successor to the New Deal." Quoted in "The Neo-Liberals Push Their Own Brand of Reform," *Business Week*, 31 January 1983, Tsongas papers, box 60C, folder 5.
67. Quoted in Osborne, "The Other Senator," 27.
68. Arguably though, for all the talk of adapting to fiscal restraint by making tough choices, this emphasis on growth essentially provided political cover to its proponents, enabling them to avoid choosing between policy priorities and potentially setting different groups in the party's coalition against one another. This approach was tested early when Reagan's economic recovery plan, which was ostensibly about encouraging growth, came before Congress in 1981. The Economic Recovery Tax Act relied on Democratic defections, particularly from members of the Conservative Democratic Forum, to ensure passage. Of those within the reform cluster, Senators Tsongas and Hart opted not to support it, as did several members of the CPE, including Ferraro, while others, including Chairman Long, voted in the affirmative. According to *CQ Press*, many of those Democrats saw supporting it as a strategic way to shift all responsibility for the economic

consequences to Reagan. "Congress Enacts President Reagan's Tax Plan," *CQ Almanac 1981*, 37th ed. (Washington, DC: Congressional Quarterly, 1982), http://library.cqpress.com/cqalmanac/cqal81-1171841, 91–104.

69. Letter from Gillis Long to HDC Members, 16 May 1983, HDC papers, box 16, folder 1, 4.

70. Hale, "New Democrats," 210.

71. "The Democrats and MITI-Minus," *NYT*, 22 September 1982.

72. Gillis Long, Statement on Rebuilding the Road to Opportunity, 21 September 1982, HDC papers, box 63, folder 1.

73. "Skirting the Fairness Issue," *WP*, 27 September 1982.

74. Minutes, 1 February 1984, HDC papers, box 19, folder 2, 25. Along with McGovern, liberal Senators Frank Church (Idaho), John Culver (Iowa), and Birch Bayh (Indiana) all lost their seats in 1980 following a targeted campaign by the National Conservative Political Action Committee. See Marc C. Johnson, *Tuesday Night Massacre: Four Senate Elections and the Radicalization of the Republican Party* (Norman: University of Oklahoma Press, 2021).

75. Long Letter, 16 May 1983, 1–7. As part of a prerecorded package, twenty-five Democrats provided the DNC response, including Senators Joe Biden and Paul Tsongas, Representatives Paul Simon and Tim Wirth, and Speaker O'Neill. https://www.c-span.org/video/?c5002903/user-clip-1983-democratic-state-union-response.

76. To be sure, Kennedy did say that "to achieve this, we do not have to call ourselves neoliberals." Edward Kennedy, Address before the Democratic Midterm Conference, 27 June 1982, TON papers, box 3, folder 3, 5.

77. Quoted in Rothenberg, *Neoliberals*, 245.

78. Gillis Long, Statement on National House Democratic Caucus, 19 July 1983, HDC papers, box 63, folder 3. Some wondered whether this move instead reflected a realization that the HDC had failed to truly impact the political status quo after three years of activity. See David Price, *Bringing Back the Parties* (Washington, DC: CQ Press, 1984), 284.

79. Press Release, "Top Democrats Form National Caucus to Promote United Party Program," 19 July 1983, HDC papers, box 63, folder 3.

80. Hale, "New Democrats," 210–211.

81. Gillis Long, Preface to "Renewing America's Promise: A Democratic Blueprint for Our Nation's Future," [n.d.], HDC papers, box 63, folder 6, v.

82. Long, Preface to "Renewing America's Promise."

83. Democratic Agenda, a liberal group formed to hold Carter to account after 1976, proposed numerous platform planks to "fight for progressive social and economic programs." Democratic Agenda Press Releases, "Open Convention Urged on Platform Issues," 12 August 1980, Theodore H. White personal papers, John F. Kennedy Presidential Library, Boston, MA, series 08.2, box 48, folder 7. Also see Stanley, *Kennedy vs. Carter*, 158–170.

84. For a comprehensive account of how reform and counterreform efforts shaped the Democratic Party, see Adam Hilton, *True Blues: The Contentious*

Transformation of the Democratic Party (Philadelphia: University of Pennsylvania Press, 2021).

85. Miroff, *Liberals' Moment*, 19–23.

86. James T. Patterson, *Grand Expectations: The United States, 1945–1974*, 2nd ed. (Oxford: Oxford University Press, 1997), 760.

87. Edsall, "Race," *The Atlantic*, May 1991.

88. Minutes, 18 November 1981, HDC papers, box 14, folder 14, 16–19.

89. Adam Clymer, "Democrats: New Views," *NYT*, 24 September 1981.

90. Minutes, 21 October 1981, HDC papers, box 14, folder 13, 26.

91. Minutes, 29 January 1981, HDC papers, box 13, folder 6, 61.

92. Excerpts from Hunt Commission Report, *NYT*, 27 March 1982; Baer, *Reinventing Democrats*, 47.

93. Minutes, 3 February 1982, HDC papers, box 15, folder 1, 9–14.

94. Minutes, 3 February 1982, HDC papers, 13.

95. Susan Estrich, "Unintended Consequences," memorandum to the Hunt Commission, 9 September 1981, in Elaine Kamarck, "A History of 'Super-Delegates' in the Democratic Party," 14 February 2008, https://www.belfercenter.org/publication/history-super-delegates-democratic-party.

96. Minutes, 3 February 1982, HDC papers, 7–10.

97. Quoted in Geraldine Ferraro, *My Story* (Evanston, IL: Northwestern University Press, 1985), 51.

98. Ferraro later noted that superdelegates were created to bring the most liberal members of the party together with its most conservative members to reach practical solutions and win elections. Geraldine Ferraro, "Got a Problem? Ask the Super," *NYT*, 25 February 2008.

99. Minutes, 21 July 1982, HDC papers, box 15, folder 7, 10–11.

100. Priscilla Southwell, "The 1984 Democratic Nomination Process: The Significance of Unpledged Superdelegates," *The American Politics Quarterly* 14, no. 1–2 (1986): 78. In later decades, the proportion of superdelegates would increase. David Nather, "Leaping Voters in a Single Bound," *Congressional Quarterly (CQ) Weekly Report*, 25 February 2008, 482.

101. Letter from Gillis Long to HDC Members, 8 June 1983, HDC papers, box 18, folder 2.

102. Quoted in Osborne, "The Other Senator," 27.

103. Diane Granat, "Whatever Happened to the Watergate Babies?" *CQ Weekly Report*, 3 March 1984.

104. Charles Peters, "Conference on Neoliberalism," 21–23 October 1983, Jefferson Reading Room, Library of Congress, Washington, DC, classification: E876. C66 1983, 1.

105. *The Nation*'s Victor Navasky described neoliberalism's appeal to racial minorities and the poor as its political flaw. Victor Ferkiss, "Neoliberalism: How New? How Liberal? How Significant? A Review Essay," *The Western Political Quarterly* 39, no. 1 (1986): 165–179, (177).

106. Peters, "Conference on Neoliberalism," 1.
107. Osborne, "The Other Senator," 58.

CHAPTER 2. PROTECTING LIBERALISM IN CONGRESS

1. Ronald Reagan, "Inaugural Address," 20 January 1981, APP, https://www.presidency.ucsb.edu/documents/inaugural-address-11.

2. Frank Newport, Jeffrey M. Jones, and Lydia Saad, "Ronald Reagan from the People's Perspective," *Gallup*, 7 June 2004, http://www.gallup.com/poll/11887/ronald-reagan-from-peoples-perspective-gallup-poll-review.aspx.

3. In a 1981 statement, Kennedy claimed that he counted his role in the passage of the VRA and its extensions as "among the most important responsibilities I have undertaken in this body." Edward Kennedy, "Statement on Introduction of the Voting Rights Amendments of 1981," 6 April 1981, Leadership Conference on Civil Rights papers (LCCR papers), Library of Congress, Washington, DC, part 2, box 66, folder 4.

4. Kennedy recounted this episode years later: Miller Center, "Interview with Edward M. Kennedy," UVA Miller Center, 31 May 2007, https://millercenter.org/the-presidency/presidential-oral-histories/edward-m-kennedy-oral-history-531 2007. Also see Ronald P. Formisano, *Boston Against Busing: Race, Class, and Ethnicity in the 1960s and 1970s* (Chapel Hill: University of North Carolina Press, 2004); and J. Anthony Lukas, *Common Ground: A Turbulent Decade in the Lives of Three American Families* (New York: Alfred A. Knopf, 1985).

5. Peter S. Canellos, *The Last Lion: The Fall and Rise of Ted Kennedy* (New York: Simon & Schuster, 2010), 237.

6. For a detailed analysis on voting rights, see Ari Berman, *Give Us the Ballot: The Modern Struggle for Voting Rights in America* (New York: Farrar, Straus and Giroux, 2015); and Jesse H. Rhodes, *Ballot Blocked: The Political Erosion of the Voting Rights Act* (Stanford, CA: Stanford University Press, 2017).

7. Jan Austin, "Edward M. Kennedy: Liberal Icon and Legendary Legislator," *CQ Almanac 2009*, 65th ed. (Washington, DC: CQ-Roll Call Group, 2010), 53–58; also see Stanley, *Kennedy vs. Carter*.

8. See Amaker, *Civil Rights*; Edsall, *Chain Reaction*; and Laham, *The Reagan Presidency*.

9. Ralph Neas, "The Untold Story Behind the Passage of the 1982 Extension of the Voting Rights Act," 27 September 1982, LCCR papers, box 8, folder 4.

10. Quoted in Canellos, *The Last Lion*, 238.

11. Eleanor Clift, "The Last Hurrah for Tip O'Neill," *Newsweek*, 17 January 1994, 22.

12. Robert Ajemian, "Tip O'Neill on the Ropes," *Time*, 18 May 1981.

13. See Martha Derthick and Steven M. Teles, "Riding the Third Rail: Social Security Reform," in *The Reagan Presidency: Pragmatic Conservatism and Its Legacies*, ed. W. Elliot Brownlee and Hugh Davis Graham (Lawrence: University Press of Kansas, 2003), 182–208.

14. Tom Morganthau, "The Third Rail of Politics," *Newsweek*, 24 May 1982, 24–26.

15. Howell Raines, "A Preview of the Democrats' New Commercials," *NYT*, 22 September 1982.

16. As Patrick Andelic argues, the recession "was less Reagan's fault than it was the Federal Reserve's, whose chairman, Paul Volcker, was determined to administer a dose of 'monetary castor oil' to finally douse the inflation that had bedeviled the American economy for a decade." Still, it badly damaged Reagan's standing, with his poll numbers going into free-fall as a result. Andelic, *Donkey Work*, 133–134; Also see Iwan Morgan, "Monetary Metamorphosis: The Volcker Fed and Inflation," *The Journal of Policy History* 24, 4 (2012): 545–571.

17. To be sure, Roosevelt (1934) and George W. Bush (2002) both gained seats in their first midterm elections, but typically presidents register losses, ranging from sixty-nine (Barack Obama, 2010) to one (JFK, 1962). See Gerhard Peters, "Seats in Congress Gained/Lost by the President's Party in Mid-Term Elections," APP, https://www.presidency.ucsb.edu/statistics/data/seats-congress-gainedlost-the-presidents-party-mid-term-elections.

18. Hedrick Smith, "Reagan Reduced," *NYT*, 7 November 1982.

19. Robert Dallek, *Flawed Giant: Lyndon Johnson and His Times, 1961–1973* (Oxford: Oxford University Press, 1998), 120.

20. While civil rights and the national Democratic Party's move to the left reconfigured partisan competition in the South from the 1960s onward, realignment in the region was a complex process that took decades to trickle down to a majority of statewide elections and local offices. See, among others, Charles S. Bullock III, Susan A. MacManus, Jeremy D. Mayer, and Mark J. Rozell, *The South and the Transformation of U.S. Politics* (Oxford: Oxford University Press, 2019).

21. At the time, a solid majority (76 percent) of the public supported passage of the VRA. George Gallup, "Voting Rights Bill Meets with Overwhelming Public Approval," Gallup Poll, 14 April 1965, Frederick Panzer papers, LBJ Library, box 179, folder marked "Civil Rights."

22. Lyndon B. Johnson, "Remarks in the Capitol Rotunda at the Signing of the VRA," 6 August 1965, APP, https://www.presidency.ucsb.edu/documents/remarks-the-capitol-rotunda-the-signing-the-voting-rights-act. Civil rights leader John Lewis wrote to President Johnson on the day of the signing, stating that the moment was just as "momentous and significant" as the Emancipation Proclamation. John Lewis, Letter to the President, 6 August 1965, White House Central Files—Legislative Background Files, LBJ Library, box 2, folder marked "Signing Ceremony in the Capitol Rotunda."

23. By 1982, nine states—Alabama, Alaska, Arizona, Georgia, Louisiana, Mississippi, South Carolina, Texas, and Virginia—and portions of thirteen others were covered by the preclearance requirements.

24. Liberal and moderate Republicans played a seminal role in advancing civil rights during the decade, with *Time* noting, for example, that "the historic civil rights bills of 1964 and 1965 would never have become law if Senate Republican

Leader Everett Dirksen had not marshaled the G.O.P. votes that quashed Southern resistance." "Civil Rights: Dirksen's Defection," *Time*, 13 May 1966.

25. Jim Rutenberg, "A Dream Undone," *NYT Magazine*, 29 July 2015.

26. Quoted in Lou Cannon, *President Reagan: The Role of a Lifetime*, 2nd ed. (New York: PublicAffairs, 2000), 458.

27. Reagan's first campaign stop after the Republican National Convention was initially scheduled to be a speech to the National Urban League, but a "scheduling problem" meant that his second stop—the Neshoba County Fair—became his first. However, as Rick Perlstein notes, whether this was a sincere "scheduling snafu" or a "deliberate strategic decision" remains contested. See Rick Perlstein, *Reaganland: America's Right Turn, 1976-1980* (New York: Simon & Schuster, 2020), 830–834.

28. Ian Haney-Lopez, *Dog Whistle Politics: How Coded Racial Appeals Have Reinvented Racism and Wrecked the Middle Class* (Oxford: Oxford University Press, 2014), 58. Certainly, as Marcus Witcher highlights, Democrats courted these voters too. Carter, for example, who received Wallace's endorsement, walked a political tightrope during his presidential campaigns by attempting to appeal to former Wallace voters without alienating African Americans. Indeed, according to Witcher, "A key element of Carter's success in 1976 was utilizing and deploying symbols of the segregationist South as surrogates." Marcus Witcher, "President Carter's Southern Strategy: The Importance of Wallace Voters in 1976 and 1980," *The Alabama Review* 72, no. 3 (2019): 178–190 [185].

29. LCCR statement and report, "Reagan Snubs Civil Rights Community," 2 November 1980, LCCR papers, box 50, folder 7.

30. See Edsall, *Chain Reaction*, 3–31.

31. Kevin P. Phillips, *The Emerging Republican Majority* (New York: Arlington House, 1969).

32. Rossinow, *The Reagan Era*, 7–8.

33. Reagan: "I've been, heart and soul all my life, active in promoting goals of that act." Quotes in H. W. Brands, *Reagan: The Life* (New York: Doubleday, 2015), 150; Leah Wright Rigueur, *The Loneliness of the Black Republican: Pragmatic Politics and the Pursuit of Power* (Princeton, NJ: Princeton University Press, 2016); and Shirley, *Rendezvous with Destiny*, 404.

34. Douglas Rossinow, "It's Time We Face the Fact That Reagan Was Hostile to Civil Rights," History News Network, 20 April 2015, http://historynewsnetwork.org/article/158887.

35. Rick Perlstein, "Lee Atwater's Infamous Interview on the Southern Strategy," *The Nation*, 13 November 2012.

36. Margaret Roberts, "This Could Be the Election in Which Black Voters Could Hold the Key to the Presidential Race," *National Journal*, 29 October 1983, 2208–2209.

37. Kiron K. Skinner, "Ronald Reagan and the African American," *National Review*, 21 February 2011.

38. Paul Downing, "The Voting Rights Act of 1965: Historical and Policy

Aspects," *Congressional Research Service*, 13 May 1981, LCCR papers, box 70, folder 1.

39. Thurmond, a former Democrat, ran as the States' Rights Democratic (also known as Dixiecrat) candidate for president in 1948, calling for continued racial segregation and opposing federal civil rights laws. He joined the Republican Party in 1964. https://www.senate.gov/senators/FeaturedBios/Featured_Bio_Thurmond.htm, accessed 25 March 2023.

40. Neas, "The Untold Story."

41. The LCCR organized a strategy meeting on 7 January 1981, just two weeks before Reagan's inauguration. "Dear Friend" letter, 3 December 1980, LCCR papers, box 68, folder 1.

42. Grounded in a firm belief that the struggle for civil rights and social justice necessitated building diverse coalitions to push for change, the LCCR was founded in 1950 as a legislative advocacy and public education organization by leaders of the civil rights movement, including A. Philip Randolph, head of the Brotherhood of Sleeping Car Porters, and the NAACP's Roy Wilkins.

43. Michael Pertschuk, *Giant Killers* (New York: W. W. Norton, 1987), 149–150; A consumer protection advocate, Pertschuk was appointed chairman of the Federal Trade Commission by President Carter in 1977. He relinquished the chairmanship after President Reagan assumed office but remained a commissioner until 1984. A sharp critic of the Reagan administration, he left office with "guns blazing," blasting that the FTC had become dominated by "economic theologians bent on stripping the commission of its power." Quoted in Mark Potts and Michael Isikoff, "Pertschuk Exits FTC with Guns Blazing," *WP*, 26 September 1984.

44. Championed by the LCCR, the 1980 Fair Housing bill would have amended Title VIII of the 1968 Civil Rights Act to revise enforcement procedures, expand coverage and protections, and increase the arsenal of mechanisms available to redress housing discrimination and neighborhood segregation. Although it passed the House, a coordinated opposition, led by Senator Orrin Hatch (R-UT), effectively blocked it in the Senate. In a VRA strategy memo two years later, Ralph Neas identified problems within the civil rights community and the inability to cope with a Senate filibuster as the key lessons to learn from the struggle. Arnold Aronson, "Memo: How the Fair Housing Bill was Defeated," 11 December 1980, LCCR papers, box 42, folder 9; Neas, "The Untold Story."

45. Neas, "The Untold Story."

46. Edward Kennedy, "Press Release—Introduction of the Voting Rights Amendments of 1981," 6 April 1981, LCCR papers, box 66, folder 4.

47. Fred Barbash, "Justices Limit Court Powers Under VRA," *WP*, 23 April 1980.

48. "VRA Fact Sheet," Joint Center for Political Studies report, [n.d.], LCCR papers, box 2, folder 1.

49. Robert Pear, "Major Fight Expected over Efforts to Extend Voting Rights Measure," *NYT*, 9 March 1981.

50. Extension of the Voting Rights Act: Hearings Before the Subcommittee on

Civil and Constitutional Rights, House of Representatives, 97th Congress, 1st sess., May–July 1981, https://catalog.hathitrust.org/Record/002758376, 173.

51. A lobbying packet encouraged activists to start grassroots "feedback" projects and focus on local media to "educate the general public and broaden support." NAACP Lobbying Packet, 10 June 1981, LCCR papers, box 66, folder 4.

52. Quoted in Thomas M. Boyd and Stephen J. Markman, "The 1982 Amendments to the VRA: A Legislative History," *Washington and Lee Law Review* 40, no. 4 (1983): http://scholarlycommons.law.wlu.edu/wlulr/vol40/iss4/3, 1368–1369. Hyde later outlined his reasoning in an op-ed. Henry Hyde, "Why I Changed My Mind on the VRA," *WP*, 21 July 1981, LCCR papers, box 69, folder 3.

53. LCCR memo to radio producers, 7 December 1981, LCCR papers, box 68, folder 2.

54. Ralph Neas, "Annual Report," 21 February 1982, LCCR papers, box 3, folder 3, 4.

55. Neas, "Annual Report," 4.

56. Ralph Neas, "Memo: The Commencement of Our Senate Strategy," 23 October 1981, LCCR papers, box 68, folder 2.

57. Memo, "VRA Extension," [n.d.], Daniel P. Moynihan papers (DPM papers), Library of Congress, Washington, DC, part 2, box 49, folder 6.

58. Ronald Reagan, "Statement About Extension of the VRA," 6 November 1981, APP, https://www.presidency.ucsb.edu/documents/statement-about-extension-the-voting-rights-act. In October 1981, Reagan called the House-passed measure "pretty extreme" and hoped that the Senate would pass "a more reasonable" bill. Quoted in David Broder, "Strange Notions," *WP*, 28 October 1981.

59. "1982 Election Material—Civil Rights," DPM papers, box 49, folder 6; Tom Wicker, "Subsidizing Racism," *NYT*, 12 January 1982.

60. In what the *New York Times* described as "another modification of his position," Reagan now promised to submit legislation to "prohibit tax exemptions for organizations that discriminate on the basis of race," declaring: "I am unalterably opposed to racial discrimination in any form." He explained that "the sole basis" of his initial decision was his opposition "to administrative agencies exercising powers that the Constitution assigns to the Congress." Ronald Reagan, "Statement on Tax Exemptions for Private, Nonprofit Educational Institutions," 12 January 1982, Ronald Reagan Presidential Library, https://www.reaganlibrary.gov/archives/speech/statement-tax-exemptions-private-nonprofit-educational-institutions-january-12-1982; Steven R. Weisman, "Reagan Acts to Bar Tax Break to Schools in Racial Bias Cases," *NYT*, 19 January 1982.

61. Bill Keller and Nadine Cohodas, "Liberal Lobby Strengthened," *Congressional Quarterly (CQ) Press*, 16 October 1982.

62. Voting Rights Act: Hearings Before the Subcommittee on the Constitution, US Senate, 97th Congress, 2nd sess., January–March 1982, https://catalog.hathitrust.org/Record/002762730, 66–76.

63. Voting Rights Act: Hearings, https://catalog.hathitrust.org/Record/002762730, 78.

64. Voting Rights Act: Hearings, https://catalog.hathitrust.org/Record/00276 2730, 243–248.

65. "Purpose v Effect, An LCCR Report," 3 November 1981, LCCR papers, box 68, folder 2; Senator Ernest Hollings (D-SC) added that results spoke louder than words of intent: "Those who discriminate do not commonly advertise their motives." Ernest Hollings, "Extend the VRA," 23 March 1982, LCCR papers, box 4, folder 9.

66. Voting Rights Act: Hearings, https://catalog.hathitrust.org/Record/00276 2730, 219.

67. LCCR, "Memo to Editors," 14 April 1982, LCCR papers, box 7, folder 7.

68. Quoted in Abigail Thernstrom, *Whose Votes Count? Affirmative Action and Minority Voting Rights* (Cambridge: Harvard University Press, 1987), 135.

69. Quoted in Adam Clymer, *Edward M. Kennedy: A Biography* (New York: Harper, 2009), 325.

70. Mary Thornton, "Senate Panel Approves Voting Act Compromise," *WP*, 5 May 1982, LCCR papers, box 69, folder 3.

71. Joanne Omang, "Senate Chokes Off VRA Filibuster, 97–0," *WP*, 18 June 1982, LCCR papers, box 69, folder 3.

72. Julia Malone, "VRA: Even Conservative Senate Heeds Civil-Rights Groups," *CSM*, 21 June 1982.

73. Quoted in Mary F. Berry, "Ronald Reagan and the Leadership Conference on Civil Rights," in *Winning While Losing: Civil Rights, the Conservative Movement, and the Presidency from Nixon to Obama*, ed. Kenneth Osgood and Derrick E. White (Gainesville: University Press of Florida, 2014), 11.

74. Ronald Reagan, "Remarks on Signing the Voting Rights Act Amendments of 1982," 29 June 1982, APP, https://www.presidency.ucsb.edu/documents/remarks-signing-the-voting-rights-act-amendments-1982.

75. Howell Raines, "VRA Signed by Reagan," *NYT*, 30 June 1982.

76. Ralph Neas, "Letter to Janet Kohn," 16 July 1982, LCCR papers, box 7, folder 7.

77. Ralph Neas, "Memo: 32nd Annual Meeting and Dinner," 23 December 1981, LCCR papers, box 2, folder 1.

78. Benjamin Hooks, "Statement of the LCCR on the VRA Extension," 29 June 1982, LCCR papers, box 67, folder 7.

79. Dianne M. Pinderhughes, "Black Interest Groups and the 1982 Extension of the Voting Rights Act," in *Blacks and the American Political System*, ed. Huey L. Perry and Wayne Parent (Gainesville: University Press of Florida, 1995), 216–217.

80. Ralph Neas, "Speaking Out," *The Civil Rights Quarterly* 14, no. 2 (Summer 1982), LCCR papers, box 4, folder 9.

81. Ralph Neas, "Letter to Edward Kennedy," 23 July 1982, LCCR papers, box 7, folder 7.

82. Edward Kennedy, "Ralph Neas—The 101st Senator for Civil Rights," *Congressional Record*, 104th Congress, 1st sess., 141:71, 2 May 1995.

83. Ralph Neas, "Annual Report," 23 January 1983, LCCR papers, box 3, folder 5.

84. Poll from William Raspberry, "Reagan's Problem with Blacks," *NYT*, 22 February 1982.
85. Quoted in Jacqueline Trescott and Eve Ferguson, "Chairman Clarence Pendleton Jr.," *WP*, 14 November 1982.
86. Juan Williams, "The Harsh Message for Blacks from Clarence Pendleton," *WP*, 12 June 1988.
87. NOW memo, "US Commission on Civil Rights," 23 August 1982, National Organization for Women papers (NOW papers), Schlesinger Library, Cambridge, MA, collection MC496, box 97, folder 3.
88. Ralph Neas, "Statement Regarding the Civil Rights Commission Compromise," 8 December 1983, LCCR papers, box 9, folder 1.
89. "Letter to Attorney General," 17 October 1986, LCCR papers, box 65, folder 4.
90. Quoted in Howard Kurtz, "Justice Dept. Won't Assess Possible Bias in Election Plans," *WP*, 30 August 1986.
91. Adrienne Jones and Andrew J. Polsky, "How to Win a 'Long Game': The Voting Rights Act, the Republican Party, and the Politics of Counter-Enforcement," *Political Science Quarterly* 136 (2021): 215–248.
92. Franklin D. Roosevelt, "Message to Congress on Social Security," 17 January 1935, APP, https://www.presidency.ucsb.edu/node/208633.
93. Robert Ball, memo: "Social Security: Making Sure It Will Be There When You Need It," 25 October 1982, DPM papers, box 293, folder 1, 3.
94. Milton Freidman, *Free to Choose: A Personal Statement* (Orlando, FL: Harcourt, 1980), 102; Stephen Chapman, "Preserving the Sanctity of SS," *Democrat and Chronicle*, 29 July 1982.
95. David Stockman, *The Triumph of Politics: How the Reagan Revolution Failed* (New York: Harper & Row, 1986), 181.
96. Edward D. Berkowitz, *Robert Ball and the Politics of Social Security* (Madison: University of Wisconsin Press, 2003), 276.
97. Ball, "Social Security: Making Sure It Will Be There When You Need It," 3.
98. Robert A. Beck, "Memo to National Commission on Social Security Reform," 8 December 1982, DPM papers, box 293, folder 3.
99. In 1980, for example, the benefit increase, as determined by an automatic indexing formula, was 14.3 percent, while wages went up only 9 percent and increased unemployment exacerbated the situation. Larry W. Dewitt, Daniel Béland, and Edward D. Berkowitz, *Social Security: A Documentary History* (Washington, DC: CQ Press, 2008), 22.
100. Ball, "Social Security: Making Sure It Will Be There When You Need It," 3.
101. Stockman, *The Triumph of Politics*, 11.
102. Stockman, *The Triumph of Politics*, 181.
103. Reagan: "It has changed from an insurance concept to a welfare concept. It should be made voluntary." Quoted in Richard Bergholz, "Reagan to Decide Soon on Running for Office," *The Los Angeles Times (LAT)*, 22 January 1965, TON papers, box 29, folder 18.

104. Douglas E. Kneeland, "Reagan Vows to Support Social Security Program," *NYT*, 8 September 1980.

105. Robert J. Myers, *Within the System: My Half Century in Social Security* (Winsted, CT: Actex, 1992), 9.

106. Ronald Reagan, Letter to Thomas O'Neill, 18 July 1981, TON papers, box 29, folder 24, 1.

107. Thomas O'Neill, Letter to Ronald Reagan, 21 July 1981, TON papers, box 29, folder 24, 1–2.

108. "Is Reagan Shredding the Safety Net," Democratic Study Group Special Report, 9 October 1981, no. 97-27, Democratic Study Group papers (DSG papers), Library of Congress, Washington, DC, part 2, box 82, folder 5, 5.

109. "Is Reagan Shredding the Safety Net," Democratic Study Group, 5.

110. Stockman, *The Triumph of Politics*, 190.

111. Statement of Secretary Richard S. Schweiker, 12 May 1981, DPM papers, box 357, folder 11; Derthick and Teles, "Riding the Third Rail," 193.

112. Quoted in Art Pine, "Democrats Vow Fight on Social Security," *WP*, 14 May 1981.

113. Daniel Patrick Moynihan, "Statement on Administration's Proposed Cuts in Social Security," 15 May 1981, DPM papers, box 50, folder 11.

114. The Associated Press credited Moynihan with leading "the Senate rebellion." Daniel P. Moynihan, "Senator Moynihan on Social Security," box 50, older 12.

115. Stockman, *The Triumph of Politics*, 192.

116. John A. Svahn, *There Must Be a Pony in Here Somewhere: Twenty Years with Ronald Reagan, A Memoir* (Minneapolis, MN: Langdon Street, 2011), 169.

117. Wilbur Cohen, "The Threat to Social Security," *New Leader*, 1 June 1981, DPM papers, box 357, folder 9.

118. Paul Light, *Still Artful Work: The Continuing Politics of Social Security Reform*, 2nd ed. (New York: McGraw-Hill, 1995), 118.

119. NOW Pamphlet, "Ronald Reagan Is No Friend of Older Americans," [n.d.], NOW papers, MC496, box 209, folder 35.

120. Quoted in David Shribman, "Lobbyists Mobilize for Battle over Social Security," *NYT*, 28 December 1982.

121. Census Bureau data showed that seven of every ten persons between sixty-five and seventy-four voted in 1980—nearly twice the rate of the youngest eligible to vote. "Voting and Registration in the Election of November 1980," US Bureau of the Census, series P-20, no. 370, https://www.census.gov/content/dam/Census/library/publications/1982/demo/p20-370.pdf.

122. "Election Polls—Vote by Groups, 1976–1980," *Gallup*.

123. Poll in "Senate Democrats Attack Reagan on Social Security," *BG*, 29 July 1981.

124. Paul Houston, "Reagan, O'Neill Escalate Political War on Social Security Cuts," *LAT*, 21 July 1981.

125. Vic Fingerhut, "Memo: What Democrats Should Do Tonight, Tomorrow,

the Day After, and Next Week in Response to the President's Speech," 24 September 1981, TON papers, box 18, folder 7, 3.

126. Ronald Reagan, *The Reagan Diaries*, vol. 1, *January 1981–October 1985*, ed. Douglas Brinkley (New York: Harper Collins, 2009), 69.

127. Stockman, *The Triumph of Politics*, 191.

128. Thomas O'Neill, Letter to Ronald Reagan, 7 October 1981, TON papers, box 29, folder 24; Claude Pepper, "Dear Friends" Letter, 6 October 1981, TON papers, box 20, folder 10.

129. Quoted in Warren Weaver Jr., "Arguing Against Social Security Cuts," *NYT*, 17 October 1981.

130. Fingerhut, "Memo," 3.

131. Memorandum from Kirk O'Donnell to Thomas O'Neill, "Political Agenda for House Democrats," 4 August 1981, TON papers, box 13, folder 16, 10.

132. "A Survey of the Political Climate in America and Voter Attitudes Toward the 1982 Elections," DNC report, January 1982, TON papers, box 3, folder 1, 9–10.

133. Patrick Caddell, "Memo to Leadership," 21 January 1982, TON papers, box 3, folder 1, 1.

134. Caddell expanded, "Women and blue-collar workers were returning to the fold. Social Security [is] rising to the top of the public's concerns.... The Democrats are granted an opportunity to fill the vacuum." Patrick Caddell, "DNC Polls, 1981–1982," 21 January 1982, TON papers, box 3, folder 1.

135. Gareth Davies, "The Welfare State," in Brownlee and Graham, *The Reagan Presidency*, 211.

136. The HDC designed the "Democratic Fairness Packet," containing statements on more than twenty specific issues to maximize this attack measure. Gillis Long, "The Democratic Fairness Packet," August 1982, TON papers, box 35, folder 7.

137. Jack Germond and Jules Witcover, "Voting Rights May Not Be a Reagan Issue," *WP*, 15 July 1981.

138. David Broder, "Party Chiefs Launch Post-Mortems of Mississippi Election Upset," *WP*, 10 July 1981, LCCR papers, box 69, folder 3.

139. Jon Margolis, "Dems See Rebellion in Dixie Vote Upset," *Chicago Tribune*, 9 July 1981.

140. Broder, "Mississippi Election Upset."

141. O'Donnell memo to O'Neill, 7–8.

142. Polls showed that the Democrats were "right in standing up to the Republicans by not cutting Social Security and Medicare, and in wanting to help the elderly, the poor, and the handicapped." "Statement from the Speaker's Rooms," July 1984, TON papers, box 10, folder 4.

143. The CBO also found that over two-thirds of Reagan's budget reductions were from programs benefiting those with incomes under $20,000. Report in Robert Pear, "The Fairness Issue: Reagan Battles His Image as a 'Rich Man's President,'" *NYT*, 25 July 1983.

144. Davies, "The Welfare State," 215.

145. Davies, "The Welfare State," 215.
146. Pear, "The Fairness Issue."
147. Herbert H. Denton, "Administration in Mighty Effort to Avoid Offence on Civil Rights," *WP*, 6 May 1982, LCCR papers, box 69, folder 3.
148. Quoted in Keller and Cohodas, "Liberal Lobby Strengthened."
149. Theodore Cross, "A Battle Plan for Blacks in 1980," *WP*, 16 September 1979.
150. Quoted in Adam Clymer, "Republicans Worry About Eroding Black Support," *NYT*, 14 April 1982.
151. Clymer, "Republicans Worry About Eroding Black Support."
152. Adam Clymer, "Talk of Social Security Cutbacks Causes Alarm in Ranks of GOP," *NYT*, 8 May 1982; Daniel Patrick Moynihan, "Special Report to New York: Budget Spurs Social Security Fight," [n.d.], DPM papers, box 50, folder 12.
153. Bill Peterson, "In a New Beginning, GOP Ads Will Retire Democratic Look-Alikes," *WP*, 20 June 1982.
154. Raines, "A Preview of the Democrats' New Commercials."
155. Quoted in Fred Barnes, "Emphasizing Security Aids Democrats," *BS*, 31 October 1982.
156. Quoted in Robert Shogan, "Democrats Score GOP Letter Suggesting Voluntary Social Security," *LAT*, 29 October 1982.
157. William J. Eaton, "Reagan to Cut Social Security, Kennedy Says," *LAT*, 31 October 1982.
158. The Democrats made a net gain of one seat in the Senate, though the party remained in the minority, 46–54.
159. Quoted in Peter McGrath, "The Next Two Years in The New Congress," *Newsweek*, 15 November 1982. In the postwar period until that point, only Truman, LBJ, and Ford had registered higher House losses in their first midterms: 45, 47, and 48, respectively. Still, as the *American Presidency Project* demonstrates, this became more common over time, with the average loss across all midterms from 1934 to 2018 in the House being twenty-eight seats. John T. Woolley, "The 2022 Midterm Elections: What the Historical Data Suggest," APP, 30 August 2022, https://www.presidency.ucsb.edu/analyses/the-2022-midterm-elections-what-the-historical-data-suggest.
160. Quoted in David Broder, "Foes' Gains Confront Reagan," *WP*, 4 November 1982.
161. Quoted in Trbovich, "How the Stage Was Set."
162. Smith, "Reagan Reduced."
163. Quoted in Svahn, *Twenty Years with Ronald Reagan*, 172.
164. Kenneth T. Walsh, "'Tip' and His Democrats: Where Now?" *U.S. News & World Report*, 26 November 1984, 30.
165. David Broder, "GOP Governors Strongly Criticize Reagan's Policies," *WP*, 16 November 1982.
166. Smith, "Reagan Reduced."
167. Quoted in Broder, "Foes."
168. Maurice Carroll, "Moynihan Wins Overwhelming Victory," *NYT*, 3 November 1982.

169. Broder, "Foes."
170. Richard A. Cloward, "There Ought Not to Be a Law," *Mother Jones*, May 1984, 9.
171. Benjamin Hooks, Letter to Ronald Reagan, 15 February 1983, Benjamin L. Hooks Collection (BH papers), Memphis Public Library, Memphis, TN, box 5, folder 2.
172. Thomas Cavanagh, "Black Gains Offset Losses in '82 Elections," *Focus*, December 1982, 4.
173. Benjamin Hooks, "Struggle on Speech," 12 July 1983, BH papers, box 8, folder 1.
174. Benjamin Hooks, "The NAACP Annual Convention Report," 14 July 1983, BH papers, box 5, folder 7.
175. Benjamin Hooks, "NAACP Long Range Plan," July 1987, BH papers, box 6, folder 1, 27–28.
176. Steven F. Lawson, *Running for Freedom: Civil Rights and Black Politics in American since 1941*, 4th ed. (West Sussex, UK: John Wiley & Sons, 2015), 219.
177. Lawson, *Running for Freedom*, 219.
178. Cloward, "There Ought Not to Be a Law," 9.
179. Daniel P. Moynihan, "Dear Colleague Letter," 20 January 1983, DPM papers, box 293, folder 7.
180. With a central recommendation not to "alter the fundamental structure of the Social Security program or undermine its fundamental principles," the commission still sought to address the budgetary shortfalls inherent in the system, which they had estimated would amount to a cumulative deficit of $150–200 billion by 1989 without remedial action. Their recommendations provided a framework to generate $168 billion across the decade in increased revenue and reduced outlays, primarily by raising Social Security taxes, postponing cost-of-living increases, and making some benefits subject to federal income tax. Seemingly moving from an ideological opponent to a defender of liberalism's most cherished achievement, Reagan welcomed the resulting bill, announcing at the signing ceremony that it "demonstrates for all time our nation's ironclad commitment to Social Security." Report of the National Commission on Social Security Reform, January 1983, DPM papers, box 293, folder 8, 2; David Shribman, "Don't Alter the Basics of Social Security, Panel Advises," *NYT*, 21 January 1983; Ronald Reagan, "Remarks on Signing the Social Security Amendments of 1983," APP, 20 April 1983, https://www.presidency.ucsb.edu/node/262675; Matthew Dallek, "Bipartisan Reagan-O'Neill Social Security Deal in 1983 Showed It Can Be Done," *US News & World Report*, 2 April 2009.
181. Gregory P. Noonan, "Social Security Under Attack: FDR's Son Defends Family Legacy," *US Law News*, February 1987, DPM papers, box 302, folder 5.
182. "What Is the National Committee," memo, [n.d.], DPM papers, box 302, folder 5.
183. "General Information," National Committee Pack, [n.d.], DPM papers, box 302, folder 5.

184. Older American reports, 31 October 1986, DPM papers, box 302, folder 5.

185. Daniel Béland, *Social Security: History and Politics from the New Deal to the Privatization Debate* (Lawrence: University Press of Kansas, 2005), 153. As Kevin Kruse and Julian Zelizer argue, the battle also "signaled to all sides on Capitol Hill and outside Washington that rumors of liberalism's death had been greatly exaggerated." Kevin M. Kruse and Julian E. Zelizer, *Fault Lines: A History of the United States since 1974* (New York: W. W. Norton, 2019), 116.

186. George H. W. Bush, "Remarks to the South Carolina State Legislature in Columbia," 15 February 1989, APP, https://www.presidency.ucsb.edu/node/247798.

187. "The Failing Presidency," *NYT*, 9 January 1983; Troy, *Morning in America*, 112.

CHAPTER 3. ADVANCING LIBERALISM ON THE GROUND

1. Collection of titles from the National Organization for Women's "Bad Press/Responses" folder, [n.d.], NOW papers, MC666, box 430, folder 9. For more on the backlash theory and stagnation argument, see Martin, *The Other Eighties*, 145–171; Zelizer, "Reflections," 367–392; Ronnee Schreiber, *Righting Feminism: Conservative Women & American Politics* (Oxford: Oxford University Press, 2008); and Susan M. Hartmann, "Liberal Feminism and the New Deal Order," in Bell and Stanley, eds., *Making Sense*, 202–228.

2. Faludi, *Backlash*, esp. 257–499.

3. NOW, established in 1966 by feminist activists, quickly emerged as the most powerful women's organization in the United States. But it is important to note that the organization was criticized from the outset due to its membership and issue orientation, which was seen to benefit white, middle-class women almost exclusively. With the white woman's experience often made synonymous with women's experiences, critics, such as bell hooks, claimed that the women's movement would "give lip-service to the idea of sisterhood and solidarity between women but at the same time dismiss black women." Still, as polls consistently demonstrated across decades, Black women (and Black men) supported NOW in higher proportions than white women or men. Moreover, NOW made efforts to address intersectionality throughout its existence, with "ending racism" and "promoting lesbian rights" as two of its six founding principles, and several of NOW's campaigns specifically tackled issues affecting working-class and minority women. Still, these criticisms persisted and should be kept in mind when considering the advances made by NOW in this period. See bell hooks, *Ain't I a Woman: Black Women and Feminism* (Boston: South End, 1981), 8–9; polling data in Jane Mansbridge, "How Did Feminism Get to Be," *American Prospect*, 19 December 2001. For nuance, see Stephanie Gilmore, ed., *Feminist Coalitions: Historical Perspectives on Second-Wave Feminism in the United States* (Champaign: University of Illinois Press, 2008), which provides a corrective to the view that the liberal feminist

movement was composed of middle-class white women unconcerned with labor or racial justice issues.

4. NOW National Conference booklet, 8–10 December 1982, NOW papers, MC496, box 21, folder 9, 15.

5. Eleanor Smeal, "Backlash to Reagan's Anti-Women Policies Fuels ERA Countdown Campaign," National Press Club speech, 15 June 1981, NOW papers, MC496, box 201, folder 25, 10.

6. Report quoted in Marisa Chappell, "Reagan's 'Gender Gap' Strategy and the Limitations of Free-Market Feminism," *Journal of Policy History*, 24 (2012): 115–134, (115–16).

7. Lee Atwater, "The Gender Gap: A Postelection Assessment," 23 November 1982, in Zelizer and Jacobs, *Conservatives in Power*, 114–117.

8. "Women Vote Differently Than Men, Feminist Bloc Emerges in 1980 Elections," *National NOW Times*, 1981, NOW papers, MC496, box 4, folder 46. Like the electorate it reflects, the gender gap is complex, but at a basic level, political observers defined it as the difference between the proportion of women and the proportion of men who support a particular politician, party, or policy position. See, among others, Carol M. Mueller, ed., *The Politics of the Gender Gap: The Social Construction of Political Influence* (London: Sage, 1988); Pamela Conover, "Feminists and the Gender Gap," *Journal of Politics* 50 (1988): 985–1010; and Carole Kennedy Chaney et al., "Explaining the Gender Gap in U.S. Presidential Elections, 1980–1992," *Political Research Quarterly* 51 (1998): 311–339.

9. In Congress, for example, a record 119 women stood for election in 1992, with 53 of them victorious. "Summary of Women Candidates for Selected Offices, 1979–2014," Center for American Women and Politics (CAWP), http://www.cawp.rutgers.edu/sites/default/files/resources/can_histsum.pdf.

10. While gender differences in presidential voting had occurred in the past, the margins were much smaller than in 1980 and generally favored the Republican Party instead; more women than men voted for Richard Nixon in 1960 (2 percent) and Gerald Ford in 1976 (3 percent). Henry C. Kenski, "The Gender Factor in a Changing Electorate" in Mueller, *Gender Gap*, 50.

11. "Gender Differences in Voter Turnout," CAWP, https://cawp.rutgers.edu/facts/voters/gender-differences-voter-turnout, accessed 9 May 2023.

12. Quoted in Anne N. Costain, "Women's Claim as a Special Interest," in *Gender Gap*, 167.

13. "Republican Party Platform," 15 July 1980, APP, https://www.presidency.ucsb.edu/node/273420.

14. Liberal Republican, Senator Charles Mathias, tried to protect the ERA, saying that to drop it would "imply that the party has backed away from its basic commitment to equal rights for women." Charles Mathias, "Letter to Colleagues," 1 July 1980, ERAmerica records, Library of Congress, Washington, DC, box 34.

15. NOW board meeting minutes, 6–7 December 1980, NOW papers, MC496, box 4, folder 46, 2.

16. "Feminist Bloc Emerges," *National NOW Times*. Evidently, the gender gap is a multifaceted, multicausal phenomenon; Jane Mansbridge produced a compelling contemporary argument challenging the extent of the ERA/gender gap connection in the 1980 elections. Jane E. Mansbridge, "Myth and Reality: The ERA and the Gender Gap in the 1980 election," *Public Opinion Quarterly* 49 (1985): 164–178.

17. In 2022, the Supreme Court overturned *Roe* in *Dobbs v. Jackson Women's Health Organization*. See https://www.supremecourt.gov/opinions/21pdf/19-1392_6j37.pdf.

18. NOW minutes, 6–7 December 1980.

19. "Double Victory for Women's Reproductive Rights," memo to NOW activists, 20 September 1982, NOW papers, MC496, box 203, folder 7.

20. Jon A. Shields, "Fighting Liberalism's Excesses: Moral Crusades During the Reagan Revolution," *The Journal of Policy History* 26 (2014): 103–120, (110).

21. Shields, "Fighting Liberalism's Excesses," 110–111; Also see, Daniel K. Williams, *God's Own Party: The Making of the Christian Right* (Oxford: Oxford University Press, 2010), 153–171.

22. The largest gender difference in presidential approval was just three points (3 percent fewer women than men approved of Nixon's job performance). Kenski, "The Gender Factor," 48.

23. Gallup polls, 8 July 1982 and 25 July 1983, NOW papers, MC666, box 361, folder 9.

24. Martin Gilens, "Gender and Support for Reagan: A Comprehensive Model of Presidential Approval," *American Journal of Political Science* 32 (1988): 19–49, (19).

25. Everett C. Ladd, "Does Reagan Have a Problem with Women?" *Public Opinion*, December 1982, 46.

26. Adam Clymer, "Women Votes Are a Reagan Woe," *NYT*, 19 November 1981.

27. NARAL is the oldest US abortion rights advocacy group, founded in 1969 to oppose restrictions and expand access to abortion.

28. "Women Can Make the Difference," NOW report, 1981, NOW papers, MC496, box 209, folder 38.

29. Judy Mann, "Women," *WP*, 21 October 1981.

30. According to the report, both parties viewed these elections as a test of Reagan's "mandate," particularly the Virginia gubernatorial race. As NOW highlighted, exit polls demonstrated that women preferred Democrat Charles Robb by a substantial margin. "Women Can Make the Difference—Revised," NOW report, January 1982, NOW papers, MC496, box 209, folder 39.

31. Kathy Bonk, "Gender Gap Update," 26 August 1982, NOW papers, MC725, box 54, folder 24.

32. In 1982, Wilson reported that a lot of women were saying "I can't be a Republican anymore." Quoted in "Women and Politics," *CQ Researcher*, 17 September 1982, 2.

33. Elizabeth Mehren, "A Faux Pas by Reagan Widens the Gender Gap," *LAT*, 11 August 1983.

34. See, among others, James T. Patterson, *America's Struggle Against Poverty in the Twentieth Century*, 4th ed. (Cambridge: Harvard University Press, 2000); and Susan Ware, *Beyond Suffrage: Women in the New Deal* (Cambridge: Harvard University Press, 1981).

35. Kiron K. Skinner, Annelise Anderson, and Martin Anderson, *Reagan's Path to Victory, The Shaping of Ronald Reagan's Vision: Selected Writings* (New York: Simon & Schuster, 2004), 75–76.

36. Kaaryn S. Gustafson, *Cheating Welfare: Public Assistance and the Criminalization of Poverty* (New York: New York University Press, 2011), 35–37; Daniel Geary also explores the intersections of racial inequality, welfare, gender, and social roles in his 2015 study *Beyond Civil Rights*. Geary, *Beyond Civil Rights: The Moynihan Report and Its Legacy* (Philadelphia: University of Pennsylvania Press, 2015).

37. Ann Mari May and Kurt Stephenson, "Women and the Great Retrenchment: The Political Economy of the 1980s," *Journal of Economic Issues* 28 (1994): 533–542, (538).

38. A 1986 study noted the inability of "social institutions to support the changing economic role of women." Suzanne Bianchi, "American Women in Transition," *NYT*, 30 December 1986.

39. "A Growing Crisis: Disadvantaged Women and Their Children," US Commission on Civil Rights, May 1983, http://babel.hathitrust.org/cgi/pt?id=uiug.301 12075634441;view=1up;seq=1, 27–33.

40. Eleanor Smeal, "Sex Discrimination in the Work Place," 28 January 1981, NOW papers, MC496, box 201, folder 24, 7. Unemployment was far more pronounced in minority communities as well, with Black unemployment sitting at over 20 percent at the time and Black women in particular often facing the double bind of structural racism and sexism. William L. Taylor and David Tatel, "The Great Society's Contribution on Civil Rights," memo to Joseph Califano, 4 April 1985, Joseph A. Califano papers, LBJ Library, box 55, folder marked "Great Society, Civil Rights," 15.

41. "Women and Politics," *CQ Researcher*, 17 September 1982, 3.

42. Ann Lewis, "Return of the Gender Gap—Just in Time for November," *Ms. Magazine*, January 1992.

43. "A Growing Crisis," 6; "Bridging the Gender Gap," *BS*, 13 July 1983.

44. Smeal, "Sex Discrimination," 7.

45. "Ronald Reagan's Budget and Women," NOW report, [n.d.], NOW papers, MC496, box 89, folder 11.

46. The NWRO, a multiracial coalition, operated from 1966 to 1975, before filing for bankruptcy. On the organization's focus, see the seminal essay by Johnnie Tillman, "Welfare Is a Women's Issue," *Ms. Magazine*, May 1972.

47. Judith Shulevitz, "Forgotten Feminisms: Johnnie Tillman's Battle Against 'The Man,'" *New York Review of Books*, 26 June 2018.

48. "NOW's Response to the Attorney General," [n.d.], NOW papers, MC666, box 371, folder 7.

49. Quoted in "Views of NOW," *NBC Today Show*, 11 October 1982.
50. Adam Clymer, "Warning on 'Gender Gap' from the White House," *NYT*, 3 December 1982.
51. Patricia Schroeder, "All but War on Women," *Houston Chronicle*, 6 November 1981.
52. Hedrick Smith, "Public's Approval of Reagan in Poll Rising but Limited," *NYT*, 3 July 1983.
53. Judy Goldsmith, Speech to the Illinois Commission on the Status of Women, 23 February 1984, NOW papers, MC496, box 201, folder 28.
54. Phyllis Schlafly, "Time Is Running Out on the E.R.A," *Phyllis Schlafly Report (PSR)*, February 1978, ERAmerica Records, box 124, 2.
55. See Donald Critchlow, *Phyllis Schlafly and Grassroots Conservatism* (Princeton, NJ: Princeton University Press, 2005).
56. Douglas Johnson, "The E.R.A./Abortion Link and How It Can Be Broken," National Right to Life factsheet, 12 January 1984, NOW papers, MC496, box 191, folder 1; Phyllis Schlafly, "Will E.R.A. Make Child-Care the State's Job?" *PSR*, November 1975, ERAmerica Records, box 124, 1.
57. Quoted in Critchlow, *Phyllis Schlafly*, 247–248.
58. "ERA Gains Highest Level of Support," *Miami Herald*, 9 August 1981.
59. As NOW pointed out, while 95 percent of candidates running were men, 20 percent of NOW's funds went to those 5 percent of female candidates. Judy Goldsmith, NOW National Conference speech, 1 October 1983, NOW papers, MC496, box 25, folder 31, 1.
60. Adam Clymer, "Women's Election Role Is Disturbing to G.O.P.," *NYT*, 18 November 1982.
61. Eleanor Smeal, *Why and How Women Will Elect the Next President* (New York: Harper & Row, 1984), 14–15.
62. Griffiths played a seminal role in getting the ERA passed in Congress in the early 1970s.
63. Smeal, *Next President*, 15.
64. Quoted in Kathy Bonk, "The Selling of the 'Gender Gap,'" in *Gender Gap*, 95.
65. With three hundred full-time staff and over seven thousand volunteers working the campaign, NOW estimated that they raised and spent over $10 million in the final year of the ERA battle. Toni Carabillo, "Looking Forward: Beyond the June 30 deadline," [n.d.], NOW papers, MC725, box 30, folder 2, 3.
66. Anastasia Toufexis, "Waking Up to the Gender Gap," *Time*, 18 October 1982.
67. NOW letter to activists, 10 January 1983, NOW papers, MC496, box 203, folder 7.
68. Betty Cuniberti, "NOW Turns to TV to Push ERA," *LAT*, 12 October 1981. A coalition of eight women's groups—including ERAmerica and NWPC—joined the media blitz. "Women Today," 8 March 1982, NOW papers, MC496, box 126, folder 8, 25.
69. NOW National Conference booklet, 8–10 December 1982, NOW papers, MC496, box 21, folder 9, 15.

70. Carabillo, "Looking Forward," 4.
71. NOW board meeting minutes, 10–11 December 1983, NOW papers, MC496, box 5, folder 41.
72. "Women and Politics," *CQ Researcher*, 17 September 1982, 8; Martin, *The Other Eighties*, 150.
73. Beverly Beyette, "NOW's Time, Say Feminists Promoting Vice Presidential Candidate in '84," *LAT*, 3 October 1983.
74. Judy Goldsmith, NOW National Conference speech, 30 September 1983, NOW papers, MC496, box 21, folder 10.
75. Press release, "Progress for Women in 1982 Elections with Significant Gains in ERA States," 4 November 1982, NOW papers, MC666, box 361, folder 9.
76. Report in David Broder, "Reagan's 'Gender Gap' Seen Widening," *WP*, 8 August 1983.
77. Eleanor Smeal, "Women and Politics: The Long Road," *Eleanor Smeal Report (ESR)*, 10 June 1983, ESR Collection, Schlesinger Library, Cambridge, MA, 1.
78. Presidential candidate forum, NOW National Conference, 1 October 1983, NOW papers, MC496, box 25, folder 34, 12–58.
79. Geraldine Ferraro, Democratic National Convention speech, 19 July 1984.
80. Judy Goldsmith, Democratic National Convention speech, 18 July 1984, NOW papers, MC496, box 201, folder 36.
81. Judy Goldsmith, NOW National Conference speech, 1 October 1983, NOW papers, MC496, box 201, folder 36, 1.
82. Quoted in Flora Davis, *Moving the Mountain: The Women's Movement in America Since 1960*, 2nd ed. (New York: Simon & Schuster, 1999), 420.
83. Judy Goldsmith, NOW National Conference speech, 30 June 1984, NOW papers, MC496, box 201, folder 36, 8–9.
84. Judy Goldsmith, Letter to NOW endorsed candidates, 2 July 1984, NOW papers, MC496, box 100, folder 35.
85. NOW national board resolution on Mondale, 10 December 1983, NOW papers, MC496, box 5, folder 41.
86. Miriam Louie and Gloria Quinones, "Women's Stake in the Rainbow Coalition," *The Black Scholar* 15 (1984): 27–32.
87. "The candidate we support can win" was point four of a confidential four-point priority plan justifying NOW's endorsement. The rest: (1) Candidate's position on and priority of women's issues; (2) Number of women in key staff positions; (3) Willingness to select a woman vice president. Memo from NOW/PAC to Judy Goldsmith, 12 February 1984, NOW papers, MC496, box 203, folder 28.
88. Eleanor Smeal, "What NOW's Endorsement of Mondale Means," *ESR*, 10 December 1983, 3.
89. According to NOW, these contributions would close the "dollar gap." NOW/PAC letter, [n.d.], NOW papers, MC496, box 203, folder 28.
90. Mary Jean Collins, "Voter Registration," memo to NOW national board, 28 June 1984, NOW papers, MC496, box 25, folder 6.

91. "Women's Truth Squad on Reagan," NOW memo, 17 February 1984, NOW papers, MC496, box 5, folder 47.

92. "Truth Squad," NOW memo, 5 May 1984, NOW papers, MC496, box 5, folder 50.

93. Judy Goldsmith, "Role of Women in the 1984 Elections," 7 April 1983, NOW papers, MC496, box 100, folder 35.

94. Registration packet to state chapters, 27 July 1984, NOW papers, MC496, box 203, folder 7.

95. Ferraro, *My Story*, 273.

96. Kirkpatrick, who was still a registered Democrat at the time and who switched to the Republicans in 1985, said that her party "behaved less like a dove or a hawk than like an ostrich—convinced it could shut out the world by hiding its head in the sand." Jeane J. Kirkpatrick, Republican National Convention speech, 20 August 1984, transcript: https://edition.cnn.com/ALLPOLITICS/1996/conventions/san.diego/facts/GOP.speeches.past/84.kirkpatrick.shtml.

97. Quoted in Martin, *The Other Eighties*, 155.

98. Arthur Miller, "Gender and the Vote: 1984," in *Gender Gap*, 266.

99. For detailed analysis of the Mondale campaign, see Steven Gillon, *The Democrats' Dilemma: Walter F. Mondale and the Liberal Legacy* (New York: Columbia University Press, 1992).

100. Quoted in James Reston, "Mondale and Who Else?" *NYT*, 24 June 1984; polls in Rossinow, *The Reagan Era*, 173.

101. Just three days after the midterms, an internal White House memo argued that "new, bold, and creative ideas are necessary to deal with the gender gap." Ronald H. Hinckley, "Memo: Gender Gap," 5 November 1982, Sara Fritz papers, Ronald Reagan Presidential Library, Simi Valley, CA, box 3, folder marked "White House Notes—December 1982," 2.

102. Before the midterms, Reagan had also appointed the first woman to the Supreme Court, Sandra Day O'Connor, in 1981. According to O'Connor, part of the calculus of this appointment was Reagan's desire to break through to women voters. Sandra Day O'Connor, "Sandra Day O'Connor's Last Times Interview," *NYT*, 1 December 2023; Linda Greenhouse, "Sandra Day O'Connor, First Woman on the Supreme Court, Is Dead at 93," *NYT*, 1 December 2023.

103. Juan Williams, "President Names Ex-Rep. Heckler as Head of HHS," *WP*, 13 January 1983.

104. Quoted in Karen Paget, "The Gender Gap Mystique," *American Prospect*, 19 December 2001.

105. Ellen Hume, "Politics '84, GOP Women Weigh Gender Gap," *Wall Street Journal (WSJ)*, 19 June 1984.

106. Hume, "Politics '84."

107. Ellen Goodman, "Yes, Ferraro Made a Difference," *WP*, 8 November 1984.

108. NOW did submit a platform report "Investing in People," and provided testimony to the Platform Committee, but Mondale's campaign was geared more toward tackling the deficit, reforming taxes, and reshaping foreign policy.

Judy Goldsmith, DNC Platform Committee speech, 12 June 1984, NOW papers, MC496, box 201, folder 28.

109. Kathleen Frankovic, "The Ferraro Factor," in *Gender Gap*, 119.

110. Support for Reagan by category. Race: white (men, 68 percent; women, 64 percent), Black (men, 12 percent; women, 6 percent). Age: eighteen-to-twenty-nine-year-olds (men, 61 percent; women, 55 percent); thirty-to-forty-four-year-olds (men, 62 percent; women, 54 percent). Marital status: married (men, 65 percent; women, 60 percent), unmarried (men, 63 percent; women, 50 percent). David Rosenbaum, "A Good Election for Poll Takers" *NYT*, 8 November 1984.

111. Walter F. Mondale, *The Good Fight: A Life in Liberal Politics* (New York: Simon & Schuster, 2010), 307.

112. Based on their ADA voting records, both Harkin (100 percent) and Kerry (85 percent) were considered quintessential liberals. Ann Lewis, *ADA Today*, January 1986, https://adaction.org/wp-content/uploads/2017/11/1985.pdf.

113. In a close race, Democrat Madeleine Kunin was boosted to victory in Vermont by a 12 percent gender gap vote. NOW board meeting minutes, 8–9 December 1984, NOW papers, MC496, box 6, folder 7.

114. NOW board meeting minutes, 8–9 December 1984, NOW papers, MC496, box 6, folder 7.

115. Eleanor Smeal, "Ferraro Euphoria," *ESR*, 25 July 1984, 1.

116. Eleanor Smeal, "The Ferraro Factor," *ESR*, 12 November 1984, 4.

117. Judy Klemesrud, "NOW's President: Assessing the Election," *NYT*, 27 July 1985.

118. See Jeffrey M. Berry, *The New Liberalism: The Rising Power of Citizen Groups* (Washington, DC: The Brookings Institution, 1999); and Ronald J. Hrebenar, *Interest Group Politics in America*, 3rd ed. (New York: M. E. Sharpe, 1997).

119. Klemesrud, "NOW's President"; "Judy Goldsmith Versus Eleanor Smeal," June-July 1985, NOW papers, box 216, folder 22.

120. Gloria Steinem, "Election Roundup: What No One Else Would Tell You About the Ferraro Campaign," *Ms. Magazine*, December 1984, 53.

121. Poll in Ferraro, *My Story*, 311.

122. Both quotes in Davis, *Moving the Mountain*, 428.

123. Ferraro, *My Story*, 311.

124. See "Summary," CAWP, http://www.cawp.rutgers.edu/sites/default/files/resources/can_histsum.pdf.

125. "Women and Politics, Election '88," NOW report, July 1988, NOW papers, MC666, box 370, folder 13, 1.

126. "Women and Politics, Election '88," NOW report, 18.

127. Paget, "Gender Gap Mystique."

CHAPTER 4. TURNING POINTS

1. Troy, *Morning in America*, 208; William Chafe, *The Unfinished Journey: America Since World War II* (Oxford: Oxford University Press, 1991), 477.

2. Peter Hart, "Reagan Job Rating," [n.d.], TON papers, box 21-2, folder 13.

3. "Prouder, Stronger, Better," 1984, The Living Room Candidate: Presidential Campaign Commercials, 1952–2020, Museum of the Moving Image, http://www.livingroomcandidate.org/commercials/1984, accessed 23 May 2023.

4. Robert Benenson, "Post-1984 Political Landscape," *Editorial Research Reports* (Washington, DC: CQ Press, 1985), 21–40.

5. Benenson, "Post-1984 Political Landscape."

6. Eric Alterman and Kevin Mattson, *The Cause: The Fight for American Liberalism from Franklin Roosevelt to Barack Obama* (New York: Viking, 2012), 317–318.

7. Quoted in Howell Raines, "Iowa Offers Hart Lessons for 1984," *NYT*, 8 December 1982.

8. Gerald Pomper, *The Election of 1984: Reports and Interpretations* (London: Chatham House, 1985), 15.

9. According to *Newsweek*, 1984 was the Year of the Yuppie: "the young urban professional who was a synecdoche of Reagan's America." "The Year of the Yuppie," *Newsweek*, 31 December 1984, 14–31.

10. Bill Hamilton, "Memo," 23 March 1984, TON papers, box 375-30, folder 3.

11. Randall Rothenberg, "The 'New Liberals' Are Here to Stay," *WSJ*, 5 June 1984.

12. Quoted in Chris Black, "Kerry Part of New Breed Liberals," *BG*, 11 November 1984.

13. Benenson, "Post-1984."

14. Quoted in Gillon, *Democrats' Dilemma*, 301.

15. Fred Barnes, "There Is a Stirring of Life Among Liberals," *BS*, 5 June 1983.

16. Judis and Teixeira, *Emerging Democratic Majority*, 123.

17. Peter Hart, "A Survey of the Political Climate in America," September 1983, TON papers, box 21-2, folder 13.

18. Gillon, *Democrats' Dilemma*, 395.

19. With members of union households voting Democratic by more than 2 to 1, according to exit polls, 20 (of 31) senatorial candidates, 237 (of 376) House candidates, and 24 (of 33) gubernatorial candidates endorsed by the AFL-CIO won election that year. Kathy Sawyer, "List Labor as One of the Midterm Winners," *WP*, 9 November 1982.

20. According to Hart years later, polls showed more than 50 percent of Democratic voters looking for a different kind of candidate: "That propelled me into the race." Quoted in Phil Hirschkorn, "America's Great Last Convention: Mondale, Jackson and Hart Dish to Salon About Wild 1984 DNC," *Salon*, 15 February 2015.

21. In 1983, Mondale tried to address this "special interest" criticism at a HDC meeting: "I have gone around speaking for the unemployed, speaking for minorities who are being discriminated against, speaking for women who have a right to have an equal rights amendment passed. . . . If that is special interest, count me in. If we let the Republicans have us sneak around and be ashamed of those organizations that broadly represent the great heart and purpose of this Democratic Party, we all ought to get out of the way and let somebody else take our place."

HDC minutes, 13 July 1983, HDC papers, box 18, folder 5, 67; Gillon, *Democrats' Dilemma*, 321.

22. Mondale told supporters that his endorsements and sophisticated organizational structure had laid the groundwork for victory early. Walter Mondale, "Letter to Supporters," 11 June 1982, TON papers, box 22-3, folder 3.

23. Pomper, *Election of 1984*, 17.

24. Jeff Greenfield, "Remember 1984: The Year of the Lengthy Primary Season We Now Long For," *Slate*, 7 September 2007.

25. Senators Alan Cranston and Ernest Hollings, former Senator George McGovern, and former Governor Reubin Askew completed the pack.

26. Hedrick Smith, "Mondale Lead over Nearest Rival in Poll sets Non-Incumbent Record," *NYT*, 28 February 1984.

27. Sidney Blumenthal, "Hart Attack: Big Politics Gets a Big Shock," *TNR*, 19 March 1984, 13–15.

28. Mondale, *The Good Fight*, 288.

29. Mondale, *The Good Fight*, 287.

30. Hedrick Smith, "Hart Surge Said to Ride on Generational Appeal," *NYT*, 13 March 1984.

31. CBS/NYT polls in Hedrick Smith, "The Campaign Reshaped," *NYT*, 29 February 1984.

32. O'Neill quoted in Gillon, *Democrats' Dilemma*, 338; David S. Broder, "Hart Defeats Mondale," *WP*, 5 March 1984.

33. Fay S. Joyce, "Jackson Admits Saying 'Hymie' and Apologizes at a Synagogue," *NYT*, 27 February 1984.

34. See Miroff, *Liberals' Moment*.

35. Hart was called the "General of McGovern's Army." Tom Watson, "Candidate Profiles: Gary Hart," *CQ Press*, 3 December 1983, DPM papers, box 88, folder 10, 2535–2539.

36. Gary Hart, *Right from the Start: A Chronicle of the McGovern Campaign* (New York: Quadrangle, 1973), 328–329; also see Gary Hart, *The Thunder and the Sunshine: Four Seasons in a Burnished Life* (Golden, CO: Fulcrum, 2010), 21–23.

37. Gary Hart, "The End of the New Deal," Remarks at the University of Denver, 25 September 1974, Gary Hart papers (Hart papers), University of Colorado, Boulder, CO, box 54, folder 11.

38. George Lardner Jr., "ACLU Report on '82 Calls Administration an 'Implacable Foe,'" *WP*, 11 October 1982. Moreover, Hart, who had received the endorsement of NOW's Colorado chapter in 1980 over his female Republican opponent—and was elected in large part due to the "gender gap"—argued his positions on numerous liberal issues in a letter to NOW supporters, pointing to his voting record on the ERA, reproductive rights, civil rights, environmental concerns, labor laws, unemployment issues, and Social Security, among others. Gary Hart, "Letter to NOW," 31 May 1983, NOW papers, MC496, box 100, folder 44, 1–40.

39. Quoted in Raines, "Iowa Offers Hart Lessons."

40. John A. Farrell, "Assessing Hart's Political Legacy," *BG*, 10 May 1987.

41. Quoted in David Shribman, "A Closer Look at the Hart Generation," *NYT*, 27 May 1984.
42. Gary Hart, "Now It's Our Turn," Speech to the Costigan-Cervi Democratic Club, 9 April 1974, Hart papers, box 53, folder 2.
43. Gary Hart, "Statement of Candidacy," 17 February 1983, Hart papers, box 233, folder 8.
44. Quoted in Gillon, *Democrats' Dilemma*, 341.
45. Gary Hart, "Letter to Supporters," [n.d.], NOW papers, MC496, box 100, folder 44; Hedrick Smith, "Senator Hart Tackles Party Renewal," *NYT*, 28 December 1981.
46. Memo, Joel Bradshaw to Hal Haddon, "Opening Gary's Option to Run for President in 1984," 9 March 1981, Hart papers, box 134, folder 1.
47. Memo, Bradshaw to Haddon, "Opening Gary's Option to Run."
48. Mary H. Cooper, "Organized Labor in the 1980s," *Editorial Research Reports* (Washington, DC: CQ Press, 1985), 437–456; Gillon, *Democrats' Dilemma*, 320–321.
49. Bernard Weinraub, "Mondale and Staff Decide to Resist Criticizing the Labor Movement," *NYT*, 14 February 1984.
50. Kathy Sawyer, "Mondale's Labor Backers Call Hart 'Two-Faced,'" *WP*, 6 March 1984.
51. Reagan's team skillfully recycled this rhetoric in the general campaign by producing a "Maybe Gary Hart Was Right" television advertisement featuring Hart criticizing Mondale as a creature of the past. A poll taken weeks after it aired in the battleground state of Ohio indicated that 45 percent of those who voted for Hart in the state's primary now favored Reagan. Ron Elving, "Mondale Feels Spring's Sting in Ohio," *The Milwaukee Journal*, 31 October 1984, Richard Gephardt papers (Gephardt papers), Missouri History Museum, St. Louis, MO, box 36, folder 12.
52. Pomper, *Election of 1984*, 68.
53. Gary Hart, Campaign Leaflet: "A New Generation of Leadership," April 1984, DPM papers, box 88, folder 13; Quoted in Shribman, "Hart Generation."
54. Watson, "Candidate Profiles: Gary Hart."
55. Hart, "Letter to Supporters."
56. Hart outlined these views at a meeting with the HDC. Minutes, 15 November 1983, HDC papers, box 18, folder 13, 50–55; Indeed, with nearly a decade on the Senate Armed Services Committee, Hart placed military reform at the center of his "new ideas" pitch, offering a wide range of proposals to reshape the military while simultaneously arguing that diplomatic and economic power, rather than military might, should be the nation's primary weapons. On the campaign trail, Hart was particularly scornful of Mondale's position on Central America, arguing that there should be no combat troops in the region whatsoever, while his reform proposals focused spending on tactical quality, rather than expensive weapons systems that required maintenance and thereby reduced readiness. Still, as the *New York Times* noted, despite nuanced differences, their views were "strikingly

similar." Kramer, "Where Does Hart Stand?" 33-34; Fay S. Joyce, "Mondale and Hart Clash on Central America," *NYT*, 28 March 1984; Fay S. Joyce, "Hart and Mondale Are Closer on Central America," *NYT*, 1 April 1984.

57. Minutes, 15 November 1983, HDC papers, box 18, folder 13, 50-55.

58. Gary Hart, "An Economic Strategy for the 1980s," 6 February 1982, TON papers, box 10, folder 8.

59. Martin Frost, "Blueprint Democrats: A New Force for Change," [n.d.], HDC papers, box 64, folder 7, 1.

60. John Dillin, "Hart or Mondale vs. Reagan," *CSM*, 16 May 1984.

61. Adam Clymer, "The 1984 National Primary," *Public Opinion*, August/September 1984, 52-53.

62. "Excerpts from Transcript of 5 Candidates' Debate in Atlanta," *NYT*, 12 March 1984.

63. Gary Hart, *A New Democracy: A Democratic Vision for the 1980s and Beyond* (New York: W. Morrow, 1983).

64. Gary Hart, "ABC News Appearance," 13 March 1984, https://www.youtube.com/watch?v=xwJB8vbOW3A.

65. Richard Cohen, "Gary Hart: Biography," *Political Profiles*, March 1984.

66. Howell Raines, "Victories by Hart Begin New Stage in Party Battle," *NYT*, 10 May 1984.

67. Hamilton, "Memo," 23 March 1984, TON papers, box 375-30, folder 3. Hart performed better than Mondale against Reagan through most of the primaries. Gallup Poll, "Presidential Test Elections," [n.d.], DSG papers, box 38, folder 1.

68. Targeting young people, women, and upwardly mobile voters, the ads argued that "the all new Democrat ideas and leadership . . . are really the same old empty promises that didn't work before and won't work now." Quoted in Ira R. Allen, "Campaign '84 moves to the Airwaves," *United Press International*, 1 April 1984; Adam Clymer, "Question of Who Can Beat Reagan: Hart's Efforts to Build a Campaign Issue," *NYT*, 16 April 1984.

69. Hart ended with twenty-five states in his column and 6,504,842 votes (35.85 percent) to Mondale's twenty-two states and 6,952,912 votes (38.32 percent); "Excerpts from Remarks of Mondale and Hart on the Race," *NYT*, 7 June 1984.

70. Thomas O'Neill, "API Notes," 6 June 1984, TON papers, box 18, folder 9.

71. Quoted in Fay S. Joyce, "Hart, Saying Race Is Not Over, Vowing to Fight On," *NYT*, 7 June 1984.

72. "Excerpts from Hart Speech to Convention Exhorting Party for Campaign," *NYT*, 19 July 1984.

73. Judis and Teixeira, *Emerging Democratic Majority*, 124.

74. Those making over $25,000 preferred Hart to Mondale, as did those under the age of thirty, who supported Hart by a 39-26 margin. Judis and Teixeira, *Emerging Democratic Majority*, 124.

75. Steven Roberts, "Hart Taps a Generation of Young Professionals," *NYT*, 18 March 1984.

76. David S. Broder, "Mondale Sets a New Theme," *WP*, 20 July 1984.

77. The Democratic Platform, 16 July 1984, APP, https://www.presidency.ucsb.edu/node/273258; Peter T. Kilborn, "Democrats Make Plans to Avoid 'Big Spender' Label," *NYT*, 8 July 1984.

78. Quoted in Ronald Smothers, "Jackson Sees Political Move in Mondale Search for No. 2," *NYT*, 20 June 1984.

79. Owen Ullmann, "Democratic Platform: Old Liberalism, New Economics," *Philadelphia Inquirer*, 22 June 1984. While the 1980 platform was a similar size, Democratic platforms have been typically around the ten-to-twenty-five-thousand-word range since the 1960s. In a stark shift from 1984, the 1988 Democratic platform was a mere 4,838 words. "Political Party Platforms of Parties Receiving Electoral Votes," APP, www.presidency.ucsb.edu/node/324129.

80. William Greider, "Give 'Em Hell, Fritz," *Rolling Stone*, 30 August 1984.

81. Rossinow, *The Reagan Era*, 173.

82. "1984 Election Review and 1985 Political Policy Preview," EF Hutton research report, 17 January 1985, DPM papers, box 88, folder 9.

83. "1984 Election Review and 1985 Political Policy Preview," EF Hutton.

84. Jon Margolis, "Reagan Wins 4 More Years," *Chicago Tribune*, 7 November 1984. Moreover, in California, according to the *Los Angeles Times*, as much as 67 percent of Hart's supporters switched to Reagan. Bill Boyarsky, "Hart Partisans Fight Doubts," *LAT*, 24 February 1986.

85. Quoted in Joyce, "Hart Sees Triumph."

86. Quoted in Fred Barnes, "Vote Sends Democrats in Search of a Message," *BS*, 8 November 1984.

87. Mondale, *The Good Fight*, 306.

88. Gillon, *Democrats' Dilemma*, 379; Iwan W. Morgan, *Beyond the Liberal Consensus: A Political History of the United States Since 1965* (London: Hurst & Company, 1994), 236.

89. Tony Coelho, "Press Release," 7 November 1984, TON papers, box 5, folder 6.

90. Alan Baron, "Report to Moynihan," 14 January 1985, no. 222, DPM papers, box 86, folder 3.

91. Thomas Ferguson and Joel Rogers, *Right Turn: The Decline of the Democrats and the Future of American Politics* (New York: Hill and Wang, 1986), 196.

92. Thomas Ferguson and Joel Rogers, "The Myth of America's Turn to the Right," *The Atlantic*, May 1986.

93. Quoted in Steven R. Weisman, "The Politics of Popularity," *NYT*, 8 November 1984.

94. Quoted in William Schneider, "Half a Realignment: Why the Voters Rejected the Democrats," *TNR*, 3 December 1984.

95. Coelho, "Press Release."

96. James Sundquist, *Constitutional Reform and Effective Government* (Washington, DC: The Brookings Institution, 1992), 117.

97. Quoted in Dan Balz, "Kennedy Challenges Party to Change," *WP*, 30 March 1985.

98. Stuart Eizenstat, "To Return to Power, The Democrats Must Win Back the Middle Class," *WP*, 25 November 1984.

99. The split was 46 percent for Reagan, 54 for Mondale. CBS/NYT Exit Polls, "How Groups Voted in 1984," Roper, 6 November 1984, https://ropercenter.cornell.edu/how-groups-voted-1984.

100. As Democratic pollster Peter Hart acknowledged in an election postmortem, "In the Sunbelt states, among younger voters and among white-collar and sales workers, the Democrats have a job to do." Quoted in "Election 84: Search for a New Coalition," Allan Shivers Election Analysis Conference, The University of Texas at Austin, 17 November 1984, Robert M. Teeter papers, Gerald R. Ford Presidential Library, Ann Arbor, MI, box 70, folder "1984—Election Analysis (2 of 2)," 9.

101. Walter Mondale, "Concession Speech," *United Press International*, 7 November 1984.

102. Quoted in Farrell, "Hart's Political Legacy."

103. Farrell, "Hart's Political Legacy."

104. Tony Coelho, "Election Analysis," [n.d.], TON papers, box 5, folder 6, 2–4.

105. Miller Center, "Interview with Paul G. Kirk, Jr.," UVA Miller Center, 23 November 2005, https://millercenter.org/the-presidency/presidential-oral-histories/paul-g-kirk-jr-oral-history-112005.

106. Ronald M. Peters Jr. and Cindy Simon Rosenthal, *Speaker Nancy Pelosi and the New American Politics* (Oxford: Oxford University Press, 2010), 32–34.

107. Thomas Oliphant, "Kirk, Pelosi Scramble for Democratic Chairmanship," *BG*, 14 January 1985.

108. Oliphant, "Kirk, Pelosi Scramble for Democratic Chairmanship."

109. Howell Raines, "Conservative Shift Is Sought as Democrats Meet to Pick Chief," *NYT*, 30 January 1985.

110. Dan Balz, "Kirk Elected Democratic Chairman: Paul Kirk to Lead Democrats," *WP*, 2 February 1985.

111. Otto Kreisher, "Kirk Heads Democrats; Minority Caucuses Angry," *The San Diego Union*, 2 February 1985.

112. Howell Raines, "Kennedy Ally Wins Test Vote for New Democratic Leader," *NYT*, 31 January 1985.

113. David Lightman, "Democrats Present Party Reins to Paul Kirk, Ex-Kennedy Aide," *The Hartford Courant*, 2 February 1985.

114. Balz, "Kirk Elected."

115. Cook, "Louisiana Liberal Dies."

116. Richard Fly, "How the Democrats' Young Turks Are Seizing Power," *Business Week*, 15 December 1986, 29.

117. Memorandum to Leon Shull from Lanny Davis, "New Direction for the ADA and 'New Politics' Liberalism," 27 November 1972, Peter R. Rosenblatt papers, LBJ Library, box 2, folder marked "ADA."

118. "DLC Press Release," 28 February 1985, TON papers, box 5, folder 2; also see Baer, *Reinventing Democrats*, 64–92.

119. Quoted in Paul Taylor, "Democrats' New Centrists Preen for '88," *WP*, 10 November 1985.
120. Phil Gailey, "From Biden to Babbitt to Nunn," *NYT*, 18 May 1986.
121. DLC, "New Directions, Enduring Values," [n.d.], Gephardt papers, box 24, folder 1.
122. Taylor, "New Centrists Preen."
123. Taylor, "New Centrists Preen."
124. Quoted in Gailey, "Biden to Babbitt."
125. Benenson, "Post-1984."
126. Taylor, "New Centrists Preen."
127. Quoted in Benenson, "Post-1984."
128. Like Hart, Kirk spoke of "new ideas" to capture the imagination of the "new generation" entering politics. HDC minutes, 29 January 1985, HDC papers, box 21, folder 8, 32; DLC, "Super Tuesday Fact Sheet," Gephardt papers, box 24, folder 1.
129. Paul Kirk, "Speech Before the National Press Club," 16 May 1985, TON papers, box 5, folder 1.
130. Baer, *Reinventing Democrats*, 61; Paul Kirk, "Speech to Democratic Governors Association," 4 December 1987, HDC papers, box 69, folder 1.
131. HDC minutes, 24 July 1985, HDC papers, box 23, folder 1, 21.
132. "Democratic Party Quotas Defended," *Chicago Tribune*, 27 April 1985.
133. Kirk, "Speech Before the National Press Club," 6.
134. Milton Coleman, "Kirk Mollifies Blacks," *WP*, 30 June 1985.
135. Jon Margolis, "Democrats Fear Kiss of Death," *Chicago Tribune*, 26 March 1985, Gephardt papers, box 9, folder 2.
136. Margolis, "Democrats Fear Kiss of Death."
137. Gailey, "Biden to Babbitt."
138. Quoted in Gailey, "Biden to Babbitt."
139. Quoted in Paul Taylor, "New Optimism for Democrats," *WP*, 12 December 1986.
140. Quoted in Taylor, "New Centrists Preen."

CHAPTER 5. THE RETURNING TIDE OF LIBERALISM

1. Martin F. Nolan, "An Election Defeat for Me-Tooism," *BG*, 17 November 1986.
2. Quoted in Michael Pertschuk and Wendy Schaetzel, *The People Rising: The Campaign Against the Bork Nomination* (New York: Thunder Mouth, 1989), 291.
3. In terms of historiography, the Bork moment is generally considered an aberration, given Reagan's overall record on judicial appointments, while scholars that do dedicate serious analysis to the matter often examine the ways in which the nomination politicized the process of judicial selection and confirmation instead. See, among others, Norman Viera and Leonard Gross, *Supreme Court Appointments: Judge Bork and the Politicization of Senate Confirmations* (Carbondale: Southern Illinois University Press, 1998); and Frank Guliuzza III, Daniel J. Reagan, and David M. Barrett, "Character, Competency, and Constitutionalism: Did

the Bork Nomination Represent a Fundamental Shift in Confirmation Criteria?" *Marquette Law Review* 73, no. 2 (1992): 409–437. For a more nuanced appraisal, see Ethan Bronner, *Battle for Justice: How the Bork Nomination Shook America* (New York: Union Square, 2007).

4. Mark Willen, "Congress Overrides Reagan's Grove City Veto," *Congressional Quarterly (CQ) Weekly Report*, 26 March 1988, LCCR papers, box 28, folder 3, 774–776.

5. Nadine Cohodas, "Grove City Rights Bill Shelved by Senate," *CQ Press*, 3 October 1984, LCCR papers, box 26, folder 5.

6. Grove City College v. Bell, 465 U.S. 555 (1984).

7. Robert Pear, "Trying to Tie Strings to Federal Aid," *NYT*, 11 March 1984.

8. Ralph Neas, "LCCR Statement in Support of the Grove City Response Legislation," 12 April 1984, LCCR papers, box 9, folder 2.

9. Quoted in Neas, "LCCR Statement in Support."

10. "Dear Senator" letter, LCCR, 2 August 1984, LCCR papers, box 26, folder 4.

11. Orrin Hatch, "The Civil Privileges Act of 1984," *Human Events*, 14 July 1984, LCCR papers, box 27, folder 1.

12. Judy Goldsmith, "Testimony Before Education and Labor Committee & Judiciary Committee," 21 May 1984, NOW papers, MC496, box 201, folder 28, 7.

13. Ralph Neas, "Statement Regarding the Dole Grove City Bill," 3 January 1985, LCCR papers, box 9, folder 5.

14. Quoted in Lavina Edmunds, "Welding a Civil Rights Coalition," *Gazette*, [n.d.], LCCR papers, box 4, folder 2.

15. With the Senate "immersed in procedural quicksand," the measure was voted down 53–45, largely across party lines (fifty Republicans were joined by three Democrats to defeat the bill; forty-one Democrats and four Republicans supported it, with two Democrats abstaining). Quoted in Cohodas, "Grove City." For voting breakdown, see "Leadership Conference Issues Voting Record for 98th Congress," 30 October 1984, LCCR papers, box 702, folder 2.

16. Edward Kennedy, "Statement on Grove City Legislation," 17 July 1985, LCCR papers, box 27, folder 9.

17. According to the LCCR, "If these substantive amendments pass, they will seriously undermine the principle of restoration. . . . The entire bill [may] unravel and die." "CRRA Stalled by Abortion Amendment," *Civil Rights Monitor*, 1, no. 2 (October 1985).

18. Benjamin L. Hooks, "Statement of LCCR Supporting the CRRA," 19 March 1987, LCCR papers, box 28, folder 1.

19. Quoted in Beverly Beyette, "NOW Election Means New Activist Course," *LAT*, 22 July 1985.

20. NAACP report, "Justice Denied: The Loss of Civil Rights After the Grove City College Decision" (March 1986) and NOW report, "Injustice Under the Law: The Impact of the Grove City College Decision on Civil Rights in America" (March 1986), LCCR papers, box 27, folder 9.

21. NAACP report, "Justice Denied" and NOW report, "Injustice Under the Law."

22. Quoted in E. J. Dionne, "Democrats Rejoice at 55–45 Senate Margin but Still Seek Agenda to Counter Reagan," *NYT*, 6 November 1986.

23. Ronald Reagan, "Remarks at the Annual Dinner of the Conservative Political Action Conference," 30 January 1986, APP, https://www.presidency.ucsb.edu/node/254254.

24. Poll cited in David S. Broder, "1986 Stakes Unusually High for Midterm Election Year," *WP*, 2 January 1986.

25. Anthony Lewis, "The End Begins," *NYT*, 6 November 1986.

26. "Shifting Power: 1981–1993," *Guide to Congress*, vol. 1, 7th ed. (Washington, DC: CQ Press, 2013).

27. These figures are cumulative for Reagan's presidency; Paul Taylor, "Senate to Have 55 Democrats," *WP*, 6 November 1986.

28. Nolan, "Me-Tooism."

29. Scott Armstrong, "Race for US Senate Seat in Colorado an Ideological Tug of War," *CSM*, 23 October 1986.

30. It is noteworthy that this was Gary Hart's seat; he had vacated it to focus on the 1988 presidential campaign. Given Wirth's role as a key Hart ally in the 1984 primary campaign and his political approach mirroring that of the senator, this can be viewed in some ways as a "third Hart term."

31. Armstrong, "Race for US Senate Seat."

32. Based on CBS/NYT Polls, NOW report, "Women and Politics, Election '88," July 1988, NOW papers, MC666, box 370, folder 13, 6.

33. All but three of these gaps were pro-Democratic, with the three pro-Republican ones being moderate-to-liberal Republicans like Senator Bob Packwood (R-OR). NOW report, "Women and Politics," 6.

34. Men split their party preference (45 percent Democrat and 45 percent Republican), whereas women were firmly in favor of the Democrats (50 percent Democrat and 40 percent Republican). Adam Clymer, "Polls Suggest Women Support Democrats in '86 Races," *NYT*, 11 May 1986; NOW 1988 Election Booklet, July 1988, NOW papers, MC666, box 370, folder 13, 8.

35. Ellie Smeal, memo to NOW leadership, 17 December 1986, NOW papers, MC496, box 203, folder 1, 4.

36. NOW report, 1. The Center for American Women and Politics (CAWP) has the figure closer to five million. "Gender Differences in Voter Turnout," CAWP, https://cawp.rutgers.edu/facts/voters/gender-differences-voter-turnout, accessed 9 May 2023.

37. NOW report, 15.

38. The voters least likely to support women candidates are consistent with this liberal/conservative demographic divide—older voters, people in small towns or rural areas, those in blue collars jobs or with lower levels of formal education, and voters in the South. NOW report, "Women and Politics," 15–18.

39. Eleanor Smeal, "Women Candidates Win Incremental—Yet Significant," *ESR*, 4, no. 10, 10 November 1986, Smeal Reports, 3.

40. "Elect Women for a Change," 1992 Organizing Packet, NOW/PAC, July 1992, NOW papers, MC496, box 330, folder 8.

41. Eleanor Smeal, "Feminization of Power Campaign Launched," *ESR*, 5, no. 6, 23 October 1987, Smeal Reports, 1.

42. According to Ferraro, "My candidacy can't be just a footnote. . . . Each point is a step in the historical process. Someday, this nation will elect a woman president." Quoted in Sam Roberts, "A History Maker Recalls the Door That She Opened," *NYT*, 18 July 1988.

43. James Ridgeway, "No Room Left on the Ticket," *Mother Jones*, September-October 1983, 31.

44. Patricia Sullivan, "Harriet Woods; Inspired Creation of Emily's List," *WP*, 10 February 2007.

45. Marylouise Oates, "For Her, the Bucks Start on Emily's List," *LAT*, 23 March 1988.

46. Rita Beamish, "In Campaign for U.S. Senate, E-M-I-L-Y Spells MONEY for Feminist Candidates," *LAT*, 13 July 1986.

47. Lena Williams, "Black Vote Courted in South," *NYT*, 19 October 1986.

48. Quoted in Williams, "Black Vote Courted."

49. Benjamin L. Hooks, "Statement of LCCR Opposing the Confirmation of William H. Rehnquist to Be Chief Justice," 28 July 1986, LCCR papers, box 61, folder 7; press release, "NOW Opposes Rehnquist Nomination," 28 July 1986, NOW papers, MC496, box 114, folder 33; Joseph L. Rauh Jr., "Rehnquist: Not a Sure Thing," *WP*, 28 July 1986.

50. Linda Williams, "1986 Elections: Major Implications for Blacks," *Focus*, 14, nos. 11/12, November-December 1986, 5.

51. Quoted in Williams, "1986 Elections," 6.

52. Memo to NOW leadership, "Year in Review," 17 December 1986, NOW papers, MC496, box 203, folder 1, 6.

53. The coalition also raised the fact that fourteen former high-ranking officials from the Johnson, Nixon, Ford, and Carter administrations had testified on behalf of the CRRA. Ralph Neas, "Enact the CRRA Now," 21 April 1987, LCCR papers, box 28, folder 1.

54. "Dear Senator" letter, LCCR, 11 June 1987, LCCR papers, box 28, folder 2.

55. Quoted in Lena Williams, "Panel Approves a Key Measure to Battle Bias," *NYT*, 21 May 1987.

56. LCCR memo, "Notes on Bork Book," [n.d.], LCCR papers, box 55, folder 5; "'Grove City' Bill Delayed by Battle over Bork," *CQ Almanac*, 43rd ed. (Washington, DC: Congressional Quarterly, 1988).

57. For Reagan's judicial legacy, see Herman Schwartz, *Packing the Courts: The Conservative Campaign to Rewrite the Constitution* (New York: Scribner, 1988); Laurence Tribe, *God Save This Honorable Court: How the Choice of Supreme Court Justices Shapes Our History* (New York: Random House, 1985); and David M. O'Brien, "Federal Judgeships in Retrospect," in *The Reagan Presidency:*

Pragmatic Conservatism and Its Legacies, ed. W. Elliot Brownlee and Hugh Davis Graham (Lawrence: University Press of Kansas, 2003).

58. Quoted in O'Brien, "Federal Judgeships," 327.

59. Angering foreign policy hawks, who saw Central America as the United States's "soft underbelly" in the global struggle against communism, the Boland Amendments in 1982 and 1984, authored by Massachusetts Democrat Edward Boland, constrained the Reagan administration by limiting military and economic assistance to the Nicaraguan Contras. See Rossinow, *The Reagan Era*, 181–200.

60. Powell was among the 7–2 majority in *Roe v. Wade* (1973) and authored the court's powerful reaffirmation of abortion rights in *Akron v. Akron Center for Reproductive Health* (1983). He also wrote the majority opinion in *Regents of the University of California v. Bakke* (1978), a landmark case that upheld the right of colleges to use race as a factor in their admissions decisions; John C. Jeffries, *Justice Lewis F. Powell Jr: A Biography* (New York: Scribner, 2001).

61. Quoted in Howard Kurtz, "Justice Powell Resigns," *WP*, 27 June 1987; Senate Democratic Whip Alan Cranston (D-CA) also urged liberals to form a "solid phalanx" of opposition to block any attempt at an "ideological court coup" by Reagan. "Senate Press Release," 29 June 1987, LCCR papers, box 58, folder 2.

62. Political analysts at the time argued that Biden's success as a candidate would be linked to his ability to defeat Bork. Clifford D. May, "Where the Opposition Makes War on Bork," *NYT*, 25 September 1987.

63. Joe Nocera, "The Ugliness Started with Bork," *NYT*, 21 October 2011.

64. Edward Kennedy, "Statement on the Nomination of Robert Bork to the Supreme Court," 1 July 1987, Clymer papers, series 4, box 7.

65. Ronald Dworkin, "From Bork to Kennedy," *The New York Review of Books*, 17 December 1987; Richard L. Worsnop, "Supreme Court Nomination," *Editorial Research Reports* (Washington, DC: CQ Press, 1987). Also see David A. Yalof, *Pursuit of Justices: Presidential Politics and the Selection of Supreme Court Nominees* (Chicago: University of Chicago Press, 2001).

66. This was according to William Taylor, the LCCR's vice chairman. Miller Center, "Interview with William Taylor," UVA Miller Center, 25 January 2007, https://millercenter.org/the-presidency/presidential-oral-histories/william-taylor-oral-history-012007.

67. See, for example, *ABC/Washington Post* poll, October 1987, iPoll Databank, The Roper Center for Public Opinion Research, University of Connecticut, https://ropercenter.cornell.edu/ipoll/.

68. By the time Reagan left office he had appointed close to half of all lower court judges, more than any other president at the time, and filled a greater percentage of the federal bench than many before him. David Mervin called this the "assiduous 'Reaganization' of the federal judiciary." David Mervin, *Ronald Reagan and the American Presidency* (New York: Longman, 1990), 146–147.

69. "Liberal" wing: Harry A. Blackmun, William J. Brennan, Thurgood

Marshall, and John Paul Stevens. "Conservative" wing: Rehnquist, O'Connor, Scalia, and Byron White.

70. Ronald Dworkin, "The Bork Nomination," *The New York Review of Books*, 13 August 1987.

71. Ronald Reagan: "Remarks Announcing the Nomination of Judge Robert H. Bork," 1 July 1987, APP, https://www.presidency.ucsb.edu/node/253179.

72. Memorandum by *People for the American Way* (PFAW) to Senator Daniel P. Moynihan, 25 August 1987, DPM papers, box 1935, folder 1.

73. PFAW memorandum.

74. "Bork Confirmation Battle," *CQ Historic Documents of 1987* (Washington, DC: CQ Press, 1988).

75. "Statements from Organizations Opposing Bork's Nomination," The Bork Report by *CHOICE*, [n.d.], NOW papers, MC666, box 365, folder 4, 4.

76. PFAW memorandum.

77. *Bowers v. Hardwick*, 478 U.S. 186 (1986). Incidentally, Powell voted in the majority, believing the case was frivolous, but later argued that he had made a "mistake." Ruth Marcus, "Powell Regrets Backing Sodomy Law," *WP*, 26 October 1990.

78. Guliuzza, Reagan, and Barrett, "Character, Competency, and Constitutionalism," 415.

79. PFAW Action Fund, "Robert Bork and the 'Saturday Night Massacre,'" [n.d.], LCCR papers, box 56, folder 2.

80. PFAW report, "Robert Bork: The Wrong Man, The Wrong Place, The Wrong Time," [n.d.], NOW papers, MC496, box 114, folder 1, 15.

81. Richard Gephardt, "NAACP Speech," 6 July 1987, Gephardt papers, box 10, folder 3.

82. PFAW, "The Selling of Robert Bork," [n.d.], LCCR papers, box 56, folder 2.

83. Ronald Reagan, "Remarks at a White House Briefing for Members of the National Law Enforcement Council," 29 July 1987, APP, https://www.presidency.ucsb.edu/node/252616.

84. "Dear Senator" letter, LCCR, 3 August 1987, LCCR papers, box 55, folder 6.

85. Pertschuk and Schaetzel, *People Rising*, 53.

86. See Richard Hodder-Williams, "The Strange Story of Judge Robert Bork and a Vacancy on the United States Supreme Court," *Political Studies* (1988): 613–637.

87. Pertschuk and Schaetzel, *People Rising*, 193.

88. "Notes on Bork," [n.d.], LCCR papers, box 55, folder 5.

89. "Statement of Benjamin L. Hooks and Ralph Neas," July 1, 1987, LCCR papers, box 55, folder 6. In a letter to members announcing a "red alert save the court campaign," NOW also described it as "the most important vote any sitting U.S. Senator will ever cast." "Dear NOW leaders," [n.d.], NOW papers, MC496, box 203, folder 1.

90. Both quotes in Clymer, *Kennedy*, 410.

91. LCCR, "Summary: Meeting of Grassroots Task Force," 13 July 1987, NOW papers, MC666, box 365, folder 3; Bronner, *Battle for Justice*, 36.

92. Michael Pertschuk and David Cohen, "The Bork Nomination: Seizing the Symbols of the Debate," *The Advocacy Institute*, 14 July 1987, NOW papers, MC666, box 365, folder 4.

93. Pertschuk and Cohen, "Seizing the Symbols."

94. Viera and Gross, *Supreme Court Appointments*, 31–32.

95. Pertschuk and Cohen, "Seizing the Symbols."

96. Press release, "Senators Announce Their Opposition to Bork," 3 October 1987, LCCR papers, box 56, folder 4.

97. Quoted in Ethan Bonner, "Passing Judgment," *BG*, 27 August 1989.

98. Pertschuk and Schaetzel, *People Rising*, 72.

99. Quoted in Pertschuk and Schaetzel, *People Rising*, 14.

100. "PFAW Action Fund's Public Education Campaign," [n.d.], LCCR papers, box 59, folder 1; Hrebenar, *Interest Group Politics*, 5.

101. PFAW Action Fund, "60 Second TV Spots," [n.d.], LCCR papers, box 59, folder 1; "PFAW Public Education Campaign."

102. "The Last Word," television advertisement, produced by PFAW, originally aired in 1987.

103. LCCR press release, 7 September 1987, LCCR papers, box 56, folder 2.

104. LCCR, "Suggested Activities for State Organizations–Grassroots Package," [n.d.], LCCR papers, box 56, folder 2.

105. Ehrman, *The Eighties*, 145.

106. Edward Kennedy, "Statement on the Bork Nomination and Civil Rights," 22 October 1987, Clymer papers, series 4, box 7, 3.

107. Quoted in Edward Walsh and Al Kamen, "Senators Question Bork's Consistency," *WP*, 17 September 1987. Also see "Transcript of Hearings Before the Committee," serial no. J-100-64, 16 September 1987, 267–277, https://archive.org/details/bork_transcripts/Bork-1/page/n319/mode/2up.

108. "Bork v Bork," a report by the NAACP & PFAW, September 1987, LCCR papers, box 57, folder 1.

109. *Oil, Chemical & Atomic Workers International Union v. American Cyanamid Company*, 741 F.2d 444 (D.C. Cir. 1984).

110. Statements of R. H. Bork on His Nomination as Associate Justice of the U.S. Supreme Court, *CQ Historic Documents of 1987*.

111. Letter from Betty J. Riggs to senators, 29 September 1987, https://archive.org/details/bork_transcripts/Bork-1/page/n319/mode/2up, 788–790.

112. "Joint Statement of Women's Groups," [n.d.], LCCR papers, box 55, folder 5.

113. Marttila Poll, LCCR papers, box 55, folder 5, Pollster Patrick Caddell said, "We knew we'd beat Bork from Marttila's poll." Quoted in Canellos, *The Last Lion*, 257.

114. Robin Toner, "Saying No to Bork, Southern Democrats Echo Black Voters," *NYT*, 8 October 1987.

115. Quoted in Pertschuk and Schaetzel, *People Rising*, 78.
116. A majority of respondents in southern states opposed the nomination. "Southern Primary—Wave 2," *Atlanta Journal-Constitution (AJC)*, September 1987.
117. A *Washington Post/ABC News* poll in mid-October showed that 56 percent of women and 48 percent of men opposed the nomination. Eleanor Smeal, "The Electoral Basis of the Anti-Bork Senate Vote," *ESR*, 5, no. 6, 23 October 1987, Smeal Reports, 2–3.
118. National Women's Law Center, "Setting the Record Straight: Judge Bork and the Future of Women's Rights," August 1987, LCCR papers, box 56, folder 5, 39.
119. Edward Kennedy, "Opening Statement, Hearings on the Bork Nomination," 15 September 1987, Clymer papers, series 4, box 7, 2.
120. Pertschuk and Schaetzel, *People Rising*, 231.
121. Mary McGrory, "The Supreme Sacrifice," *WP*, 6 October 1987.
122. Quoted in McGrory, "The Supreme Sacrifice."
123. David Lauter and Ronald J. Ostrow, "Nominee's Strategists Overwhelmed: How Liberal Spectrum Fought to Block Bork," *LAT*, 8 October 1987.
124. William T. Coleman, "Why Judge Bork Is Unacceptable," *NYT*, 15 September 1987.
125. Among them, Atlanta Mayor Andrew Young described Bork as "an extremist whose zealous dogmatic view of the world allows him to travel many rationalized paths to his negative ends." Andrew Young, "Testimony," 21 September 1987, LCCR papers, box 54, folder 3.
126. Memorandum, "Keep Up the Great Work," 14 October 1987, LCCR papers, box 56, folder 2.
127. Kenneth B. Noble, "Heflin, at Last Voting No, Weathers the Intense Heat on the Uncommitted," *NYT*, 7 October 1987.
128. Toner, "Saying No to Bork."
129. Barbara Jordan, "Robert Bork: The Continuing Controversy, The Lasting Lessons," [n.d.], Michael Pertschuk papers, Library of Congress, Washington, DC, box 1, folder 8, 7.
130. The split was mainly along partisan lines—fifty-two Democrats and six Republicans voted against confirmation; forty Republicans and two Democrats voted for confirmation.
131. Quoted in Don Irwin, "Reagan Asks Public to Back Bork," *LAT*, 4 October 1987.
132. Stuart Taylor Jr., "The Bork Hearings; A Disparity of Images," *NYT*, 27 September 1987.
133. Quoted in Linda Greenhouse, "Bork's Nomination Is Rejected, 58–42; Reagan 'Saddened,'" *NYT*, 24 October 1987.
134. NOW also pointed to Kennedy's hiring practices on the Ninth Circuit Court of Appeals and his "long-time memberships in segregated clubs" as further justification for their opposition. Molly Yard, "Testimony Before the Senate Judiciary Committee," 16 December 1987, NOW papers, MC496, box 114, folder 26.

135. Todd Ruger, "Reagan Aides Foresaw Kennedy Gay-Rights Views That Conservatives Now Lament," *CQ Press*, 26 June 2015.
136. Quoted in Linda Greenhouse, "Reagan Nominates Anthony Kennedy to Supreme Court," *NYT*, 12 November 1987.
137. Ruger, "Reagan Aides."
138. Ruger, "Reagan Aides."
139. Quoted in Pertschuk and Schaetzel, *People Rising*, 279.
140. Mary McGrory, "Democratic Unity and Disarray," *WP*, 8 October 1987, Gephardt papers, box 12, folder 2.
141. Quoted in Pertschuk and Schaetzel, *People Rising*, 1.
142. Quoted in Peter Baker, "Defeat of '87 Nomination a Model for Liberals, a Lesson for Conservatives," *WP*, 12 July 2005.
143. Linda Greenhouse, "After Bork, the Liberals' Silence on Judge Kennedy Is Deafening," *WP*, 4 December 1987.
144. Quoted in Pertschuk and Schaetzel, *People Rising*, 291.
145. "Dear Senator" letter, LCCR, 20 January 1988, LCCR papers, box 28, folder 2.
146. Letter to Ronald Reagan, LCCR, 8 March 1988, LCCR papers, box 28, folder 2.
147. Republican Senator Rudy Boschwitz pleaded with the president: "I implore you to sign the bill." Rudy Boschwitz, "Letter to Ronald Reagan," 3 March 1988, LCCR papers, box 28, folder 2.
148. Quoted in Helen Dewar, "Congress Overrides Civil Rights Law Veto," *WP*, 23 March 1988.
149. Ralph Neas, "Congress Acts to Prohibit the Federal Funding of Discrimination," 2 April 1988, LCCR papers, box 28, folder 2.
150. Quoted in Cohodas, "Senate Passes Civil Rights Bill," 215.
151. Arnold Aronson, "How the Fair Housing Bill Was Defeated," LCCR report, 11 December 1980, LCCR papers, box 42, folder 9.
152. Ralph Neas, "LCCR Hails the Enactment of the Fair Housing Law," 13 September 1988, LCCR papers, box 42, folder 10.
153. Neas, "LCCR Hails." A 1983 report also criticized the Justice Department's retreat on enforcement measures. "A Decent Home: A Report on the Continuing Failure of the Federal Government to Provide Equal Housing Opportunity," *Citizens' Commission on Civil Rights*, April 1983, LCCR papers, box 43, folder 4.
154. Ralph Neas, "LCCR Applauds the Introduction of the FHA," 19 February 1987, LCCR papers, box 42, folder 10.
155. "Some Questions and Answers on the FHA," [n.d.], LCCR papers, box 42, folder 10.
156. Berry, "Reagan and the LCCR," 13–14.
157. Neas, "Enactment of the Fair Housing Law"; Ralph Neas, "The Civil Rights Legacy of the Reagan Presidency: Forcing the Nation to Refight Battles Won Long Ago," LCCR memo, October 1989, LCCR papers, box 10, folder 2.
158. Neas, "Civil Rights Legacy."

159. Willen, "Congress Overrides," 774–776.
160. Willen, "Congress Overrides," 774–776.
161. "NAACP Delegates Cheer Jesse Jackson's Anti-Bork Stance," WP, 8 July 1987, Gephardt papers, box 10, folder 3.
162. Amaker, *Civil Rights*, 160.
163. Laham, *The Reagan Presidency*, 2.

CHAPTER 6. "WAKE UP, LIBERALS, YOUR TIME HAS COME"

1. Arthur Schlesinger Jr., "Wake Up, Liberals, Your Time Has Come," WP, 1 May 1988.
2. JoAnn Wypijewski, "The Rainbow's Gravity," *The Nation*, 15 July 2004.
3. R. W. Apple Jr., "Jackson Is Seen as Winning a Solid Place in History," NYT, 29 April 1988.
4. Jesse Jackson, "On Winning," NYT, 5 May 1984.
5. Frank Clemente, *Keep Hope Alive: Jesse Jackson's 1988 Presidential Campaign* (Boston: South End, 1989), 6.
6. Clemente, *Jackson's 1988 Presidential Campaign*, 6.
7. Clemente, *Jackson's 1988 Presidential Campaign*, 233.
8. Penn Kimble, *Keep Hope Alive: Super Tuesday and Jesse Jackson's 1988 Campaign for the Presidency* (Washington, DC: Joint Center for Political and Economic Studies Press, 1992), 10.
9. Jesse Jackson, "Address Before the Democratic National Convention," 18 July 1984, transcript: http://www.pbs.org/wgbh/pages/frontline/jesse/speeches/jesse 84speech.html.
10. The name "testified to Jackson's roots in the urban political tradition that had served as a pathway for black political success," according to historians Kruse and Zelizer, highlighting the Rainbow Coalition of African Americans, Hispanics, labor, and white liberals who had supported Harold Washington's upset over Chicago's incumbent mayor, Jane Byrne, in 1983. Kruse and Zelizer, *Fault Lines*, 129.
11. Quoted in Michael Cheers, "Campaign Earns Jackson Major Voice in Dem. Party's Future," *Jet*, 20 June 1988, 4.
12. Quoted in Cheers, "Campaign Earns Jackson," 4.
13. Polls in Robin Toner, "Hart, Stressing Ideals, Formally Enters the 1988 Race," NYT, 14 April 1987.
14. Chris Black, "Hart Sets Sights on '88 Campaign; Faneuil Hall Speech Urges Party Revival," BG, 5 February 1985.
15. William Schneider, "The Democrats in '88," *The Atlantic*, April 1987, Gephardt papers, box 9, folder 4, 37–59, (40).
16. Ronald Brownstein, "The Lessons of 1984," *National Journal*, 20 July 1985, Gephardt papers, box 9, folder 2, 1666–1670.
17. E. J. Dionne, "Gary Hart, The Elusive Front-Runner," *NYT Magazine*, 3 May 1987.

18. Jack W. Germond and Jules Witcover, *Whose Broad Strips and Bright Stars: The Trivial Pursuit of the Presidency 1988* (New York: Warner Books, 1989), 44.

19. Dionne, "Gary Hart."

20. After pictures surfaced of Hart and Donna Rice, a model, aboard a yacht ironically named "Monkey Business," the national press ran an exposé on Hart's supposed adultery, and the rumors were eventually substantiated; E. J. Dionne, "Courting Danger: The Fall of Gary Hart," *NYT*, 9 May 1987.

21. Warren Weaver, "Schroeder, Assailing the System, Decides Not to Run for President," *NYT*, September 29, 1987; NOW leadership memo, "Schroeder 1988? Fundraising," 4 September 1987, NOW papers, MC496, box 203, folder 2.

22. Dorothy Bland, "Women Hope to Build on Lesson of '84," *USA Today*, 20 July 1987, Michael Dukakis Presidential Campaign Records (Dukakis papers), Archives and Special Collections, Northeastern University, Boston, MA, box 19, folder 751; John A. Farrell, "Schroeder Seen Advancing Women's Candidacy," *BG*, 12 October 1987, Dukakis papers, box 16, folder 870.

23. Asked "Why Dukakis" by the *Washington Post*, a former Hart aide said: "He's the most liberal and electable of the candidates remaining." Maralee Schwartz, "Hart Staff Looks East for Candidate to Back in 1988," *WP*, 14 May 1987, Gephardt papers, box 9, folder 3; Jack Germond and Jules Witcover, "Dukakis Is Prime Beneficiary of Hart Departure—So Far," *BS*, 7 June 1988, Dukakis papers, box 19, folder 769.

24. Michael Dukakis, "On the Issues: Idealism That Works," [n.d.], Dukakis papers, box 5, folder 312.

25. David Shribman, "As Gary Hart Throws Hat Back in the Ring, Republicans Rejoice," *WSJ*, 16 December 1987; "No Money, No Headquarters, No Staff but 'I'm Back in the Race,'" *NYT*, 16 December 1987, Dukakis papers, box 17, folder 852.

26. Laura B. Randolph, "Can Jesse Jackson Win?" *Ebony*, March 1988, 154–162.

27. Joyce Purnick, "Jesse Jackson Aims for the Mainstream," *NYT*, 29 November 1987.

28. Sylvester Monroe and Howard Fineman, "Now It's Jesse Mainstream," *Newsweek*, 25 May 1987, Gephardt papers, box 9, folder 6.

29. Hal Straus, "Jackson Claims Common Cause with Democratic Moderates," *AJC*, 22 June 1987, Gephardt papers, box 10, folder 1. Quoted in Kimble, *Keep Hope Alive*, 94.

30. In 1987 the Census Bureau reported that the Black poverty rate had risen to 33.1 percent, while the white rate had fallen to 10.5. Martin Tolchin, "Minority Poverty on Rise but White Poor Decline," *NYT*, 1 September 1988.

31. Quoted in Robert Gillette, "Jackson to Whites: Focus on 'Common Ground,'" *LAT*, 20 February 1988.

32. Richard Gephardt, position papers, [n.d.], Gephardt papers, box 32, folder 8.

33. Sidney Blumenthal, "Richard Gephardt, The Insider as Populist," *WP*, 13 February 1988.

34. Richard Gephardt, "Policy Positions, Q&As," [n.d.], Gephardt papers, box 32, folder 8.

35. Paul Taylor, "Gephardt Declares for Presidency," *WP*, 24 February 1987, Gephardt papers, box 9, folder 3.

36. Similarly, liberal labor groups (AFL-CIO) rated Gephardt 61 percent in 1980 and 100 percent in 1989, while the conservative Chamber of Commerce gave him 64 percent in 1980 and 0 percent in 1989. "Ratings by Public Interest Groups for Rep. Richard Gephardt," [n.d.], Gephardt papers, box 36, folder 19.

37. Blumenthal, "Gephardt."

38. DLC, "Super Tuesday Fact Sheet," Gephardt papers, box 24, folder 1.

39. Clemente, *Jackson's 1988 Presidential Campaign*, 10.

40. Kimble, *Keep Hope Alive*, 97; Jackson would eventually attract 2.1 million white voters overall, with particular support coming from young professionals. E. J. Dionne, "Jackson Share of Votes by Whites Triples in '88," *NYT*, 13 June 1988.

41. Quoted in Tom Buckham, "Super Tuesday Lifts NOW's Morale," *Buffalo News*, 10 March 1988, NOW papers, MC666, box 370, folder 13.

42. Polls in Sidney Blumenthal, "Jockeying for Position: Only 1,000 Days to Go," *WP*, 2 September 1986, Gephardt papers, box 9, folder 2.

43. Poll in John W. Mashek, "Hart, Bush Lead in Poll of South," *Arkansas Gazette*, 15 March 1987, Gephardt papers, box 9, folder 4.

44. Andrew Blake, "Dukakis Camp: Aware of New Reality," *BG*, 29 March 1988, Dukakis papers, box 18, folder 931.

45. Quoted in Clemente, *Jackson's 1988 Presidential Campaign*, 14.

46. Schneider, "The Democrats in '88," 57.

47. "Intoxicated Democrats," *NYT*, 31 March 1988.

48. Quoted in Philip Geyelin, "But He Still Has an Accommodating Streak," *WP*, 13 July 1988, Gephardt papers, box 36, folder 9.

49. "Jackson Turned Aside on 3 Platform Issues," *NYT*, 20 July 1988.

50. Quoted in Apple Jr., "Winning a Solid Place in History."

51. Barack Obama, "Victory Speech," 4 November 2008, transcript: http://edition.cnn.com/2008/POLITICS/11/04/obama.transcript/index.html?iref=nextin.

52. Steve Cobble, "For Half a Century, Jesse Jackson Has Helped Lead Fight for Progressive Politics," *The Nation*, 29 July 2010.

53. Lawson, *Running for Freedom*, 233.

54. Quoted in Apple Jr., "Winning a Solid Place in History."

55. "What Now?" *TNR*, 26 November 1984.

56. Editorial, "The East," *WP*, 6 November 1986; Joe Klein, "Ready for the Duke," *New York Magazine*, 17 August 1987, Gephardt papers, box 11, folder 3, 30.

57. Jack Beatty, "Suburbs Key in '88 Vote, Dukakis Can Attract Non-City Vote for Dems," *LAT*, 8 May 1988; Michele Cohen, "Many Yuppie Republicans Find Dukakis Appealing," *Sun-Sentinel*, 21 July 1988.

58. William Schneider, "The Suburban Century Begins," *The Atlantic*, July 1992.

59. Democratic Policy Commission Report, "Democrats Making It Work: Opportunity for All, Mike Dukakis," [n.d.], Dukakis papers, box 5, folder 270.
60. Gailey, "Biden to Babbitt."
61. Michael Dukakis, "On the Issues: The Massachusetts Success Story," [n.d.], Dukakis papers, box 4, folder 253.
62. Dukakis, "Idealism That Works"; Ronald Brownstein, "Running on His Record," *National Journal*, 18 July 1987, 1830–1835.
63. Klein, "Ready for the Duke," 30.
64. Polls demonstrated that Kennedy was popular with the younger generation, and crucially for the Democrats, particularly with those who voted for Reagan in 1984. David Broder, "Dukakis, Another JFK?" *Sarasota Herald-Tribune*, 10 October 1988.
65. Broder, "Dukakis, Another JFK?"
66. Richard Reeves, "The Atlanta Democrats," *BS*, 15 July 1988, Gephardt papers, box 36, folder 9.
67. Michael Dukakis, "Address Accepting the Presidential Nomination at the Democratic National Convention in Atlanta," 21 July 1988, APP, https://www.presidency.ucsb.edu/node/216671.
68. Gallup Poll in "Dukakis Lead Widens, According to New Poll," *NYT*, 26 July 1988. Although it is common for a candidate to receive a convention bump in the polls, Dukakis held significant leads before the convention as well, including a sixteen-point lead in May and a fourteen-point lead in June according to Gallup. See "Gallup Presidential Election Trial-Heat Trends, 1936–2008," https://news.gallup.com/poll/110548/gallup-presidential-election-trial-heat-trends.aspx, accessed 30 April 2023.
69. George Bush campaign leaflet, "Values," Issues File: Bush, Negative Campaign, [n.d.], Dukakis papers, box 3, folder 174.
70. Michael Dukakis, "Lies and Distortions in Latest Bush/Quayle Defense/Foreign Policy Ad," 21 October 1988, Dukakis papers, box 1, folder 17.
71. Bush campaign leaflet, "Values."
72. See William Rabbie, "Above the Fray: The Lessons of Dukakis '88," *MSNBC*, 18 December 2014.
73. Sidney Blumenthal, "Willie Horton and the Making of an Election Issue," *WP*, 28 October 1988.
74. Blumenthal, "Willie Horton."
75. Quoted in Rossinow, *The Reagan Era*, 247.
76. Quoted in Blumenthal, "Willie Horton."
77. He also apologized to Horton for vilifying him and, in effect, orchestrating his lynching by the media. "Gravely Ill Atwater Offers Apology," *NYT*, 13 January 1991.
78. Bush campaign leaflet, "Values."
79. "The Revolving Door," 1988, http://www.livingroomcandidate.org/commercials/1988/revolving-door#4121, accessed 30 April 2023.
80. Michael Oreskes, "TV's Role in '88: The Medium Is the Election," *NYT*, 30

October 1988; Darrell M. West, *Air Wars: Television Advertising and Social Media in Election Campaigns, 1952–2012*, 6th ed. (Washington, DC: CQ Press, 2014), 105.

81. Blumenthal, "Willie Horton."

82. Memo, "Furlough from the Truth," Dukakis papers, [n.d.], box 1, folder 17.

83. Memo, "Talking Points for 'Counter Punch' and 'Furlough from the Truth,'" [n.d.], Dukakis papers, box 1, folder 17.

84. Carole Ashkinaze, "Taking the High Road in Campaign May Cost Dukakis the Election," *AJC*, 9 September 1988, Dukakis papers, box 21, folder 1031.

85. Gallup Polls in Steve Neal, "Dukakis Trails by 10 Percent; 68 Percent Predict Bush Win," *Chicago Sun-Times*, 26 October 1988, Dukakis papers, box 21, folder 1104.

86. Ronald Reagan, "Remarks at a Republican Campaign Rally in Mount Clements, Michigan," 5 November 1988, Ronald Reagan Presidential Library, https://www.reaganlibrary.gov/archives/speech/remarks-republican-campaign-rally-mount-clements-michigan; John M. Broder, "Reagan Launches Stern Attack on 'Liberal' Foes," *LAT*, 15 August 1988.

87. Dukakis would try to spin this attack by arguing that his "L-word is Leadership" but the damage had been done. Andrew Rosenthal, "Dukakis Asserts That His 'L Word' Is 'Leadership,'" *NYT*, 16 August 1988.

88. Quoted in Robin Toner, "Dukakis Asserts He Is a 'Liberal,' but in Old Tradition of His Party," *NYT*, 31 October 1988.

89. Quoted in Toner, "Dukakis Asserts He Is a 'Liberal.'"

90. Quoted in Bruce Mohl, "Former Speaker Rebuts Bush's 'Liberal' Charge," *BG*, 28 September 1988, Dukakis papers, box 20, folder 1051.

91. Bush had also cast the tie-breaking vote in 1986 to wipe out cost-of-living adjustments. Michael Dukakis, campaign material: "George Bush and Danforth Quayle: The Uncola Ticket," 21 September 1988, box 3, folder 185. Quoted in Ben Bradlee Jr., "Dukakis Vows Support for Social Security," *BG*, 28 September 1988, Dukakis papers, box 20, folder 1051.

92. Michael Dukakis, campaign material: "Reagan/Bush Record on Civil Rights," [n.d.], Dukakis papers, box 3, folder 161.

93. Michael Dukakis, campaign material: "Black Americans," [n.d.], Dukakis papers, box 4, folder 223.

94. Quoted in Christopher Blake, "Jackson Stumps for 'Duke,'" *The Bridgeport Post*, 3 November 1988, Dukakis papers, box 2, folder 67; Jesse Jackson, "10 Reasons Why We Must Work For, Fight For, Vote For Michael Dukakis," [n.d.], Dukakis papers, box 2, folder 67.

95. Poll in Lillian Williams, "Blacks Seen Leaning Tepidly Toward Dukakis," *Chicago Sun-Times*, 28 October 1988, Dukakis papers, box 21, folder 1104.

96. Lawson, *Running for Freedom*, 275; Paul Taylor, "The Growing Electoral Clout of Blacks Is Driven by Turnout, Not Demographics," *Pew Research*, 26 December 2012, https://www.pewresearch.org/social-trends/2012/12/26/the-growing-electoral-clout-of-blacks-is-driven-by-turnout-not-demographics/.

97. Michael Dukakis, campaign material: "Judge Robert Bork," [n.d.], Dukakis papers, box 5, folder 316.

98. Memo, "Judges," 14 October 1988, Dukakis papers, box 5, folder 316. A separate letter also discussed Bork's role in the sterilization case and its ability to attract working women. Letter to Bill Woodward, "Working Women Theme," 18 October 1988, Dukakis papers, box 5, folder 316.

99. The fact that three liberal justices were over eighty heightened the stakes further. Memo, "People Interested in the Future of the Supreme Court," 24 October 1988, Dukakis papers, box 5, folder 316.

100. Memo, "Ideas for Grassroots Activities," [n.d.], Dukakis papers, box 5, folder 316.

101. Quoted in Anne Kornhauser, "One Year Later, Bork Enters the Campaign," *Legal Times*, 24 October 1988, Dukakis papers, box 5, folder 316.

102. Quoted in Josh King, "Dukakis and the Tank," *Politico*, 17 November 2013. Dukakis eventually released a series of ads to address each one of Bush's criticisms. Press release, "'Fed Up' with Bush's Campaign Tactics, Dukakis Campaign Unleashes New TV Ads to 'Set Record Straight,'" 21 October 1988, Dukakis papers, box 1, folder 17.

103. Poll in E. J. Dionne, "Bush Still Ahead as End Nears, but Dukakis Gains in Survey," *NYT*, 6 November 1988, Dukakis papers, box 21, folder 1105.

104. Overall, 1988 witnessed the lowest turnout since 1924. "Voter Turnout in Presidential Elections: 1828–2012," APP, http://www.presidency.ucsb.edu/data/turnout.php.

105. "Voter Turnout in Presidential Elections," APP, http://www.presidency.ucsb.edu/data/turnout.php.

106. "Voter Turnout in Presidential Elections," APP, http://www.presidency.ucsb.edu/data/turnout.php.

107. Baer, *Reinventing Democrats*, 123.

108. Kevin Phillips, "The Electoral College: Easy for the GOP in 1988 but Trouble to Come?" *The American Political Report*, 14 October 1988, TON papers, box 28, folder 10.

109. *Time* cover, 21 November 1988.

110. Baer, *Reinventing Democrats*, 120–125; Bloodworth, *Losing the Center*, 9–10.

111. Quoted in E. J. Dionne, "A 'New Centrism' Quietly Creeps into Campaign," *NYT*, 17 May 1987, Gephardt papers, box 9, folder 3.

112. E. J. Dionne, "Polls Show Dukakis Leads Bush; Reagan Backers Shift Sides," *NYT*, 17 May 1988.

113. Andrew Mollison, "Liberals Like Look of Democratic Field Seeking Presidency," *AJC*, 22 June 1987, Gephardt papers, box 10, folder 1.

114. David Nyhan, "A Full-Court Press" *BG*, 18 April 1988, Dukakis papers, box 19, folder 951.

115. Christopher Madison, "Message Bearer," *National Journal*, 1 December 1990, Gephardt papers, box 13, folder 6, 2906.

116. Poll/quote in Stanley Greenberg, "Reconstructing a Democratic Vision," *The American Prospect* (Spring 1990).

CHAPTER 7. EMERGING FROM THE SHADOW

1. Linda Campbell, "Groups Unleash Lobbying Blitz on Rights Bill," *Chicago Tribune*, 27 May 1991.

2. John E. Jacob, keynote address to National Urban League Annual Conference, 21 July 1991, Nelson Lund files, George H.W. Bush presidential records (Bush presidential records), White House Counsel's Office (WHCO), George H. W. Bush Presidential Library (Bush Library), College Station, Texas, folder marked "Civil Rights File, Civil Rights: Letters Concerning Bill [1]," OA/ID: 45401-004, 11.

3. Though it varied, Dukakis enjoyed significant gender gap leads in the spring/summer, with a *WP/ABC News* poll recording the 61–33 gap and a *CBS/NYT* poll showcasing a 53–35 preference, for example. Walter Robinson, "Gender Gap Seen as Pitfall for Bush," *BG*, 5 June 1988; Judy Mann, "Political Gender Gap," *WP*, 15 June 1988.

4. "Elect Women for a Change," NOW papers, box 330, folder 8.

5. Molly Yard, Democratic platform committee speech, 10 May 1988, NOW papers, MC496, box 201, folder 33.

6. Marilyn Gardner, "Women Seek to Win More Attention in 1988 Campaign," *CSM*, 7 December 1987.

7. Ethel Klein, "Gender Politics 1988: Earning the Women's Vote," NOW press conference, 7 July 1988, NOW papers, MC666, box 370, folder 13.

8. Paget, "Gender Gap Mystique."

9. According to Estrich, "The symbolism was very powerful.... Women said it scared the living daylights out of them." Quoted in West, *Air Wars*, 106.

10. Eleanor Smeal, "Gender Gap—1988 Elections and Beyond," *ESR*, 6, no. 4, 2 November 1988, Smeal Reports, 2.

11. Memo, "Ms. Magazine Endorses Dukakis," 21 October 1988, Dukakis papers, box 3, folder 192; DNC, "Campaign '88: Democrats Launch 'Women at Work' Tour," 1 November 1988, Dukakis papers, box 3, folder 192; Michael Dukakis, "Women's Issues: Results," [n.d.], Dukakis papers, box 7, folder 408.

12. Gwen Ifill, "Dukakis Gender Gap Advantage, Once Formidable, Has Vanished: Bush's Kinder, Gentler Image and Pronouncements Seen as Key," *WP*, 17 October 1988.

13. Polls showed that the gender gap provided Democratic Senate gains for New Jersey, Connecticut, Nevada, and Wisconsin. Smeal, "Gender Gap," 3.

14. According to the National Abortion Federation (NAF), between 1977 and 1994 pro-life activists participated in 634 clinic blockades and 7,768 pickets, and they were arrested 33,661 times. "NAF Violence and Disruption Statistics," https://prochoice.org/wp-content/uploads/Stats_Table_2014.pdf, accessed 6 February 2023.

15. Judy Goldsmith, NOW conference speech, 19 July 1985, NOW papers, MC496, box 201, folder 36, 7.

16. Judy Goldsmith, speech to the National Press Club, 12 February 1985, NOW papers, MC496, box 201, folder 36, 1; Eleanor Smeal, "National March for Women's Lives—Largest Women's Rights Demonstration in History," *ESR*, 3, no. 19, 25 March 1986, Smeal Reports, 1.

17. NOW report, "Why a Justice Department Investigation of the Anti-Abortion Violence is Necessary," [n.d.], NOW papers, MC496, box 95, folder 14.

18. This was the single largest demonstration in the nation's capital; Molly Yard, "Welcome Speech," NOW 1989 National Conference, 21–23 July 1989, NOW papers, MC496, box 21, folder 16, 2.

19. Eloise Salholz, "Pro-Choice: 'A Sleeping Giant' Awakes," *Newsweek*, 24 April 1989, 39.

20. Eleanor Smeal, "Public Support for Preserving Roe Increasing—Especially Among Young," *ESR*, 6, no. 9, 13 February 1989, Smeal Reports, 3.

21. Julian Zelizer, "The Unexpected Endurance of the New Deal Order: Liberalism in the Age of Reagan" in *Beyond the New Deal: U.S. Politics from the Great Depression to the Great Recession*, ed. Gary Gerstle, Nelson Lichtenstein, and Alice O'Connor (Philadelphia: University of Pennsylvania Press, 2019), 83.

22. Quoted in Maralee Schwartz, "Illinois Senate Race: A Matter of Choice," *WP*, 2 June 1990.

23. Bill Kristol, "Note to the Vice President," 4 June 1990, Lee S. Liberman files, Bush presidential records, WHCO, Bush Library, folder marked "General Subject File, Abortion [4]," OA/ID: 45271-004.

24. Eleanor Smeal, "Massive Gender Gaps in State Legislatures' Votes on Anti-Abortion Bills," *ESR*, 7, no. 2, 27 March 1990, Smeal Reports, 1. The White House welcomed the *Webster* decision, noting that the court "has begun to restore to the people the ability to legislate protection for the unborn. We continue to believe that Roe v Wade was incorrectly decided, and will work for its full overturning." White House release, 3 July 1989, William Roper files, Bush presidential records, White House Office of Policy Development, Bush Library, folder marked "Subject Files, Abortion [1]," OA/ID: 01669-001.

25. Karen Tumulty, "Pro-Choice Advocates Rally Coast-to-Coast," *LAT*, 13 November 1989.

26. "Abortion: Historical Trends," *Gallup*, www.gallup.com/poll/1576/abortion.aspx, accessed 9 February 2023.

27. Martin P. Wattenberg, "Why Clinton Won and Dukakis Lost: An Analysis of the Candidate-Centered Nature of American Party Politics," *Party Politics* 1, no. 2 (1995): 254–256.

28. Michael Oreskes, "Virginia Campaign Watched as Test on Abortion Rights," *NYT*, 29 October 1989.

29. Oreskes, "Virginia Campaign Watched."

30. Undoubtedly, race played a part too—Wilder became the first African American to occupy Virginia's statehouse—but pollsters suggested that the abortion

issue was actually used to defuse any concerns voters might have had about Wilder's race. William Schneider, "1989 Election: The Flip Side of 1988: Abortion & Negative Campaigning," *LAT*, 12 November 1989.

31. Eleanor Smeal, "Abortion and the Gender Gap Decisive in 1989 Gubernatorial Elections," *ESR*, 6, no. 22, 17 November 1989, Smeal Reports, 1–2; Quoted in Paget, "Gender Gap Mystique."

32. Ann Lewis, "Return of the Gender Gap—Just in Time for November," *Ms. Magazine*, January 1992; Ann Richards, a keynote speaker at the 1988 Democratic Convention, used abortion to mobilize the pro-choice community in Texas and win the governor's race with a significant gender advantage. Paget, "Gender Gap Mystique."

33. Wattenberg, "Why Clinton Won and Dukakis Lost," 254–256.

34. Between 1980 and 1992, the number of women in the House went from twenty-one to forty-eight, and from two to seven in the Senate. "Summary of Women Candidates," CAWP.

35. NOW was the first organization to support Pelosi's 1987 bid for California's 5th District. Eleanor Smeal, "Nancy Pelosi Wins NOW Endorsement," *ESR*, 4, no. 16, 28 February 1987, Smeal Reports, 3; Pelosi also served a second stint as speaker from 2019 to 2023.

36. "History of Women in the U.S. Congress," CAWP, http://www.cawp.rutgers.edu/history-women-us-congress, accessed 19 February 2023.

37. Michael Oreskes, "The 1990 Elections," *NYT*, 7 November 1990.

38. According to Julian Zelizer, these "groups were the reason that Bush felt compelled to sign the Clean Air Act in 1990." Zelizer, "Unexpected Endurance," 82.

39. Tom Harkin, press release, 9 May 1989, LCCR papers, part 3, box 68, folder 4.

40. Lex Frieden, one of principal architects of the Americans with Disabilities Act, appeared before the Senate during CRRA consideration in 1987, arguing that while a more comprehensive solution to discrimination against people with disabilities was needed, "an absolutely necessary first step is to return the scope of coverage of Section 504 and the other civil rights laws to their status before the Supreme Court's ruling in the Grove City case." Lex Frieden, "Testimony Before the U.S. Senate Committee on Labor and Human Resources, 1 April 1987," Lex Frieden Collection, George H.W. Bush Presidential Library, College Station, TX, box 4, folder marked "CR [Civil Rights] Restoration Act [Testimony—1987]," 4.

41. Wards Cove Packing Co. v. Atonio, 490 U.S. 642 (1989).

42. "Compromise Civil Rights Bill Passed" *CQ Almanac 1991*, 47th ed. (Washington, DC: Congressional Quarterly, 1992), 251–261.

43. Patterson v. McLean Credit Union, 491 U.S. 164 (1989).

44. Ralph Neas, "The Civil Rights Legacy of the Reagan Years," *USA Today Magazine*, March 1990, LCCR papers, part 3, box 54, folder 7, 18.

45. According to the NAACP's Benjamin Hooks at the time, the new "Reaganized" court "is more dangerous to civil rights than any Bull Connors with his fire hoses." Neas, "Civil Rights Legacy," 18.

46. "Dear Representative" letter, LCCR, 31 January 1990, LCCR papers, part 3, box 53, folder 6. The White House took a different view, with an internal memo to the president months earlier noting: "The Court simply has not undermined the goals of the civil rights laws or set up unnecessary barriers to legitimate victims of discrimination. Rather, it has allocated responsibility among the parties to litigation so as to treat employers, minority employees, and white employees in a way that is fair to all." C. Boyden Gray, "Memo for the President, Subject: Recent Civil Rights Decisions by the Supreme Court," 26 June 1989, C. Boyden Gray files, Bush presidential records, WHCO, Bush Library, folder marked "Subject File, Civil Rights 1989," OA/ID: 45064-041.

47. King would later write directly to Bush, warning of the consequences of a presidential veto: "Mr. President, your veto of this legislation would be a major set-back for the goals and objectives for which my husband gave his life and it would set a regressive tone in race relations throughout our nation." Coretta Scott King, "Letter to the President," 18 October 1990, Lund files, folder marked "Civil Rights File, Civil Rights: Letters Concerning Bill [3]," OA/ID: 45402-001.

48. PFAW news release, "Report Documents 'Severe' Human Impact of Supreme Court Rollback of Civil Rights," 5 February 1990, LCCR papers, part 3, box 53, folder 7.

49. Statement of Women's Legal Defense Fund president Judith Lichtman, "Back to the Future," 7 February 1990, LCCR papers, part 3, box 53, folder 7.

50. LCCR memo, "Civil Rights Act of 1990," 6 February 1990, LCCR papers, part 3, box 53, folder 7; quoted in Arch Parson and Lyle Denniston, "Congress Unveils Bill for Revitalizing Civil Rights Laws,'" *BS*, 8 February 1990.

51. Ralph Neas, LCCR press release, 27 February 1990, LCCR papers, part 3, box 54, folder 2.

52. "Dear Representative" letter, LCCR, 31 January 1990, LCCR papers, part 3, box 53, folder 6.

53. The LCCR tied success directly to grassroots participation in a "massive national campaign," outlining five key approaches to victory: "Write, Visit, Call, Inform, Organize." LCCR letter to "LCCR Presidents, Representatives, and Friends. RE: Grassroots Activities on Behalf of the Civil Rights Act of 1990," 16 March 1990, LCCR papers, part 3, box 54, folder 6, 2.

54. LCCR letter to "LCCR Presidents and Representatives, RE: Civil Rights Act of 1990," 5 March 1990, LCCR papers, part 3, box 54, folder 4, 2.

55. LCCR "Media Task Force" memo [n.d., folder marked "May 1990"], LCCR papers, part 3, box 55, folder 6.

56. "Dear Senator" letter, LCCR, enclosed with William T. Coleman Jr., "A False 'Quota' Call," *WP*, 23 February 1990, LCCR papers, part 3, box 54, folder 2; quoted in Chinta Strausberg, "Jackson urges Bush to sign 90s Civil Rights Act," *Chicago Defender*, 19 May 1990.

57. "A New Civil Rights Debate: Liberals in Congress Take On the Supreme Court over Job Bias," *US News & World Report*, 12 February 1990.

58. Quoted in Joan Biskupic, "Partisan Rancor Marks Vote on Civil Rights Measure," *CQ Press*, 21 July 1990, 2312–2313.

59. Quoted in Biskupic, "Partisan Rancor," 2314.

60. Colorado's William Lester Armstrong (R) did not vote. S.2104 (101st): Civil Rights Act of 1990, 18 July 1990.

61. Quoted in Biskupic, "Partisan Rancor," 2314.

62. Biskupic, "Partisan Rancor," 2316.

63. Quoted in Joan Biskupic, "House Joins in the Standoff over Civil Rights Measure," *CQ Press*, 4 August 1990, 2517.

64. H.R. 4000 (101st): Civil Rights Act of 1990, 3 August 1990.

65. LCCR memo, "Legislative Alert," 20 August 1990, LCCR papers, part 3, box 57, folder 2.

66. LCCR memo, "Update on Civil Rights Act of 1990," 15 October 1990, LCCR papers, part 3, box 57, folder 5, 2.

67. Hatch withdrew formal support when the White House signaled that it still opposed the bill, despite the compromises. "Dear Representative" letter, LCCR, 15 October 1990, LCCR papers, part 3, box 57, folder 5; [author unknown], "Mr. Bush, Against the Tide," *NYT*, 15 October 1990.

68. David Hamilton Golland, *A Terrible Thing to Waste: Arthur Fletcher and the Conundrum of the Black Republican* (Lawrence: University Press of Kansas, 2019), 253.

69. In his veto message, Bush wrote: "Despite the use of the term 'civil rights' in the title . . . the bill actually employs a maze of highly legalistic language to introduce the destructive force of quotas into our Nation's employment system." George H. W. Bush, "Message to the Senate Returning Without Approval the Civil Rights Act of 1990," 22 October 1990, APP, https://www.presidency.ucsb.edu/node/265179.

70. Ralph Neas, "Statement Regarding President George Bush's Announced Intention to Veto the Civil Rights Act of 1990," 17 October 1990, LCCR papers, part 3, box 57, folder 5.

71. Quoted in "Compromise," *CQ Almanac 1991*.

72. "Compromise," *CQ Almanac 1991*.

73. "Compromise," *CQ Almanac 1991*.

74. Ann Chipley, "Letter to LCCR President, 18 January 1991," LCCR papers, part 3, box 58, folder 5.

75. "The Bill and Women" was talking point number 2, behind "The Bill and Quotas" in the new strategy pack, while "The Bill and Racial Minorities" was point 6. "Dear Friend" letter, LCCR, 26 March 1991, LCCR papers, part 3, box 58, folder 7.

76. Quoted in Joan Biskupic, "New Struggle over Civil Rights Brings Shift in Strategy," *CQ Press*, 9 February 1991, LCCR papers, part 3, box 58, folder 6, 372.

77. LCCR memo, 10 May 1991, LCCR papers, part 3, box 59, folder 1. At the same time, an internal White House memo also argued that the Democrats were

succeeding in turning "Willie Horton into the codeword of the decade.... It means: Republicans are racists.... Horton's transformation from embarrassment into rallying cry offers a case study in the politics of deliberate division." "Memorandum to Gov. Sununu, RE: The Use and Abuse of Willie Horton," 3 June 1991, Gray files, folder marked "Subject File, Civil Rights 5/91–8/91 [1]," OA/ID: 45064, 1.

78. Cosigners included Benjamin Hooks, Joseph Lowery, and Rep. Edolphus Towns (D-NY). "Press Release," 3 June 1991, Mink papers, box 2070, folder 1, 2.

79. Quoted in Andrew Rosenthal, "Marshall Retires from High Court; Blow to Liberals," *NYT*, 28 June 1991.

80. The liberal group Alliance for Justice framed its opposition through the broader CRA fight at the time, writing: "Thomas has taken positions on federal laws prohibiting employment discrimination on the basis of race, sex, national origin and age, which have undermined their effectiveness.... [He has] an overall disdain for the rule of law." Nan Aron, Alliance for Justice memo, "RE: Nomination of Clarence Thomas," 13 September 1989, LCCR papers, part 3, box 91, folder 2.

81. "Thomas Talking Points for Congressional Black Caucus," [n.d.], LCCR papers, part 3, box 91, folder 3.

82. Flo Kennedy reportedly said that the "game plan" was to "Bork" Thomas: "NOW to Fight Confirmation of Thomas: Supreme Court," *LAT*, 6 July 1991. Moreover, in NOW's "Take Action" pamphlet sent to its mailing list, it advised supporters to form "BORK THOMAS coalitions." "Clarence Thomas: Talking Points," [n.d.], NOW papers, MC666, box 366, folder 2.

83. Neil A. Lewis, "Thomas Ends Testimony but Senators Grumble over Elusive Views," *NYT*, 17 September 1991.

84. Joseph L. Rauh, "Statement," 19 September 1991, Rauh papers, box 271, folder 6, 3–4.

85. "Clarence Thomas: Then and Now," PFAW media packet, DPM papers, part 2, box 606, folder 8. Appearing on Court TV, Robert Bork jumped to Thomas's defense, blaming "White House image specialists" for packaging Thomas "too cautiously" and suggesting he should simply say he has "changed his mind." Quoted in Walter Goodman, "Bork as Analyst: Past Loser Views Today's Game," *NYT*, 13 September 1991.

86. This fear was ultimately realized in the landmark June 2022 case *Dobbs v. Jackson Women's Health Organization*, with Thomas voting to overturn *Roe*; "Dear Senator" letter, NARAL, 13 September 1991, DPM papers, part 2, box 606, folder 11.

87. Ralph Neas, "Statement Opposing the Confirmation of Judge Clarence Thomas to the US Supreme Court," 7 August 1991, LCCR papers, part 3, box 91, folder 3, 1.

88. Julian Bond, "My Case Against Clarence Thomas," *WP*, 8 September 1991.

89. Bond, "Case Against Clarence Thomas."

90. Alliance for Justice memo, "Study Shows Thomas Lowest Rated Supreme Court Nominee," 29 August 1991, DPM papers, part 2, box 607, folder 7.

91. "LCCR Talking Points on the Thomas Nomination," 23 July 1991, LCCR papers, part 3, box 91, folder 3, 4–5.
92. "Clarence Thomas Wins Senate Confirmation," in *CQ Almanac 1991*, 274–285.
93. Moreover, with his reputation for womanizing, and his nephew, William Kennedy Smith, facing an impending rape trial for an alleged incident that occurred in Palm Beach while holidaying with the senator, Kennedy, the "Bork-Slayer," was uncharacteristically quiet during the hearings, looking "grimly uncomfortable" according to John Farrell. Consequently, had it not been for the senator's transgressions, Farrell argues, Thomas might well have been kept off the Supreme Court. John A. Farrell, *Ted Kennedy: A Life* (New York: Penguin, 2022), 477–478.
94. Jill Abramson, "Image of Anita Hill, Brighter in Hindsight, Galvanizes Campaigns," *WSJ*, 5 October 1992.
95. Patsy Mink, letter to supporter, 11 June 1992, Mink papers, box 1072, folder 7.
96. "Compromise," *CQ Almanac 1991*.
97. "Compromise," *CQ Almanac 1991*.
98. William T. Coleman Jr. and Vernon B. Jordan Jr., "How the Civil Rights Bill Was Really Passed," *WP*, 18 November 1991.
99. James Simon, *The Center Holds: The Power Struggle Inside the Rehnquist Court* (New York: Simon & Schuster, 1995), 81.
100. "Compromise," *CQ Almanac 1991*.
101. LCCR memo, "Summary of President George Bush's Record on Civil Rights," 13 August 1992, Rauh papers, box 271, folder 6, 1–7.
102. Elizabeth Drew, "A Win for Bill Clinton, the Candidate of Change," *The New Yorker*, 8 November 1992.
103. Richard L. Berke, "The 1992 Campaign: In 1992, Willie Horton Is Democrats' Weapon," *NYT*, 25 August 1992.
104. Wilentz, *Age of Reagan*, 289.
105. Sidney Blumenthal, "Celebrating Bill Clinton's Candidacy," *Politico*, 30 September 2011.
106. Blumenthal, "Celebrating Bill Clinton's Candidacy."
107. Richard L. Berke, "Gingrich, in Duel with White House, Stays True to His Role as an Outsider," *NYT*, 5 October 1990.
108. See Julian E. Zelizer, *Burning Down the House: Newt Gingrich, the Fall of a Speaker, and the Rise of the New Republican Party* (New York: Penguin, 2020).
109. Zelizer, *Burning Down the House*, 87.
110. Quoted in John M. Barry, "The House of Jim Wright," *Politico*, 7 May 2015.
111. Barry, "The House of Jim Wright"; Zelizer, *Burning Down the House*, 8, 133.
112. In his resignation speech, Wright pleaded with his colleagues for civility, arguing that "all of us, in both political parties, must resolve to bring this period of mindless cannibalism to an end." But the episode was, in many ways, a Crossing the Rubicon moment for the type of combative hyper-partisanship that now

dominates the sclerotic institution. Jim Wright, "Resignation Speech," *C-SPAN*, 31 May 1989, https://www.c-span.org/video/?c4730601/jim-wright-resignation.

113. Zelizer, *Burning Down the House*, 283.

114. Berke, "Gingrich."

115. Zelizer, "Unexpected Endurance," 85.

116. Witcher, *Getting Right with Reagan*, 67.

117. Still, for all his charisma, Clinton's first real foray into national politics was "an unmitigated disaster," according to his home-state newspaper, the *Arkansas Gazette*. As a rising star and "a leading voice of the new South," Clinton was selected by Dukakis to nominate him at the 1988 Democratic Convention. But the governor notoriously gave a long-winded and lackluster speech that lasted thirty-three minutes, rather than the allotted fifteen, interrupted by boos and chants, and it was so poorly received that the audience cheered when he said, "In conclusion." Stephen Kurkjian and Curtis Wilkie, "Ark. Governor Winces over a Failed Nominating Speech," *BG*, 22 July 1988; E. J. Dionne Jr., "Night of Triumph," *NYT*, 20 July 1988.

118. Wilentz, *Age of Reagan*, 31.

119. Baer, *Reinventing Democrats*, 2.

120. Martin Walker, *Clinton: The President They Deserve* (London: Vintage, 1997), 8.

121. Here, Clinton tried to frame some of these arguments through a liberal prism, promising to reform the welfare system as a means of "reviving liberalism," for example. According to Jason DeParle, Clinton believed that welfare had poisoned the politics of poverty and race, discrediting government and aggravating the worst racial stereotypes by casting poor people as "shirkers" and the Democrats as "the party of giveaways." Jason DeParle, *American Dream: Three Women, Ten Kids, and a Nation's Drive to End Welfare* (New York: Viking Penguin, 2004), 150.

122. Judis and Teixeira, *Emerging Democratic Majority*, 28.

123. David Greenberg, "Reinventing Democrats: The Politics of Liberalism from Reagan to Clinton by Kenneth Baer," *The Journal of Interdisciplinary History*, 32, no. 2 (2001): 339–341, (340).

124. Robin Toner, "A Revival and a Party Transformed", *NYT*, 27 December 2000.

125. Greenberg, "Reinventing Democrats," 340.

126. Richard Rothstein, "Friends of Bill? Why Liberals Should Let Up on Clinton," *The American Prospect*, 19 December 2001.

127. According to Francis Fowler, Clinton's election represented the moment that the "neoliberal wing of the Democratic Party came to power." Fowler justifies this by arguing that Clinton, Vice President Al Gore, Secretary of Labor Robert Reich, and Secretary of the Interior Bruce Babbitt had all "long been considered members of the neoliberal inner circle." Francis C. Fowler, "The Neoliberal Value Shift and Its Implications for Federal Education Policy Under Clinton," *Educational Administration Quarterly* 31, no. 1 (1995): 38–60.

128. "Clinton Sets His Sights Beyond '88," *AJC*, 16 July 1987, Dukakis papers, box 6, folder 753.
129. Judis and Teixeira, *Emerging Democratic Majority*, 133.
130. Andelic, *Donkey Work*, 179.
131. David Broder, "Something Owed to Tsongas," *NYT*, 26 January 1997.
132. Jeff Jacoby, "Liberalism's Debt to Paul Tsongas," *BS*, 29 January 1997.
133. Paul Berman, "Left Behind," *TNR*, 18 September 2000.
134. Zelizer, "Reflections," 382–383.
135. Lisa Young, *Feminists and Party Politics* (Toronto: UBC Press, 2000), 48–49.
136. Matthew S. Scott, "Up for Grabs: The Black Vote," *Black Enterprise*, August 1995, 183. Clinton would continue to enjoy strong support from Black voters, with Nobel laureate Toni Morrison famously labeling him the "first black president" in 1998. Toni Morrison, "The Talk of the Town," *The New Yorker*, 5 October 1998.
137. According to Byron Shafer, the Clinton administration set out its policy stances for all to see early: "sharply liberal on cultural-national issues, and clearly liberal on economic-welfare issues too." Shafer, *Two Majorities*, 68; Thomas L. Friedman, "Clinton's Cabinet Choices Put Him at Center, Balancing Competing Factions," *NYT*, 27 December 1992; Sean Wilentz, "20 Years Later: How Bill Clinton Saved Liberalism from Itself," *TNR*, 1 October 2011.
138. According to California representative Henry Waxman (D): "In one day, no President has ever done more to affirm the right of women to make personal reproductive choices." Quoted in Karen Tumulty and Marlene Cimons, "Clinton Revokes Abortion Curbs," *LAT*, 23 January 1993.
139. Baer, *Reinventing Democrats*, 219.
140. Although Perot drew support from both, he damaged Bush disproportionately more than Clinton, owing to his harsh attacks against the incumbent and the timing of both his departure and re-entry into the 1992 campaign; "American President: Biography of Bill Clinton," UVA Miller Center, http://millercenter.org/president/clinton/essays/biography/print, accessed 9 April 2023.
141. NAFTA represented a free trade agreement among the United States, Mexico, and Canada. Initially brokered by Bush, it became an important issue during the 1992 campaign, with Clinton struggling to take a position at first. He would eventually endorse NAFTA but only if Mexico and Canada agreed to additional side provisions addressing the concerns of labor and environmental groups, two key Democratic constituencies. Peter Behr, "Clinton's Conversion on NAFTA," *WP*, 19 September 1993.
142. While Clinton received over three million more votes than Dukakis, the Democrats recorded a 3 percent decrease in their share of the popular vote compared to 1988 due to higher turnout rates and the Perot candidacy in 1992.
143. Polls in Wattenberg, "Why Clinton Won and Dukakis Lost," 254–256.
144. A record-breaking 119 women stood for Congress in 1992, with 53 of them winning seats. "Summary" CAWP; "From Anita Hill to Capitol Hill," *Time*, 16 November 1992.

145. Jacob Weisberg, "Ellen Malcolm: The Woman Behind All Those Women Candidates," *LAT*, 8 November 1992.

146. Joseph A. Califano Jr., *Governing America: An Insider's Report from the White House and the Cabinet* (New York: Simon & Schuster, 1981), 97. While the bill was not the nationalized single-payer program that many liberals had been demanding, with Clinton pushing for a more market-based, technocratic intervention instead, it was still, according to Julian Zelizer, "the most sweeping health-care proposal to come out of the White House since Medicare." Zelizer, "Reflections," 383.

147. With turnout among women the lowest since 1974, Democratic pollster Celinda Lake attributed the 1994 loss to the gender gap, arguing that "Democrats would have retained control of both the House and Senate if women had been as excited about the Democrats as men were about the Republicans." Quoted in Steven Stark, "Gap Politics," *The American Prospect*, July 1996.

148. Richard L. Berke, "The 1994 Elections; The Overview," *NYT*, 9 November 1994.

149. As the *Washington Post* noted in 1995, for example, "Big Government has become too woven into society's fabric to be unthreaded. It does too many people too much good and has created too many defenders." Robert J. Samuelson, "Big Government Is Here to Stay," *WP*, 20 June 1995. Also see Andelic, *Donkey Work*, 181–187.

150. Becky Little, "How a Petty Snub Led to Clinton's Government Shutdown," *History*, 12 December 2018.

151. After 1994, when many within the party were advising Clinton to move to the right, Senator Kennedy urged the president to stay true to themes that had long been identified with traditional Democratic Party liberalism: protecting Medicare, Medicaid, and education, raising the minimum wage, etc. As the *New Yorker* argued, while Clinton did effectively neutralize the Republicans by co-opting some of their issues, "the real foundation" of his reelection in 1996 was "a liberal agenda, not a conservative one. . . . The message of the Clinton reelection campaign—of the more than eighty-five million dollars' worth of ads—was defined and driven by Edward Kennedy." Elsa Walsh, "Kennedy's Hidden Campaign," *The New Yorker*, 31 March 1997, 66–81.

152. Toner, "A Revival."

CONCLUSION: RECKONING WITH THE "REAGAN ERA"

1. Historian Hugh Heclo later argued that Reagan's legacy was to "consolidate rather than roll back" the welfare state. Hugh Heclo, "The Mixed Legacies of Ronald Reagan," *Presidential Studies Quarterly* 38, no. 4 (2008): 558.

2. Kruse and Zelizer, *Fault Lines*, 132.

3. Political scientists, such as Paul Pierson, have explored this process of policy feedback in depth, whereby established policies "create strong electoral constituencies, nurture interest group networks, and transform public opinion, so they are

very hard to undo even if partisan politics changes dramatically." Zelizer, "Unexpected Endurance," 77.

4. Certainly, some important works have started to address this: Gareth Davies, for instance, has used his innovative study of federal education policy since 1965 to detail how government expanded in tandem with the supposed conservative revolution, while Robert Mason has convincingly shown how conservatism unfolded in a dialectical fashion with liberalism, rather than as a replacement to it in the 1960s and 1970s. Gareth Davies, *See Government Grow: Education Politics from Johnson to Reagan* (Lawrence: University Press of Kansas, 2007); Robert Mason, *The Republican Party and American Politics from Hoover to Reagan* (Cambridge: Cambridge University Press, 2012).

5. Lloyd A. Free and Hadley Cantril, *The Political Beliefs of Americans: A Study of Public Opinion* (New York: Simon & Schuster, 1968).

6. Zelizer, "Unexpected Endurance," 89.

7. Lily Geismer has also demonstrated how some of the cross-class, interracial coalitions that developed to push for change on a national level struggled to translate when certain issues were reduced to a local level, like fair housing. See Geismer's *Don't Blame Us*.

8. The Bork nomination altered the way that law and politics intersect as everything from the shape of the confirmation hearings to the trajectory of the gay rights movement was affected. His name was even transformed from a noun into a verb: to "Bork" became a politico-judicial attack phrase in Washington parlance.

9. Rossinow, *The Reagan Era*, 241. Also see Andrew Hartman, *A War for the Soul of America: A History of the Culture Wars* (Chicago: University of Chicago Press, 2015).

10. Hale, "New Democrats," 216.

11. Baer, *Reinventing Democrats*.

12. Bloodworth, *Losing the Center*, 13.

13. Galston and Kamarck set up and demolished a series of straw men, the supposed myths through which "liberal fundamentalists" succeeded in getting the Democrats to evade reality, including the mobilization myth—that greater mobilization of nonparticipants, principally minorities, equaled victory—and the myth of the congressional bastion—that Democratic control of Congress allowed liberals to obscure the fact that a clear realignment was taking place. William Galston and Elaine Kamarck, "The Politics of Evasion: Democrats and the Presidency," Progressive Policy Institute, September 1989, http://www.progressivepolicy.org/wp-content/uploads/2013/03/Politics_of_Evasion.pdf; Jeff Faux, "The Myth of the New Democrats," *The American Prospect* (Fall 1993).

14. Historian Iwan Morgan has also shown commonalities between Carter's response to stagflation and Clinton's economic governance model—both placed a greater reliance on the market, prioritized inflation over unemployment, and used supply-side measures to enhance investment. Iwan Morgan, "Jimmy Carter, Bill Clinton, and the New Democratic Economics," *The Historical Journal* 47, no. 4 (2004): 1015–1039.

15. Wilentz, "20 Years Later."

16. Gretchen Reynolds, "Vote of Confidence," *Chicago Magazine*, 1 January 1993.

17. The so-called non-white share of the electorate as a whole (the proportion of racial minorities) nearly doubled in the years between 1988 and 2008 (from 15 to 26 percent) and backed Obama by over 80 percent in 2008 and 2012. According to Census Bureau data, the number of women registered to vote continued to climb after the 1980s, with more than ten million more women than men voters by 2012. Since 1980, a gender gap of 4 to 11 percent appeared in every presidential election. In 2008, and especially in 2012 when male voters swung against Obama, women voters provided the winning margin (in 2008, Obama carried women by 56 to 43 percent, with a slim 49 to 48 percent lead among men; in 2012, Obama carried women 55 to 44, while losing men 45 to 52). Finally, the professional class expanded considerably as America moved from an industrial to a postindustrial economy (from 7 percent of the electorate in the 1960s to 17 percent by the 1990s). These voters supported Obama by 58 to 40 percent in 2008 (higher turnout rates among professionals also meant that they accounted for 21 percent of voters). See Ruy Teixeira, "The Emerging Democratic Majority Turns 10," *The Atlantic*, 9 November 2012; "The Gender Gap: Voting Choices in Presidential Elections," CAWP, January 2017, http://www.cawp.rutgers.edu/sites/default/files/resources/ggpresvote.pdf; and Ruy Teixeira, "Demographic Change and the Future of the Parties," Center for American Progress, 16 June 2010, https://www.americanprogressaction.org/article/demographic-change-and-the-future-of-the-parties/.

18. According to Julian Zelizer, Obama is part "of a generation of liberals who have been lost in the historiographical focus on the 'rise of the right' after the 1960s. He is one of the many liberal leaders who remained alive and well—and politically active at all levels of government—in the conservative era that followed Ronald Reagan's victory in 1980." Julian E. Zelizer, ed., *The Presidency of Barack Obama: A First Historical Assessment* (Princeton, NJ: Princeton University Press, 2018), 3.

Bibliography

ARCHIVES

Ann Arbor, Michigan
    Gerald R. Ford Presidential Library
        Papers of Robert M. Teeter
        President Ford Committee Campaign Records

Austin, Texas
    Lyndon B. Johnson Presidential Library
        Papers of Joseph A. Califano
        Papers of Lyndon B. Johnson, White House Central Files
        Papers of Frederick Panzer
        Papers of Peter R. Rosenblatt

Boston, Massachusetts
    Boston College, John J. Burns Library
        Papers of Thomas P. O'Neill Jr.
    John F. Kennedy Presidential Library
        Edward M. Kennedy Senate Files
        Papers of Adam Clymer
        Papers of Arthur M. Schlesinger Jr.
        Papers of John Kenneth Galbraith
        Papers of Nancy F. Korman
        Papers of Theodore C. Sorensen
        Papers of Theodore H. White
    Northeastern University, Archives and Special Collections
        Michael Dukakis Presidential Campaign Records

Boulder, Colorado
    University of Colorado, Boulder
        Papers of Gary W. Hart

Cambridge, Massachusetts
    Schlesinger Library, Harvard University
        Collection of Eleanor Smeal Reports
        Organizational Papers of the National Organization for Women

College Station, Texas
    George H. W. Bush Presidential Library
        Lex Frieden Collection
        George H. W. Bush Presidential Records
            C. Boyden Gray Files
            Lee S. Liberman Files

　　　　Nelson Lund Files
　　　　William Roper Files
　Memphis, Tennessee
　　　Memphis Public Library
　　　　Benjamin L. Hooks Collection
　Lowell, Massachusetts
　　　University of Massachusetts, Lowell, Center for Lowell History
　　　　Paul E. Tsongas Congressional Collection
　Simi Valley, California
　　　Ronald Reagan Presidential Library
　　　　Sara Fritz Papers
　St. Louis, Missouri
　　　Missouri Historical Society, Library Research Center
　　　　Richard A. Gephardt Congressional Collection
　Washington, DC
　　　Library of Congress, Manuscript Reading Room
　　　　ERAmerica Records
　　　　Organizational Papers of the Leadership Conference on Civil Rights
　　　　Papers of Robert Bork
　　　　Papers of the House Democratic Caucus
　　　　Papers of the Democratic Study Group
　　　　Papers of Mary McGrory
　　　　Papers of Patsy T. Mink
　　　　Papers of Daniel Patrick Moynihan
　　　　Papers of Michael Pertschuk
　　　　Papers of Joseph L. Rauh
　　　　U.S. Capitol Historical Society Oral History Collection

SECONDARY SOURCES

Books

Alterman, Eric. *Why We're Liberals: A Political Handbook for Post-Bush America.* New York: Penguin Group, 2008.

Alterman, Eric, and Kevin Mattson. *The Cause: The Fight for American Liberalism from Franklin Roosevelt to Barack Obama.* New York: Viking, 2012.

Amaker, Norman C. *Civil Rights and the Reagan Administration.* Washington, DC: Urban Institute, 1988.

Ambar, Saladin M. *American Cicero: Mario Cuomo and the Defense of American Liberalism.* Oxford: Oxford University Press, 2018.

Andelic, Patrick. *Donkey Work: Congressional Democrats in Conservative America, 1972–1994.* Lawrence: University Press of Kansas, 2019.

Andelic, Patrick, Mark McLay, and Robert Mason, eds. *Midterms and Mandates: Electoral Reassessments of Presidents and Parties.* Edinburgh: Edinburgh University Press, 2022.

Andrew, John A. *Lyndon Johnson and the Great Society*. Chicago: Ivan R. Dee, 1999.
Aronowitz, Stanley. *The Death and Rebirth of American Radicalism*. New York: Routledge, 1996.
Baer, Kenneth S. *Reinventing Democrats: The Politics of Liberalism from Reagan to Clinton*. Lawrence: University Press of Kansas, 2000.
Barker, Lucius J., and Ronald W. Walters, eds. *Jesse Jackson's 1984 Presidential Campaign: Challenge and Change in American Politics*. Champaign: University of Illinois Press, 1989.
Battista, Andrew. *The Revival of Labor Liberalism*. Champaign: University of Illinois Press, 2008.
Batza, Katie. *Before AIDS: Gay Health Politics in the 1970s*. Philadelphia: University of Pennsylvania Press, 2018.
Béland, Daniel. *Social Security: History and Politics from the New Deal to the Privatization Debate*. Lawrence: University Press of Kansas, 2005.
Bell, Jonathan. *California Crucible: The Forging of Modern American Liberalism*. Philadelphia: University of Pennsylvania Press, 2012.
Bell, Jonathan, and Timothy Stanley, eds. *Making Sense of American Liberalism*. Champaign: University of Illinois Press, 2012.
Berkowitz, Edward D. *America's Welfare State: From Roosevelt to Reagan*. Baltimore, MD: John Hopkins University Press, 1996.
———. *Mr. Social Security: The Life of Wilbur J. Cohen*. Lawrence: University Press of Kansas, 1995.
———. *Robert Ball and the Politics of Social Security*. Madison: University of Wisconsin Press, 2003.
———. *Something Happened: A Political and Cultural Overview of the Seventies*. New York: Columbia University Press, 2006.
Berman, Ari. *Give Us the Ballot: The Modern Struggle for Voting Rights in America*. New York: Farrar, Straus and Giroux, 2015.
Berry, Jeffrey M. *The New Liberalism: The Rising Power of Citizen Groups*. Washington, DC: Brookings, 1999.
Biven, W. Carl. *Jimmy Carter's Economy: Policy in an Age of Limits*. Chapel Hill: University of North Carolina Press, 2002.
Bloodworth, Jeffrey. *Losing the Center: The Decline of American Liberalism, 1968–1992*. Lexington: University of Kentucky Press, 2013.
Blumenthal, Sidney, and Thomas Byrne Edsall, eds. *The Reagan Legacy*. New York: Pantheon Books, 1988.
Brands, H. W. *Reagan: The Life*. New York: Doubleday, 2015.
———. *The Strange Death of American Liberalism*. New Haven, CT: Yale University Press, 2001.
Brandt, Karl Gerald. *Ronald Reagan and the House Democrats: Gridlock, Partisanship, and the Fiscal Crisis*. Columbia: University of Missouri Press, 2009.
Brinkley, Alan. *The End of Reform: New Deal Liberalism in Recession and War*. New York: Vintage Books, 1995.

———. *Liberalism and Its Discontents*. Cambridge: Harvard University Press, 1998.
Bronner, Ethan. *Battle for Justice: How the Bork Nomination Shook America*. New York: Union Square, 2007.
Brownlee, W. Elliot, and Hugh Davis Graham, eds. *The Reagan Presidency: Pragmatic Conservatism and Its Legacies*. Lawrence: University Press of Kansas, 2003.
Bullock, Charles S., III, Susan A. MacManus, Jeremy D. Mayer, and Mark J. Rozell. *The South and the Transformation of U.S. Politics*. Oxford: Oxford University Press, 2019.
Bunch, Will. *Tear Down This Myth: How the Reagan Legacy Has Distorted Our Politics and Haunts Our Future*. New York: Free Press, 2009.
Burnham, Walter Dean. *Critical Elections and the Mainsprings of American Politics*. New York: W. W. Norton, 1971.
Busch, Andrew. *Reagan's Victory: The Presidential Election of 1980 and the Rise of the Right*. Lawrence: University Press of Kansas, 2005.
Califano, Joseph A., Jr. *Governing America: An Insider's Report from the White House and the Cabinet*. New York: Simon & Schuster, 1981.
Canellos, Peter S. *The Last Lion: The Fall and Rise of Ted Kennedy*. New York: Simon & Schuster, 2010.
Cannon, Lou. *President Reagan: The Role of a Lifetime*, 2nd ed. New York: PublicAffairs, 2000.
Cantril, Albert H., and Susan Davis Cantril. *Reading Mixed Signals: Ambivalence in American Public Opinion About Government*. Washington, DC: Woodrow Wilson Center, 1999.
Carroll, Peter N. *It Seemed Like Nothing Happened: America in the 1970s*, 3rd ed. New Brunswick, NJ: Rutgers University Press, 2000.
Carter, Dan T. *From George Wallace to Newt Gingrich: Race in the Conservative Counterrevolution, 1963–1994*. Baton Rouge: Louisiana State University Press, 1996.
———. *The Politics of Rage: George Wallace, the Origins of the New Conservatism, and the Transformation of American Politics*, 2nd ed. Baton Rouge: Louisiana State University Press, 2000.
Carter, Jimmy. *White House Diary*. New York: Farrar, Straus and Giroux, 2010.
Casey, Susan Berry. *Hart and Soul: Gary Hart's New Hampshire Odyssey . . . and Beyond*. Concord, NH: NHI Press, 1986.
Cebul, Brent, Lily Geismer, and Mason B. Williams, eds. *Shaped by the State: Toward a New Political History of the Twentieth Century*. Chicago: University of Chicago Press, 2019.
Chafe, William H. *The Achievement of American Liberalism: The New Deal and Its Legacies*. New York: Columbia University Press, 2003.
———. *The Unfinished Journey: America Since World War II*. Oxford: Oxford University Press, 1991.
Clemente, Frank. *Keep Hope Alive: Jesse Jackson's 1988 Presidential Campaign*. Boston: South End, 1989.

Clymer, Adam. *Edward M. Kennedy: A Biography*. New York: Harper, 2009.
Conley, Richard S. *The Presidency, Congress, and Divided Government: A Postwar Assessment*. College Station: Texas A&M University Press, 2003.
Courtwright, David T. *No Right Turn: Conservative Politics in a Liberal America*. Cambridge: Harvard University Press, 2010.
Critchlow, Donald T. *The Conservative Ascendancy: How the GOP Right Made Political History*. Cambridge: Harvard University Press, 2007.
———. *Phyllis Schlafly and Grassroots Conservatism*. Princeton, NJ: Princeton University Press, 2005.
Critchlow, Donald T., and W. J. Rorabaugh. *Takeover: How the Left's Quest for Social Justice Corrupted Liberalism*. Wilmington, DE: ISI Books, 2012.
Crothers, Lane, and Nancy S. Lind. *Presidents from Reagan Through Clinton, 1981–2001: Debating the Issues in Pro and Con Primary Documents*. Westport, CT: Greenwood, 2002.
Dallek, Matthew. *The Right Moment: Ronald Reagan's First Victory and the Decisive Turning Point in American Politics*. New York: Free Press, 2000.
Dallek, Robert. *Flawed Giant: Lyndon Johnson and His Times, 1961–1973*. Oxford: Oxford University Press, 1998.
Dalton, Russell J. *The Apartisan American: Dealignment and Changing Electoral Politics*. Washington, DC: CQ Press, 2013.
Davies, Gareth. *From Opportunity to Entitlement: The Transformation and Decline of Great Society Liberalism*. Lawrence: University Press of Kansas, 1996.
———. *See Government Grow: Education Politics from Johnson to Reagan*. Lawrence: University Press of Kansas, 2007.
Davies, Gareth, and Julian E Zelizer, eds. *America at the Ballot Box: Elections and Political History*. Philadelphia: University of Pennsylvania Press, 2015.
Davis, Flora. *Moving the Mountain: The Women's Movement in America Since 1960*, 2nd ed. New York: Simon & Schuster, 1999.
Davis, Lanny J. *The Emerging Democratic Majority: Lessons and Legacies from the New Politics*. New York: Stein and Day, 1974.
DeParle, Jason. *American Dream: Three Women, Ten Kids, and a Nation's Drive to End Welfare*. New York: Viking Penguin, 2004.
Depoe, Stephen P. *Arthur M. Schlesinger, Jr., and the Ideological History of American Liberalism*. Tuscaloosa: University of Alabama Press, 1994.
Derthick, Martha. *Policymaking for Social Security*. Washington, DC: Brookings, 1979.
Dewitt, Larry W., Daniel Béland, and Edward D. Berkowitz, eds. *Social Security: A Documentary History*. Washington, DC: CQ Press, 2008.
Diggins, John Patrick, ed. *The Liberal Persuasion: Arthur Schlesinger, Jr., and the Challenge of the American Past*. Princeton, NJ: Princeton University Press, 1997.
Drew, Elizabeth. *Campaign Journal: The Political Events of 1983–1984*. New York: Macmillan, 1985.
———. *Election Journal: The Political Events of 1987–1988*. New York: W. Morrow, 1989.

———. *On the Edge: The Clinton Presidency.* New York: Touchstone, 1994.
———. *Portrait of an Election: The 1980 Presidential Campaign.* New York: Simon & Schuster, 1981.
———. *Showdown: The Struggle Between the Gingrich Congress and the Clinton White House.* New York: Touchstone, 1996.
Dye, Thomas R., and Luther Harmon Zeigler. *American Politics in the Media Age.* Pacific Grove, CA: Brooks/Cole, 1986.
Edsall, Thomas Byrne. *Chain Reaction: The Impact of Race, Rights, and Taxes on American Politics.* New York: W. W. Norton, 1991.
Ehrman, John. *The Eighties: America in the Age of Reagan,* New Haven, CT: Yale University Press, 2005.
———. *The Rise of Neoconservatism: Intellectuals and Foreign Affairs, 1945–1994.* New Haven, CT: Yale University Press, 1995.
Ehrman, John, and Michael W. Flamm. *Debating the Reagan Presidency.* New York: Rowman & Littlefield, 2009.
Faludi, Susan. *Backlash: The Undeclared War Against American Women.* London: Vintage, 1992.
Farrell, John A. *Ted Kennedy: A Life.* New York: Penguin, 2022.
———. *Tip O'Neill and the Democratic Century.* Boston: Little, Brown, 2002.
Ferguson, Thomas, and Joel Rogers. *Right Turn: The Decline of the Democrats and the Future of American Politics.* New York: Hill and Wang, 1986.
Ferraro, Geraldine. *My Story.* Evanston, IL: Northwestern University Press, 1985.
Fink, Gary M., and Hugh Davis Graham, eds. *The Carter Presidency: Policy Choices in the Post–New Deal Era.* Lawrence: University Press of Kansas, 1998.
Fisher, Klaus. *America in White, Black, and Grey: A History of the Stormy 1960s.* New York: Continuum, 2006.
Foley, Michael Stewart. *Front Porch Politics: The Forgotten Heyday of American Activism in the 1970s and 1980s.* New York: Hill and Wang, 2013.
Formisano, Ronald P. *Boston Against Busing: Race, Class, and Ethnicity in the 1960s and 1970s.* Chapel Hill: University of North Carolina Press, 2004.
Frank, Barney. *Speaking Frankly: What's Wrong with the Democrats and How to Fix it.* New York: Random House, 1992.
Frank, Thomas. *What's the Matter with Kansas? How Conservatives Won the Heart of America.* New York: Henry Holt, 2007.
Fraser, Steve, and Gary Gerstle. *The Rise and Fall of the New Deal Order, 1930–1980.* Princeton, NJ: Princeton University Press, 1989.
Free, Lloyd A., and Hadley Cantril. *The Political Beliefs of Americans: A Study of Public Opinion.* New York: Simon & Schuster, 1968.
Freidman, Milton. *Free to Choose: A Personal Statement.* Orlando, FL: Harcourt, 1980.
From, Al. *The New Democrats and the Return to Power.* New York: St. Martin's, 2013.
Geary, Daniel. *Beyond Civil Rights: The Moynihan Report and its Legacy.* Philadelphia, University of Pennsylvania Press, 2015.
Geismer, Lily. *Don't Blame Us: Suburban Liberals and the Transformation of the Democratic Party.* Princeton, NJ: Princeton University Press, 2014.

Germond, Jack W., and Jules Witcover. *Blue Smoke & Mirrors: How Reagan Won & Why Carter Lost the Election of 1980.* New York: Viking, 1981.
———. *Mad as Hell: Revolt at the Ballot Box, 1992.* New York: Warner Books, 1993.
———. *Wake Us When It's Over: Presidential Politics of 1984.* New York: Simon & Schuster, 1985.
———. *Whose Broad Strips and Bright Stars: The Trivial Pursuit of the Presidency 1988.* New York: Warner Books, 1989.
Gerstle, Gary, Nelson Lichtenstein, and Alice O'Connor, eds. *Beyond the New Deal: U.S. Politics from the Great Depression to the Great Recession.* Philadelphia: University of Pennsylvania Press, 2019.
Gillon, Steven. *The Democrats' Dilemma: Walter F. Mondale and the Liberal Legacy.* New York: Columbia University Press, 1992.
———. *Politics and Vision: The ADA and American Liberalism, 1947–1985.* Oxford: Oxford University Press, 1987.
Gillmore, Robert. *Liberalism & the Politics of Plunder: The Conscience of a Neo-Liberal.* Dublin, NH: W. L. Bauhan, 1987.
Gilmore, Stephanie, ed. *Feminist Coalitions: Historical Perspectives on Second-Wave Feminism in the United States.* Champaign: University of Illinois Press, 2008.
Golland, David Hamilton. *A Terrible Thing to Waste: Arthur Fletcher and the Conundrum of the Black Republican.* Lawrence: University Press of Kansas, 2019.
Gould, Lewis L. *1968: The Election That Changed America,* 2nd ed. Chicago: Ivan R. Dee, 2010.
Gustafson, Kaaryn S. *Cheating Welfare: Public Assistance and the Criminalization of Poverty.* New York: New York University Press, 2011.
Hamby, Alonzo. *Beyond the New Deal: Harry S. Truman and American Liberalism.* New York: Columbia University Press, 1973.
———. *Liberalism and Its Challengers: From F.D.R. to Bush,* 2nd ed. Oxford: Oxford University Press, 1992.
Haney-Lopez, Ian. *Dog Whistle Politics: How Coded Racial Appeals Have Reinvented Racism and Wrecked the Middle Class.* Oxford: Oxford University Press, 2014.
Hannam, June. *Feminism,* 2nd ed. New York: Routledge, 2014.
Hart, Gary W. *A New Democracy: A Democratic Vision for the 1980s and Beyond.* New York: W. Morrow, 1983.
———. *Right from the Start: A Chronicle of the McGovern Campaign.* New York: Quadrangle, 1973.
———. *The Thunder and the Sunshine: Four Seasons in a Burnished Life.* Golden, CO: Fulcrum, 2010.
Hartman, Andrew. *A War for the Soul of America: A History of the Culture Wars.* Chicago: University of Chicago Press, 2015.
Hays, Samuel P. *Beauty, Health and Permanence: Environmental Politics in the United States, 1955–1985.* Cambridge: Cambridge University Press, 1987.
Hayward, Steven F. *The Age of Reagan: The Fall of the Old Liberal Order: 1964–1980.* New York: Random House, 2001.

———. *The Age of Reagan: The Conservative Counterrevolution, 1980–1989*. New York: Three Rivers, 2009.
Hersh, Burton. *The Shadow President: Ted Kennedy in Opposition*. Hanover, NH: Steerforth, 1997.
Hilton, Adam. *True Blues: The Contentious Transformation of the Democratic Party*. Philadelphia: University of Pennsylvania Press, 2021.
Hodgson, Godfrey. *American in Our Time: From World War II to Nixon—What Happened and Why*. Princeton, NJ: Princeton University Press, 1976.
———. *The Gentleman from New York: Daniel Patrick Moynihan, A Biography*. New York: Houghton Mifflin, 2000.
hooks, bell. *Ain't I a Woman: Black Women and Feminism*. Boston: South End, 1981.
HoSang, Daniel Martinez, and Joseph E Lowndes. *Producers, Parasites, Patriots: Race and the New Right-Wing Politics of Precarity*. Minneapolis: University of Minnesota Press, 2019.
Hrebenar, Ronald J. *Interest Group Politics in America*, 3rd ed. New York: M. E. Sharpe, 1997.
Hudson, Cheryl, and Gareth Davies, eds. *Ronald Reagan and the 1980s: Perceptions, Policies, Legacies*. New York: Palgrave Macmillan, 2008.
Inglehart, Ronald. *Culture Shift in Advanced Industrial Society*. Princeton, NJ: Princeton University Press, 1990.
Jeffries, John C. *Justice Lewis F. Powell Jr: A Biography*. New York: Scribner, 2001.
Judis, John. *The Paradox of American Democracy: Elites, Special Interests, and the Betrayal of the Public Trust*. New York: Routledge, 2001.
Judis, John B., and Ruy Teixeira. *The Emerging Democratic Majority*. New York: Scribner, 2002.
Johnson, Haynes. *Sleepwalking Through History: America in the Reagan Years*. New York: W. W. Norton, 2003.
Johnson, Marc C. *Tuesday Night Massacre: Four Senate Elections and the Radicalization of the Republican Party*. Norman, OK: University of Oklahoma Press, 2021.
Kalman, Laura. *Right Star Rising: A New Politics, 1974–1980*. New York: W. W. Norton, 2010.
Kamarck, Elaine C. *Primary Politics: How Presidential Candidates Have Shaped the Modern Nominating System*. Washington, DC: Brookings, 2009.
Kennedy, Edward M. *True Compass: A Memoir*. New York: Twelve, 2009.
Kimble, Penn. *Keep Hope Alive: Super Tuesday and Jesse Jackson's 1988 Campaign for the Presidency*. Washington, DC: Joint Center for Political and Economic Studies, 1992.
Kruse, Kevin M., and Julian E. Zelizer. *Fault Lines: A History of the United States Since 1974*. New York: W. W. Norton, 2019.
Kuttner, Robert. *The Life of the Party: Democratic Prospects in 1988 and Beyond*. New York: Penguin Group, 1987.
Laham, Nicholas. *The Reagan Presidency and the Politics of Race*. Westport, CT: Praeger, 1998.

Lassiter, Matthew D. *The Silent Majority: Suburban Politics in the Sunbelt South.* Princeton, NJ: Princeton University Press, 2006.
Laursen, Eric. *The People's Pension: The Struggle to Defend Social Security Since Reagan.* Oakland, CA: AK Press, 2012.
Lawrence, John A. *The Class of '74: Congress After Watergate and the Roots of Partisanship.* Baltimore, MD: John Hopkins University Press, 2018.
Lawson, Steven F. *Running for Freedom: Civil Rights and Black Politics in American Since 1941*, 4th ed. West Sussex, UK: John Wiley & Sons, 2015.
Light, Paul. *Still Artful Work: The Continuing Politics of Social Security Reform*, 2nd ed. New York: McGraw-Hill, 1995.
Loomis, Burdett A. *The New American Politician: Ambition, Entrepreneurship, and the Changing Face of Political Life.* New York: Basic Books, 1988.
Lucks, Daniel S. *Reconsidering Reagan: Racism, Republicans, and the Road to Trump.* Boston: Beacon, 2020.
Lukas, J. Anthony. *Common Ground: A Turbulent Decade in the Lives of Three American Families.* New York: Alfred A. Knopf, 1985.
Luker, Kristin. *Abortion & the Politics of Motherhood.* Berkeley: University of California Press, 1984.
Mann, Robert. *Becoming Ronald Reagan: The Rise of a Conservative Icon.* Lincoln: University of Nebraska Press, 2019.
Martin, Bradford. *The Other Eighties: A Secret History of America in the Age of Reagan.* New York: Hill and Wang, 2011.
Mason, Robert. *The Republican Party and American Politics from Hoover to Reagan.* Cambridge: Cambridge University Press, 2012.
———. *Richard Nixon and the Quest for a New Majority.* Chapel Hill: University of North Carolina Press, 2004.
Matusow, Allen J. *The Unraveling of America: A History of Liberalism in the 1960s.* New York: Harper & Row, 1984.
Mayer, William G. *The Divided Democrats: Ideological Unity, Party Reform, and Presidential Elections.* Boulder, CO: Westview, 1996.
McAdam, Doug, and Karina Kloos. *Deeply Divided: Racial Politics and Social Movements in Postwar America.* Oxford: Oxford University Press, 2014.
McGirr, Lisa. *Suburban Warriors: The Origins of the New American Right.* Princeton, NJ: Princeton University Press, 2001.
McGovern, George. *Grassroots: The Autobiography of George McGovern.* New York: Random House, 1977.
———. *What It Means to Be a Democrat.* New York: Blue Rider, 2011.
McGuigan, Patrick B., and Dawn M. Weyrich. *Ninth Justice: The Fight for Bork.* Washington, DC: Free Congress Research & Education Foundation, 1991.
Mervin, David. *Ronald Reagan and the American Presidency.* New York: Longman, 1990.
Milkis, Sidney M., and Jerome M. Mileur, eds. *The Great Society and the High Tide of Liberalism.* Boston: University of Massachusetts Press, 2005.

———. *The New Deal and the Triumph of Liberalism.* Boston: University of Massachusetts Press, 2002.

Milkis, Sidney M., and Daniel J. Tichenor. *Rivalry and Reform: Presidents, Social Movements, and the Transformation of American Politics.* Chicago: University of Chicago Press, 2019.

Miroff, Bruce. *The Liberals' Moment: The McGovern Insurgency and the Identity Crisis of the Democratic Party.* Lawrence: University Press of Kansas, 2009.

Mondale, Walter F. *The Good Fight: A Life in Liberal Politics.* New York: Simon & Schuster, 2010.

Morgan, Iwan W. *The Age of Deficits: Presidents and Unbalanced Budgets from Jimmy Carter to George W. Bush.* Lawrence: University Press of Kansas, 2009.

———. *Beyond the Liberal Consensus: A Political History of the United States Since 1965.* London: Hurst, 1994.

———. *Reagan: American Icon.* London: I.B. Tauris, 2016.

Mould, Tom. *Overthrowing the Queen: Telling Stories of Welfare in America.* Bloomington: Indiana University Press, 2020.

Moynihan, Daniel P. *Came the Revolution: Argument in the Reagan Era.* New York: Harcourt, 1988.

———. *Coping: Essays on the Practice of Government.* New York: Vintage Books, 1973.

———. *Daniel Patrick Moynihan: A Portrait in Letters of an American Visionary,* ed. Steven R. Weisman. New York: PublicAffairs, 2010.

Mueller, Carol M., ed. *The Politics of the Gender Gap: The Social Construction of Political Influence.* London: Sage, 1988.

Myers, Robert J. *Within the System: My Half Century in Social Security.* Winsted, CT: Actex, 1992.

O'Neill, Thomas P., Jr., and William Novak. *Man of the House: The Life and Political Memoirs of Speaker Tip O'Neill.* New York: Random House, 1987.

Osgood, Kenneth, and Daniel E. White, eds. *Winning While Losing: Civil Rights, the Conservative Movement, and the Presidency from Nixon to Obama.* Gainesville: University Press of Florida, 2014.

Patterson, James T. *America's Struggle Against Poverty in the Twentieth Century,* 4th ed. Cambridge: Harvard University Press, 2000.

———. *Grand Expectations: The United States, 1945–1974,* 2nd ed. Oxford: Oxford University Press, 1997.

———. *Restless Giant: The United States from Watergate to Bush v. Gore.* Oxford: Oxford University Press, 2005.

Perlstein, Rick. *Before the Storm: Barry Goldwater and the Unmaking of the American Consensus.* New York: Hill and Wang, 2001.

———. *The Invisible Bridge: The Fall of Nixon and the Rise of Reagan.* New York: Simon & Schuster, 2014.

———. *Nixonland: The Rise of a President and the Fracturing of America.* New York: Scribner, 2008.

———. *Reaganland: America's Right Turn, 1976–1980*. New York: Simon & Schuster, 2020.
Perry, Huey L., and Wayne Parent, eds. *Blacks and the American Political System*. Gainesville: University Press of Florida, 1995.
Pertschuk, Michael. *Giant Killers*. New York: W. W. Norton, 1987.
Pertschuk, Michael, and Wendy Schaetzel. *The People Rising: The Campaign Against the Bork Nomination*. New York: Thunder Mouth, 1989.
Peters, Charles, and Phillip Keisling. *A New Road for America: The Neoliberal Movement*. Lanham, MD: Madison Books, 1985.
Peters, Ronald M., Jr., and Cindy Simon Rosenthal. *Speaker Nancy Pelosi and the New American Politics*. Oxford: Oxford University Press, 2010.
Phillips, Kevin P. *The Emerging Republican Majority*. New York: Arlington House, 1969.
Phillips-Fein, Kim, and Julian E. Zelizer, eds. *What's Good for Business: Business and American Politics Since World War II*. Oxford: Oxford University Press, 2012.
Pierson, Paul. *Dismantling the Welfare State: Reagan, Thatcher, and the Politics of Retrenchment*. Cambridge: Cambridge University Press, 1994.
Piper, J. Richard. *Ideologies and Institutions: American Conservative and Liberal Governance Prescriptions Since 1933*. New York: Rowman & Littlefield, 1997.
Pomper, Gerald, ed. *The Election of 1980: Reports and Interpretations*. London: Chatham House, 1981.
———. *The Election of 1984: Reports and Interpretations*. London: Chatham House, 1985.
———. *The Election of 1988: Reports and Interpretations*. London: Chatham House, 1989.
Poole, Keith T., and Howard Rosenthal. *Ideology & Congress*, 2nd ed. New York: Routledge, 2017.
Price, David. *Bringing Back the Parties*. Washington, DC: CQ Press, 1984.
Rae, Nicol C. *The Decline and Fall of the Liberal Republicans: From 1952 to the Present*. Oxford: Oxford University Press, 1989.
Reagan, Ronald. *Ronald Reagan: An American Life*. New York: Simon & Schuster, 1990.
Reagan, Ronald. *The Reagan Diaries*, Vol. 1, *January 1981–October 1985*, edited by Douglas Brinkley. New York: Harper Collins, 2009.
Reich, Robert B. *The Resurgent Liberal (And Other Unfashionable Prophecies)*. New York: Vintage Books, 1991.
Rhodes, Jesse H. *Ballot Blocked: The Political Erosion of the Voting Rights Act*. Stanford, CA: Stanford University Press, 2017.
Rigueur, Leah Wright. *The Loneliness of the Black Republican: Pragmatic Politics and the Pursuit of Power*. Princeton, NJ: Princeton University Press, 2016.
Rossinow, Douglas. *The Reagan Era: A History of the 1980s*. New York: Columbia University Press, 2015.

———. *Visions of Progress: The Left-Liberal Tradition in America*. Philadelphia: University of Pennsylvania Press, 2008.

Rothenberg, Randall. *The Neoliberals: Creating the New American Politics*. New York: Simon & Schuster, 1984.

Ryan, Barbara, ed. *Identity Politics in the Women's Movement*. New York: New York University Press, 2001.

Sabin, Paul. *Public Citizens: The Attack on Big Government and the Remaking of American Liberalism*. New York: W. W. Norton, 2021.

Sandbrook, Dominic. *Eugene McCarthy: The Rise and Fall of Postwar American Liberalism*. New York: Random House, 2004.

———. *Mad as Hell: The Crisis of the 1970s and the Rise of the Populist Right*. New York: Alfred A. Knopf, 2011.

Scammon, Richard M., and Ben J. Wattenberg. *The Real Majority*. New York: Coward-McCann, 1970.

Schaller, Michael. *Reckoning with Reagan: America and Its President in the 1980s*. Oxford: Oxford University Press, 1992.

———. *Right Turn: American Life in the Reagan-Bush Era, 1980–1992*. Oxford: Oxford University Press, 1996.

Schickler, Eric. *Racial Realignment: The Transformation of American Liberalism, 1932–1965*. Princeton, NJ: Princeton University Press, 2016.

Schlesinger, Arthur M., Sr. *Paths to the Present*. New York: Macmillan, 1949.

Schlesinger, Arthur M., Jr. *The Cycles of American History*, 2nd ed. New York: Houghton Mifflin, 1999.

———. *Journals, 1952–2000*, edited by Andrew Schlesinger and Stephen Schlesinger. London: Atlantic Books, 2008.

———. *The Vital Center: The Politics of Freedom*. New York: Houghton Mifflin, 1949.

Schoenwald, Jonathan. *A Time for Choosing: The Rise of Modern American Conservatism*. Oxford: Oxford University Press, 2001.

Schreiber, Ronnee. *Righting Feminism: Conservative Women & American Politics*. Oxford: Oxford University Press, 2008.

Schulman, Bruce J. *Lyndon B. Johnson and American Liberalism: A Brief Biography with Documents*. Boston: Bedford/St. Martin's, 1995.

———. *The Seventies: The Great Shift in American Culture, Society, and Politics*. New York: Free Press, 2001.

Schulman, Bruce J., and Julian E. Zelizer. *Rightward Bound: Making America Conservative in the 1970s*. Cambridge: Harvard University Press, 2008.

Schwab, Larry M. *The Illusion of a Conservative Reagan Revolution*. New York: Routledge, 2016.

Schwartz, Herman. *Packing the Courts: The Conservative Campaign to Rewrite the Constitution*. New York: Scribner, 1988.

Shafer, Byron E., ed. *The End of Realignment? Interpreting American Electoral Eras*. Madison: University of Wisconsin Press, 1991.

———. *The Two Majorities and the Puzzle of Modern American Politics.* Lawrence: University Press of Kansas, 2003.

Shafer, Byron E., and Anthony J. Badger, eds. *Contesting Democracy: Substance and Structure in American Political History, 1775–2000.* Lawrence: University Press of Kansas, 2001.

Shirley, Craig. *Rendezvous with Destiny: Ronald Reagan and the Campaign That Changed America.* Wilmington, DE: Intercollegiate Studies Institute, 2009.

Simon, James. *The Center Holds: The Power Struggle Inside the Rehnquist Court.* New York: Simon & Schuster, 1995.

Skinner, Kiron K., Annelise Anderson, and Martin Anderson. *Reagan's Path to Victory: The Shaping of Ronald Reagan's Vision: Selected Writings.* New York: Simon & Schuster, 2004.

Smeal, Eleanor. *Why and How Women Will Elect the Next President.* New York: Harper & Row, 1984.

Smith, Hedrick. *The Power Game: How Washington Works.* New York: Ballantine Books, 1988.

Smith, Steven S., and Melanie J. Springer, eds. *Reforming the Presidential Nomination Process.* Washington, DC: Brookings, 2009.

Stanfield, James R. *John Kenneth Galbraith.* London: Palgrave Macmillan, 2011.

Stanley, Timothy. *Kennedy vs. Carter: The 1980 Battle for the Democratic Party's Soul.* Lawrence: University Press of Kansas, 2010.

Stimson, James A. *Tides of Consent: How Public Opinion Shapes American Politics,* 2nd ed. Cambridge: Cambridge University Press, 2015.

Stockman, David. *The Triumph of Politics: How the Reagan Revolution Failed.* New York: Harper & Row, 1986.

Sundquist, James L. *Constitutional Reform and Effective Government.* Washington, DC: Brookings, 1992.

———. *Dynamics of the Party System: Alignment and Realignment of Political Parties in the United States.* Washington, DC: Brookings, 1983.

Svahn, John A. *There Must Be a Pony in Here Somewhere: Twenty Years with Ronald Reagan: A Memoir.* Minneapolis, MN: Langdon Street, 2011.

Tarrow, Sidney G. *Power in Movement: Social Movements and Contentious Politics,* 3rd ed. Cambridge: Cambridge University Press, 2011.

Thernstrom, Abigail M. *Whose Votes Count? Affirmative Action and Minority Voting Rights.* Cambridge: Harvard University Press, 1987.

Tribe, Laurence. *God Save This Honorable Court: How the Choice of Supreme Court Justices Shapes Our History.* New York: Random House, 1985.

Troy, Gil. *Morning in America: How Ronald Reagan Invented the 1980s.* Princeton, NJ: Princeton University Press, 2007.

———. *The Reagan Revolution: A Very Short Introduction.* Oxford: Oxford University Press, 2009.

Tsongas, Paul. *Heading Home.* New York: Alfred A. Knopf, 1984.

———. *The Road from Here: Liberalism and Realities in the 1980s.* New York: Alfred A. Knopf, 1981.
Tuck, Stephen. *We Ain't What We Ought to Be: The Black Freedom Struggle from Emancipation to Obama.* Cambridge: Harvard University Press, 2010.
Viera, Norman, and Leonard Gross. *Supreme Court Appointments: Judge Bork and the Politicization of Senate Confirmations.* Carbondale: Southern Illinois University Press, 1998.
Volle, Jeffrey J. *The Political Legacies of Barry Goldwater and George McGovern: Shifting Party Paradigms.* New York: Palgrave Macmillan, 2010.
von Bothmer, Bernard. *Framing the Sixties: The Use and Abuse of a Decade from Ronald Reagan to George W. Bush.* Boston: University of Massachusetts Press, 2010.
Waldman, Tom. *Not Much Left: The Fate of American Liberalism.* Berkeley: University of California Press, 2008.
Walker, Martin. *Clinton: The President They Deserve.* London: Vintage, 1997.
Ware, Susan. *Beyond Suffrage: Women in the New Deal.* Cambridge: Harvard University Press, 1981.
Wattenberg, Martin P. *The Decline of American Political Parties, 1952–1980.* Cambridge: Harvard University Press, 1984.
Weisberg, Jacob. *Ronald Reagan.* New York: Times Books, 2016.
West, Darrell M. *Air Wars: Television Advertising and Social Media in Election Campaigns, 1952–2012,* 6th ed. Washington, DC: CQ Press, 2014.
White, John Kenneth. *Barack Obama's America: How New Conceptions of Race, Family, and Religion Ended the Reagan Era.* Ann Arbor: University of Michigan Press, 2009.
Wickham, DeWayne. *Bill Clinton and Black America.* New York: Ballantine Books, 2002.
Wilentz, Sean. *The Age of Reagan: A History 1974–2008.* New York: HarperCollins, 2008.
Williams, Daniel K. *God's Own Party: The Making of the Christian Right.* Oxford: Oxford University Press, 2010
Witcher, Marcus M. *Getting Right with Reagan: The Struggle for True Conservatism, 1980–2016.* Lawrence: University Press of Kansas, 2019.
Yalof, David Alistair. *Pursuit of Justices: Presidential Politics and the Selection of Supreme Court Nominees.* Chicago: University of Chicago Press, 2001.
Young, James P. *Reconsidering American Liberalism: The Troubled Odyssey of the Liberal Idea.* Boulder, CO: Westview, 1996.
Young, Lisa. *Feminists and Party Politics.* Toronto: UBC Press, 2000.
Zelizer, Julian E. *Burning Down the House: Newt Gingrich, the Fall of a Speaker, and the Rise of the New Republican Party.* New York: Penguin, 2020.
———. *Jimmy Carter.* New York: Henry Holt, 2010.
———. *On Capitol Hill: The Struggle to Reform and Its Consequences, 1948–2000.* Cambridge: Cambridge University Press, 2004.
———. ed. *The American Congress: The Building of Democracy.* New York: Houghton Mifflin, 2004.

———. ed. *The Presidency of Barack Obama: A First Historical Assessment*. Princeton, NJ: Princeton University Press, 2018.
Zelizer, Julian E., and Meg Jacobs. *Conservatives in Power: The Reagan Years, 1981–1989: A Brief History with Documents*. Boston: Bedford/St. Martin's, 2011.

Journal Articles

Boyd, Thomas M., and Stephen J. Markman. "The 1982 Amendments to the VRA: A Legislative History." *Washington and Lee Law Review* 40, no. 4 (1983): 1347–1428.
Brandt, Karl Gerard. "The Ideological Origins of the New Democrat Movement." *Journal of the Louisiana Historical Association* 48, no. 3 (2007): 273–294.
Brinkley, Alan. "The Problem of American Conservatism." *American Historical Review* 99, no. 2 (1994): 409–429.
Cerulo, Karen A. "Identity Construction: New Issues, New Directions." *Annual Review of Sociology* 23 (1997): 385–409.
Chappell, Marisa. "Reagan's 'Gender Gap' Strategy and the Limitations of Free-Market Feminism." *Journal of Policy History* 24, no. 1 (2012): 115–134.
Cochran, Thomas C. "The 'Presidential Synthesis' in American History." *American Historical Review* 53, no. 4 (1948): 748–759.
Delton, Jennifer. "Rethinking Post-World War II Anticommunism." *Journal of the Historical Society* 10, no. 1 (2010): 1–41.
Ehrman, John. "The Age of Reagan? Three Questions for Future Research." *Journal of Historical Society* 11, no. 1 (2011): 111–131.
Ferkiss, Victor. "Neoliberalism: How New? How Liberal? How Significant? A Review Essay." *Western Political Quarterly* 39, no. 1 (1986): 165–179.
Fowler, Francis C. "The Neoliberal Value Shift and Its Implications for Federal Education Policy Under Clinton." *Educational Administration Quarterly* 31, no. 1 (1995): 38–60.
Galston, William, and Elaine Kamarck. "The Politics of Evasion: Democrats and the Presidency." *Progressive Policy Institute* (September 1989).
Gerstle, Gary. "The Protean Characteristics of American Liberalism." *American Historical Review* 99, no. 4 (1994): 1043–1073.
Gilens, Martin. "Gender and Support for Reagan: A Comprehensive Model of Presidential Approval." *American Journal of Political Science* 32, no. 1 (1988): 19–49.
Greenberg, David. "Reinventing Democrats: The Politics of Liberalism from Reagan to Clinton by Kenneth Baer." *Journal of Interdisciplinary History* 32, no. 2 (2001): 339–341.
Guliuzza, Frank, III, Daniel J. Reagan, and David M. Barrett. "Character, Competency, and Constitutionalism: Did the Bork Nomination Represent a Fundamental Shift in Confirmation Criteria?" *Marquette Law Review* 73, no. 2 (1992): 409–437.
Hale, Jon F. "The Making of the New Democrats." *Political Science Quarterly* 110, no. 2 (1995): 207–232.

Heclo, Hugo. "The Mixed Legacies of Ronald Reagan." *Presidential Studies Quarterly* 38, no. 4 (2008): 555–574.
Hodder-Williams, Richard. "The Strange Story of Judge Robert Bork and a Vacancy on the United States Supreme Court." *Political Studies* (1988): 613–637.
Jones, Adrienne, and Andrew J. Polsky. "How to Win a 'Long Game': The Voting Rights Act, the Republican Party, and the Politics of Counter-Enforcement." *Political Science Quarterly* 136 (2021): 215–248.
Jung, Courtney. "Why Liberals Should Value 'Identity Politics.'" *Daedalus, Journal of the American Academy of Arts & Sciences* 135, no. 4 (2006): 32–39.
Key, V. O. "A Theory of Critical Elections." *Journal of Politics* 17, no. 1 (1955): 3–18.
Kato, Kenneth, and Elizabeth Rybicki. "Congressional History: A Literature Review." *OAH Magazine of History* 12, no. 4 (1998): 5–12.
Ladd, Everett C. "The Brittle Mandate: Electoral Dealignment and the 1980 Presidential Election." *Political Science Quarterly* 96 (1981): 1–25.
May, Ann Mari, and Kurt Stephenson. "Women and the Great Retrenchment: The Political Economy of the 1980s." *Journal of Economic Issues* 28, no. 2 (1994): 533–542.
Morgan, Iwan. "Jimmy Carter, Bill Clinton, and the New Democratic Economics." *Historical Journal* 47, no. 4 (2004): 1015–1039.
———. "Monetary Metamorphosis: The Volcker Fed and Inflation." *Journal of Policy History* 24, no. 4 (2012): 545–571.
Ogundele, Ayo, and Linda Camp Keith. "Reexamining the Impact of the Bork Nomination to the Supreme Court." *Political Research Quarterly* 52, no. 2 (1999): 403–420.
Sandalow, Terence. "The Supreme Court in Politics." *Michigan Law Review* 88 (1990): 1300–1325.
Scott, Joan W. "Gender: A Useful Category of Historical Analysis." *American Historical Review* 91, no. 5 (1986): 1053–1075.
Shields, Jon A. "Fighting Liberalism's Excesses: Moral Crusades During the Reagan Revolution." *Journal of Policy History* 26, no. 1 (2014): 103–120.
Southwell, Priscilla. "The 1984 Democratic Nomination Process: The Significance of Unpledged Superdelegates." *American Politics Quarterly* 14, no. 1–2 (1986): 75–88.
Wattenberg, Martin P. "Why Clinton Won and Dukakis Lost: An Analysis of the Candidate-Centered Nature of American Party Politics." *Party Politics* 1, no. 2 (1995): 245–260.
Witcher, Marcus. "President Carter's Southern Strategy: The Importance of Wallace Voters in 1976 and 1980." *Alabama Review* 72, no. 3 (2019): 178–190.
Zeitz, Joshua. "Rejecting the Center: Radical Grassroots Politics in the 1970s: Second-wave Feminism as a Case Study." *Journal of Contemporary History* 43, no. 4 (2008): 673–688.
Zelizer, Julian E. "Reflections: Rethinking the History of American Conservatism." *Reviews in American History* 38, no. 2 (2010): 367–392.

Index

ABC/Washington Post poll, 145
abortion, 16, 64, 76, 146; access to, 104, 202n27; attack on, 63; as personal choice, 150; restrictions on, 148
abortion issue, 9–10, 61, 67, 102–103, 109, 111, 119, 148–151, 158, 230–231n30
abortion rights, 9, 79, 102–103, 137; advocacy for, 202n27; reaffirmation of, 218n60
activism, 8, 123; government, 2, 22; grassroots, 3, 11, 15, 31, 42, 179n27, 180n31; neoliberalism and, 21; pro-choice, 10, 63, 231n32; pro-life, 10, 149, 229n14
ADA. *See* Americans for Democratic Action
Advocacy Institute, 109, 114
AFDC. *See* Aid to Families with Dependent Children
affirmative action, 48, 109, 121, 141, 154, 156, 159, 168
AFL-CIO, 75, 97, 208n19, 225n36; Mondale and, 82, 86; Reagan and, 82; Social Security and, 51
African Americans. *See* Blacks
Age Discrimination Act (1975), 101
Aid to Families with Dependent Children (AFDC), 64, 65
Akron City Council, 149
Alliance for Justice, 121, 234n80
American Association of Retired Persons (AARP), 51
American Bar Association, 158–159
American Civil Liberties Union, 84, 138
American Presidency Project, 198n159
Americans for Democratic Action (ADA), 2, 3, 93, 96, 104, 133, 143, 144, 174, 177n4, 177n8, 183n12, 184n26; Carter and, 23; DLC and, 95; Kennedy and, 23, 25; Long and, 26; Tsongas and, 20, 165, 175; voting records, 207n112
Americans with Disabilities Act, 152, 231n40

Andelic, Patrick, 7, 165, 190n16
Anderson, John B., 23
Andrews, Rob, 166
antiabortion movement, 60, 149
antidiscrimination laws, 100, 125, 146, 152
antitrust law, 109
Arkansas Gazette, 236n117
Armstrong, Scott, 104
Armstrong, William Lester, 233n60
Aron, Nan, 121, 142
Askew, Reubin, 209n25
Associated Press, 196n114
Atari Democrats, 27, 186n60
Atlanta Journal-Constitution, 118, 140
Atwater, Lee, 41, 61, 139

Babbitt, Bruce, 94, 236n127
Baby Boomers, 8, 80, 86, 97, 131
Backlash: The Undeclared War Against American Women (Faludi), 60
Baer, Kenneth, 163, 174
Baker, James, 91
Ball, Robert, 49, 52
Barnes, Clifford, 139
Barnes, Fred, 81
Baron, Alan, 91
Barone, Michael, 30
Bell, Jonathan, 179n28
Bentsen, Lloyd, 137
Biden, Joseph R., 218n62; Bork and, 109, 119, 120
Bill of Rights (NOW), 66
Black Enterprise, 166
Blackmun, Harry A., 218n69
Blacks, 26, 55, 120, 159, 191n28; Democratic Party and, 40; election of, 43; Jackson and, 141; marginalization of, 180n32; NOW and, 200n3; opportunity for, 66; Reagan's performance and, 48; structural racism/sexism and, 203n40; VRA and, 39

257

Black vote, 133–134; attracting, 107; Clinton and, 166
Blanchard, Richard, 68
Block Bork campaign, 15, 112, 113, 115, 117, 120, 136, 142; Bush and, 128; impact of, 118, 119; Kennedy nomination and, 123; legacy of, 122–123; strategists for, 114. *See also* Bork, Robert H.
Block Bush campaign, 142
Bloodworth, Jeffrey, 4, 174
Blumenthal, Sidney, 133
Bob Jones University, 44, 45, 101, 155
Boland, Edward, 218n59
Boland Amendments, 218n59
Boll Weevil Democrats, 26, 56, 106
Book of Bork, 115
Bork, Robert H., 100–108, 157, 158, 159, 214n3, 221n125, 234n82, 235n93; abortion issue and, 111; campaign against, 14–15, 16, 120, 122, 172; campaign for, 112–116; civil rights and, 111; criticism of, 109, 110, 112, 114, 115–116, 118; defeat of, 110, 116–120, 120–123, 125, 127, 130, 218n62; Dukakis and, 141–142; judicial philosophy of, 113, 114; nomination of, 14, 99–100, 108–123, 171, 239n8; opponents of, 111, 112, 113, 114–115, 117, 118, 122; privacy issues and, 111; race/gender and, 119; record of, 112, 115, 118, 158; sterilization case and, 228n98; testimony of, 117–118, 119; Watergate and, 112
Boston Globe, 104
Boxer, Barbara, 151
Brandt, Karl Gerard, 26
Braun, Carol Moseley, 159, 176
Breaux, John, 104
Brennan, William J., 218n69
Broder, David, 54, 56, 83
Brotherhood of Sleeping Car Porters, 192n42
Brown, Ronald, 135, 144, 164
Brown, Willie, 129
Buchanan, Patrick, 18, 161
Burnham, Walter Dean, 6
Burton, Phillip, 93
Bush, George H. W., 16, 156, 227n91, 231n40, 237n141; campaign of, 128, 162; civil rights and, 141, 154, 233n69; CRA and, 161; criticism by, 228n102; Dukakis and, 140, 141; election of, 146; Gingrich and, 162; King and, 232n47; liberalism and, 128, 138; Perot and, 237n140; popularity of, 161; quotas and, 159, 160; Reagan and, 156; Social Security and, 58; Supreme Court pick and, 157; Thomas and, 159; vote for, 142
Bush, George W., 190n17
"Bush's Furlough from the Truth" (advertisement), 140
Business Roundtable, LCCR and, 157
Byrne, Jane, 223n10

Caddell, Patrick, 53, 55, 76, 197n134
"Campaign '92: The Race to Avoid Being the Guy Who Loses to Bush" (*Saturday Night Live*), 161
Campaign to Save Women's Lives, 149
Canellos, Peter, 36
Cantril, Hadley, 170
Carabillo, Toni, 69
Carswell, G. Harrold, 159
Carter, Jimmy, 2, 31, 56, 92, 192n43, 217n53, 239n14; ADA and, 23; conservative approach of, 21–22; ERA and, 62; gender gap and, 62; Kennedy and, 7, 23; malaise speech of, 22; repudiation of, 18; stagflation and, 25; tax increase by, 49; vote for, 22, 62; Wallace endorsement and, 191n28
CBS, 134
CBS/New York Times poll, 66, 140, 143; abortion issue and, 150
Census Bureau, 71, 105, 196n121, 224n30, 240n17
Center for New Democracy, 130
Chamber of Commerce, 225n36
Christian Science Monitor, 46
Church, Frank, 24, 187n74
City of Akron v. Akron Center for Reproductive Health (1983), 149, 218n60
civil rights, 2, 9, 10, 16, 36, 37, 41, 42, 44, 4546, 54, 80, 102, 103, 107–109, 111, 113–116, 120, 121, 124, 125; abandonment of,

67, 69; opposition to, 62, 67, 68, 102, 204n65
ERAmerica, 204n68
Estrich, Susan, 32, 139, 229n9

Fair Housing Act (1980), 15, 42, 192n44
Fair Housing Amendment Act (1988), 124–125
fairness issue, 13, 38, 53, 54, 55, 59, 66, 82, 92, 96
Faludi, Susan, 60
Farrell, John, 84, 235n93
Federal Reserve, 38, 190n16
Federal Trade Commission (FTC), 192n43
Federation of Business and Professional Women, 166
Feinstein, Dianne, 151
feminism, 114, 173, 200n3; ERA and, 67; second-wave, 9, 180n31; stagnation of, 60
Feminist Majority Foundation, 106
feminist organizations, 33, 105, 106, 147, 164. *See also* women's movement
Feminization of Power campaign, 105, 147
Fenwick, Millicent, 67
Ferguson, Thomas, 91
Ferraro, Geraldine, 31, 32, 76–77, 105, 131; candidacy of, 72–73, 75, 79, 188n98, 217n42; compromise by, 33; influence of, 70–76; Jackson and, 135; Task Force on Women and, 27; women candidates and, 106
Fifteenth Amendment, 39
Finch, Atticus, 115
Fingerhut, Vic, 52
Fitzwater, Marlin, 155
Fletcher, Arthur, 156
Foley, Tom, 26
food stamps, 64, 65
Ford, Gerald, 22, 23, 198n159, 201n10, 217n53
Ford, Wendall, 56
Fortune, 3
Fourteenth Amendment, 121
Fowler, Francis, 236n127
Frank, Barney, 67, 168
Frankfurter, Felix, 112
Free, Lloyd, 170
Frieden, Lex, 231n40

Friedman, Milton, 49
Friends of Bill, 164
From, Al, 27, 163
Frost, Martin, 87
fundamentalism, liberal, 175, 239n13

Gallup polls, 52, 63, 67, 76, 130, 141, 150, 226n68
Galston, William, 90, 174, 239n13
gay rights movement, 239n8
Geary, Daniel, 203n36
Geismer, Lily, 7, 239n7
gender, 19, 157, 170, 180n32, 181n34, 203n36; issues of, 9, 160
gender gap, 13, 15, 61, 105, 147–151, 166, 201n8, 206n101, 207n113, 209n38, 229n3, 229n13, 231n32, 238n147; birth of, 6264; Democratic Party and, 76; electoral significance of, 70–71, 105; ERA and, 68, 202n16; exploiting, 73, 231n32; impact of, 72, 75; NOW and, 65, 67, 68, 70, 71, 74, 75; presidential elections and, 240n17; Reagan and, 64, 73, 76; Republican Party and, 73; women's issues and, 68
"Gender Gap Update" (NOW), 64
Gephardt, Richard, 21, 28, 112, 144; labor groups and, 225n36; Reaganomics and, 133; vote for, 134
gerrymandering, 43, 45
Gillon, Steven, 85
Gingrich, Newt, 161, 162, 167, 168
Gingrich's Revolution, 167
Ginsburg, Douglas, 120, 121
Glass Ceiling Commission, 156, 160
Glenn, John, 27–28, 83
Goldsmith, Judy, 70–71, 74, 75–76
Goldwater, Barry, 18, 39, 40, 41, 185n38
Goodman, Ellen, 74
Gore, Al, 133, 144, 236n127
Gradison, Bill, 162
grassroots organizations, 3, 7, 8, 11, 30, 31, 35, 37, 61, 76, 84, 96, 154, 165–166; Bork and, 15; Democratic Party and, 33, 128; identity politics and, 12; liberal, 15, 34, 100, 147; power of, 14, 16; women and, 67
Gray, William H., III, 154
Gray Lobby, 52

Great Depression, 49, 79
Great Society, 13, 19, 20, 21, 36, 80, 131, 138; Clinton campaign and, 164–165; hostility for, 50; protecting, 38–49; VRA and, 49
Greenberg, David, 163
Greer, Frank, 150
Greider, William, 90
Griffiths, Martha, 68, 204n62
Griggs v. Duke Power Co. (1971), 160
Griswold v. Connecticut (1965), 111
Grove City College, 100, 101
Grove City v. Bell (1984), civil rights and, 103
Gulf War, 161

Hale, Jon, 28
Hamilton, Bill, 88
Harkin, Tom, 75, 152, 207n112
Harris poll, 52
Hart, Gary, 11, 70, 94, 95, 97, 104, 133, 134, 164, 166, 173, 183n11, 186n66, 208n20, 209n35, 211n67, 214n128, 224n20; appeal of, 82–83, 85–86, 87; Armed Services Committee and, 210n56; book by, 88; campaign of, 80, 81, 84–90, 130; defeat of, 93, 131–132; Democratic Party and, 131; Dukakis and, 131–132; HDC and, 87; Kennedy and, 84; labor unions and, 87; on leadership, 90; liberalism and, 80, 85, 86, 90, 92, 131, 141; McGovern and, 84; Mondale and, 80, 83–88, 211n69, 211n74; neoliberalism and, 21, 89; New Generation Democrats and, 126, 175; NOW and, 209n38; Reagan and, 88, 90, 210n51, 212n84; Reagan Revolution and, 84; Schroeder and, 131; special interests and, 88; vote for, 14, 82–83; Wirth and, 89, 216n30
Hart, Peter, 23, 81–82, 83, 213n100
Hatch, Orrin, 45, 46, 102, 107, 192n44, 233n67; CRRA and, 155; HLA and, 63
Haynsworth, Clement, 159
HDC. *See* House Democratic Caucus
Headlee, Richard, 68
health care, 22, 141, 163, 165, 167, 175
Heckler, Margaret, 67, 73
Heclo, Hugh, 238n151

Heflin, Howell, 119, 120
Helms, Jesse, 46, 54
Hightower, Jim, 98
Hill, Anita, 159
Hodgson, Godfrey, 19
Hollings, Ernest, 194n65, 209n25
hooks, bell, 200n3
Hooks, Benjamin: on Black unemployment, 57; on discrimination, 45; on Reagan/civil rights, 46, 231n45; voter enrollment and, 57; VRA and, 47
Horton, Willie, 157, 160, 161, 172; apology for, 226n77; political advertisement about, 139–140; Republican racism and, 234n77
House Democratic Caucus (HDC), 12, 27–28, 30, 31, 32, 34, 35, 97, 173, 187n78, 208n21; Democratic Fairness Packet and, 197n136; Hart and, 87; new direction for, 26; reform process and, 94; reviving, 26; superdelegates and, 33
House Education and Labor Committee, 156
housing: benefits, 64; bill, 124; women and, 65
Human Life Amendment (HLA), 62–63
Humphrey, Hubert, 80, 90, 137
Hunt, James, 31
Hunt Commission, 31, 32
Hyde, Henry, 43, 44, 193n52

identity, 7, 8, 11, 12, 14, 17, 19, 27, 31, 171; collective, 9; formation, 10; groups, 47, 95; issues, 16, 33, 146, 160; political, 20, 51, 135; social, 172
identity politics, 10, 32, 34, 40, 85, 99, 166, 173, 175; concepts of, 14; emergence of, 9, 11, 12, 19; focus on, 7; incorporating, 33; Jackson and, 129; move away from, 31, 95
ideology, 3, 8, 17, 28, 40, 112, 136–140, 141, 144, 170, 185n38
inflation, 21, 22, 38, 49, 79, 183n17, 190n16, 241n14
Internal Revenue Service, 4445
"Investing in Our Economy" (Wirth and Gephardt), 28
"Investing in People" (NOW), 206n108

Iran-Contra scandal, 108, 112, 116, 117, 120
Ireland, Patricia, 134

Jackson, Andrew, 34
Jackson, Jesse, 43, 83, 89, 106, 139, 154, 166, 173, 174, 223n10; Black America and, 57; campaign of, 15, 127–128, 128–136, 144; civil rights and, 125, 130; Democratic Party and, 98, 134; on DLC, 95; Dukakis and, 133, 137, 141; Ferraro and, 135; identity politics and, 129–130; King and, 128–129; liberalism and, 132; Obama and, 135; policy/institutional changes and, 134–135; racism and, 71; support for, 71, 83, 134, 136, 225n40
Jackson, Maynard, 98
Jackson, Robert, 112
Jet magazine, 130
Jim Crow laws, 39
Johnson, Lyndon B., 83, 85, 90, 190n22, 198n159, 217n53; Great Society and, 19, 36, 38, 39, 40
Joint Center for Political Studies, 107
Jordan, Barbara, 120
Jordan, Vernon, 160
Joyce, Fay, 28
Judiciary Committee, 42, 109, 116, 120
Judis, John, 81, 180n32
"Justice Denied" (PFAW report), 153
"just say no" campaign, 157

Kamarck, Elaine, 174, 239n13
Kauffman, L. A., 10
Kennedy, Anthony: confirmation of, 121, 123; *Obergefell* and, 121
Kennedy, Edward, 2, 31, 32, 34, 36, 42, 93, 107, 109, 133, 166, 184n27, 184n30, 185n46, 187n76, 189n3, 238n151; ADA and, 23, 25; Bork and, 110, 113, 114, 117, 118, 120, 235n93; Carter and, 7, 23; civil rights and, 37, 45–46, 124; concessions forced by, 170; CRA and, 154–155; CRRA and, 123, 154–155; on discrimination, 102; Dukakis and, 137; Hart and, 84; LCCR and, 101; liberal rating of, 143–144; Mondale and, 90; on Neas, 47–48; neoliberalism and, 25, 29; on perception problem, 92; on Reagan, 55; support for, 22, 226n64; Tsongas and, 3; VRA and, 44
Kennedy, Flo, 234n82
Kennedy, John F., 27, 37, 85, 86–87, 98, 141, 166, 180n32, 190n17; on racial discrimination, 101; revival of, 137–138
Kerry, John, 75, 207n112
Key, V. O., 6
King, Coretta Scott, 153, 232n47
King, Martin Luther, Jr., 41, 53, 153; Jackson and, 128–129; poor people's crusade and, 129
Kirk, Paul, 93, 97–98, 173–174, 214n128; DLC and, 96; DPC and, 96; Dukakis and, 136; interest groups and, 97; labor unions and, 94; liberal activists and, 97
Kirkpatrick, Jeane J., 73, 206n96
Klopp, Arthur, 115
Kondracke, Morton, 18, 22
Kopkind, Andrew, 130
Kramer, Ken, 104
Kruse, Kevin, 200n185, 223n10
Ku Klux Klan, 160
Kunin, Madeleine, 207n113

Labor and Human Resources Committee, 102, 107
labor unions, 2, 8, 11, 21, 82, 85, 87, 94, 165, 173
Ladd, Everett C., 6
Laffer, Arthur, 54
Laham, Nicholas, 125
Lake, Celinda, 238n147
Lake, James, 74
Lautenberg, Frank, 67
Lawson, Steven, 136
Leadership Conference on Civil Rights (LCCR), 7, 8, 37, 42, 43, 45, 46, 47, 72, 101, 103, 110, 122, 123, 153, 155, 158, 160, 171; agenda of, 156–157; Bork and, 112, 113, 142; Bush and, 156, 159; Business Roundtable and, 157; coalition building and, 125; CRA and, 146, 154; fair housing and, 124; founding of, 192n42; grassroots participation and, 232n53; organization of, 192n41; Title IX and, 102; Women's Caucus, 156, 180n31
Leahy, Patrick, 117

Lewis, Ann, 56, 65, 143; Bork campaign and, 123; on Hart, 93
Lewis, Anthony, 18
Lewis, John, 160, 190n22
liberalism: caricatured version of, 140; Cold War, 3; crossroads for, 88–89; cultural shift in, 20; decline of, 5, 7, 17, 41, 84; Democratic Party and, 3, 4, 9, 10, 11, 81, 84, 135; development of, 4, 9, 10, 11, 12, 28, 53, 128; discrediting, 18, 20, 64, 138; future of, 12–13, 31; limits of, 5, 172; neoliberalism and, 20; new approaches to, 24, 26, 34, 165; packaging/marketing, 100; persistence of, 128; Reaganism and, 79–80; recalibrating, 5, 12, 16, 18–19, 20, 21, 22, 24–25, 29, 96, 147; resurgence of, 15, 81, 123–126; social, 3, 23, 134; support for, 10, 28, 29, 37, 143, 146, 169, 174; updating, 25, 86, 130, 131, 165
Lightman, David, 94
Lincoln, Abraham, 156
Long, Gillis, 94, 96, 185n50; ADA and, 26; Hunt Commission and, 32; "Liberal Laboratory" and, 12, 25–31
Long, Speedy, 25
Los Angeles Times, 69, 167, 212n84
Lowery, Joseph, 118, 123, 234n78

MacNeil-Lehrer Report, 18
Mager, Mimi, 142
Malcolm, Ellen, 106
Manatt, Charles, 32, 55, 93
Mann, Judy, 64
Mansbridge, Jane, 202n16
March for Women's Lives, 149
Marshall, Thurgood, 157, 218–219n69
Martin, Bradford, 7
Martin, Lynn, 149
Marttila, John, 118
Maryland Republican Party, Horton flyer by, 140
Mason, Robert, 239n4
Massachusetts Miracle, 137, 138
Mathias, Charles, 10, 201n14
May, Ann Mari, 65
"Maybe Gary Hart Was Right?" (advertisement), 210n51

McCarthy, Eugene, 31, 83
McGovern, George, 29, 163, 164, 209n25; campaign of, 19; defeat of, 95; Hart and, 84
McGrory, Mary, 122–123
Medicaid, 19, 145, 167, 238n151; abortion funding and, 150
Medicare, 19, 58, 64, 167, 197n142, 238n146, 238n151; support for, 84, 145; women and, 65
Meese, Edwin, 108, 114
Mervin, David, 218n68
Me-Tooism, 98, 104
Mikulski, Barbara, 104, 105, 106
Miller, Angela, 139
Miller, Warren, 145
Mineta, Norman, 26
Mink, Patsy, 2, 25, 159
Mitchell, George, 55
Mobile v. Bolden (1980), 43, 47
mobilization strategies, 11, 14, 57, 59, 172, 173
Mondale, Walter, 11, 25, 74, 79, 80, 89, 90, 94, 97, 131, 173, 206n108, 209n22, 210n56, 213n99; AFL-CIO and, 82, 86; campaign of, 81–84; civil rights and, 130; defeat of, 70, 76, 77, 81, 93, 99, 136; endorsements for, 72, 82, 92; fairness concept and, 82; gender gap and, 72; Hart and, 80, 83–88, 210n51, 211n69, 211n74; Kennedy and, 90; New Deal and, 87; popularity of, 73; on Reagan, 75; special interests and, 88, 208n21; superdelegates and, 32; vote for, 14
Morgan, Iwan, 239n14
"Morning Again in America" (advertisement), 75, 79, 104
Morrison, Toni, 237n136
Moynihan, Daniel Patrick, 25, 58, 196n114; election of, 56; liberalism and, 28; Social Security and, 51, 55; VRA and, 44, 185n49
Ms. Magazine, 148
Myers, Robert, 50

NAACP, 32, 54, 158, 192n42, 231n45; civil rights and, 125; voter enrollment, 57
Nader, Ralph, 113

NAFTA. *See* North Atlantic Free Trade Agreement
NARAL. *See* National Abortion Rights Action League
Nation, The, 135
National Abortion Federation (NAF), 229n14
National Abortion Rights Action League (NARAL), 8, 63, 123, 202n27; Democratic Party and, 77; Thomas and, 158; *Webster* and, 149; Wilder and, 150
National Advisory Council on Economic Opportunity, 65
National Association of Realtors, 124
National Committee to Preserve Social Security and Medicare, 58
National Council of Senior Citizens, 51
National Election Study, 74
National Governors Association, 164
National House Democratic Caucus (NHDC), 30, 34
National Journal, 10, 130
National Organization for Women (NOW), 7, 8, 32, 33, 48, 51, 61–62, 97, 105, 110, 123, 134, 148, 150, 171, 180n31, 202n30, 204n59, 204n65, 206n108, 219n89, 221n134, 234n82; Black women/men and, 200n3; campaign by, 68, 149; coalition building by, 77; conservative backlash and, 60; CRRA and, 103; Democratic Party and, 13, 75, 76, 77; endorsement from, 205n87, 209n38; ERA and, 61, 67, 69; formation of, 69, 72; gender gap and, 65, 67, 68, 70, 71, 74, 75, 147; HLA and, 63; NWRO and, 66; PACs by, 69; Pelosi and, 231n35; as political force, 75, 77; Senate control and, 107–108; strategy of, 105; symposium by, 70; Thomas and, 158; Title IX and, 102; voter registration drive by, 72, 75, 77; women voters and, 64, 73–74
National Press Club, 24
National Rainbow Coalition, 130
National Review, The, 177n3
National Security Council, 117
National Urban League, 191n27

National Welfare Rights Organization (NWRO), 65, 66, 203n46
National Women's Political Caucus (NWPC), 64, 106, 147, 204n68; conference, 71
Neas, Ralph, 125, 153, 155; Bork and, 113, 114, 119; civil rights and, 47–48, 152; CRRA and, 108, 123; LCCR and, 37, 42; VRA and, 44, 46, 47, 192n44
neoliberalism, 15, 18, 22, 27, 28, 34, 89, 144, 188n105; activism and, 21; criticism of, 24; development of, 81; growing interest in, 25, 30; liberalism and, 20
Neoliberal's Manifesto, A, 24–25
Neshoba County Fair, 40, 191n27
New Deal, 1, 3, 4, 9, 11, 14–17, 19, 20, 21, 25, 36, 38, 40, 58, 65, 77, 80, 81, 82, 85, 86, 87, 89, 90, 131, 138, 163, 164, 173; defending, 49–53; framework of, 84; Social Security and, 49
New Democracy, A (Hart), 88
New Democrats, 145, 165, 175
New Generation Democrats, 130, 175
New Republic, The, 3, 23, 136
New Right, 54, 63, 177n3
New Yorker, 238n151
New York Post, 112, 144
New York Times, 18, 21, 23, 28, 38, 43, 45, 53, 56, 67, 74, 83, 105, 130–131, 141, 142, 143, 165, 186n60, 193n60; Book of Bork and, 115; Bork and, 119; civil rights organizations and, 107; deficit reduction and, 54; on Democratic goals, 29; gender gap and, 68; on Hart, 89, 131, 210n56; on Jackson, 127, 132, 134, 135; on Reagan's power, 104; on Thomas, 158
Newman, Paul, 91
Newsweek, 132
NHDC. *See* National House Democratic Caucus
Nineteenth Amendment (1920), 66
97th Congress, 42, 47
Ninth Circuit Court of Appeals, 221n134
Nixon, Richard M., 18, 19, 90, 143, 180n32, 202n22, 217n53; Bork and, 112; civil rights and, 41; gender differences

Nixon, Richard M. (*cont.*)
  in voting for, 201n10; Southern
    Strategy and, 40
North, Oliver, 117
North Atlantic Free Trade Agreement
  (NAFTA), 166, 237n141
NOW. *See* National Organization for
  Women
Nuclear Freeze movement, 7
Nunn, Sam, 95
NWPC. *See* National Women's Political
  Caucus
NWRO. *See* National Welfare Rights
  Organization

Obama, Barack, 190n17, 240n18;
  campaign by, 175–176; Jackson and,
  135; male/female vote and, 240n17;
  political identity of, 135
Obergefell v. Hodges (2015), 121
O'Connor, Sandra Day, 108, 206n102,
  219n69
O'Donnell, Kirk, 53, 54, 56
Omnibus Budget and Reconciliation Act
  (1981), 36
100th Congress, 125, 127
O'Neill, Thomas P. "Tip," 27, 36, 37, 53,
  55, 161; concessions forced by, 170;
  on Dukakis, 141; Hart and, 80, 83, 88;
  Mondale and, 80; NHDC and, 30;
  policy statements and, 29; Reagan
  and, 52, 91; on Reagan Revolution,
  103; retirement of, 90, 103; Social
  Security and, 38, 50, 51, 56
Operation PUSH, 129
Osborne, David, 35

Packwood, Bob, 216n33
PACs. *See* political action committees
Patterson v. McLean Credit Union (1989),
  152
Paul, Alice, 6667
Peck, Gregory, 115–116, 171
Pelosi, Nancy, 151, 231n35; political
  education of, 93; Sanford and, 94
Pendleton, Clarence, Jr., 48
People for the American Way (PFAW),
  112, 114, 153, 157

Pepper, Claude, 52
Perlstein, Rick, 191n27
Perot, Ross, 166, 237n140, 237n142
Pertschuk, Michael, 42, 192n43
Peters, Charles, 20, 24, 34, 35
PFAW. *See* People for the American Way
Philadelphia Plan (1969), 156
Phillips, Kevin, 143
Pierson, Paul, 238n3
Podesta, Anthony, 114
political action committees (PACs), 58,
  60, 69
politics: conservative, 9; feminist, 60;
  feminization of, 66–70; identity, 7, 9,
  11–12, 19, 21, 31, 32, 34, 77, 8586, 98, 129,
  166, 172, 173, 175; national, 6; partisan,
  3–4; racial, 40, 156, 159, 160; remaking,
  170, 179n24
Politics of Evasion, The, 174, 175
populism, 40, 134, 163
poverty, 19, 54, 132, 236n121; Black/
  White, 224n30; feminization of,
  64–66, 70, 72
Powell, Lewis F., 108, 109, 110, 112, 113,
  218n60, 219n77
privacy issues, 111, 113, 114, 115, 116, 148
Public Opinion, 63

racial minorities, 8, 9, 11, 13, 16, 29, 43,
  48, 57, 141, 180n32; agenda of, 128;
  Clinton and, 166; Democratic Party
  and, 135; power of, 135–136; social
  welfare programs and, 14
racism, 44, 71, 111, 200n3; politics and,
  156; Republican, 234n77; structural,
  203n40; Wallace-style, 41
Randolph, A. Philip, 192n42
Rauh, Joseph L., 23, 46, 99, 158
Reagan, Nancy, 157
Reagan, Ronald: AFL-CIO and, 82; Bob
  Jones and, 45; Bork and, 108, 109, 116,
  119–120; budget policies of, 57; Bush
  and, 156; civil rights and, 41, 51, 124,
  151–161, 231n45; Democratic Party
  and, 91; Dukakis and, 138; economic
  policies of, 95; election of, 12–13, 14, 18,
  21, 25, 26, 34, 173; ERA and, 62; gender
  gap and, 64, 73, 76; Goldwater and,

40; Hart and, 88, 90, 210n51, 212n84; HLA and, 62–63; ideological agenda of, 37, 58; judicial appointments by, 112, 214n3, 218n68; Kennedy and, 121; legacy of, 176, 178n16, 238n151; liberalism and, 100, 171; liberal programs/policies and, 16–17; neoliberalism and, 80; O'Connor and, 206n102; O'Neill and, 52, 91; popularity of, 36, 63, 73, 79, 91–92; racial minorities and, 48; reckoning with, 22–25; rhetoric of, 76–77; role of government and, 169; Social Security and, 50, 52; supply-side economics and, 38; support for, 207n110, 226n64; tax cuts by, 54; vote for, 22, 23, 62–63, 64, 78; VRA and, 44, 46, 47, 53–54; welfare cuts and, 66
Reagan Democrats, 22–23, 148, 166
Reagan Era, 6, 7, 14, 16, 25, 29, 61, 76, 121, 127, 143, 146, 151, 159, 160, 161; Bork and, 122; liberalism and, 34, 132; marketing in, 114; social change across, 8
Reaganism, 3, 14, 24, 34, 59, 60, 87, 172; end of, 127; inequities of, 104; liberalism and, 79–80; responding to, 130
Reaganomics, 14, 66, 84, 133
Reagan Revolution, 4–5, 7, 12, 24, 52, 81, 91, 127, 169, 175; arrival of, 36; Bork and, 121; end of, 59, 103; Hart and, 84; institutionalization of, 108; Social Security and, 50
Rebuilding the Road to Opportunity (CPE), 27
Reconstruction, 39, 41
Reeves, Richard, 24
Regents of the University v. Bakke (1978), 218n60
Rehabilitation Act (1973), Section 504 of, 101, 231n40
Rehnquist, William, 107, 108, 113, 219n69
Reich, Robert, 123, 164, 236n127
Reinventing Democrats (Baer), 174
Renewing America's Promise (NHDC), 30
reproductive rights, 15, 114, 118, 209n38, 237n138

Republican National Committee, Hart ads by, 88
Republican Party, 39, 98, 141; civil rights and, 190–191n24; conservative direction of, 13; divisions within, 161; ERA and, 62; federal judgeships and, 108; gender differences in voting and, 201n10; gender gap and, 73; losses for, 103; Social Security and, 55, 58, 170; VRA and, 170; welfare state and, 66; white voters and, 19; women voters and, 63, 73–74
Reuss, Pat, 62, 102
"revolving door" advertisement, impact of, 139–140, 148
Rice, Donna, 224n20
Richards, Ann, 231n32
Richardson, Elliot, 112
Riggs, Betty, 118
Road from Here, The (Tsongas), 165
Robb, Charles, 94, 202n30
Robinson, Jackie, 128, 129
Roe v. Wade (1973), 111, 218n60, 230n24; overturning, 62–63, 158, 202n17; reaffirmation of, 149; reasoning in, 148
Rogers, Joel, 91
Roosevelt, Franklin D., 36, 49, 50, 58, 85, 95, 138, 141; election of, 6; midterm elections and, 190n17; New Deal and, 40; welfare state and, 1
Roosevelt, James, 58
Roosevelt, Theodore, 166
Rossinow, Douglas, 41, 90, 177n2
Roth, William, Jr., 51
Rothstein, Richard, 164
Ruckelshaus, William, 112
Russell Senate Office Building, 117

same-sex couples, 121
Sanford, Terry, 94, 95, 106, 107
Saturday Night Live, 161
Saturday Night Massacre, 112
Save Our Security (SOS), 51
Scalia, Antonin, 108, 219n69
Schlafly, Phyllis, 67
Schlesinger, Arthur, Jr., 3, 6, 24, 127, 177n8, 184n30
Schneider, William, 20

Schroeder, Patricia, 66, 131
Schweiker, Richard, 51
Section 504 (Rehabilitation Act). *See* Rehabilitation Act (1973), Section 504 of
segregation, 39, 40, 109, 121, 192n44; racial, 36, 192n39
Senate Armed Services Committee, 210n56
Senate Committee on Foreign Relations, 24
"Senate Unanimously Rebuffs President on Social Security" (*Washington Post*), 51
Setting the Record Straight: Judge Bork and the Future of Women's Rights (NWLC), 118
sexuality, 9, 10, 64, 111, 121, 181n39
Shafer, Byron, 179n24, 237n137
Shaw, Bernard, 138
Shelby, Richard, 104, 107, 120
Shull, Leon, 96, 177n4
Siegel, Mark, 33
Sierra Club, 152
Simmons, Althea T. L., 54
Simon, James, 160
Simon, Paul, 133, 149
Simpson, Alan, 117, 119
Slagle, Bob, 94
Smeal, Eleanor, 70, 148; endorsement by, 72; on Ferraro nomination, 75; gender gap and, 61; midterms and, 105; NOW and, 76
Smith, Hedrick, 179n22
Smith, William French, 45
Smith, William Kennedy, 235n93
social issues, 1, 8, 19, 28, 30, 36, 80, 86
social justice, 20, 21, 141, 192n42
Social Security, 19, 37, 38, 52, 59, 64, 141, 165, 167, 170; campaign against, 50, 52–53, 53–54; cuts for, 50, 56, 199n180; as election issue, 56; fairness issue and, 55; liberalism and, 58; protecting, 53, 56, 59; reforming, 50–51; Republican Party and, 55, 58, 170; stagflation and, 49; support for, 53, 84, 145; women and, 65
Social Security Act (1935), 13, 36

social welfare, 132, 279n24
sodomy law, 111
Sorensen, Theodore, 137
Southern Christian Leadership Conference, 118
Southern Crusade, 129
Southern Democrats, 130, 148
Southern Strategy, 40, 41, 120
special interests, 27–28, 82, 85, 88, 89, 92, 95, 97, 113, 120, 122, 208n21
Specter, Arlen, 119
stagflation, 21, 25, 49, 183n17, 239n14
Stanley, Timothy, 7
States' Rights Democrats, 39, 192
Steinem, Gloria, 74, 76
Stephenson, Kurt, 65
Stevens, John Paul, 219n69
Stevenson, Adlai, 85, 87
Stockman, David, 50; Social Security and, 49, 51, 52
Subcommittee on Civil and Constitutional Rights, 43
Sunbelt states, 52; Democrats and, 186n56, 213n100
Sundquist, James, 178n20
superdelegates, 31–34, 88, 135, 188n98, 188n100
Super Tuesday, 83–84, 87, 88, 133, 134, 174
supply-side model, 21, 38, 54, 161, 239n14
Sutherland, George, 113
Svahn, John, 51

Tarr-Whalen, Keith, 58
Task Force on Women, 27
Taylor, William, 122, 218n66
Teeter, Robert, 55
Teixeira, Ruy, 81, 180n32
Teles, Steven, 51
Third Way, 16, 147, 175
Thomas, Clarence, 234n82; abortion issue and, 158; civil rights record of, 157–158; employment discrimination and, 234n80; hearings for, 161; nomination of, 157, 158, 159–160; racial politics and, 160; *Roe* and, 234n86; sexual harassment and, 159
Thurmond, Strom, 42, 45, 107, 192n39
Time, on Dukakis, 143

Tipps, Paul, 81
Title VI (Civil Rights Act), 101
Title VIII (Civil Rights Act), 124, 192n44
Title IX (Education Amendments), 100, 101, 102
To Kill a Mockingbird, 115–116
Troy, Gil, 5
Truman, Harry S., 141, 198n159
Tsongas, Paul, 4, 10, 19; ADA and, 20, 165, 175; Clinton and, 164–165; Kennedy and, 3; liberalism and, 1, 2, 3, 12, 28, 34; on Mondale, 81; on Reaganism, 24
Tully, Paul, 131

unemployment, 22, 38, 82, 137, 183n17, 195n99, 209n38, 239n14; Black, 57, 203n40; drop in, 79; as election issue, 56; rising, 21; women and, 65. *See also* employment
USCCR. *See* US Commission on Civil Rights
US Commission on Civil Rights (USCCR), 48, 65, 156
US Conference of Catholic Bishops, 102
US Constitution, original intent of, 111
US House of Representatives, 150; Democratic control of, 12; women in, 77
US Justice Department, 39
US News & World Report, 154
US Senate, Democratic loss of, 18
US Supreme Court, 45, 74, 99, 107, 115, 116, 138, 146, 158, 202n17, 206n102, 231n40, 235n93; antidiscrimination laws and, 152; Bob Jones and, 101; Bork nomination and, 14, 110, 111, 117, 120; civil rights and, 121, 153; as judicial forum, 110–111; nominations to, 149; Reagan transformation of, 111; *Roe* and, 62–63, 148, 149, 202n16; social justice and, 121

Van Dyk, Ted, 136
Vietnam War, 19, 20, 73, 80, 85, 89, 183n11
Viguerie, Richard, 63
Volcker, Paul, 190n16
Voter Awareness Programs, 57

voter registration, 39–40, 57–58, 71, 72, 75, 77, 129, 130; drives for, 136
voting blocs, 13, 27, 180n32, 240n17
voting rights, 36, 180n32; campaign for, 42–49
Voting Rights Act (VRA) (1982), 19, 36–37, 38, 39, 40, 41, 49, 58, 129, 135, 141, 196; campaign for, 47, 48, 54–55; extending, 42, 46, 57, 99; fairness issue and, 55; lobbying against, 45; protecting, 13, 53, 56, 59; Republican Party and, 170; support for, 53; undermining, 36, 43
Vrdolyak, Edward, 97

"Wake Up, Liberals, Your Time Has Come" (Schlesinger), 127
Wallace, George, 19, 40, 41, 191n28
Wall Street Journal, 80–81, 159
Wards Cove Packing Co. v. Atonio (1989), 152
War on Drugs, 140
Warren, Earl, 138
Washington, Craig, 160
Washington, Harold, 129, 223n10
Washington Monthly, The, 20
Washington Post, 29, 33, 43, 48, 51, 54, 64, 67, 73, 122, 127, 154, 160; on Bork, 118; on DLC, 96; on gender gap, 148
Washington Post/ABC News poll, 103
Watergate, 3, 19, 85, 89, 164, 172; Bork and, 112
Watergate Babies, 15, 19, 20, 24, 29, 34, 84, 172
Wattenberg, Martin, 150
Waxman, Henry, 237n138
Webster v. Reproductive Health Services (1989), 148, 150, 159, 230n24; abortion debate and, 151; impact of, 149
welfare, 40, 61, 203n36; cuts in, 64, 66; fraud, 64–65; liberalism and, 236n121; policy, 136; programs, 19; women and, 65, 68
welfare queen, 64–65
welfare state, 1, 49, 72, 86, 238n1; defending, 170; Democratic Party and, 170; Republican Party and, 66; women and, 66

Wendy's, advertisement by, 87–88, 130–131
White, Byron, 219n69
White, John, 95
White, Mark, 68
White, Theodore, 73
Wilder, Douglas, 150, 230–231n30
Wilderness Society, 152
Wilentz, Sean, 5
Wilkins, Roy, 192n42
Will, George: Reagan and, 18
Williams, Liles, 53–54
Wilson, Kathy, 64, 202n32
Wirth, Tim, 28, 104; gender gap and, 105; Hart and, 89, 216n30
Witcher, Marcus, 162, 178n16, 191n28
Women Can Make the Difference (NOW), 63–64
Women DO Make the Difference (NOW), 68
"Women in Politics" (NOW), 70
Women's Equity Action League, 62
women's issues, 61, 62, 64, 68, 73, 113, 148, 156
Women's Legal Defense Fund, CRA and, 153
women's movement, 60, 72; *See also* feminist organizations
"Women's Truth Squad on Reagan," 72
Women's Vote Project, 72
women voters, 14, 70, 73, 146, 148, 206n102, 240n17; gender gap and, 13; social welfare programs and, 14
Woods, Harriet, 105
Working Group on Women, 73
World War II, civil rights after, 9
Wright, Jim, 55–56, 161–162, 235–236n112

Yard, Molly, 147
Year of the Woman, 61, 167
yellow booklet, 27, 30
Young, Andrew, 221n125

Zelizer, Julian, 5, 170, 200n185, 223n10, 231n38, 238n46, 240n18

www.ingramcontent.com/pod-product-compliance
Lightning Source LLC
Chambersburg PA
CBHW031802220426
43662CB00007B/498